DATE DUE

POVERTY KNOWLEDGE

POLITICS AND SOCIETY IN TWENTIETH-CENTURY AMERICA

SERIES EDITORS

William Chafe, Gary Gerstle, and Linda Gordon

A list of titles

in this series appears

at the back of

the book

POVERTY KNOWLEDGE

SOCIAL SCIENCE, SOCIAL POLICY,
AND THE POOR IN TWENTIETH-CENTURY
U.S. HISTORY

Alice O'Connor

PRINCETON UNIVERSITY PRESS   PRINCETON AND OXFORD

Library of Congress Cataloging-in-Publication Data

O'Connor, Alice, 1958–
Poverty knowledge : social science, social policy,
and the poor in twentieth-century U.S. History /
Alice O'Connor.
p.   cm.—(Politics and society in twentieth-century America)
Includes bibliographical references and index.
ISBN 0-691-00917-1 (alk. paper)
1. Poverty—United States—History—20th century. 2. Poor—United States—
History—20th century. 3. Economic assistance, Domestic—United States—History—
20th century. I. Title. II. Series.
HC110.P6 O33 2000
362.5′0973′0904—dc21   00-034682

This book has been composed in Times New Roman

The paper used in this publication meets the minimum requirements
of ANSI/NISO Z39.48-1992 (R1997) (*Permanence of Paper*)

www.pup.princeton.edu

Printed in the United States of America

3   5   7   9   10   8   6   4

In Memory of My Mother

Contents

Acknowledgments

THIS BOOK is the product of my own somewhat unconventional pathway into the historical profession, which has taken me back and forth between academic and more "applied" research and policy settings, and leaves me with many people and institutions to thank.

I first began to explore the history of social scientific ideas about poverty in my doctoral dissertation at Johns Hopkins University, with support from a Woodrow Wilson Foundation doctoral fellowship. I am grateful to my advisor, Kenneth S. Lynn, for the often spirited, always instructive conversations we had about my research in progress, and to Ron Walters for his careful reading and generous assistance in shepherding the dissertation through. I also learned a great deal about both social science and social policy while working at the Ford Foundation, which put me in touch with a wide variety of social welfare policy makers and practitioners, as well as with a great many scholars from outside my own discipline. My thanks to several foundation colleagues who encouraged and helped me to pursue this inquiry in the first place, including Gordon Berlin, Shepard Forman, Charles V. Hamilton, David Arnold, Mil Duncan, and Susan Sechler, and to the interdisciplinary group of scholars with whom I had the pleasure of working on the Project on Social Welfare and the American Future, especially Fay Cook, Edward Gramlich, Hugh Heclo, Ira Katznelson, Jack Meyer, Robert Reischauer, and William Julius Wilson. At the Social Science Research Council, I also encountered colleagues and interdisciplinary working groups who urged me to incorporate what I was learning about social knowledge in the making into my historical research, including Martha Gephart, Leslie Dwight, Larry Aber, Sheldon Danziger, Jim Johnson, Melvin Oliver, and Rob Hollister. I am especially fortunate to have had the opportunity to work with historian Michael B. Katz, who as archivist to the SSRC Program for Research on the Urban Underclass conducted several vital oral history interviews, and whose writings on the history of poverty and welfare offer a model of scholarship I can only hope to emulate.

A National Science Foundation postdoctoral fellowship at the University of Chicago's Center for the Study of Urban Inequality gave me the opportunity to reflect and follow through on what I had learned from these professional experiences, and to expand my original inquiry into a study of knowledge-making institutions and politics as well as ideas. While at the Center, I had the opportunity to engage in ongoing discussion about my own and related research with Rebecca Blank, Christopher Jencks, William J. Wilson, Jim Quane, Susan Lloyd, Tom Jackson, and other participants in the seminar on race and poverty cosponsored by Northwestern University. The Russell Sage Foundation, where I was in residence as a visiting scholar, provided a wonderful atmosphere for research and writing, as well as a stimulating environment for interdisciplinary exchange. Special thanks to Eric Wanner for making the opportunity available, and to Madge Spitaleri, Cheryl Seleski, and the RSF staff for the extraordinary range and level of assistance they provided.

For all that I have learned from collaborating with scholars from other disciplines, I have found a real intellectual home in the Department of History at the University of California, Santa Barbara, where I have the pleasure of working with a number of colleagues and students who share my interests in poverty, welfare, and social knowledge, and in a department that has made a strong institutional commitment to the history of policy. Sharon Farmer, Carl Harris, Stephan Miescher, and Erika Rappaport offered helpful comments on various chapters. My deepest thanks go to my colleague Mary Furner, who has been extraordinarily generous in the time and care she has taken to read and comment on the entire manuscript. Thanks also to Sarah Case, Melissa Davis, Colleen Egan, and Vicki Fama for research and editorial assistance.

I would also like to thank several other people who have offered comments on all or parts of the manuscript, including Betsy Blackmar, Michael Bernstein, Don Critchlow, Herbert Gans, Jess Gilbert, Rob Hollister, Allen Hunter, Tom Jackson, Michael Katz, Jim Quane, Dorothy Ross, Bruce Schulman, Carol Stack, and Tom Sugrue. Many thanks as well to series editors Linda Gordon, Gary Gerstle and Bill Chafe for their thorough and helpful readings.

Among the pleasures of researching this book were the interviews I conducted with several people who were witness to or who themselves took part in shaping poverty research as a field in the wake of the War on Poverty, including James Bonnen, Glen Cain, Tom Corbett, Sheldon Danziger, Leonard Duhl, Betty Evanson, Herbert Gans, Thomas Glennan, Edward Gramlich, Alvin Hansen, Robert Haveman, Rob Hollister, Sanford Kravitz, Robert Lampman, Myron Lefkowitz, Robert Levine, Hylan Lewis, Charles Manski, S. M. Miller, Walter Miller, Peter Rossi, Alvin Schorr, Elizabeth Uhr, Burton Weisbrod, and Walter Williams. I also appreciate the assistance of the extremely knowledgeable archivists and research librarians I have encountered, and would especially like to thank staff members at the Lyndon B. Johnson Presidential Library, the Urban Institute, the Manpower Demonstration Research Corporation, and Faith Coleman and Alan Divack at the Ford Foundation Archives for their help in tracking down material. I was extremely fortunate to have access to many boxes of records at The Institute for Research on Poverty at the University of Wisconsin, and to have an excellent guide to what I might find in those boxes in the person of Betty Evanson. My thanks to the Institute, and to director Barbara Wolfe for permission to use these materials.

I have also been fortunate in the generous financial support for my research at each stage. In addition to fellowship support from the Woodrow Wilson Foundation, the National Science Foundation, and the Russell Sage Foundation, grants from the Lyndon B. Johnson and Gerald R. Ford Presidential Libraries helped to offset the costs of travel to archives.

My most lasting debt is to many friends and family members, who have offered support, encouragement, and much-needed perspective throughout the various stages of this project. Thanks to my siblings—Frank, Katie, Jimmy, Eileen, Kevin, Mary Beth, and Brendan—and to Scott Ellsworth, Susan Gallagher, Ethel Klein, Anne Kubisch, Leslie McCuaig, Karen McGuinness, Amy Moore, Jim Pearson, and Mary Stanton for keeping me going in ways I can only begin to appreciate.

POVERTY KNOWLEDGE

Introduction

THE IDEA that scientific knowledge holds the key to solving social problems has long been an article of faith in American liberalism. Nowhere is this more apparent than when it comes to solving the "poverty problem." For well over a century, liberal social investigators have scrutinized poor people in the hopes of creating a knowledge base for informed social action. Their studies have generated massive amounts of data and a widening array of research techniques, from the community-based social surveys of the Progressive Era, to the ethnographic neighborhood studies conducted by Chicago-school social scientists in the 1920s, to the technically sophisticated econometric analysis that forms the basis of the poverty research industry today. Although its origins can be traced to what historian Daniel Rodgers calls the transatlantic "borrowings" of late nineteenth- and early twentieth-century progressives, contemporary poverty research is very much an American invention, with a degree of specialization and an institutional apparatus that is unmatched in other parts of the world.[1] And yet, poverty remains a fact of life for millions in the world's most prosperous economy, stubbornly resistant to all that social scientists have learned about its "causes, consequences, and cures."[2]

Frustrated by what they routinely refer to as the "paradox" of "poverty amidst plenty," liberal social scientists often charge that politics and ideology are to blame. We know what to do about poverty, they believe, but ideologically motivated policy makers from both sides of the aisle lack the political will to do the right, scientifically informed thing. A powerful expression of such frustration came in response to the "end of welfare as we know it" in 1996, when three highly respected Department of Health and Human Services Department officials resigned in protest over President Clinton's decision to sign the harsh, Republican-sponsored Personal Responsibility and Work Opportunity Reconciliation Act—now widely referred to as welfare repeal. "The passage of this new law tells us what we already knew," wrote HHS Assistant Secretary Peter Edelman in explaining his actions. "[P]oliticians make decisions that are not based on research and experience." Welfare reform was a triumph of politics and ideology over knowledge, that is, and a defeat for the policy analysts who had mustered an enormous amount of scientific data showing that the bill would send millions more children into poverty—very much in the hope of preventing politicians from doing the wrong thing.[3]

Accurate though it may be in its characterization of recent welfare reform, this explanation for what happened in 1996 has one overriding problem: it fails to acknowledge the role that scientific poverty expertise played in bringing welfare as we knew it to an end. Following a well-established pattern in post–

Great Society policy analysis, the Clinton administration's poverty experts had already embraced and defined the parameters of a sweeping welfare reform featuring proposals that promised to change the behavior of poor people while paying little more than rhetorical attention to the problems of low-wage work, rising income inequality, or structural economic change, and none at all to the steadily mounting political disenfranchisement of the postindustrial working class. Approaching the poverty problem within the narrow conceptual frame of individual failings rather than structural inequality, of cultural and skill "deficits" rather than the unequal distribution of power and wealth, the social scientific architects of President Clinton's original, comparatively less punitive welfare reform proposal made "dependency" their principal target and then stood by helpless as congressional conservatives took their logic to its radical extreme. Their helplessness in the matter was not just a matter of "bad" politics laying "good" scientific knowledge to waste. It was also a failure of the knowledge itself.

Taken on its own, the recent "end of welfare" offers evidence for one of the central arguments of this book: that building an antipoverty agenda will require a basic change in the way we as a society think collectively about "the poverty problem," a change that begins with a redirection in contemporary social scientific poverty knowledge. Here I am referring to the body of knowledge that, very much as a legacy of Lyndon Johnson's War on Poverty, has attained a kind of quasi-official status in defining "the poverty problem" and assessing how social programs affect the poor. Besides being social scientific, this knowledge is based principally on quantitative, national-level data. It is produced by a network of public agencies, think tanks, university-based and privately operated research institutes that traffics in the shared language and recognized methods of applied economics and policy analysis. Although liberal in origins, poverty knowledge rests on an ethos of political and ideological neutrality that has sustained it through a period of vast political change. Very much for this reason, it can also be distinguished by what it is not: contemporary poverty knowledge does not define itself as an inquiry into the political economy and culture of late twentieth-century capitalism; it is knowledge about the characteristics and behavior and, especially in recent years, about the welfare status of the poor. Nor does it much countenance knowledge honed in direct action or everyday experience, whether generated from activism, program implementation, or, especially, from living poor in the United States. Historically devalued as "impressionistic," "feminized," or "ideological," this kind of knowledge simply does not translate into the measurable variables that are the common currency of "objective," "scientific," and hence authoritative poverty research.

Certainly I am not the first to make the argument that poverty knowledge, as currently constituted, needs to change. On occasion such an argument has been sounded by recognized poverty experts, exasperated, for example, by how their colleagues have allowed the political obsession with welfare dependency to overshadow the problems of wage decline, labor market failure, and rising inequality that continually get shunted off to the side in the poverty/welfare debate.[4] More often, though, the argument for change finds expression in the not-always-articulated frustration of people on the periphery of the poverty research industry—the program administrators, advocates, legislators, community activists, or, as in my own case, the foundation program officers—who since the 1980s have grown increasingly dissatisfied with the narrow, individualized focus of poverty research, who feel cut off from its technical language and decontextualized, rational choice models of human behavior, and who rankle at its refusal to acknowledge the value judgments underlying measures of welfare "dependency" that have come to play such a prominent role in recent policy. To be sure, thanks to poverty knowledge we now have a more accurate statistical portrait of who suffers from substandard incomes, housing, nutrition, and medical care—a far more diversified and shifting population than lingering stereotypes of the "other America" would allow. So, too, has poverty knowledge provided an indispensable picture of actual program spending and benefit levels that contradicts popular notions of welfare mothers living off the fat of the state. Poverty experts have also amassed convincing evidence about the links between poverty and macroeconomic performance, and about the extraordinary effectiveness of Social Security in reducing poverty among the elderly. And yet, however impressive its data or sophisticated its models, poverty knowledge has proved unable to provide an analysis or, equally important, a convincing narrative to counter the powerful, albeit simplistic story of welfare state failure and moral decline—a narrative that, with the help of well-organized conservative analysts, has come to inform policy discourse to a degree hardly imaginable twenty years ago.

I got my first introduction to poverty knowledge as a new assistant program officer at the Ford Foundation in the mid-1980s, when the liberal research establishment was still reeling from the impact of Charles Murray's just-released missive, *Losing Ground*. In that book, Murray used data and techniques earlier honed in predominantly liberal think tanks to argue that the liberal welfare state was to blame for a whole host of social problems, including poverty, family breakup, and crime.[5] From an empirical standpoint, Murray's argument proved easy to demolish, and a number of poverty experts rose convincingly to the task. But their careful empirical analyses were no match at all for *Losing Ground* as an ideological manifesto: couched, as they were, in the language and conventions of ideologically neutral objectivity, these critiques alone were inadequate as a response to Murray's attack on both the value premises and the performance record of the welfare state. Nor were poverty experts organized to counter the network of explicitly ideological conservative and libertarian think tanks that had managed, through their own organizing and publicity, to gain control of the terms of the poverty debate.

Along with many others at the time, then, I welcomed what has since become a perennial conversation about how liberal and progressive philanthropy can use knowledge more effectively to shape rather than react to public debate. At the same time, I was struck by what is still a pervasive assumption in the network of research institutes that make up the core of the poverty research industry: that knowledge, in order to meet the standards of empirical testing and rigorous scientific scrutiny, must—indeed that it ever is or can be—apolitical if not entirely value- and ideology-free.

In my job as assistant director of the Ford Foundation's Project on Social Welfare and the American Future, I was responsible for managing a portfolio of research grants that purposely ranged across the broad spectrum of social welfare policies, but that inevitably concentrated on the hotly contested issues of poverty, welfare, and what was becoming widely known as the "underclass." This proved my first introduction to the enormous influence of foundations and government agencies in setting social scientific research agendas, through control not just over what and who gets funding, but also over what, at any given time, constitutes policy expertise. To the extent that poverty research agendas were driven by "the science" (a standard foundation question: "what do we know and what do we need to know?"), it was always with an eye to making social science more "policy-relevant"—a virtual guarantee, during an era of rising deficits and antiliberal, antigovernment backlash, that poverty research would confine itself to an ever-shrinking realm of political possibility. The parameters of research were similarly narrow, as captured in what at the time was repeatedly characterized as the central fault line in the social scientific debate: whether poverty was "structural," and hence "caused" by an absence of human capital, or "cultural," as measured through various indicators of bad behavior, including whether dependency and single parenthood were somehow passed along as intergenerational character traits. In neither case was poverty defined as anything other than an individual condition, nor was it seen as susceptible to any other than individual-level reform. Most striking to me, though, was how rarely anyone acknowledged that this constricted, strangely either-or debate was not at all new, and not one that had ever been definitively settled through recourse to empirical data and social scientific models alone. Here again I agreed with the still-current assessment that poverty knowledge needed to be more interdisciplinary, qualitative as well as quantitative, and much broader in scope—and that it could use a good deal more of what we on the Social Welfare Project took to calling "blue sky" thinking in analyzing the possibilities for reform.

A few years later, as a staff associate assigned to the Social Science Research Council's Program for Research on the Urban Underclass, I had an opportunity to work more directly with social scientists to attempt such a broad, interdisciplinary approach, for the purposes of understanding at least one dimension of contemporary poverty—the dramatic economic decline of racially segregated neighborhoods in the nation's postindustrial urban core. That project, which I joined in the early 1990s, used the work of sociologist William Julius Wilson as the starting point for what was to be a more structural as well as interdisciplinary understanding of the roots of ghetto poverty, one that, in the eyes of its sponsor, the Rockefeller Foundation, could inform the design of community-based programs as well as national policy debates. These aims, as I soon discovered, were more easily stated than achieved. On the one hand were the methodological, conceptual, even linguistic barriers between disciplines, all exaggerated by our effort to broaden the conversation to disciplines that had been sidelined within established poverty research networks in recent years. On the other there were the divisions separating "academic" from "applied" policy research, and social scientists from neighborhood residents and practitioners—divisions rooted as much in professional cultures as in conflicting ideas about what constituted "usable" knowledge for purposes of policy and program. Especially telling, though, was that the efforts to "operationalize" and test the underclass concept continued to rest far more heavily on indicators of individual and group behavior than on comparable measures of structural economic and/or institutional decline in urban neighborhoods—reinforcing the notion that some form of behavioral "pathology" was what caused and sustained the underclass. When the SSRC Underclass Program was ending, in late 1993 and early 1994, it had just barely begun to broach the institutionalized barriers to collaboration and to address the limitations of conventional measures for documenting structural and community-level change. By then, too, poverty researchers had started to pay more attention to the growth in inequality and the decline of wages as defining, structurally rooted conditions of late twentieth-century poverty. Still, social science was a long way from realizing a genuinely different kind of poverty knowledge, one that revolved more around the problems of political economy than the behavioral problems of the poor.

Coming, as it did, from a planning group led by prominent poverty experts, the Clinton administration's 1994 proposal to "end welfare as we know it" seemed more a step backwards than a reflection of the powerful evidence emerging from recent research—particularly in the administration's willingness to make dependency the issue without adequately addressing the more pressing issues of declining wages and available work. Protest though they might once conservative Republicans took over, it was difficult to deny that welfare reform drew its logic from a so-called "consensus" on dependency that the administration's poverty experts had helped to construct—or that welfare, especially in recent memory, was simply not an issue that would be decided on the basis of high-minded, nonideological debate. And yet, the end of welfare has decidedly not spurred efforts to rethink the premises, the organization, or the overwhelmingly individualized focus of poverty research. If anything, it has been the occasion for growth and expansion in the existing research industry—in response to the well-warranted concern for keeping track of what actually happens to people under the new rules.

For me, then, the role of liberal social science in ending welfare confirmed the need to reexamine, and ultimately to reconstruct, the foundations of contemporary poverty knowledge. But while this view is informed by my experience as a funder and a kind of participant observer, it has been more deeply informed by historical research. Through historical analysis I have come to appreciate why poverty knowledge is so loaded with meaning: why "knowing" poverty generates such controversy and so much attention; why what is recognized as expertise can be so consequential—though rarely in ways the experts anticipate—for the poor; and why as a body of knowledge that has been historically constructed, it must be assessed as a part of historical trends in ideology, politics, institutions, culture, and political economy far more than as a disembodied store of learning about poverty's "causes" and "cures." By way of introduction, then, and in the chapters that follow, I highlight several insights that can be drawn from historical understanding of poverty knowledge, and that inform my conclusion that reconstructing poverty knowledge is more than simply a matter of generating new research questions for social scientists to pursue.

First and foremost among these insights is that poverty knowledge is fundamentally ideological in nature: It is above all a project of twentieth-century liberalism, dating most immediately from the 1960s and the Great Society, but more deeply rooted in the rise of the "new liberalism" that emerged in late nineteenth-century Euro-American political culture as an alternative to the laissez-faire individualism of the industrial age.[6] Originating, as it did, in this formative period of twentieth-century liberalism, poverty knowledge rests on several characteristic commitments and beliefs: a commitment to using rational empirical investigation for the purposes of statecraft and social reform; a belief that the state, in varying degrees of cooperation with organized civil society, is a necessary protection against the hazards of industrial capitalism and extreme concentrations of poverty and wealth; a commitment, nevertheless, to maintaining a capitalist economy based on private ownership and market principles, however much it need be tamed or managed by public intervention; and, finally, a distinctly secular faith in human progress, not just through the accumulation of knowledge, but through the capacity to apply it for the common good. These core beliefs, to be sure, have been subject to varying interpretations, to internal conflict, and to revision over time. Nevertheless, in one form or another they have defined poverty knowledge as a *liberal* as well as a scientific enterprise, starting with the efforts by Progressive-era social investigators to de-pauperize thinking about poverty—to make it a matter of social rather than individual morality—by turning attention from the "dependent" to the wage-earning poor.

As a historically liberal enterprise, poverty knowledge also reflects the diversity and internal tensions within twentieth-century liberal social thought: differences between labor/ left and corporate/centrist liberals over how to manage the economy; between "top-down," elite-driven and "bottom-up," politically empowering approaches to reform; and even between class-based vs. cultural or "identity" politics, as can be seen in a long-enduring debate pitting "race" against "class" as alternative frameworks for explaining and responding to poverty among African Americans. Most fundamentally though, poverty knowledge reflects a central tension within liberal thought about the nature of inequality—not so much over whether inequality is innate or environmental in origin, but whether it is best understood and addressed at the level of individual experience or as a matter of structural and institutional reform. That this tension has more often been resolved in favor of the individualist interpretation can be seen in several oft-noted features in poverty research. One is the virtual absence of class as an analytic category, at least as compared with more individualized measures of status such as family background and human capital. A similar individualizing tendency can be seen in the reduction of race and gender to little more than demographic, rather than structurally constituted, categories. Poverty research treats the market and the two-parent, male-headed family in much the same way, as inevitable, naturally occurring ways of ordering human relations rather than as institutions that are socially created and maintained. The point is that these have not always been prevailing characteristics in poverty knowledge; nor are they simply a reflection of a shift towards economics as its disciplinary base. They grew just as much out of ongoing struggles within liberalism over the ideological boundaries of reform—the outcomes of which, in the name of remaining realistic or "relevant" for political purposes, have repeatedly eclipsed an alternative, more institutionalist and social democratic research tradition, that has challenged liberalism's individualistic assumptions from within. Nor, for this very reason, should we see the outcome in terms of some self-generating, inevitable ideological trajectory, or in terms of an irreversible end to an expansive, social democratic, or participatory vision of liberal reform. Indeed, the ideological boundaries of poverty knowledge have been drawn and redrawn amidst changing political and economic circumstances, and in an ongoing process of negotiation and debate.

Thus, by paying attention to the history of poverty knowledge, we can see that its very development as a science has been closely tied to the shifting preoccupations, to the political fortunes, and certainly to the major crusades of twentieth-century liberalism. Not all of these crusades were tied so obviously to the expansion of social welfare provision: World War II and the Cold War underwrote the anthropological studies in developing countries that fostered Oscar Lewis's infamous theory of the "culture of poverty." So, too, did they provide the occasion for the use of systems analysis in a burgeoning postwar defense industry—a weapon, so to speak, that federal research administrators imported directly from the Pentagon when it came time to fight the War on Poverty. Poverty knowledge was also shaped by domestic social welfare considerations, and none more powerfully than the experience of postwar economic affluence. Eager to push the expansive economy to its "full growth potential," Keynesian economists in the Kennedy administration cultivated an analysis that linked poverty to sluggish growth and less-than-full employment, and its solution to what skeptics considered the unlikely device of a growth-stimulating tax cut. And it was amidst the great African American migrations of the two post–world war periods that poverty knowledge began gradually to exhibit an assimilationist racial egalitarianism, brilliantly synthesized in Gunnar Myrdal's *An American Dilemma* during the 1940s, that explained differences of race *and* class in terms of culture rather than biology while implicating cultural exclusion and pathology in the persistence of black poverty. Here in particular poverty knowledge proved capable of accommodating, and to some degree anticipating, the social movements and world transformations that were reshaping liberalism at the time, and that made it sufficiently flexible as an ideology to sustain a loose consensus within a diverse constituency during the decades after World War II.

Nevertheless, as with liberalism, the capaciousness of poverty knowledge could only extend so far before bearing the brunt of internal conflict and battering from without. Thus, by the late 1960s both the culture of poverty and racial assimilationism had generated deeply divisive debates within a social scientific community that was itself being transformed by civil rights and women's movement politics. Similarly, with the end of postwar affluence and the collapse of the "Keynesian consensus," poverty knowledge lost both its link to macroeconomic policy and its central organizing idea. More recently, poverty knowledge has been profoundly shaken by the rise of the political Right, with its ideological, not-always secularist approach to knowledge and its extraordinary success in keeping the locus of discourse away from the economics of rising inequality and centered squarely on issues framed as "family values," "big government," and the decline of personal responsibility. It is in this context that the direction poverty knowledge has taken in the past two decades reflects the fragmentation of liberalism, and its subsequent efforts to reinvent itself on a more limited social base—this time in the guise of the "third way," "new Democrat," or market-oriented neoliberalism that ushered in the end of welfare while wholeheartedly embracing the private market as the ultimate arbiter of individual well-being and the common good. With the turn to dependency as its central concept, the contemporary neoliberal drift in poverty research marks an important break with the earlier "new liberal" past, for it in effect re-pauperizes the poverty issue while emphasizing individual, rather than social, morality.

A second major insight from historical analysis is that poverty knowledge is highly political in nature, in ways that go beyond its close association with the trajectory of liberalism, and that have led to the emergence of professional social science as the dominant source of expertise on poverty and welfare policy. To some degree this can be understood as part of the politics of knowledge—the ability of well-placed research entrepreneurs to act as advocates for particular approaches, theoretical frameworks, and for the necessity of social scientific expertise as the basis of enlightened policy. It is thanks to such efforts that poverty knowledge bears the markers of professionalization—specialization, standardized data, experimental methods, a body of theory, or at least a series of "testable hypotheses"—along with the mechanisms for training future generations to uphold established standards of scientific expertise. But the triumph of social science as a way of knowing poverty can also be understood as part of the politics of class, race, and gender in determining who qualifies and can participate as an authority—and who not—in the broader public sphere. Seen in this light, poverty knowledge can be characterized as the project of an increasingly credentialed, formally educated segment of the middle class—one that, despite important contributions from prominent female and nonwhite social scientists, has for most of its history been predominantly white and male. Moreover, the claim to scientific objectivity rests on technical skills, methods, information, and professional networks that historically have excluded those groups most vulnerable to poverty: minorities, women, and especially the relatively less-educated working class, putting poverty knowledge in a position not just to reflect but to replicate the social inequalities it means to investigate.

This is not to say that poverty knowledge can be reduced to a playing out of material class interest (populist and conservative critics to the contrary, there really is *not* much money or professional glamour to be had from studying the poor), nor to deny that individual social scientists have been capable of transcending their class, race, and gender-bound identities. It is to recognize, though, that not only despite but because of its quest for a particular scientific standard, poverty knowledge has been filtered, not just through the experiences and cultural biases of the privileged, but through the social position of "the professors" in relation to "the poor." It is in this regard that recent changes in political economy take on a special significance for poverty knowledge, not just as they affect the demographic "composition" of poverty, but as they pit the more- against the less-educated in the distribution of economic punishments and rewards. In the "new," information-hungry, postindustrial economy, poverty experts are in a position to benefit from the transformations that have destabilized the industrial working class; in economists' language, it is an economy that brings ever-greater "returns" to education while devaluing industrial skills. And yet, poverty experts show little inclination to question whether their own stake in the "new economy" might affect their interpretation that its disparities can be explained primarily as differences in education and skill—

suggesting, in a way reminiscent of earlier cultural criticism, that the poor should simply strive to be more like us.

It is this disparity of status and interest that make poverty research an inescapably political act: It is an exercise of power, in this instance of an educated elite to categorize, stigmatize, but above all to neutralize the poor and disadvantaged through analysis that obscures the political nature of social and economic inequality. By the same token, it is the power to construct and give scientific weight to ideas of what is natural, "functional," or socially desirable, in terms that are exclusive of, if not in direct opposition to, the poor. Finally, it is the power to constitute or at least to influence the categories of social policy in ways that are of material consequence to the poor, whether those categories have to do with determining the particulars of who is eligible (or "deserving") of public assistance or with establishing the broader parameters of the welfare state.

The question of categorization in turn highlights a third important insight from historical analysis, and that is the degree to which poverty knowledge has been influenced by social welfare institutions and the categories they establish for channeling (or denying) aid to people who are poor. For just as social scientists and social research have played a part in shaping policy, so, too, has the structure of U.S. social welfare policy played a central role in designating what constitutes poverty knowledge, and in distinguishing it from labor, or economic, or other bureaucratically influenced categories of research. It was not until the War on Poverty in the 1960s that the state officially recognized poverty as a category for investigation, launching a research operation within the newly created Office of Economic Opportunity, adding poverty statistics to the federal census, and adopting an official "poverty line." Before then, the study of poverty had been segmented according to the categories and constituencies of social policy, acknowledged within the bureaucracy as an aspect of maternal and child welfare, old age, or unemployment but not privileged as a problem worthy of an elaborate investigatory apparatus in its own right. Even when infused with the crusading spirit of the Great Society, poverty could hardly be considered a truly "privileged" research category. Ever aware of its negative connotations, research bureaucrats continually struggled with ways to keep the word "poverty" out of their initiatives, while the institutionalized stigma assigned to "poor people's" or "welfare" programs created an incentive for agencies to sharpen, rather than break down, the distinctions between their own constituencies and the poor.

Poverty knowledge reflects the influence of institutional arrangements in other ways as well, and in particular the uneasy, and changing, relations between the state, civil society, and the private market economy that have characterized the twentieth-century American polity. Made possible from the start by the frequently cooperative ventures of state /federal research bureaus and corporate philanthropy, poverty knowledge has been cultivated primarily within a changing array of nonprofit research organizations and social policy "intermediaries" which, though established to be nonpartisan sources of knowledge, presumably independent of politics or the state, have themselves been affected by three major developments in the public/private "mix."

The first is what was, at least up until the 1980s, a fairly steady expansion of the state in the production of social scientific knowledge, resulting in a proliferation of agency research bureaus, along with opportunities for social scientists to move in and out of official government posts. It was not until after World War II, however, that the prospect of often large federal government contracts became a mainstay, as well as a source of legitimacy, in social scientific research. Like other large-scale government undertakings, the War on Poverty played a pivotal role in this regard, generating the impetus for the elaboration of a whole new set of specialized research institutions designed specifically to meet federal demands for policy research. Thus constituted, poverty research developed what by contemporary welfare criteria would have to be considered an unhealthy, long-term "dependence" on the state—certainly a tendency to follow, rather than to set, the parameters of policy debate. A second development, somewhat paradoxically, was the simultaneous tendency to embrace the values of the private market in the organization and production of knowledge—a competitive approach to procuring, and using, research in a federal social research "market" that was constructed to meet political as well as administrative needs. Nowhere was the competitive principle more operative than in the rise, expansion, and ultimate survival of the poverty research industry, due largely to its entrepreneurial capacity to win government contracts even after successive administrations began to dismantle the apparatus of the Great Society welfare state. Indeed, the dramatic devolution of federal welfare responsibility since the 1980s has actually sped the competitive pulse, as state and local think tanks proliferate and state agencies become increasingly important sources of funding once federally controlled.[7] Contrary to stated expectations, however, the embrace of competitive principles has hardly been a guarantee of independent thought; if anything, it has tied poverty knowledge more closely than ever to a contract market defined by agency needs, and to a narrowly construed policy agenda that has given far higher priority to reforming welfare than to improving living standards for the working class. Thus, the most recent historical development is perhaps most paradoxical of all, and that is the rise of an alternative network of conservative and libertarian knowledge-producing institutions that have managed to exert far greater policy influence by eschewing government contracts, while embracing competitive market principles as the basis for policy as well as for aggressively publicizing their wares.

A fourth set of insights from historical analysis has to do with the nature of poverty knowledge as science: to some degree in the enlightenment sense of progressively accumulated knowledge, but more fundamentally as a product and shaping force in culture—a source of language, interpretive frameworks, even of the stylized rituals of investigation that give expression to broader social understandings of the human condition and of social change. Judged according to the norms of rational enlightenment, poverty knowledge can indeed be credited with certain achievements, even if they have more to do with documenting unequal or substandard conditions than with explaining why they persist. With the help, for example, of longitudinal data, social experimentation, and a wide array of evaluation studies, social scientists have systematically challenged the stubborn mythology that poor people are lazy, nonworking, or for that matter that poor people are all alike. As welfare debates never cease to remind us, however, very little in this body of presumably established learning is uncontested—scientists arrive at very different conclusions even when they use the same data and methodologies—nor has it, as learning, extended much beyond an expert elite. In contrast, scientific poverty knowledge has had a far more lasting impact on the American cultural and social policy vocabulary, albeit with ambiguous, at times contradictory results.

On the one hand is the notion, put forward initially by nineteenth-century social investigators, that poverty is an objective, quantifiable condition—measurable against a scientifically calculated standard of need known as the *poverty line*. This measure of poverty has since been absorbed into bureaucratic, political, and to a more limited degree popular culture—a way of determining program eligibility as well as an indictment of society's neglect. Equally important, at least in the eyes of its original proponents, is the social conviction the measure implies: poverty is not a mystery of nature; it can be explained, reduced, or eliminated by rational means. On the other hand, and far more ubiquitous in political and popular culture, have been the many social scientific variations on precisely the opposite theme: the notion, variously expressed in concepts such as social "disorganization," "deviance," or "dysfunction"; in metaphors such as the "vicious circle" or the self-perpetuating "tangle of pathology"; and in totalizing theories of the "culture of poverty," or, most recently, the "underclass," that poverty is deeply ingrained in "intractable" psychological and cultural processes that may very well be beyond rehabilitation or reform. Despite its current association with conservative politics, the culture of poverty and its variants gained the imprimatur of scientific objectivity within a liberal research tradition. As can be seen in recent efforts to measure the underclass according to behavioral indicators, they have since achieved the status of quantifiable fact—a status that at least some poverty experts, unable to control the politics of "blaming the victim," have subsequently come to regret. In this sense, at least, poverty experts have proved to be rather ineffective cultural brokers: even when offered in the name of social criticism or as a call to action, their formulations of cultural deviance have been used far more readily and regularly to stigmatize, isolate, and deny assistance to the poor.

Alongside the language that has been absorbed into popular and political culture, over the past three decades poverty knowledge has also cultivated an increasingly technical jargon as the common, if not exclusive, language of poverty expertise. More than simply a question of quantification—the "amateur" researchers of the social survey movement were every bit as quantitative as current-day econometricians—the technical jargon of recent decades has taken poverty knowledge to a level of abstraction and exclusivity that it had not known before. It is a language laced with acronyms that themselves speak of particular data sets, policies, and analytic techniques (PSID, NLSY, TRIM, FAP, PBJI, EITC, and, albeit without a detectable sense of irony, Five Year Plans and a model known as the KGB). It also speaks of a self-contained system of reasoning that is largely devoid of political or historical context, in which individuals are the units of analysis and markets the principal arbiters of human exchange. The effect has been to put entire questions and categories of inquiry outside the boundaries of critical scientific discourse—capitalism, for example, like the institutionalized systems of race and gender relations, does not translate into variables that can be scrutinized within these models of cause and effect.

On the whole, though, poverty knowledge has been perhaps most effective as a form of cultural affirmation: a powerful reassurance that poverty occurs outside or in spite of core American values and practices, whether those are defined in terms of capitalist markets, political democracy, self-reliance, and/ or a two-parent, white, middle-class family ideal. Although present in much of the social scientific literature before then, it was not until the 1960s that this theme became virtually institutionalized in research. That, after all, was when federal officials, designating "poverty" as a distinct social, policy, and analytic category, quite consciously detached it from the language of income distribution, class, and racial inequality. Poverty, to use the terminology of the day, occurs in some "other," separate America; as an aberration, an exception, a "paradox" of plenty rather than as an integral or necessary condition of the affluent society.[8] Built on this premise, poverty knowledge continues to hold out a certain promise: doing something about, even eliminating, poverty will not require radical change; whether through social engineering, wage subsidies, economic growth, or the new/old-fashioned strategy of pushing people into the market, the paradox can be resolved without resorting to a massive redistribution of power and wealth. It also offers a substitute language, of deviance and deprivation, for the language of inequality. Most important from a policy perspective, it conceptually disenfranchises poor people from the larger political community—experts refer to the "working poor," not the "working class"—and in this way has helped to confine the reform conversation to the problem of welfare rather than the problems of political economy and work.

In addition to these insights about the nature of poverty knowledge, historical analysis provides the basis of a narrative that weaves the various dimensions of poverty knowledge together—ideological, political, institutional, cultural—while paying attention to the ever-changing contingencies of politics, social movements, and critical events. This narrative, as laid out in the next several chapters, is a story of transformation: over the course of the twentieth century, the study of poverty has changed. What started out as a series of reform-minded, sometimes "amateur" investigations into the political, or "social" economy of industrial capitalism has become an ostensibly more detached, highly professionalized and technically proficient inquiry that takes postindustrial capitalism as a given and focuses primarily on evaluating welfare programs, as well as on measuring and modeling the demographic and behavioral characteristics of the poor. This transformation did not occur as a smooth, one-directional, or cumulative progression, but more as a series of "turns," or paradigm shifts. Nor did it take place along a single, clear-cut political or ideological continuum so much as along liberalism's complicated twists and turns. Moreover, within this narrative of transformation are several continuities, in particular an enduring tension that has only recently become polarized along liberal/conservative lines, between a discourse that associates poverty with some form of cultural pathology or difference and one that points to structural barriers in society and political economy. As we shall see, the tension between "culture" and "structure," while long-standing, has not always been sharply drawn. For many, indeed, the existence of a poor, presumably pathological subculture has been both a product of and a reason for redressing structural inequities in the political economy. It is also the case that the tension has been bound up just as much in disciplinary rivalries as in prescriptions for policy. Nevertheless, as poverty knowledge became more and more about poor people and less and less about culture or political economy more broadly defined, the terms of the question became more oppositional: what differentiates poor people—money or culture—from everyone else? It is in this context that "culture" vs. "structure" has come to be regarded as an either/or choice.

Two other themes warrant special mention in this narrative of transformation, and indeed help to explain its twists and turns. One is just how deeply race has influenced the course of poverty knowledge, in the form of racial ideology and racial politics, as well as in the racialized nature of poverty and social policy. Thus, for example, it was at least in part the battle against pseudo-biological justifications for racism that, in the early decades of the twentieth century, helped to draw racially liberal social scientists to culture, both as a way of explaining racial differences and inequities and as a way of showing that they were neither natural nor inevitable. By the 1960s, though, culture was itself becoming a suspect category in poverty knowledge, largely in reaction to an unrelenting, heavily psychologized imagery of black cultural deviance and pathology that, many suspected, had come to replace biology as a basis for scientific racism. In other instances, race has exerted an equally powerful influence as an unacknowledged variable, in analyses that, for political and ideological as well as for scientific reasons, have diminished the importance of racially discriminatory institutions and social practices in explaining racialized patterns of poverty. In this context, poverty has been conceptualized as an alternative to rather than as a dimension of racial inequality—and itself a problem that can be addressed without explicit "race-targeted" policies. Nevertheless, the reality that poverty, and particularly welfare, have themselves become such racially charged political problems has consistently undermined the very possibility of "race-neutral" antipoverty policy.

A second theme running throughout the narrative is that poverty knowledge, especially in recent decades, has frequently assumed far different political meanings than what is envisioned by social scientists. Nowhere is this more apparent than in the transformation of the culture of poverty in the late 1960s and early 1970s from an argument for liberal intervention if not radical social revolution (as Oscar Lewis occasionally hinted) to an argument for conservative withdrawal from the welfare state—a transformation brought about as much by liberal and left critics who drew out the implications of the behavioristic cast of Lewis's theory as by an outright conservative embrace of the culture of poverty theory. While themselves avoiding thorny issues of culture, economists affiliated with the War on Poverty similarly saw their research used for unintended political purposes, when conservative policy analysts effectively appropriated their methods, findings, and to some degree their style of discourse to undermine support for the welfare state in the 1980s. It is not only the culture of poverty, then, that has been absorbed into conservative policy thinking—Charles Murray, indeed, insisted that unmarried mothers grown dependent on welfare were simply responding as *any* rational actor would to the perverse incentives of the liberal welfare state. It is more a matter of a knowledge base that, however unintentionally, has opened itself to conservative interpretation by locating the crux of the poverty problem in the characteristics of the poor. But the use of poverty knowledge for overtly conservative purposes also reveals an aspect of the relationship between knowledge and policy that liberal or purportedly "neutral" social scientists have continually underestimated—no matter how many times the best-laid plans of empirically informed policy intellectuals have gone either unattended or misconstrued. What matters in determining whether and how knowledge connects to policy is not only the classical enlightenment properties of rationality and verifiability; nor is it only the way knowledge is mobilized, packaged, and circulated; nor even whether the knowledge corresponds with (or effectively shatters) popularly held values and conventional wisdom. All of these things have, indeed, proved important in affecting the course of poverty and welfare policy. Even more important in determining the political meaning and policy consequences of poverty knowledge, though, has been the power to establish the terms of debate—to contest, gain, and ultimately to exercise ideological hegemony over the boundaries of political discourse. It is within this broader context, of ideological battle that for the past two decades has been dominated by the conservative right, that poverty knowledge has been used most effectively for politically conservative ends.

Part One of this book begins with a discussion of what was known during the Progressive Era as "social" economy and its efforts, most fully realized in the social survey movement, to recast public understanding of poverty by emphasizing its roots in unemployment, low wages, labor exploitation, political disfranchisement, and more generally in the social disruptions associated with large-scale urbanization and industrial capitalism. To be sure, Progressive social investigators wrote with conviction about what they considered to be the moral and cultural deficiencies of poor people. But they also used their investigations to frame a much different kind of critical discourse: in the case of the famed Hull House and Pittsburgh surveys, about the policies and institutional practices of corporate capital; about the history and political economy of racial discrimination in the case of W.E.B. DuBois; and even, in studies of women in industrial, agricultural, and household work, about the burdens created by the gendered division of labor. In this way, Progressive social investigators sought to extend the boundaries of antipoverty thinking to issues of industrial democracy, political reform, and trade union organizing as well as to the kind of community-based cultural uplift for which the settlement houses have become renowned.

In chapter 1 I trace the shift from this Progressive "social" economy to Chicago-school "social ecology" as the dominant paradigm in poverty research. With substantial funding from the Rockefeller Foundation, Chicago-school sociologists built a formidable research and training institution, with an emphasis on theory-based, "objectivist" research as the appropriate knowledge base for policy. Emulating the rigors and experimental techniques of the natural sciences, Robert E. Park, Ernest W. Burgess, and their students treated local neighborhoods more as laboratories for research and experimentation than as sites for political organizing, social uplift, or industrial reform. Their naturalistic models of urbanization, assimilation, and social "disorganization" explained poverty as an inevitable by-product of modernization, and looked to more limited attempts to achieve neighborhood and family "reorganization" in response. By the late 1920s, this model of community study and action had largely displaced Progressive-era reform investigation as a source of expertise, while reinforcing a growing professional and gender divide between academic social science and feminized or "amateur" reform research. Equally important, the Chicago-school turn in social investigation marked a shift away from political economy as a framework for understanding poverty, and an embrace of the newer, social psychological and cultural approaches of sociology and anthropology. The implications of these developments were profound: social disorganization and cultural lag, not industrial capitalism, were at the root of the poverty problem in the new social science, and cultural, not industrial, "reorganization" was the cure.

In chapter 2, I show how these themes and methods continued to frame social scientific understanding of poverty during the Great Depression, amidst renewed concern over unemployment, low wages, and class polarization. Shifting away from an initial, anti-statist emphasis in social ecology, however, sociologists and social anthropologists used the techniques of cultural analysis, social psychology, and laboratory-like community study to reintroduce and invigorate the case for progressive-style political and economic reform. In landmark community studies by Robert S. Lynd, W. Lloyd Warner, and E. Wight Bakke, poverty was indeed a problem of corporate restructuring, and unregulated capitalist markets, but it was also a sign of the cultural "lags" of a society unable to adjust to the need for a welfare state. At the same time, according to these scholars, poverty also led to deep-seated, potentially self-perpetuating cultural and psychological disorders that stood as powerful evidence of the need for enhanced social engineering to accompany the project of relief and reform. So, too, according to regionalist sociologists at the University of North Carolina, had poverty hardened into cultural affliction in the backward, "colonial" political economy that had earned the South recognition as the nation's "number one economic problem."

In chapter 3 I draw out the ambiguities of this turn to culture as manifest in the sociology of poverty and race, showing how racially liberal social scientists used the concept of culture as at once a challenge to the biological racism of earlier social science and as a powerfully stigmatizing way of explaining why such a large proportion of the African American population remained mired in poverty. Drawing alternately from Chicago-school social ecology and social anthropology, sociologists in the 1930s and 1940s arrived at competing explanations for the high rates of poverty among blacks. Those explanations came together, though, in treating poverty as a form of cultural deviance or pathology—whether a legacy of the cultural damage done by slavery, or an expression of the psychologically distorting influence of persistent white racism. It was this formulation of cultural pathology that would most heavily engage social scientific thinking about race and poverty for decades to come, and that, even when invoked as a rationale for greater social and economic inclusion, reinforced the imagery of a basically unassimilable black lower class.

The analytic emphasis on social psychology and culture redoubled in the postwar decades, fueled by a combination of widening prosperity, Cold War politics, and especially by the tremendous expansion in funding for research in the behavioral sciences by private foundations and federal government agencies. Turning away once again from political economy as the focus of investigation or intervention, postwar sociologists and anthropologists concentrated instead on the unique culture and psychology of what they regarded as an isolated class of poor people, sharply distinguished from the more respectable working class, in an otherwise affluent society. As discussed in chapter 4, this notion of cultural isolation also rested on an increasingly psychological understanding of the family, and specifically of gender relations within low-income, and particularly within black families, that drew heightened attention to poor women's reproductive behavior while ignoring their economic role. These ideas about gender relations, expressed powerfully in studies of the impact of the "mother-centered" or "matriarchal" family, were central to the culture of poverty theory developed by Oscar Lewis, and widely accepted in liberal social science by the late 1950s and early 1960s. As discussed in chapter 5, this and other theories of cultural deprivation and social disorganization became the basis of a whole series of sociologically informed, community-based, primarily urban social interventions sponsored by foundations and government agencies, that served as testing grounds for the War on Poverty. Depicting the poor as socially isolated, and culturally deprived, these experiments proved inadequate as a response to the ongoing problems of racial discrimination, suburbanization, and industrial decline that were then reshaping the urban United States. At least in their earliest stages, they also embraced an essentially apolitical vision of deliberative, rational, "top-down" change that the actual experience of community action in the 1960s would quite literally explode.

Part Two of this book focuses on a set of developments that pulled poverty knowledge in a somewhat different direction. It begins, in chapter 6, with the emergence of a new political economy of poverty in the decades following World War II, ushered in by the Keynesian and human capital "revolutions" in economic thought and by the growing influence of economists in the expanding policy apparatus of the federal government. Grounded in market-centered, neoclassical economics, the new political economy returned to the older categories of income, wages, and employment in its definition of the poverty problem, but explained it as an indicator of inadequate economic growth, high unemployment, and individual human capital deficiencies rather than relating it to the unequal distribution of wealth and opportunity. Like its predecessors, this formulation of the poverty problem reflected political and ideological concerns as much as new analytic approaches. Aware of the political hazards, administration economists made a conscious effort to avoid mention of redistribution or economic restructuring in their proposals, emphasizing instead the power of macroeconomic growth, high employment, and individual human capital investment to bring poverty to an end. They also presented their antipoverty initiative as essentially "race-neutral," confident once again that growth and tight labor markets would diminish the need for more overt, politically risky, antidiscrimination policies. In many ways, this approach shared more in common with the psychology and culture of modernist social science than with the political economy of Progressive reform: poverty stemmed not from the economic and institutional relationships of industrial capitalism, but from the individual—in this case skill—deficiencies of the poor. Thus, while uncomfortable with psychological renditions of a problem they sought to redress with economic measures, administration economists nevertheless incorporated the notion of a culture of poverty in their blueprint for the War on Poverty in 1964, and called for programs that would break the "vicious cycle" that had captured the poor.

The tensions within the Great Society idea of poverty soon started coming unraveled, however, when social scientists became embroiled in a series of disputes that left their tenuous "consensus" in disarray. In chapter 7 I discuss some of the less visible of these disputes, between economists and community action administrators in the Office of Economic Opportunity over the *kind* of social knowledge that was needed to fight poverty. This time, ironically, it was the new political economy, armed with "hard" quantitative data, econometric modeling techniques, and cost/benefit policy analysis, that laid claim to the mantle of objectivity and political neutrality—and that, with the swift political demise of community action, displaced sociology as the dominant framework for poverty knowledge in the OEO. Borrowing from the experience of postwar defense research, OEO economists led the way in creating the institutional infrastructure for a poverty research industry—an industry designed with the needs and interests of government policy makers in mind, principally reliant on federal agencies for funding, and thriving long after the War on Poverty had been abandoned. Chapter 8 then turns to the more public and visible of the poverty "wars" of the mid-to-late 1960s, tracing a series of highly polarized debates over the ideas about culture, race, and poverty underlying administration policy, most prominent among them the debate over the Moynihan Report on the Negro Family following the Watts riot in 1965.

Part Three of *Poverty Knowledge* follows the fortunes of the poverty research industry in the aftermath of the War on Poverty, when, in the face of growing inequality, wage deterioration, urban deindustrialization, and a profound ideological challenge to the liberal welfare state, the social scientific poverty discourse narrowed even further to focus principally on understanding the "dynamics" of welfare dependency, the skill deficits of the "working poor," and the size and characteristics of the urban "underclass." In chapter 9 I outline the political origins and institutional structure of the poverty research industry, in the form of an interlocking network of government agencies, private foundations, and nonprofit research institutes that operated together to define and contain the boundaries of scientific poverty research. Reflecting a research agenda that was substantially defined by the political obsession with welfare reform, poverty researchers acquiesced to the shrinking parameters of social policy by confining their sights to diagnoses and interventions targeting poor people and their behavior while avoiding the pressing issue of growing disparities in income and wealth. Nor could analysis offer anything more than limited, mostly descriptive explanations for why poverty was on the rise—explanations that, confined as they were to what was measurable in existing databases, invariably pointed to individual-level characteristics as the cause. In chapter 10 I show the poverty research industry faced with challenges that these individualized models could not explain—growing inequality, wage deterioration, deindustrialization, concentrated urban poverty—while grappling with an even more fundamental ideological challenge from the political right. Little wonder, then, that poverty analysts were overshadowed by the more explicitly ideological, heavily publicized explanations offered by Charles Murray and other conservative social scientists who, nominally using the same "neutral" analytic techniques perfected by economists at the OEO, blamed the rise of poverty on the liberal welfare state. In two ways, I conclude in chapter 11, liberal poverty knowledge contributed to the end of welfare in 1996—its acquiescence to a political agenda that had less to do with reducing poverty than with reducing the welfare rolls, and its failure to provide an explanatory knowledge base for an alternative agenda of political and economic reform.

It is with these failures in mind that I conclude by outlining what a reconstructed poverty knowledge might look like, a project that would draw upon the insights from historical analysis to take in the political, ideological, institutional, and cultural as well as the more immediate research agenda-setting dimensions of the task. I aim, with this outline, to start a conversation rather than to offer precise prescriptions for change. The first task is to redefine the conceptual basis for poverty knowledge, above all by shifting the analytic framework from its current narrow focus on explaining individual deprivation to a more systemic and structural focus on explaining—and addressing—inequalities in the distribution of power, wealth, and opportunity. A second is to broaden the empirical basis for poverty knowledge—recognizing that studying poverty is not the same thing as studying the poor—by turning empirical attention to political, economic, institutional and historical conditions, to the policy decisions that shape the distribution of power and wealth, and to interventions that seek to change the conditions of structural inequality rather than narrowly focusing on changing the poor. A third task is to change the way poverty knowledge is produced and organized, shifting away from the state-centered "research industry" model created during the War on Poverty in order to generate more independence and diversity in setting research agendas. A fourth is to challenge the distinctions that associate narrowly construed, hypothesis-testing models of inquiry with "objectivity" while denigrating more theoretical, historical, and structural analyses as "advocacy" or ideology. Above all, a reconstructed poverty knowledge would challenge two fallacies that, despite having been subject to frequent criticism, continue to inform the quest for more or better knowledge about the poor: one, that good social science is a necessarily apolitical, ideology- or "value-free" endeavor; the other, that rational, scientific knowledge about poverty will yield a rational, scientific "cure."

PART ONE

CHAPTER 1.

Origins: Poverty and Social Science in The Era of Progressive Reform

AT THE END of the nineteenth century social investigators in several of the world's most advanced industrial societies set out to bring new scientific understanding to the problem of poverty. In this they were very much caught up in the international wave of organizing, policy innovation, state building, and, above all, social learning that characterized the decades between 1880 and the beginning of World War I as an era of progressive reform.[1] They were also moved by the central paradox Henry George referred to in the title of his wildly popular *Progress and Poverty* (1879) and in subsequent lecture tours: that great wealth and unprecedented productive capacity brought increasing poverty. So, too, were they dedicated to challenging the precepts of "laissez-faire," a doctrine they associated with unbridled free market capitalism, the narrow pursuit of individual self-interest, and the rise of a social scientific justification for inequality and concentrated wealth.[2] Drawing on a combination of classical economics and Social Darwinism, Yale University sociologist William Graham Sumner had argued that inequality was a social expression of the natural laws of economic competition—the survival and dominance of the fittest— and that any attempt to intervene in the free market system would simply set progress back on its heels.[3] Poverty was not only inevitable but, in Sumner's words, "the best policy": deprived by their own or by nature's doing, the poor had no special claim on society at large.

The new knowledge, in contrast, would distinguish itself from other types of "scientific" investigation in several ways, which together make the Progressive Era a foundational period for twentieth-century poverty research. In the first instance it would be rigorously empirical—for the most part, quantitative—distinguishing it from the more abstract discourse of classical economics that inscribed poverty, along with the operation of markets, with the aura of natural law. The new poverty knowledge would take its cue instead from the insurgent, German-influenced "new economics" expounded by Richard T. Ely, Henry Carter Adams, and other founders of the American Economic Association in 1885, which embraced a more historical and institutional, but above all, social and ethical understanding of how the capitalist economy had evolved.[4] Second, the new poverty knowledge would be rigorously objective, as distinct from the morally judgmental inquiries of charity work, and would devote itself to devising more and ever-better scientific methods for gathering, categorizing, and analyzing the facts of social, as opposed to merely individual, circumstance. Third, the new poverty knowledge would in no other sense be neutral; it would, without bias toward specifics, serve the interests of reform. Moreover, the new knowledge would be instrumental in other ways as well, serving the institution-building objectives of a burgeoning array of public and private organizations—social settlements, philanthropies, professional and civic groups, state and federal bureaus of research—that were beginning to look beyond the patchwork of local poor laws and private charities for ways of prevention rather than relief.[5] The first order of business for the new poverty knowledge, then, was not only to denaturalize but to depauperize the "poverty problem," by redirecting attention from individual dependency to social and, especially, to labor conditions as underlying cause.[6]

To be sure, the new poverty knowledge was not without moral judgment; it, too, deemed relief a corrupting influence and distinguished between deserving and undeserving poor. But Progressive investigators took some care to distinguish social research from individual casework, to make theirs a study of *poverty* rather than the poor. It was above all this shift in sensibility that set the stage for the future development of poverty knowledge as a social scientific research field, informing at once the extraordinary outpouring of investigation into social conditions and the wave of philanthropic institution-building that marked the Progressive Era. Ironically, it was in the name of this very same sensibility that succeeding generations of social scientists would seek to distinguish theirs from that early Progressive project, with an approach to knowledge that was at once more recognizably scientific and less immediately attached to reform. It was thus as a more naturalistic, behavioral science that the new poverty knowledge would seek to establish its cultural and political authority. By the 1920s, University of Chicago sociologists had taken a first step in that direction, with an "ecological" analysis of poverty that focused more on issues of identity and culture than on employment and wages, and that provided the conceptual underpinnings for programs of community action against poverty in the second half of the twentieth century.

POVERTY AND INDUSTRIAL REFORM:
THE SOCIAL SURVEY MOVEMENT

Of all the methods of Progressive Era social investigation none better captures the blend of social science and reform sensibility—of advocacy *through* objectivity—than the social surveys conducted in the cities that were home to industrial capital and, in the U.S., to an increasingly immigrant and nonwhite working class. The earliest and most renowned of the surveys—in London, Chicago, Philadelphia, and Pittsburgh—have since been recognized as precursors to the emergence of the more sophisticated sample survey methodology familiar to our own time. But the social surveys of the Progressive Era are relevant for reasons that go well beyond methodology, most importantly for establishing a framework within which poverty could be investigated as a problem of political or social economy—of low wages, un- and "under"-employment, long hours, hazardous work conditions—and of the policies and practices governing the distribution of income and wealth. It was a framework, moreover, within which investigators could, however sporadically, examine the political economy of racial and gender as well as class inequality—here again by scrutinizing the discriminatory policies and practices that shaped the labor market and even, tentatively, relationships within the working-class family. Equally important, the social survey aimed to be both comprehensive and contextual, an aim that drew attention beyond individuals and households to the community, the neighborhood, the workplace, and to the details of associational life.

The social survey was also notable as an effort to join research with reform in several ways: by devoting as much energy to displaying and publicizing as to amassing the data; by using it as the basis for local organizing and community action; and by making research a collective endeavor that engaged the energies of amateur as well as professional social scientists—although not, as later models of action research would, working-class community residents themselves. Finally, at its height the social survey joined forces with the new, more institutionalized private philanthropies to create a space outside either the state or the university to generate knowledge for Progressive reform. As a movement, more than in any single community study, the social survey quite literally began to map out the substantive and institutional terrain of poverty knowledge that would be explored by future generations of social scientists, some with much different models and concerns in mind.

In terms of sheer size and international attention, nothing in the social survey movement could approach Charles Booth's *Life and Labour of the People in London*, a seventeen-volume study published between 1889 and 1903, considered in its time and subsequently to be "the first great empirical study in the social survey tradition."[7] Booth himself may have appeared something of an unlikely poverty surveyor—a wealthy shipping merchant turned amateur social scientist, a member of the Royal Statistical Society who financed his own research and made it his personal avocation—but he was no stranger to reform circles. Active as a philanthropist since early in his career, he was consistently a voice for individual self-reliance and welfare capitalism, who nonetheless envisioned a substantial role for the state in providing for the elderly and certain categories among the poor: at one point he toyed with the not-uncommon idea of state-run labor colonies for the most "shiftless" of London's poor. He was also known to engage in respectful, albeit oppositional, debate with British socialists, including his cousin by marriage and co-investigator, Beatrice Potter Webb.[8]

Booth's study was notable for its painstaking and detailed data, but what truly drew attention was his use of graphic and statistical display, best illustrated in his famous "Descriptive Map of London Poverty" (published in 1891), which soon became a kind of traveling centerpiece of social economy exhibits around the world. To be sure, there were many revelations in Booth's statistical findings, which American investigators were eager to reproduce. Not in the least of these was what Booth found about the extent and causes of poverty, reportedly a surprise even to him: 30 percent of Londoners lived below or just at his somewhat impressionistically defined "line of poverty," and problems with employment—lack of jobs, low wages, or intermittent work—were chiefly to blame. Contrary to popular opinion, "habit" and behavior could account for only a small proportion of London's poverty; the lowest, virtually self-reproducing class of "semi-criminals" measured less than 1 percent of the population at large. The other leading causes, besides employment, were illness and family size. Indeed, contemporary readers may be struck with a certain sense of déjà vu: Booth's findings touch on the contemporary contours of poverty, as well as on the myths contemporary poverty knowledge seeks continuously to dispel. Equally striking in this regard was Booth's emphasis on the heterogeneity of the poor, who made up the bottom half of an elaborate eight-part scheme of social classes—A for the "lowest class of occasional labourers, loafers, and semi-criminals," B for the marginally employed "very poor," C for seasonal laborers, D for the low-paid, regularly employed poor— on a scale that went from there to skilled laborers on through to the wealthy "upper middle class."[9]

But it was the maps, as much if not more than the voluminously reported findings, that offered a distinctive way to *look* at poverty—in a way, in contrast to the poignant but voyeuristic and individualized photographs published in Jacob Riis's *How the Other Half Lives* (1890), that appealed to middle-class intellect rather than mere sentiment. For there, in color-coded relief, Booth and his assistants made poverty a part of the social and industrial fabric, of what would later be called its social ecology, and still later its "built environment," by locating each of his eight classes in residential neighborhoods to create a dramatic illustration of the social geography of poverty and wealth.[10] The maps also made poverty concrete and compelling, as a social problem to be reckoned with, to an educated middle class. Indeed, Booth's study, which helped to launch the social survey movement in the United States, was entirely filtered through middle-class perceptions: For all the extraordinary detail of its data, there was no direct testimony—no actual household survey—to back it up. Booth's survey relied instead on the observations and estimates of amateur investigators and local school board home visitors for statistical and qualitative data on everything from occupations, income, expenditures, and housing conditions to the street life of the neighborhoods.

The maps were the most direct link to the first and most well-known of the U.S. settlement house surveys inspired by Booth's example, *Hull House Maps and Papers*, published in 1895. Acknowledging the "greater minuteness" of the territory—the study was confined to the third of a square mile immediately to the east of Hull House, in Chicago's 19th ward—its authors invoked the "great interest" generated by Booth's maps as a source of "warm encouragement" for their own work.[11] Their debt was most visible in the now-famous color-coded Hull House maps, which graphically displayed the wage levels, diversity, and the residential density in that working-class neighborhood. But *Hull House* differed from Booth's work in several important respects, indicating both the distinctive characteristics of urban poverty, and some of the more homegrown roots of the new poverty knowledge in the United States.[12]

First, the Hull House maps underscored the degree to which race and ethnicity were essential dimensions of social stratification, and a central preoccupation in American reform. The issues were particularly salient for Hull House residents, who had founded their settlement in 1889 amidst the vast "new immigration" that brought thousands of racially "other" Southern and Eastern Europeans to a city that was already home to large concentrations of British, Irish, and German immigrants. The results were in plain view in the most pronounced of the Hull House innovations: accompanying the color-coded Map of Wages was a color-coded Map of Nationalities, which had no counterpart in Booth's work. There, observers could see not only the intermingling of "eighteen nations . . . in this small section of Chicago," but also their segmentation into "little colonies" that reflected an internal hierarchy in the slums—blacks ("colored") were clustered on the least desirable blocks; Italians and Jews frequently relegated to the rear apartments in larger tenements.[13] Here the "minuteness" of the study area was in fact its strength, capturing in miniature the multilayered patterns of wage inequality and residential segregation that would only later harden into a stark separation between black and white. In this regard, though, the great visual contribution of the maps did not extend to the analysis in the accompanying papers. Save for a largely descriptive and methodological opening comment by resident Agnes Holbrook, the neighborhood data plotted on the maps are nowhere discussed in the book. The Hull House *Papers*, instead, amount to an eclectic compilation of essays by various residents and associates based on their own independent research, featuring exposés of child labor and the infamous "sweating system" by Florence Kelley, a comparative study of cloakmakers in New York and Chicago by a young resident named Isabel Eaton, a series of separate essays on the Jews, the Bohemians, and the Italians of the 19th ward, and a contribution from Hull House founder Jane Addams on the role of settlements in the movement for industrial democracy. The purpose of the maps was to "present conditions rather than to advance theories," Holbrook noted.[14] Connecting the patterns of workers' earnings and racial segregation would await the more systematic and concentrated efforts of W.E.B. DuBois.

In fact, the absence of a visible editorial hand or even common database in the volume points to a second distinctive aspect of the Hull House survey, and, in the 1890s, social policy investigation in the U.S. more generally. Unlike *Life and Labours*, which originated as a personal act of investigation and philanthropy, *Hull House Maps and Papers* grew out of a much more scattered sequence of connections that linked the settlement house to both university-trained scholars and government research bureaus in what remained a decidedly ad hoc process of generating knowledge for the work of policy and reform. Indeed, Booth was quite consciously responding to a generalized but "evident demand for information" emanating from contemporary policy debates. He also, by virtue of his social standing and connections, had ready access to the relatively more enclosed, centralized London policy making elite.[15] The Hull House residents, in contrast, drew from several different empirical investigations, conducted independently for a scattered array of agencies and designed to meet more immediate, specifically targeted policy needs. In at least one instance this made for an important improvement, due in part to the relatively advanced state of publicly gathered labor statistics in the U.S.: the statistical data for the Hull House maps was based on actual household surveys, supervised by then-resident Florence E. Kelley and commissioned as part of a study of urban slums by U.S. Bureau of Labor Statistics director Carroll D. Wright. Kelley herself was an experienced social investigator, with graduate training at the University of Zurich that had introduced her to the philosophic underpinnings of the "new economics" as well as to the leading figures in European socialism. By the early 1890s, she was beginning to gain notice as an expert on female and child labor—an expertise, due to the bars of gender, she and other women social scientists had cultivated outside the formal academy. When Wright commissioned her for the BLS study she was already immersed in her duties as a special agent of the Illinois Bureau of Labor Statistics, charged with investigating child labor and the sweating system—the subjects of her contributions to the *Hull House* text. Still, in the hopes of having a policy impact beyond these bureau connections, Kelley turned to the academy: *Hull House Maps and Papers* was published under the auspices of Richard T. Ely's Library of Economics and Politics, and was subject to Ely's review.[16]

But if *Hull House Maps and Papers* exhibited a certain ad hoc–ness, it was at least in part because Addams and Kelley wanted it that way: social investigation, Addams believed, could best advance the multifaceted settlement mission by remaining independent of the state or the university. Like Toynbee Hall, their counterpart in London, settlement house members established residence in working-class neighborhoods to stem the threat of class polarization through programs of education and cultural uplift, but even more

so through actually "sharing," as Jane Addams put it, "the life of the poor."
Also unlike the British movement, the American settlement aimed to channel
the talents and energies of educated, middle-class Progressive women, for
whom it offered an alternative pathway to reform leadership and professional-
ism in the face of restricted opportunities in more traditionally male-dominated
venues.[17] Social science was integral to both of these objectives: One of the
first Hull House endeavors was the Working People's Social Science Club, a
neighborhood forum on "social and economic topics" that drew speakers and
participants from around the world.[18] The settlement also proved an excellent
venue for female residents to practice—and acquire—the skills of empirical
investigation, and eventually to see their work in published form.[19] For the
Hull House investigators, fulfilling these aspects of the settlement house mission could be put to scientific advantage: as neighborhood residents, they actually lived with the dense tenement crowding, hidden sweatshops, lack of services, and constant changeover that might escape the otherwise untrained eye,
as Agnes Holbrook noted in her opening essay. Their status as neighbors further helped, she believed, not only in smoothing the "insistent probing into the
lives of the poor," but in matters of statistical measurement as well. So, too,
did their status as women make a difference. The question of family income
was a case in point. The Hull House residents were aware of the essential
contributions of women and children to family income, Holbrook wrote: "In
this neighborhood . . . a wife and children are sources of income as well as
avenues of expense." Accordingly, they relinquished the practice of treating
wives and adult children as dependents and instead counted them as separate
wage-earning units contributing to household income. "The theory that 'every
man supports his own family' is as idle in a district like this as the fiction that
'every man can get work if he wants it,' " Holbrook explained, drawing on her
neighborhood familiarity as well as her gender as sources of authority that no
university could provide.[20]

Moreover, social science was also a way of fulfilling the settlement's ultimate mission: not "sociological investigation," as Jane Addams wrote in the
preface to *Hull House Maps and Papers*, but "constructive work."[21] On one
level that meant using investigation as the basis of wide-reaching programs
of community mobilization and action—to identify neighborhood problems,
agitate for municipal response, and, especially, to form cooperative neighborhood ventures to serve local needs through child care, communal kitchens,
recreational facilities, savings and loans and a host of neighborhood clubs. It
also meant using investigation as the basis of publicity, for settlement work as
well as for working-class needs. Indeed, the entire research project would be
"unendurable and unpardonable," wrote Agnes Holbrook, without the "conviction that the public conscience when roused must demand better surroundings
for the most inert and long-suffering citizens of the commonwealth."[22] Moreover, social science was a way to put a distance between settlement work and

charity or individual casework, albeit without ever completely severing the tie. "It is, of course, a very easy thing to give a man who asks for a meal some food and send him on, but it is very bad for the man," wrote University of Chicago social scientist and longtime Hull House resident Sophonisba Breckinridge reflecting on the activities of the settlement's Relief Committee. For Breckinridge it was more important to "find out why he is tramping and after investigating put him in a way of getting work."[23] To the social scientist this was much more than a matter of individual casework; Breckinridge herself took part in several pioneering studies of local housing, workplace conditions, immigrant labor, juvenile delinquency, and, on a national level, female and child labor. Such investigations, of which *Hull House Maps and Papers* was an early example, gave the settlement a voice in numerous reform campaigns and a knowledge base, as Jane Addams urged in her closing chapter, for cooperation between the settlements and the labor movement in the project of "industrial organization."[24]

Indeed, in *Hull House Maps and Papers*, as in so many other Progressive Era contributions to poverty knowledge, it was the "labor question," as opposed to the "poverty question," that took center stage. The volume appeared at the height of labor radicalism, less than a year after the bloody Pullman strike tore Chicago—and much of the country—apart. In this context, and more generally as part of the movement for industrial democracy, investigations could be a vehicle for organizing the fight for better wages and working conditions, Addams urged.[25] "Poverty," then, was not itself the central focus or conceptual underpinning for the Hull House inquiry, as it had been in Booth's *Life and Labour*, but merely one aspect of a complex of working-class problems that needed to be addressed through a combination of community organizing, uplift, public education, and labor reform. While roughly corresponding to Booth's income cutoffs, the class categorizations in *Hull House* kept the focus on the problem of inadequate wages rather than spending patterns or family size, and shied away from using Booth's qualitative typology for differentiating among different classes of the poor. Kelley and Holbrook produced a "wage-earning" rather than a "poverty" map, that graphically illustrated the large number of low-wage earners in the district, but made no attempt, aside from a statement that families earning $5–$10 per week represented "probably the largest class in the district," to calculate the numbers or percentages of people living below Booth's "line of poverty."[26] Here again settlement residents distinguished theirs from charity work, cutting through the symptoms to go directly to the cause: low wages, the sweating system, labor subdivision, and the lack of organization—political as well as social—in working-class neighborhoods.

This is not to say that American investigators rejected poverty as a category for analysis—in fact, on both sides of the ocean it was becoming recognizably more scientific as a measure, and more distinguishable from morally tinged measures of "pauperism," or dependency. British businessman/philanthropist B. Seebohm Rowntree gave poverty a more precise and purposely narrow definition in his "town study" of York, published in 1902. Basing his calculations on what he repeatedly emphasized were the minimal costs of adequate nutrition ("physical efficiency"), rent, and household necessities, Rowntree developed a standard that allowed for families of various compositions and sizes and called it the "poverty line." Corroborating Booth, he found 27.9 percent of York's population living in poverty. More than half of the incidence of poverty, he determined, was due to low wages, and nearly 40 percent to the death of the chief wage earner or to family size. Unlike Booth, and in anticipation of American economists in the 1960s, he eschewed behavioral indicators in favor of income as a way to classify the poor—strongly suggesting, though not explicitly endorsing, better wages and income as the first line of defense. This did not mean that Rowntree eschewed moral judgment; he readily denounced drinking and gambling as "growing evils," which along with "ignorant or careless housekeeping, and other improvident expenditure," contributed to poverty rates. Even these, though, had to be understood in context, as "the outcome of adverse conditions under which too many of the working classes live." [27] Picking up on the rapid advances in measurement, American reformer and sometime settlement house resident Robert Hunter took an even bolder step toward distinguishing poverty from pauperism, in his ambitious effort to educate "blissfully ignorant" Americans about the nationwide extent of, as he titled his 1904 book, *Poverty*. Relying on official data and other published reports, Hunter counted a minimum of 10 million in poverty, taking care to distinguish between the vast majority, "who are poor as a result of social wrongs," and the most undeserving, "who are poor because of their own folly and vice."[28] "The pauper" had to be understood as the product of the massive failure of policy, in the first instance to prevent dependency with adequate jobs, wages, and social protections, in the second to reform the irreversibly debilitating provision of relief.[29] Pauperism and vice, however, were not the crux of the problem. It was the large but, as Hunter put it, "forgotten class" of people who were working for inadequate wages, in substandard conditions, at unsteady jobs, who, in the absence of some kind of mediating influence— whether from trade unions, the state, and/or the settlement house—were powerless against exploitation and social neglect. The Hull House survey underscored this distinction by shying away from the language of "poverty," in favor of the categories of wage-earning and ethnicity. In the process, it helped to open up a conversation about poverty that would turn on work, community, and ethnic relations, rather than on providing relief for the poor.

Work was also the central issue in what stands out as the most impressive of the Progressive-era social surveys, W.E.B. DuBois's *The Philadelphia Negro* (1899). A comprehensive survey of economic, social, political, cultural, and residential conditions in what was at that time the largest black community in the urban North, the study was based on original data collected from the "historic centre of the Negro population," the city's 7th ward, supplemented with official census statistics, a survey of black institutions and neighborhood conditions throughout the city, and the observations of the author himself.[30] It shared several of the characteristic features of the social survey—including a house-to-house survey of the ward's nine thousand black residents—and built on the literature's conceptual and methodological innovations.[31] Like Booth, DuBois collected data on household expenditure as well as income, using what he learned to make qualitative distinctions among different categories of poor people, and also as an occasion to scold. "Probably few poor nations waste more money by thoughtless and unreasonable expenditures than the American Negro," he wrote, advising the community to learn from "the Jew and Italian as to living within his means."[32] Like the Hull House residents, DuBois also cast his study within the broader context of immigration, albeit principally with an aim to understanding the condition of native-born blacks. The more direct link to the Hull House survey came in the person of Isabel Eaton, who worked as DuBois's lone assistant and published a pioneering study of domestic labor as an appendix to *The Philadelphia Negro*. DuBois also adopted what were fast becoming the standard income categories for determining class status, and plotted them, as his predecessors had, on block-by-block color-coded maps. But what stands out most about *The Philadelphia Negro* is how it departed from, stretched, and went beyond the existing survey tradition, revealing at once DuBois's deep commitment to systematic social research, and the racial stratification of social research and reform.

In contrast to the other major surveys, DuBois conducted his as a solitary rather than a collective endeavor—with no canvassers and one research assistant—leaving DuBois to administer his questionnaires personally in five thousand households. Much of this had to do with the shabby treatment he received from the University of Pennsylvania, which commissioned DuBois for the "pitiful stipend" of $800 per year, and appointed him an "assistant" in sociology despite his Harvard Ph.D., his sociological training in Germany, and his previous academic appointment at Wilberforce College in Ohio. But DuBois's independence also reflected his own skepticism about the motivations of his philanthropic sponsors, who included some of the city's leading Progressive reformers. Susan P. Wharton, a Quaker humanitarian whose family was the chief benefactor of the University's Wharton College, had originally proposed the study in the aftermath of a frustrated good government reform campaign that had been unable to woo black Philadelphians away from the local Republican machine. Behind the study was a larger transformation, that the Hull House maps at the time could not anticipate: the "new immigration" that had so visibly changed the demography of Chicago had been accompanied in Philadelphia by a surge in post–Civil War black migration from the South—leaving blacks still a small percentage of the growing population, but an ever-visible presence in the city, and in the neighborhoods of its cultural elite.[33] Anxiety among whites was expressed in the widely held "theory," DuBois later reflected, that black "crime and venality" were sending their city "to the dogs." The Whartons were one of several wealthy white families who lived in the 7th ward, just outside the ghetto, and were affiliated with the Philadelphia College Settlement Association, which maintained a residence there. DuBois rented an apartment above the Settlement-run cafeteria, but otherwise kept his distance. In his mind, the "stupidity" of the white reform network was part of the problem, an "evil" which only "knowledge based on scientific investigation" could "cure."[34] His response was to be as rigorous and complete as the circumstances would allow, and to be especially vigilant in his own efforts to keep the study free of error and bias. The researcher must "ever tremble," he wrote in his introductory comments, "lest some personal bias, some moral conviction or some unconscious trend of thought due to previous training, has to a degree distorted the picture in his view." Aware that "even the most cold-blooded scientific research" could never be free of moral conviction, he pledged himself to the "heart-quality of fairness, and an earnest desire for the truth despite its possible unpleasantness."[35]

DuBois's quest for scientific detachment did not prevent him from denouncing the prejudices of white Philadelphians or from showing his personal disdain for recent black migrants from the South. But it did lead him into more thorough and conceptually sophisticated analysis than any previous survey had achieved. DuBois made extensive use of comparative analysis, for example, regularly checking his own findings for the 7th ward against statistics for blacks throughout the city, both to "correct the errors" and to "illustrate the meaning of the statistical material obtained in the house-to-house canvass."[36] More revealing, and conceptually original, were findings from systematic comparative analyses between blacks and whites. Black men and women worked more than their white counterparts, he showed, but were disproportionately concentrated in low-paying personal service and unskilled labor positions and vastly underrepresented in the professions. He illustrated these findings in graphic displays comparing black with overall occupational distribution for both men and women, displays that would later be replicated in such sociological classics as *Black Metropolis*.[37] Comparative analysis also helped to give meaning to black mortality statistics, which, although not abnormally high in absolute terms, were far higher than death rates among whites.[38] DuBois also used comparative analysis to put black gender and family dynamics—later to become a virtual obsession in poverty knowledge—in the broader context of the working-class family economy. "All of the forces that are impelling white women to become breadwinners, are emphasized in the case of Negro women," he wrote, referring to the low wages and limited job opportunities open to black men, and to an "excess" of females in the black urban population in general. "[Y]et among Negro women, where the restriction in occupation reaches its greatest limit nevertheless 43% are breadwinners," as compared to 16 percent and 24 percent among native-born white and immigrant women, respectively. Nor were black children contributing wages to the household, he explained, not due to wishes of their parents so much as to the restricted demands for black child labor.[39]

In light of prevailing beliefs about racial inferiority, DuBois could hardly afford to let these data and graphs speak for themselves. Keeping his focus on the relative as well as the absolute status of blacks, DuBois offered a complex explanation that put his findings in the context of history, environment, and white racial beliefs and practices. The legacy of slavery was manifest, he believed, in the skill, education, and moral deficiencies he attributed to new migrants from the South. But three equally powerful historical forces had also combined to frustrate black progress, and they continued to operate in the Philadelphia of 1896. One was the periodic influx of white European immigrants, who repeatedly invaded the skilled trades where blacks had found a niche and did their best to keep blacks out of unskilled laboring jobs by controlling trade union practice. The second was industrialization and economic change, which created new skill demands that the continuing stream of untrained black migrants were unprepared to meet. And third was the "great fact of race prejudice," that distinguished the black experience from that of all other low-status groups. These combined forces—competition from immigration, industrial change, and white racial discrimination—were nowhere more evident than in "the question of employment," for Negroes the "most pressing of the day." And they were expressed in the "contradictory economic policy" that first confined blacks to menial jobs and then displaced them with better-prepared white immigrant competitors.[40] DuBois was never entirely clear on how far he would take the policy implications of this analysis—whether he would include, for example, restrictions on immigration. But when it came to the critical tasks of training, education, and diversifying employment opportunities for blacks, he made it clear that the responsibility rested with whites. "[M]en have a right to object to a race so poor and ignorant and inefficient as the mass of the Negroes; but if their policy in the past is parent of much of this condition, and if to-day by shutting black boys and girls out of most avenues of decent employment they are increasing pauperism and vice, then they must hold themselves largely responsible for the deplorable results," he wrote in his "final word" on "the duty of whites." Whites were responsible for the "narrow opportunities afforded negroes for earning a decent living," he continued. "Such discrimination is morally wrong, politically dangerous, industrially wasteful, and socially silly. It is the duty of whites to stop it, and to do so primarily for their own sakes." Without a change the social cost, in the form of crime and pauperism, would only grow.[41]

The distinctive features of DuBois's approach also came through in his treatment of poverty—where, in notable contrast to the Hull House investigators, he maintained Booth's language and categorizations, only further to underscore the distinctiveness of the African American, as opposed to the white immigrant experience. Nearly 20 percent of 7th ward Negroes fell into the "very poor" or "poor" category in wage calculations—that is to say, they earned less than $5.00 per week. This group included the criminals, paupers, and vagrants who hovered in the "submerged tenth" of the larger black population as well as the more honest, if "improvident" and "inefficient" who earned their living in irregular work. Another 47 percent earned between $5 and $10, classifying them as "fair" in DuBois's earnings calculations. They represent the "great hard-working laboring class . . . which is, on the whole, most truly representative of the masses." The rest of the 7th ward could be characterized as "comfortable" (25%) with $10–15 in weekly earnings or in "good circumstances" (8%) at $15 and above. Juxtaposing his charts against Booth's, however, DuBois illustrated a larger point: when judged according to the measured standards of London's white working class, a far higher percentage of 7th ward residents would be designated "poor." More important, the "great mass" of London whites looked far better off than Philadelphia blacks in the overall distribution of income: two-thirds of Booth's families could be rated "comfortable" or "middle class" as compared to the one-third who had achieved that status in DuBois's sample.[42] The "germ of a great middle class," these highly successful black families carried the "responsibilities of an aristocracy," but were prevented by discrimination, and their own ambivalence about being associated with the lower elements, from taking on the full burden of race leadership.

When explaining the high incidence of pauperism, DuBois once again emphasized the unique experience of blacks. Seventy percent of black poverty could be explained by sickness or lack of work, he calculated, echoing Booth's central theme, and the rest by crime, laziness, improvidence, and intemperate drinking.[43] All of these problems had been greatly exaggerated by the economic depression of the 1890s, which explained recent rises in poverty and crime following a period of decline. So far there was little new or "exceptional" in these findings, he continued, to distinguish blacks from other low-status groups. Beyond these standard explanations there were deeper forces, however, "which can rightly be called Negro problems: they arise from the peculiar history of the American Negro." Recounting the themes he had been emphasizing all along, DuBois pointed to three "peculiarities" that made blacks more vulnerable to poverty than whites: "slavery and emancipation, with their attendant phenomena of ignorance, lack of discipline and moral weakness; immigration with its increased competition and moral influence"; and, "possibly greater in its influence than the other two," the "strange social environment" in which blacks found themselves in Philadelphia. That "environment," characterized by segregation, economic exclusion, and the family instability they encouraged, was the product of active white racial discrimination, founded in the "widespread feeling all over the land . . . that the Negro is something less than an American and ought not to be much more than he is."[44]

In drawing attention to what was unique about black poverty, DuBois boldly departed from the Progressive practice of folding "coloreds" in with other immigrants or treating class as a common bond that could transcend ethnic differences. Neither class, ethnicity, nor the disadvantages of unskilled new migrants, that is, could alone explain the patterns of black/white inequality; those problems were infinitely compounded by white racism. He also directly challenged the view that the economy operated on color-blind competitive principles, noting how often "men" had ignored their "economic advantage" if it involved "association, even in a causal and business way, with Negroes."[45] Nor, again in contrast to the Hull House survey, did his analysis point to the trade unions or the settlements as solutions: the unions, because they had themselves become instruments of racial segmentation; the settlements, as his own experience suggested, because they were decidedly uncomfortable with their black neighbors, whether as residents or wards.[46] The answers, which DuBois left implicit in the analysis, hinged on bringing racial discrimination to an end—a solution that would itself require changes in existing economic policies—and in continuous efforts at Negro self-help and racial uplift. In all of these ways, he anticipated the central themes that would emerge decades later in social scientific debates over the nature of poverty and its connection to race. Equally important, DuBois demonstrated how the social survey could be used to sketch out a political economy of poverty and race that brought both concreteness and agency to the ongoing construction of the "color line"—here using the tools of measurement and objectivity to render it subject to change.

The problem was that the same color line that divided black from white Philadelphia also kept *The Philadelphia Negro* out of the contemporary mainstream of social science and reform. The *American Journal of Sociology* ignored it altogether, as if to suggest that the subject was not worthy of recognition. It was favorably received in other scholarly and popular journals, many of which, in what would become a familiar pattern, overlooked its contribution to political economy to commend DuBois for his honesty in dealing with the faults and social handicaps of his own race. DuBois himself did not entirely discourage this interpretation; in newspaper and journal articles around the time of publication, he listed as the "first" among the interrelated complex of "Negro problems" the vast ignorance and cultural deficiency, expressed in "sexual immorality, disease and crime," of the black lower class. That there was a "second," indeed inseparable dimension to the Negro problem was a message that even DuBois's Progressive sponsors were in a position to avoid—and, for the most part, did. DuBois's contribution to political economy never got much play in broader social work and philanthropic networks, which were themselves heavily segregated, as well as segregation*ist* in their treatment of blacks.[47] Nor did *The Philadelphia Negro* enter into the liberal social scientific canon, where the color line had only recently begun to allow African Americans entree to graduate training, and continued to deny access to professorships at elite white universities, as well as to the professional recognition and institutional resources that would have allowed DuBois to realize his ambitious plans to make a comprehensive sociological and historical study of the "Negro problem" in the United States.[48] For the next three decades, race remained submerged as a category separable from class or ethnicity in poverty knowledge. When it did reemerge, it was in a debate that would turn more on the nature and origins of black lower-class pathology than on the origins of poverty itself.

By the early twentieth century, the social survey had become thoroughly absorbed into the wider world of Progressive reform and social investigation, as any number of local tenement, public health, and child welfare studies can attest. The survey had also proved itself as a form of middle-class, especially female, activism; so much so that it was formally adopted by the consolidated network of charity and social work institutions that had grown out of an official 1905 merger between the settlements and the older charity organization movement.[49] The product of a time when certain boundaries—between public and private, and between policy domains—were not sharply drawn, this network extended its reach to embrace local neighborhood improvement, city planning, environmental cleanup, Americanization, child welfare, and labor protections among its causes, and made its presence felt on the municipal as well as the state and federal levels of government.[50] In 1909, the network's leading journal changed its name, from *Charities and the Commons* to *Survey*, in effect placing social investigation at the heart of a broader process of institutional transformation that aimed to link the disparate strands of charity and reform work through an emphasis on standardization, poverty prevention, and professional expertise. Through these means, and especially by advancing their own brand of social scientific knowledge, the emerging social work network would attempt to establish itself as an independent voice for a host of Progressive reforms, undertaken in the name of the public interest, in national and municipal policy.

Nothing was more important to this process of transformation than the arrival, in the first decade of the twentieth century, of large-scale, corporately organized private philanthropy.[51] A small number of the new "general purpose" foundations dominated from the outset, as did the names of the country's wealthiest and most famous corporate industrialists, Andrew Carnegie and John D. Rockefeller. But no single foundation identified itself more completely with social welfare than the Russell Sage Foundation (RSF), established in 1907 by Margaret Olivia Sage, widow of the lumber, railroad, and banking tycoon for whom the foundation was named. From the beginning, the foundation identified its mission as principally one of social investigation, generally for the "improvement of social and economic conditions," but more specifically for the nominally consolidated charity organization and settlement movements from which RSF drew its trustees and staff. Its first major research undertaking, the Pittsburgh Survey, heralded a new phase in social investigation; hitherto, poverty knowledge would be shaped by the shifting relationship between research and organized philanthropy.

The Pittsburgh Survey benefited immediately from RSF's financial support (totaling the then-substantial sum of $27,000), growing from an initial plan for "quick journalistic diagnoses" to what was truly the first American counterpart to Booth's *Life and Labour*—in fact, had the seeds of a survey not already been planted in Pittsburgh, RSF just might have taken the suggestion of an early solicitor that it do for its home town, New York City, what Booth had done for his.[52] Along with RSF sponsorship came a kind of instantaneous prestige: directed by *Survey* editor Paul Kellogg, the study drew on the expertise of such notables as Florence Kelley, settlement house leader Robert Woods, economist John R. Commons, and many others, all well aware of what RSF could do to put scientific social study on the map.[53] RSF support subsequently helped to keep the study in the limelight: serialized in the foundation-subsidized *Survey*, the study findings were extensively documented in a traveling exhibit of maps and photographs, and published by the foundation in six volumes released between 1909 and 1914. What's more, with a regular staff and a team of paid and volunteer researchers that by one count reached seventy-four, the study surpassed all previous inquiries in scope. Its subject, broadly speaking, was the impact of industrial capitalism on everything from the working-class family and household to Pittsburgh's politics and physical environment. Its investigations, focused heavily on the dominant steel industry, included detailed surveys of workplace accidents, company real estate holdings, corporate labor practices, workers' income and household conditions, female labor force participation, and the panoply of institutions organized—however inadequately—to protect and aid the working class. So, too, did its recommendations read like a roster of Progressive reform causes: protection against industrial accidents, workers' compensation, trade unionism, hours and wage regulation topped the list. Surveyors also pointed to the need for environmental cleanup, urban planning, better housing, immigrant education, and Americanization. All told, the Pittsburgh Survey was by far the most extensive expression of the "new view" of poverty produced in the United States to date, leaving little doubt that economic exploitation, embodied in the swelling ranks of underpaid, overworked laborers, was the underlying cause of social distress.[54]

Like other surveys, Pittsburgh's also created a number of nonacademic research opportunities for women, opportunities extended, at RSF, into positions of influence in organized philanthropy. Three of the six volumes were written and based on independent research by women: *Homestead: The Households of a Mill Town* by Margaret Byington; *Women and the Trades* by Elizabeth

Beardsley Butler; and Crystal Eastman's *Work Accidents and the Law. The Steel Workers*, by John Fitch, was the only other monograph in the series; the other two volumes were compilations of articles edited by Paul Kellogg. Meanwhile, RSF was actually putting women in a position to influence the course of research. At Olivia Sage's insistence, women were well represented on the original board of trustees (4 out of 9), a gender balance that only began to shift in the 1930s, gradually yielding an all-male board by 1938.[55] Staff appointments proved more important, though, as the careers of longtime RSF department heads Mary Richmond and Mary van Kleeck suggest. Richmond, already a leading figure in social work when she came to head the foundation's Charity Organization Department in 1909, undertook an extraordinarily influential program to promote social work professionalization and standards during her almost twenty-year tenure, helping to establish several of the country's leading graduate schools of social work, and publishing her own textbook, *Social Diagnosis*, laying out the principles of charity investigation and casework.[56] Van Kleeck, in contrast, came to the foundation as a still relatively novice College Settlements Association fellow, a graduate of Smith College who had recently completed investigations of child labor and women's overtime work in New York. As head of the RSF Department of Women's Work (renamed Industrial Studies in 1916), she directed or commissioned numerous studies of women wage earners, channeling that expertise into temporary appointments running the Labor Department's Women in Industry Service during World War I, and its newly created Women's Bureau in 1919. Like the foundation, she continued to expand her portfolio to less gender-specific labor issues, which she used as a platform for promoting scientific management and economic planning until retiring from the foundation in 1948.[57]

As suggested by the Pittsburgh Survey, there was a certain amount of unresolved tension to be found in RSF's strong emphasis on investigating "women's work" as a vehicle for raising broader questions about industrial change, labor market segmentation, and the need for a living wage. Elizabeth Beardsley Butler's study showed women at the low-skilled, low-wage end of an industrial labor market segmented by gender and race (significantly, though, her "racial analysis" of employment included white "Americans," Italians, "Slavs," and "Jewesses," but made no mention of African American women, who were concentrated in domestic employment). Commenting on the high turnover among single, marriage-age women, Butler explicitly rejected this and other traditional explanations for the gender gap. The problem was not, she insisted, that women were incapable, without breadwinning responsibilities, or not in the industrial labor force to stay, but that employers were able to exploit such "theories" to thwart organizing and training efforts and to keep wages low. Nevertheless, in her own proposals for "trade training," Butler was quick to reassure male unionists that women would not violate gender norms by competing for skilled industrial jobs. Nor would training undermine the female commitment to "intelligent home making"; if anything, higher wages and productivity would enhance the working woman's capacity to perform her duties at home.[58] In *Homestead*, Margaret Byington also showed women engaged in productive, in this case household, work, "due not primarily to any theory as to women's sphere, but the simple fact that the one industry [steel] cannot use the work of women and children." Women's work, in this context, was to manage the household on her husband's substandard wage, a task that inspired "elements of genius" in the intelligent and thrifty housewife, but that led to waste, neglect, poor nutrition, and, occasionally, immorality in the house of the "poor, unintelligent" woman. And yet, while emphasizing the housewife's role as a worker in the household economy, for Byington the key lesson to draw was about substandard wages, long hours, dangerous working conditions—and the feelings of powerlessness and apathy they generated among working class *men*.[59] Investigating women's work, then, could be used at once to challenge and to reinforce traditional gender norms.

From the perspective of past and future poverty knowledge, however, what was most significant was that women's work was getting recognition at all. For as Florence Kelley, Carroll Wright, Edith Abbott, and a handful of pioneering social scientists had long since recognized, female participation in the industrial workforce was not likely to draw attention or reward in traditional academic venues. At RSF, and later under van Kleeck's direction at the Department of Labor's Women's Bureau, working-class women's wages and work opportunities would gain recognition and institutional stability as legitimate questions for social scientific inquiry. So, too, would the structural limitations women faced in the labor force enter into the broader poverty discourse.

Ultimately it was here that the Russell Sage Foundation made its singular contribution to Progressive social investigation: in institutionalizing the space, outside government and outside the academy, where reform-minded women *and* men could engage in social scientific exploration and have it recognized as such. As with many institutionalizing projects, this one tended to domesticate the more radical aspects of Progressive research and reform. As the survey itself became more institutionalized, even centralized, it was easy to lose sight of the sense of community residence and collective action the Hull House investigators had written about, and to shift the balance toward the more distant kind of social engineering that also occupied an important place in Progressive social thought. RSF, like most organized philanthropy, showed little interest in the kind of "bottom-up" community initiative Jane Addams envisioned, far more in using its investigations to speak on behalf of rather than in concert with the impoverished working class. Nor would social investigators ever entirely distance themselves from the tinge of charity under RSF sponsorship—the foundation, with a board and staff heavily weighted toward the leading lights of charity organization, was popularly known as the "Charity Trust."[60] And while RSF provided a berth wide and comfortable enough for the broad spectrum of Progressive ideology, its own stance was resolutely neutral and moderate. As van Kleeck said with reference to her own program, "The Foundation is concerned with the labor movement from the viewpoint neither of employers nor workers, but as representing the public interest . . . its investigators have sought not to influence conclusions, but to help to establish the habit of making facts, rather than prejudice or self-interest, the basis for conclusions."[61]

If institutionalization tipped the balance on some tensions within Progressive social investigation, it left many others unresolved, chief among them the failure of the unbiased investigators to leave their own class, cultural, and racial biases aside. The Pittsburgh surveyors were often contemptuous of Pittsburgh's "Slavic" immigrants, routinely treating them as a separate caste of "dull" or "subservient" workers who, as cheap and exploitable labor, threatened to keep industrial wages low.[62] DuBois, clearly identifying with the "better class of Negroes" he elsewhere labeled the "talented tenth," did not hide his disapproval of the "submerged tenth" of criminals, "lewd women," and their "aiders and abettors" who populated Philadelphia's slums and set the stereotype by which whites judged all of black Philadelphia. Frustrated by public blindness to the hard-working "respectable" working and upper classes who constituted the majority of Philadelphia Negroes, DuBois was also disdainful when writing about "the poor and unfortunate and the casual laborers," who had not been able to secure a place in the urban economy due to the "good-natured, but unreliable and shiftless" ways they brought with them from the South.[63] While Jane Addams often spoke of the need to appreciate immigrant culture, other Hull House investigators resorted to ethnic stereotypes in their characterizations of neighborhood residents, whether writing of the "drunken" Irish, the "incorrigible" Italians or the cutthroat "trading instinct" of the Jew. Whether or not they undermined the underlying structural analysis, these biases did undermine the surveyors' capacity to understand either the culture or the political agency of the people they studied as a force that could be mobilized for change.

Moreover, important though they may have been in drawing public attention to industrial poverty and labor conditions, the social surveys had little discernible impact on policy, or at least not the direct, immediate impact their sponsors envisioned. The Pittsburgh survey was denounced as biased and sensational by the local business leaders it was aimed at, who then went on to commission a competing study that challenged its bleak depiction of local conditions and called on the business community to undertake modest, voluntaristic reforms.[64] Equally problematic was the Progressive tendency to assume that enlightened social investigation, properly publicized through mechanisms such as traveling exhibits and the *Survey*, would be sufficient to mobilize political support for change. But the more important problem with the survey movement's vision of policy influence was that it was rapidly being displaced by a different model of social scientific influence in policy making, actively promoted by foundations as well as by Herbert Hoover in his capacity first as U.S. Secretary of Commerce and later as president. Expertise, in this model, would continue to be organized around objective understanding of economic and social processes, but it would remain detached from particular reform causes or even proposals. It would also be targeted at a more select, enclosed audience of administrators, legislators, elite citizens, and, of course, professional social scientists who were in a position to influence policy decisions directly. The quintessential expression of this effort to introduce more objectivity and expertise into policy making, the survey of *Recent Social Trends* commissioned by Hoover in 1929, made no mention whatever of the social survey movement or its findings.[65]

Nevertheless, as part of the broader tradition of Progressive political economy, the social survey made several lasting, albeit unacknowledged, contributions to later poverty expertise. Especially important, the surveys shifted the focus of inquiry, from pauperism to poverty, from the "dependent" poor to the conditions of the working class, and from individual behavior to industrial capitalism as the main source of economic deprivation. The survey movement also laid the groundwork for many of the research techniques that would later become essential to more self-consciously "scientific" poverty expertise. One of its chief innovations, the household budget-based poverty line, would be resurrected in the 1960s as the basis of official measurement of national poverty rates. More immediately, the movement's pioneering use of social mapping and graphic display provided the foundations for the Chicago-school social ecology that came to dominate sociology in the 1920s. Similarly, the movement's holistic approach to community surveys, combining quantitative data-gathering with case studies and personal observation, were precursors to the anthropological community studies of a later generation.

Equally important were the possibilities investigators developed within the survey framework that were either eclipsed by later developments or never fully realized in the survey movement itself: DuBois's documentation of racial discrimination as a structural component of political economy; the attention investigators brought to women as wage earners and to gender segmentation in the labor market; the importance the movement placed on making its findings accessible to a broad general audience; and the recognition that knowledge-gathering, never a perfectly "objective" endeavor in the first place, need not be "value-free" in order to be legitimate. In all of these ways, the social surveyors mapped out the terrain for a much broader approach to poverty knowledge than we have come to know today. To a remarkable degree, they also anticipated what would remain the central tensions—over issues of class, culture, objectivity, and, especially, the "significance" of gender and race—in liberal poverty knowledge for the rest of the twentieth century.

POVERTY, ASSIMILATION, AND SOCIAL DISORGANIZATION: THE CHICAGO SCHOOL

Ultimately, it was a significantly altered vision of community research and action that would be remembered as the first truly *social scientific* contribution to poverty knowledge. Grounded in the theories of sociology at the University of Chicago, it did not so much reject as shift the focus of Progressive Era poverty knowledge from political economy to "social ecology," from class to racial and ethnic identity, and from employment and wages to social disorganization and cultural lag. No doubt this shift in focus had a great deal to do with the tenor of the times. Enjoying their heyday in the 1920s, a decade that started out with race riots and a wave of restrictive anti-immigrant legislation, Chicago sociologists offered a reassuring framework for understanding ethnic conflict as an inevitable part of urban growth and modernization—a path that would eventually lead to assimilation. At a time, too, when national politicians were urging a return to "normalcy" and singing the praises of welfare capitalism, they looked to urban neighborhoods primarily as laboratories for research rather than proving grounds for labor organizing or other varieties of reform, while raising skepticism about Progressive schemes for taming the market and reserving a special, almost personal animosity for social casework. In the Chicago-school vision, community action was to be more strictly bottom-up, but it was also to smooth the process of assimilation rather than to challenge existing social arrangements. But what proved most important to assuring the longevity of the Chicago-school vision of community research and action was its attachment to a formidable research and training institution, which was itself a harbinger of a movement within organized philanthropy to build a more academic, theoretically grounded social science as the knowledge base for policy. Amply subsidized by the newly created Laura Spelman Rockefeller Memorial, Chicago-school sociologists wielded tremendous influence in the discipline, and established the wide-ranging research and policy networks through which their ideas about poverty, social disorganization, and community-based intervention would find a way first into local practice and eventually into the War on Poverty, three decades after the department's heyday had come and gone.[66]

The Chicago approach to sociology was really no single approach at all. Embracing a wide range of statistical, ethnographic, quantitative, and qualitative techniques, the department's real trademark was the tradition of theory-based urban ethnography inspired by Chicago's first truly pathbreaking study, W. I. Thomas and Florian Znaniecki's *The Polish Peasant* (5 vols., 1918–20).[67] In that study, Thomas (working with research assistance from Znaniecki, a Polish philosophy student who emigrated to the U.S. during World War I) developed an anthropological approach to studying ethnic communities that marked his as a research rather than as a "practical" reform or, as he saw it, morally judgmental enterprise. Equally important, he developed the cyclical concept of social organization-disorganization-reorganization that Chicago-trained sociologists would use to explain what happened to peasant communities in the throes of transition from rural village to a more modern, urbanized, and, for immigrants, culturally alien way of life. Poverty, as part of the broader symptomology of "social disorganization," could be attributed to temporary cultural breakdown as much if not more than to the wage structure of the industrial economy.[68]

Thomas based his ideas about social disorganization among immigrants on a comparative study of "adjustment and maladjustment" among newly urbanized peasants in Poland and in Chicago's Polish neighborhoods.[69] In Poland, he traced the initial breakdown of traditional peasant customs and social controls under the atomizing influences of urbanization and industrial development. The result was social "disorganization," reflected in increased crime, loss of religious faith, sexual promiscuity, family breakup, and economic dependency. But Thomas also saw signs that the former villagers were emerging as a "reorganized" social group, for which he credited education, the press, and, especially, the new institutions and customs they had constructed from elements of the old. Most important among these were the large number of cooperative economic institutions—agricultural and commercial associations, cooperative shops, savings and loans—through which peasant groups were seeking to improve their collective welfare, and, more important, collectively absorbing the social learning that would help their adjustment to urban life.[70] In Chicago, though, Thomas found it harder to see past the signs of disorganization—even though, as historians have subsequently emphasized, Chicago Poles maintained a rich and extensive network of mutual aid, political, and church-based associations. In his eyes, filtered through data collected primarily by Znaniecki, Chicago's Polish-American "colonies" remained cultural backwaters, barriers to the process of adjustment that would allow "real Americanization" to begin. In at least part of this judgment, Thomas was not entirely wrong: there was strong resistance to Americanization among Polish immigrants, especially from the church. Significantly, though, in Thomas's framework of cultural adjustment, such resistance was a sign of social disorganization rather than political agency.[71]

The Polish Peasant marked a turning point in social investigation in methodological as well as conceptual terms. By no means the first to characterize the "new immigrant" as a cultural challenge, Thomas and Znaniecki turned the tables and asked their readers to view the challenge of "readjustment" from the inside. To do that, they discarded the quantifying conventions of the social survey and used personal documents such as letters, diaries, newspaper accounts, and life history interviews as the essential "facts" of their account. It was, after all, the "subjective" data that made poverty, delinquency, family

breakup, and other familiar indicators of disorganization comprehensible. Ultimately, the "subjective" held the key to solving the immigrant problem as well.
Social work was on the wrong track, they argued, because its casework methods failed to recognize that assimilation was a group, not an individual, process. At the same time, American-run community centers, including settlements, came as artificial and unfamiliar impositions from the outside. Instead,
in what would later become a cardinal principle in community action, Thomas
hinted that the truly authentic leadership for neighborhood reorganization
should come not from middle-class American neighbors, but from within the
immigrant community, and envisioned a network of cooperative, deliberately
cross-ethnic economic associations to serve the dual purpose of self-help and
Americanization.[72]

It is interesting that Thomas distanced himself not only from social work
but, at least obliquely, from the settlement house as well. A friend and associate
of Jane Addams, he received the generous sum of $50,000 from Hull House
benefactor Helen Culver to underwrite the research. Certainly Thomas was no
stranger to Hull House research: in 1912, when he started work on *The Polish
Peasant*, Hull House remained the linchpin of a social work community that
frequently crossed academic and nonacademic lines to produce the vast majority of research about the city and its immigrant neighborhoods.[73] But Thomas,
like his colleagues at the University of Chicago, was eager to distinguish his
sociology from social work and reform, among other ways by locating themselves as detached, nonjudgmental observers rather than as helping neighbors
or political allies. The distinctions grew sharper in the years following the
release of *The Polish Peasant* in 1918. In 1920, the University formally separated social work from sociology by establishing the School of Social Service
Administration. Under the leadership of Hull House alumnae and Chicago-
trained social scientists Sophonisba P. Breckinridge and Edith Abbott (Breckinridge held Ph.D.s from the University in political science and law, Abbott in
economics), SSA promoted a decidedly activist, policy-oriented approach to
research, and, with a major grant from the Russell Sage Foundation, emphasized the importance of both research and casework in its graduate curriculum.[74] Sociology, under emerging new leadership, was taking the opposite direction. Thomas himself was forced out of the University, his academic career
cut short by his highly publicized arrest in a Chicago hotel room with the wife
of an American serviceman. But his ideas and methods formed the basis of an
extensive program of fieldwork and theoretical training using Chicago, and
especially its poor neighborhoods, as a laboratory for experimentation and
empirical research. The leading figures in this expansion were Robert E. Park
and Ernest W. Burgess, who together helped to make Chicago the most productive and influential sociology department of its day.

Park, a former journalist and press agent for Booker T. Washington, had
been recruited to Chicago after first meeting Thomas at Tuskegee, and arrived

as a part-time lecturer in 1913.[75] A relative latecomer to the profession—he was forty-nine when he started teaching at Chicago—Park quickly rose to a position of eminence in the department after Thomas's departure, and was considered by many to be a major intellectual light. He was a vociferous advocate of detaching research from reform—Park showed disdain for "do-gooders" and planners, as he did for the survey as a research technique, calling it a "high form of journalism" designed to bring about "radical reform."[76] Burgess, who got his degree from Chicago the year Park arrived, was more willing to recognize the legitimacy of nonacademic research and had been briefly affiliated with Hull House in his graduate student days. While teaching at the University of Kansas, he had worked on two local social surveys, and continued to regard the basic method as a valuable source of data.[77] By the time they took the lead in graduate training, however, both Park and Burgess were eager to distinguish the department as a training ground for a different kind of social science: theoretical, experimental, devoted to uncovering the natural laws of human and social development.

In this Park and Burgess were the immediate beneficiaries of a major new player in social scientific philanthropy, the Laura Spelman Rockefeller Memorial, established in 1922. By far the biggest player in the field (its grant expenditures amounted to more than $58 million through 1929, as compared to the Russell Sage Foundation's $9 million between 1907 and 1946) the new Rockefeller fund was exclusively devoted to upgrading the stature and scientific credo of the social sciences. It also embraced a strict policy of neutrality—a not-so-subtle response to earlier charges that John D.'s parent foundation had tried to slant industrial relations studies in his favor following the infamous Ludlow Massacre, which brought a bloody end to a 1913–14 coal miners' strike against the Rockefeller's Colorado Fuel and Iron Company. Though frequently an RSF partner and endowed with the same "practical knowledge" rhetoric, the Laura Spelman Rockefeller Memorial took a far more academic—more "basic" than "applied"—approach to the task. Under the direction of Chicago-trained psychologist Beardsley Ruml, the fund subsidized scores of empirical research and discipline-building efforts. Most effective, though, was its more open-ended support for institutions, including the Social Science Research Council, the National Bureau of Economic Research, and the social sciences at the University of Chicago, that were officially apolitical, disinterested purveyors of social science knowledge, organized less around specific social problems than around more generic categories of human activity and policy. For much of the 1920s, the Memorial was at the hub of a network that would parallel if not compete with the network linking settlement and social work intellectuals to the Russell Sage Foundation and the U.S. Children's and Women's Bureaus. When Herbert Hoover mobilized policy intellectuals to form the Committee on Social Trends, RSF had a seat at the table, but most of the funding and the heaviest representation came via Rockefeller, the University of Chicago, the National Bureau of Economic Research, and the SSRC.[78] With support from the Memorial, Park and Burgess were able to sustain a large number of graduate students in fieldwork positions, a sizeable research and support staff that was virtually unheard of in other sociology departments, and regular subventions for publications that kept the department visible in sociological and local policy circles. They also provided a model of the kind of detached social science that, although enormously political in its implications, allowed foundations to take a strong role in shaping policy knowledge, while remaining distant from partisan political controversy. In addition, Park and Burgess published several works on theory and method, including *Introduction to the Science of Sociology* (1921) and *The City* (1925), which for years were considered the definitive texts in the field.[79]

If Chicago sociology appeared apolitical, one reason may have been that its "ecological" model of social development explained such touchy subjects as ethnic relations and the rise of industrial capitalism as part of a natural evolutionary process. Like an organism, society was constantly evolving according to the laws of four interacting human instincts. The most fundamental was *competition*, leading inevitably to *conflict*, and from there to the control mechanisms, or *accommodations* through which societies established temporary equilibrium and maintained the social interactions that would eventually lead to *assimilation*. Social change occurred when the state of equilibrium was disrupted—and it frequently was—by some naturally occurring "invasion" such as large-scale migration or technological advance, which in turn started the cycle all over again. The entire process, which could be described as one of ecological "succession," was continuous, evolutionary, and irreversible.[80] While not exactly survival of the fittest, it was also not especially amenable to intervention from the state or from social reform.

The city was an extraordinary laboratory for research from the ecological viewpoint, as Park and Burgess noted in their influential volume entitled *The City* (1925). There, the differences with Progressive political economy were laid bare. In that volume, which collected essays written over the previous ten years, they presented the rise of the industrial city as the most advanced stage of human evolution—the "outstanding fact of modern society," that captured industrial growth, migration, and all of the "inevitable processes of human nature" within the boundaries of its geographic space.[81] As a research project, urban ecology would focus not merely on concrete "factors" behind specific, isolated "events," as the social survey had, but on the abstract "social forces" that shaped the whole of urban life.[82] Similarly, it would use such familiar survey methods as mapping to explain social geography in abstracted, ecological—and wholly apolitical—terms.

Dividing the city into a series of concentric "zones," what Burgess outlined as the ecological base map was meant to reflect not the constructed hierarchies of power, wealth, and poverty but the natural logic of urban growth and residential distribution. Industry, commerce, and population migration were the driving forces, and distributed themselves as if by nature from the innermost "loop," or central business district, through areas of "transition" and "deterioration," where the city's slums, ghettos, and criminal "underworlds" could be found, and eventually to the outermost "residential" and "commuter" zones where the comforts of single-family dwellings and suburban life beckoned as a "promised land."[83] Thus abstracted, the ecological map offered a contrast to the story of industrial exploitation depicted in the Hull House maps of wages and nationalities. The slum, the Jewish ghetto, and the black belt were all part of an organic sorting process, creating "natural areas" for immigrant groups when they first arrived in the city. Segregation was itself a natural process, "which sifts and sorts and relocates individuals and groups by residence and occupation."[84] So, too, was social disorganization, as a feature of certain characteristically unstable central city neighborhoods. Part of the "natural, if not normal, life of a city," these areas could breed deviance like a "contagion," if they remained too isolated from the mainstream moral code.[85] For most, however, they were temporary way stations, where disorganization was not "pathological," but "normal," a preliminary stage in the "reorganization of attitudes and conduct [that] is almost invariably the lot of the newcomer to the city."[86] Similarly, certain areas would be natural sites of interethnic conflict, as newcomers competed with more established residents for space, but again as a stage in a natural progression towards accommodation and ultimate assimilation into the ever-evolving urban culture. Given these natural progressions, there was a certain futility in efforts at planning or control. Urban reform was both ubiquitous and dangerous, Park wrote derisively, in its attempts to impose government regulation on processes over which it had little control. This was not to say that social ecology was without practical application; it was not simply a justification for laissez-faire. Reform, to be meaningful and effective, had to be in harmony with social ecology and, by implication, circumscribed enough to avoid interference with the natural progression of industrial growth and ethnic assimilation.[87]

Indeed, under Park and Burgess, urban ecology was to become not only Chicago's preeminent sociological project, but a new, more "scientific basis" for community action, or "neighborhood work."[88] Its methods and implications would be spelled out in dozens of dissertations, whose titles and authors included the most renowned in urban sociology, including Frederic Thrasher's *The Gang* (1927), Louis Wirth's *The Ghetto* (1928), Harvey Zorbaugh's *The Gold Coast and the Slum* (1929), and E. Franklin Frazier's *The Negro Family in Chicago* (1931). It would also find its way into several official reports commissioned through the department's local policy connections, most prominent among them Charles S. Johnson's *The Negro in Chicago* (1922) on the summer race riot of 1919, and *Social Factors in Juvenile Delinquency* (1931) by Clifford Shaw and Henry D. McKay.[89]

It was in the field of juvenile delinquency that urban ecology would have its most concrete, transformative effect, and in which Chicago sociologists would lay out the vision of community action later adopted by federal officials in the War on Poverty. As a central target for urban Progressive reform and investigation since the turn of the century, juvenile delinquency was, in Park's mind, a field ripe for more "searching" scientific inquiry and experimentation, based on the principles of sociology rather than on moral concern. "Delinquency is not primarily a problem of the individual but of the group," he wrote, in criticism of prevailing treatments. One by-product of the vast, and inevitable, dislocations brought about by urban and industrial growth, the high rates of delinquency found in poor immigrant neighborhoods were a reflection of the breakdown of traditional social controls—family, church, rural village—under the pressures of modernization. "Delinquency is, in fact, in some sense a measure of the failure of our community organizations to function."[90] Although he was critical of such Progressive anti-delinquency proposals as playground-building, Park heralded the prospect of a "new social science" that their "frankly experimental" approach had helped to spawn. Based on these experiments, he hoped, academic social science would now examine, "redefine," and eventually come up with new approaches to the delinquency problem, approaches informed by the new learning about human nature and social processes more generally.

For the next decade, drawing on their own expanding connections in the local social service bureaucracy, Chicago-school sociologists followed through on Park's mandate, and by the late 1920s the department was providing both research and staff members for leading criminal justice agencies.[91] Working, thanks to Burgess's connections, in tandem with the Illinois Institute of Juvenile Research, Chicago graduate students gained access to police records, social agency case files, and juvenile court proceedings. They supplemented these with life history interviews and neighborhood ethnographies and plotted extensive ecological maps linking delinquency with neighborhood traits. Although by no means the first to "map" the incidence of delinquency in Chicago—Sophonisba Breckinridge and Edith Abbott had created a delinquency map published by the Russell Sage Foundation in 1912—Chicago-trained sociologists noted that their own studies were based on more sophisticated statistical calculations, putting them in a better position to generalize about the links between delinquency and place.[92] The findings from these studies were reported in a series of publications beginning with *Delinquency Areas* (1929) by Burgess student and IJR research director Clifford R. Shaw. Delinquency, Shaw concluded, was concentrated "in a characteristic type of area," where the combination of industrial "invasion" and the "influx of foreign nationals" had caused a "disintegration of the community as a unit of social control." In ecological terms, as Shaw demonstrated by plotting his data on the now-familiar Chicago-school maps, the delinquency area was the "zone in transition"; in more pedestrian terms, it was the immigrant slum. Delinquency, as Park had earlier hypothesized, could now be shown to be a community, not an individual, problem, a product of urban growth and neighborhood instability, and not of the pathological behavior of immigrant youth. Indeed, it was a normal response to the breakdown in traditional mechanisms of social control. The solution, then, was not to be found in the impersonal, individualized juvenile justice system that Progressive reformers had helped to create. Nor was it simply in efforts to improve external neighborhood living conditions, which would only aim at the symptoms of the underlying disorganization. Fighting delinquency called for more comprehensive community reorganization, a restoration of internal social controls, and to be effective it had to build from within the community.[93]

At the time it was published, *Delinquency Areas* offered a new way of looking at youth criminal behavior, opening up a field once dominated by individualized, psychological perspectives to a "sociological, or cultural, approach." For the Chicago sociologists, it also represented applied social science at its best, as knowledge about human nature and social processes that could be used in redirecting ill-fated reforms. In 1932 Shaw and other Chicago-trained sociologists took that next step, creating the Chicago Area Project (CAP) as a community-based experiment in delinquency prevention. Targeting six "transitional" neighborhoods known for their high delinquency rates, Shaw and his staff joined forces with neighborhood residents, local churches, businesses, and labor and other groups to create what they called "a program of community action." Operating as a nonprofit corporation with a board made up of prominent Chicago citizens, CAP sponsored boys' clubs, summer camps, recreational and educational activities, and initiated a program known as "curbstone counseling" using neighborhood peers to work with members of youth gangs. These activities were planned and managed by neighborhood or community councils, which raised funds for new initiatives, recruited volunteers to supplement the paid staff, and, most importantly, were set up to put neighborhood residents in charge. The idea was to generate a sense of local autonomy and solidarity, to emphasize neighborhood rather than law enforcement or social work solutions, and eventually to reconstitute the community as a mechanism of social control.[94]

In this emphasis CAP was quite consciously an application of Chicago-school theory, and also an affront to the more casework-oriented local social work establishment. Residents would be spared the "humiliations" of receiving outside philanthropy. "Indigenous workers" would replace trained professionals as program staff. "Individualized" treatment would give way to community methods, building on the resources at hand. "Outside" professionals would retain a role in these initiatives, Shaw insisted, but it would be under the guidance of local residents. Understandably, CAP came under fire from local social welfare officials, but its well-placed city connections helped to diffuse their criticisms. More damaging to its credibility, especially as the Depression deepened, was what critics came to recognize as CAP's narrow focus on social services and the absence of a strategy for addressing the underlying conditions of neighborhood poverty. Such a strategy would require a more overtly political approach to neighborhood organizing, in the eyes of Chicago graduate student and onetime CAP organizer Saul Alinsky, and would of necessity look outside the neighborhood for the sources of distress and the targets for change. Frustrated by the limited aims of the anti-delinquency effort, Alinsky broke off to help establish the Back of the Yards Neighborhood Council in the working-class community adjacent to Chicago's stockyards, already famous as the setting for Upton Sinclair's novel *The Jungle* (1906). Alinsky spoke little of social "disorganization," assimilation, or the need to reestablish internal social control; instead, he sought to merge existing community institutions—especially the church and the unions—to create immediate pressure for better municipal services, while organizing to demand broader economic and political reform.[95]

In the 1950s and early 1960s, Chicago-school ideas about community reorganization found expression in dozens of foundation and government-funded experiments to combat juvenile delinquency and poverty in urban neighborhoods, which in turn provided the models for Community Action in the War on Poverty.[96] But the Chicago-school impact on poverty knowledge was at once more immediate and more far-reaching than that. Working from a more secure institutional base and in the more conservative political climate of the 1920s, Chicago sociologists took social scientific community research in a direction not contemplated in Progressive social inquiry. In their hands, poverty knowledge became an academic rather than so exclusively a reform-minded endeavor, a contribution to theory-building, and a "scientific basis" for a more limited (though it would not remain that way) kind of community action. Their social ecology naturalized urban poverty and segregation as well as the underlying "forces" social surveyors had attributed to capitalist expansion and racial discrimination. It also established sociology as a science of human behavior and social psychology, leaving the "social" or political economy of previous investigators to less strictly "scientific" minds. As a program of research, social ecology neutralized the conceptual terrain mapped out in the social surveys; as a program for action, it redirected the aims of intervention, away from wages and work and living conditions, and toward the more circumscribed objectives of community "reorganization" and assimilation into the existing social mainstream.

And yet, for all its limitations, social ecology provided the tools for a more basically sympathetic understanding of immigrant and working-class culture than most Progressive inquiry to date, providing a framework for understanding the unfamiliar and presumably "pathological" as adaptive to the disruptions of social change. Steeped though it was in the language of "disorganization," social ecology started from a recognition of not only the importance but the legitimate variability of cultures within changing historical circumstances. And despite its own reaffirmation of the competitive impulse and the individualistic economic system laissez-faire had shaped, in practice social ecology took the community as its unit of analysis, and as a perspective from which to challenge the assumptions of individualized social casework. Finally, for all the talk about natural forces and assimilation, social ecology was not simply or always an affirmation of the evolutionary social order. Reworked and put into practice by a later generation of community activists, Chicago sociology lent theoretical grounding to the concept of community empowerment as a vehicle for broader social change.

CHAPTER 2.

Poverty Knowledge as Cultural Critique:
The Great Depression

IT MAY SEEM odd that, amidst the vast unemployment and structural dislocations of the Great Depression, social scientific poverty knowledge should make
culture an overriding theme. This, too, alongside the unprecedented demand
for economic and more traditionally defined social welfare knowledge coming
from the expanding apparatus of New Deal, state, and private agencies—all
clamoring for knowledge, as Franklin D. Roosevelt himself might have put it,
to get government *out* of the business of relief through programs of prevention,
social insurance, and economic reform. Drawing insights from Progressive as
well as a newer, Keynesian political economy, social work and economic policy intellectuals carved out plans for addressing the economic risks of unemployment, old age, maternal widowhood, agricultural crisis, and, more generally, laissez-faire capitalism.[1] And yet, for all the accumulated statistics on
unemployment, income levels, housing conditions, relief rolls, and other indicators of economic decline, the more pronounced, and immediate legacy of
the Great Depression for poverty knowledge was in the social scientific study
of how poverty was at once a cause and a consequence of psychological depression, the distinctive values associated with lower-class culture, and the
broader problem of a society unable to cope with the challenge of mass
economic breakdown due to its own cultural "lag." The most sustained and
comprehensive study of unemployment from the 1930s, reported in E. Wight
Bakke's companion volumes *The Unemployed Worker* and *Citizens Without
Work*, was as much concerned with its psychological and cultural as with its
economic costs.[2]

But if there was some tension between economic and cultural understandings of poverty, the differentiation was not at all as sharp or politicized as it
would later become. Indeed, for Chicago's rival "schools" in the 1920s and
1930s, the turn to culture was not a break from Progressive political economy
so much as a new way to illuminate its central themes: class polarization,
the dangers of laissez-faire individualism, and the necessity of planned social
reform. It was in this spirit that Robert and Helen Lynd came up with a new,
more anthropological approach to community study and with it dissected the
cultural contradictions that industrial capitalism had wrought. Others, including students of anthropologist W. Lloyd Warner, uncovered the elements of a
distinctive and coherent lower-class culture that helped poor people cope with

the conditions of social and economic deprivation, and for which poor people were routinely stigmatized by a society bent on individual advance. A third group, the regional sociologists at the University of North Carolina, wrote about the stubborn economic and cultural traditions that kept the South from modernizing and that, by the 1930s, had earned the region recognition as the nation's "number one economic problem." In all three instances, social scientists associated with these "schools" of thinking drew on the concept of culture, and on the methods of the behavioral sciences more generally, to make a case for centralized planning and social engineering in aid of the poor.

Certainly the Depression-era emphasis on behavior and culture was not for want of economic analyses that could explain poverty. For many, the breadlines, homelessness, agricultural dislocation, and above all the spectacle of mass unemployment provided powerful and visible evidence that the economy, it not capitalism itself, had failed. But while large-scale poverty was indeed recognized as a sign of economic failure, poverty itself was not the central problem nor even a central analytic category in economic knowledge. The issue was not, as in the familiar Progressive formulation, the puzzle of "poverty amidst plenty," but the puzzle of wholesale, and enduring, economic collapse. Unemployment, underconsumption, wage and wealth maldistribution, underdevelopment: these could be, and were, identified as systemic causes of poverty, but economic policy intellectuals did not conceptualize their task in terms of alleviating, let alone ending, poverty but in terms of how their often competing analyses would translate into programs of economic recovery and reform.[3]

Nor, in marked contrast to the 1960s, when a Democratic administration did pledge to bring poverty in America to an end, did the New Deal establish a clear-cut place within its shifting panoply of agencies for gathering knowledge about poverty. Statistic-gathering, though plentiful, was more scattered and directly mission-oriented, and more apt to hone in on a poverty-related problem—unemployment, old age, disability, the absence of a (male) breadwinner—than on poverty per se.[4] Agency knowledge also reflected the concerns of particular constituencies and advocates—organized labor, old-age pension advocates, tenant farmers, "maternalist" reformers—at least some of whom were eager to maintain a distance between themselves and a more generically defined poor or lower class. Bureaucratic poverty knowledge, as a result, was fragmented and categorical—much like the emerging welfare state—leaving little trace of established method or centrally accumulated statistical information for future generations to build upon. Instead, the legacy of New Deal agency-based social and economic investigation would be realized in future poverty knowledge in more indirect, albeit powerful ways. One was in the Roosevelt administration's eventual turn to full employment as the key to economic recovery and health. Nearly three decades later, this became the central economic doctrine, and the basis of economic knowledge-gathering, for the War on Poverty. A second was in the segmentation of knowledge along the lines of a welfare state that drew sharp lines between how it would provide for men and women, old and young, white and nonwhite, and, especially, poor and nonpoor, by segregating universalistic, relatively more generous, non-stigmatized programs such as social insurance from means-tested, ungenerous, stigmatized "welfare" programs for the poor.[5] Here again, this aspect of the New Deal legacy would be most fully realized decades hence, this time amidst the decline of postwar prosperity and liberalism, when poverty knowledge became almost wholly absorbed in a long and drawn-out struggle over the most stigmatized of the welfare programs created in the 1930s, Aid to Families with Dependent Children.

In contrast, anthropological and sociological studies exploring issues of social class and caste, community, and culture—often supported by funds from the Works Progress Administration and other New Deal agencies—had a more immediate impact on the course of poverty knowledge. For without necessarily identifying "poverty" as their central concern, these studies established the methods and the conceptual apparatus of what amounted to a new, or at least newly developing, line of inquiry that made culture a factor in understanding poverty in ways that it had not been before: not, as in Chicago-school sociology, as a reflection of internal "disorganization," but as itself a dimension of the structural inequalities that liberal reformers were trying to redress.

POVERTY, CLASS, AND CULTURE IN SOCIAL ANTHROPOLOGY

Culture, of course, had not been absent from Progressive political economy. To social surveyors, long hours, low pay, and the tenements were as much breeding grounds for cultural deprivation as for material want. But it was a different tradition of cultural analysis, aimed at the broader culture and inspired by the economist Thorstein Veblen, that influenced Robert S. Lynd. It was within this tradition, of broadly aimed cultural criticism rather than anxiety over cultural deprivation, that Lynd implicated culture in the problems of class polarization and unemployment in 1920s and Depression-era America. Best known for *The Theory of the Leisure Class* (1899), Veblen had introduced such concepts as "conspicuous consumption" and the "pecuniary" or money culture into the vocabulary of American social criticism, using them to illuminate the nature of economic inequality in the era of rising consumer capitalism. In consumerism Veblen recognized not only a source of class division, but a powerful means of suppressing radical consciousness within the working class. In the money culture, symbolized by high finance, he recognized a powerful threat to the ethos of workmanship and physically productive labor that constituted the true source of value in the economy. Together, Veblen thought, these signposts of capitalist culture threatened to leave society in a state of arrested development, spiritually sapped by materialism and unable to organize a more democratic polity. That criticism in turn provided an essential intellectual back-drop for Robert and Helen Lynd's classic sociological bestseller *Middletown*, a study of cultural transformation and consumer capitalism in "that common-denominator of America, the Middle West." There, in statistical surveys, archi-val research, interviews, and participant observations conducted originally in 1924 and in a separate follow-up study in 1935, the Lynds found a class-polarized society, unable to cope with the problems of low wages, unemploy-ment, and "caring for the unable" because of its own cultural commitment to consumerism and individual gain.[6]

While building from within the Progressive intellectual tradition, the Lynds were also eager to branch out in directions suggested by more contemporary social scientific trends. This turned out to be a matter of some contention with the project's sponsoring agency, the Rockefeller-backed Institute of Social and Religious Research, which in 1923 commissioned Robert Lynd to conduct one in what was to be a series of social surveys on religion in modern industrial life. Lynd was not exactly a natural choice for the commission; though a minis-ter-in-training at the Union Theological Seminary, he had just recently pub-lished a scathing exposé in *The Survey* criticizing Rockefeller's Standard Oil Company for exploitative labor practices at Elk Basin, a Wyoming oil camp. Nevertheless, having gotten the job with the help of a friend, an influential Laura Spelman Rockefeller Memorial official, he shifted the study's frame-work from what his sponsors initially envisioned as a heavily statistical survey of religious practices to a study of cultural transformation using the methods of anthropology.[7]

It was thus both social surveyors and as resident anthropologists that the Lynds established themselves in Muncie, Indiana, in 1924. And it was as cul-tural as well as social surveyors that they measured the impact of Muncie's economic transformation from small-town manufacturer to large-scale indus-trial capitalism. Using Veblenesque categories, they traced the economic and political disparities between Middletown's producer, or working (71%) and its commercial, or business (29%) class.[8] But they were especially keen to illumi-nate the power of consumer culture as a mechanism for maintaining class disparities. The business class was rapidly consolidating its power, with orga-nizations to promote pride in "Magic Middletown" and to bolster more indus-try, more consumerism, and more "free market" growth. Meanwhile, a once-thriving trade union movement had dwindled to almost nothing, its energy sapped by the disappearance of craftsmanship and the mechanization of labor, and its psychological "satisfactions" replaced by the pursuit of more and more consumer goods. Everyone in Middletown was "running for dear life" to keep up with their new "subjective wants," but it was the working class that paid the price. Only one-fourth of the workers in a sample of one hundred made more than the Bureau of Labor Statistics minimum standard of living. All of them lived with the constant threat of "bad times" and unemployment hanging over their heads. For these very reasons, it was the working class who fed the ranks of "the unable," who could not "secure the necessary food, shelter and care of health under the economic system by which people live in Middletown." And yet, the vast working class had little collective consciousness of its own exploitation; few seemed to realize that they were being lulled into complacency by the advertiser's appeal to consumption as "a new necessity," and the businessman's promise that a return to "free competition" was in the interest of all.[9]

It was not just consumerism that exposed the working class to poverty. On an even deeper level, it was the cultural commitment to laissez-faire. Here the Lynds saw the starkest example of what sociologist William Ogburn had called "cultural lag": having made the transition to a complex industrial economy, the community steadfastly clung to its outmoded individualistic ways. Thus, "a man may get his living by operating a twentieth century machine and at the same time hunt for a job under a *laissez-faire* individualism which dates back more than a century." The same contradiction characterized the way the city provided assistance for the poor. Although transformed from the old tradition of neighborly help and Christian charity, the modern, business-like way of giving was still regulated by the old philosophy of "individual responsibility" which held the poor responsible for their misfortunes—and ignored the systemic problems of unemployment and low pay. Far from any thought of "change in the social or industrial system," Middletown preferred to go on feeling good about giving charity to "people in actual need," while doing its best to "get the unpleasant business over with and out of sight as soon as possible!"[10]

As a description of 1920s America, the Lynds' analysis of cultural lag took the tone of sharp but not necessarily urgent social criticism. Published in 1929, on the verge of the Great Depression, *Middletown* offered few concrete prescriptions for change. After a follow-up study to see how Muncie was coping with the Depression, however, the Lynds quickly abandoned that complacent tone. For even though unemployment had grown and the social structure was more fragmented, and even though power was more concentrated in the hands of a small circle of corporate elites, Middletown nevertheless remained stuck in "a culture suckled on the lion's milk of getting ahead by personal exploitative powers." The working class was still largely unorganized, swayed by the symbolism of laissez-faire opportunity and individual gain. Worse still, the spirit of the Chamber of Commerce–sponsored "Magic Middletown" campaign, with its "solvent remedy of more and better possessions and socially distinguished goods" was alive and well among the workers, once again diverting them from organized opposition to the very system that was leaving them, as the Lynds saw it, on an ever-more crowded shop floor, where the mythical ladder of opportunity was "becoming shorter, harder to climb and leading nowhere in particular."[11]

Middletown's changed circumstances were also reflected in the Lynds' prescriptions, now more urgent and explicit than at first. In 1929 the Lynds had concluded by tentatively suggesting a reexamination of local institutions, perhaps hoping that Middletowners would recognize and correct the symptoms of cultural lag, and urged "would-be reformers" to relinquish the "widely current method of a head-long assault upon established institutions" in favor of a more organic, community-based process of change.[12] By 1936, with all hope of enlightened community-based reform abandoned, the Lynds painted two stark alternatives. In one, Middletowners succumbed to the appeal of an authoritarian leader. In the other, they came to accept the leadership of enlightened New Deal planners. The Lynds revealed their own predilections in their lengthy chapter on "Caring for the Unable," now no longer an "inconspicuous" feature of Middletown life as it had been the decade before. Alone among the areas surveyed, social welfare had shown real progress, and the reason was the sudden, transforming "interjection of Federal planning into the local scene." Relief remained unpopular, among both the working and the business classes, but the fact was that more than one-fourth of the population relied on public assistance, and local leaders had learned how to provide it in a coordinated, rational way. Although the locals were eager to go back to the old ways once prosperity returned, New Deal intervention had established a better way of doing things, a "bench mark for social change" from which, despite local resistance, even Middletown could never completely retreat.[13]

In the context of the Great Depression, then, the Lynds' cultural criticism reconnected with the reform urgency of Progressive-era social investigation. But the tone of fatalism in the Lynds' conclusion also suggested a loss of at least some articles of Progressive faith—certainly in the informed citizenry, but also in the power of social scientific knowledge to effect change. On the one hand, they portrayed a town utterly incapable of comprehending, let along resolving, its cultural dilemmas without enlightened leadership from above. On the other, as social scientists they had seen how little their investigations had penetrated local consciousness, how powerless they as experts were in the face of cultural resistance to change. Most significant, though, was the sense in the Lynds' follow-up study that control over Middletown's economic future—for good or for ill—lay ineluctably in the hands of the large "outside" forces of corporate capitalism and the federal government. Like it or not, the new, mass consumer-driven political economy was here to stay, and, as Robert Lynd recognized in his own shift toward consumer politics, the locus of organized resistance would come not from working-class producers but from citizens in their capacity as consumers—if at all. In the new political economy, the reformist objectives of knowledge were more important than ever, but changed; now, reformers hoped to reorganize culture in response to the inevitable forces of economic change.[14]

One study of an impoverished, Depression-era farm community suggests the ambiguous implications of applying this perspective in the social science of poverty. With *Middletown* as his template, anthropologist Carl Withers examined small-town transformation under the impact of a commercializing agricultural economy. Although he endorsed the modernizing objectives of New Deal agricultural planners, Withers mourned the passing of the traditional farm community. "The greater problem for all 'backwards' and 'poor' communities like Plainville is one which doubled or even tripled income will not solve," he concluded. "For better or for worse, they are doomed as 'traditional' communities. As their ancient value systems crumble under the blows of a new 'tradition' imposed from outside, their problem is to learn to participate more fully in the cultural rewards of the greater society."[15] In this Withers anticipated what would later emerge as a central theme in postwar and particularly in Cold War–era studies of impoverished, "backward," and "underdeveloped" communities around the world. In Withers's eyes, it was not necessarily the dominant culture that stood in the way of a more equitable and universal enjoyment of the fruits of modernization; it was the culture of the poor.

The first volume of *Middletown* was packaged as a new genre in social science, a "social anthropology of contemporary life."[16] By then, though, anticipating the much more pervasive, heavily endowed behavioral science "revolution" after World War II, the fascination with studying culture as a dimension of human behavior was starting to become more pronounced and institutionalized. In 1929, the Rockefeller Foundation provided funds for the establishment of the Institute of Human Relations at Yale University, an interdisciplinary center for the study of human behavior that would map out the field of "personality and culture" in several collaborative studies over the next several years. Two years later, the Social Science Research Council followed suit, with a committee on Personality and Culture that counted Robert Lynd among its most active supporters, and that hoped to encourage comparative cross-cultural research.[17] At the same time, and especially in the wake of *Middletown's* success, young anthropologists immersed in the study of far-off "primitive" cultures were becoming impressed by the possibilities for research in "typical" American communities, and, as Depression set in, by the importance of cultural knowledge for the work of reform. In communities with fictionalized names like Plainville, Yankee City, Southerntown, and Jonesville they began to uncover the elements of a distinctive lower-class culture, locating its origins not merely in the response to conditions of economic deprivation, but also in the deeper recesses of psychological and social identity.

No figure was more important in generating opportunities for the study of lower-class culture than W. Lloyd Warner, an anthropologist with fieldwork techniques honed in the study of Australian aboriginal tribes, who made the American community study a lifelong academic career. During the 1930s Warner directed major studies of Newburyport, Massachusetts ("Yankee City"), and Natchez, Mississippi ("Deep South"), and helped to supervise the field-work in Chicago's South Side black belt ("Bronzeville") that provided the basis for St. Clair Drake and Horace Cayton's *Black Metropolis*. In the early to mid-1940s, he put together a community study of Morris, Illinois ("Jones-ville"), as the war was ending and before the apparent impact of postwar economic prosperity. To staff these ambitious and highly labor intensive studies Warner proved particularly adept at tapping into philanthropic, university, and, at the height of the Great Depression, federal research funding under the auspices of the Works Progress Administration (WPA). Later on, he would connect up to the booming postwar market for demographic profiling in advertising and private industry. He also positioned his approach as an alternative to Chicago-school social ecology—like the Lynds, he specialized in the "total community" study and considered class a "fundamental structure" in American society—in a rivalry that became a running battle once Warner joined the University of Chicago sociology department (at the time not yet separate from anthropology) in 1935. As the momentum behind Chicago-school neighborhood studies began to fade during the 1930s, Warner's high-visibility team projects provided training grounds—not to mention employment—for aspiring ethnographic researchers and helped to sustain the community study as a legitimate and ongoing academic enterprise. Even more than the Lynds, Warner also introduced a generation of students trained in the 1930s and 1940s to the notion that class stratification had a deep-seated cultural dimension that operated independently of economic relationships.[18]

Warner's trademark was the detailed, easily parodied, but widely embraced scheme he devised for measuring social class, a technique that—not unlike Charles Booth's—enlisted the services of strategically placed community residents to help rank their neighbors on a status hierarchy that ranged from "upper-upper" to "lower-lower," with a slew of sometimes-oxymoronic categories ("lower-upper," "upper-lower") in between. This method, which Warner called "Evaluated Participation," complemented the more conventional "Index of Status Characteristics" (occupation, amount and source of income, neighborhood, housing type) that Warner's research teams compiled for every family in the community.[19] These measures, along with scores of interviews, ethnographies, and, in later studies, psychological tests, provided the empirical basis for Warner's central theme: that class and status hierarchy, as Warner claimed to have "discovered" in Yankee City, was determined by "something more" than income and wealth. Behind it was an elaborate system of formal social institutions, informal cliques, and, especially, class-specific cultural practices that socialized and prepared individuals for their inherited stations in the social order—and that made upward mobility a difficult, potentially hazardous climb.[20] Of these subcultures, Warner himself showed most fascination with the upper-uppers, and most appreciation for the psychological drama ("status anxiety") of the "strivers" below. But he also laid out a typology of lower-class subcultures that brought culture into poverty knowledge in a new, albeit in some respects familiar, way.

Thus, like legions of investigators before him, Warner based his lower-class typology on a barely masked distinction between the "deserving" and "undeserving" poor. The unskilled, low-wage laborers in the "upper-lower" group were "honest but poor," lived orderly lives in stable but undesirable neighborhoods, and took pride in their ability to get by without relief. They believed in educating their children in the hopes of a better life, and yet they themselves remained loyal to the ethnic associations and cliques that would hamper mobility into higher-status groups; they preferred the company, that is, of "people like us." The "lower-lowers," on the other hand, cared little about education and resisted outside attempts to improve their lot. They were marginally employed, disorderly and "shiftless," and lived on the "wrong side of the tracks." Concerned more with meeting bare necessities than with getting ahead, they satisfied themselves with immediate gratifications, and lived by a quasi-criminal, sexually uninhibited moral code. If these themes resonated with earlier Progressive-era social investigation, one did not: Together constituting more than half of Yankee City's population, Warner's lower classes were not only culturally well-adapted but generally satisfied with their place on the status hierarchy. To their credit, they showed few signs of the anxiety and personality disorder rampant among their striving middle- and upper-class counterparts. Even the town's extended 1933 shoe factory strike, to Warner, could be interpreted as a sign of lower-class complacency: what the workers wanted was not necessarily a say in the workplace, but a return to the old craft-based hierarchy and paternalistic welfare capitalism that were being threatened by the arrival of an outside corporate conglomerate.[21] Indeed, despite frequent rhetorical nods to the "basic contradiction" between American dream and social reality, Warner thought that lower-class culture played a vital integrating function in a "complex society" that needed status rankings to "get its work done."[22]

Warner himself, then, was no reformer—knowledge of class, he wrote in a primer first published in the late 1940s, was a "corrective instrument" to help people "adapt themselves to social reality and fit their dreams and aspirations to what is possible."[23] But for students of lower-class culture in the 1930s and 1940s Warner's functionalist framework provided the basis for what later commentators would dismiss as a "muckraking," culturally relativist, and romanticized approach—one that pointed to a need for cultural rehabilitation *and* economic reform.[24] Lower-class culture had its "rewards and punishments," wrote anthropologist and Warner student Allison Davis, who had gotten his first significant fieldwork experience in the mid-1930s as a principal investigator for Warner's community study of Natchez, Mississippi. Facing a future of low wages and unrewarding work, the "underprivileged worker" got powerful compensation from "the pleasures that he actually can attain by following his underprivileged culture. He gets strong biological enjoyment. He spends a great deal of his nights in sexual exploration . . . he lives in a world where visceral, genital and emotional gratification is far more available than it is in a middle-class world."[25] Elsewhere, Davis argued that lower-class values of toughness and aggression were functional in a way outsiders would never understand, reflecting a "realistic and adaptive" response to living in neighborhoods where "physical aggression is as much a normal, socially approved and socially inculcated type of behavior as it is in frontier communities."[26] Similarly, the behavior of the underprivileged worker was sensible in light of his limited circumstances. "The habits of 'shiftlessness,' 'irresponsibility,' lack of 'ambition,' absenteeism, of quitting the job, which management usually regards as a result of the 'innate' perversity of underprivileged white and negro workers, are in fact *normal responses* that the worker has learned from his physical and social environment." Critical of the "ethnocentric" views of the helping professions, Davis insisted that these habits had to be understood before they could be changed. Ultimately, it would require "real rewards" to "repay" the worker for "the hard work and self-denial required to change his old habits, and to compete with the rewards of a physical kind that he already gets." Assisting the underprivileged worker thus called for a two-pronged approach: the first, most immediate, was to raise the standard of living with better pay, working, and housing conditions so that poor workers would increase their own "consciousness of economic needs"; second, more difficult, was to raise the worker's "cultural goals" for education, respectability, enlightened child rearing, and hard work. Only then could society break the "circle" of material and cultural deprivation that trapped the poor in a substandard way of life.[27]

With its emphasis on class and the coherence of lower-class culture, Warner's anthropological framework also offered an alternative to the Chicago-school's ecological image of "disorganized" slum neighborhoods. "Cornerville's problem is not lack of organization but a failure of its own social organization to mesh with the structure of the society around it," wrote William Foote Whyte in his influential ethnography of Boston's Italian North End, *Street Corner Society* (1943). The neighborhood actually had a stable social structure, Whyte observed, dominated by racketeers, ward politicians, street gangs, and family networks, all tied together by a "hierarchy of personal relations based upon a system of reciprocal obligation." Judged backwards and inferior by individualistic middle-class standards, the Cornerville world was in fact highly functional when viewed from the inside, providing jobs, services, and, especially, a cohesive identity in a generally unaccepting social environment. Nor was "the problem of Cornerville" simply one of ethnicity—the neighborhood's "symbolic attachment to Italy" could be understood as a lower-class defense mechanism against both upper-class disapproval and middle-class professional reform.[28] Davis, too, emphasized class as the more fundamental dividing line, this time extending the analysis across racial lines. In *Children of Bondage* (1940), a collaborative study with Yale sociologist John Dollard, he concluded that child rearing and related cultural practices differed more profoundly along class than along racial lines.[29] Davis confirmed these conclusions in later research with sociologist Robert J. Havighurst, finding "considerable social class differences in child-rearing practices, and these differences are greater than the differences between negroes and whites of the same social class." Likewise, black and white children faced similar punishments from "our thoroughly middle-class teachers and school systems." In school they were "humiliated and punished too severely *for having the lower-class culture* which their own mothers, fathers and siblings approve" (emphasis in original). Anticipating the arguments that he and other liberal education reformers made in the 1960s, Davis argued that these punishments could help to explain differences in school achievement between the classes, and called on educators to understand and "remove the class punishments" from the lower-class child's behavior.[30]

With encouragement from Warner and in various applied research projects, by the mid-1930s the concept of lower-class culture was taking on increasingly psychological overtones. *Children of Bondage* was one of several studies commissioned by the Rockefeller-backed American Council on Education to understand the impact of racial stratification on black adolescent personality development. In this study, Davis and Dollard, attempting to blend Freudian and behaviorist theory, focused exclusively on child rearing practices as gleaned from psychological interviews. Although offering an unconventional argument with their emphasis on class as the dominant influence, Davis and Dollard anticipated a more general trend in the literature by assessing psychological damage as a measure of social disadvantage, and by tracing its origins to the lower-class family. Stripped, in this context, of her "functions" as either a breadwinner or a household manager, the lower-class mother loomed large as the instigator of a lower-class personality type—undisciplined, aggressive, unable to defer gratification because raised without sexual or impulse control—that in turn, Davis and Dollard warned, left children without the basic personality traits, such as anxiety and frustration, that motivated achievement.[31] Although tempering their psychological prognoses with the conviction that motivation could, given better "rewards," be learned, their emphasis on the permanence, even the predictive value of child rearing would seem to undercut the rehabilitative capacity of economic or school reform.

More important, such behavioristic theories were attached to what was becoming an ever-more stylized profile of lower-class culture that, as the tests became more routinized and the typology more abstracted, did more to reify than to challenge or get beyond existing stereotypes. It was a culture that, for all their aversion to middle-class ethnocentrism, social anthropologists were hardly eager to preserve. "We should not be so naïve," Davis warned, "as to think that lower-class life is a happy hunting ground given over to complete impulse expression." The lower-class child was exposed to frequent violence and family instability, and was handicapped by such "accepted class ways" as gambling, superstition, aggression, and sexual promiscuity.[32] Even Whyte, who admired the solidarity within the "corner boy" gang, found it to be narrow and circumscribed as a way of life. The corner boys were "blocked" by "their own organized society," as well as by the "outside world."[33] However "adaptive" to the vicissitudes of lower-class circumstances, the issue was not whether but how to bring about change in a culture that, left unchecked, would perpetuate deviant behavior and poverty. Starting out from the conviction that middle-class culture, however "striving" and stultifying, was what led to achievement in life, functionalist social anthropology was limited as a way of understanding the lower class. On the one hand, the work of Whyte, Davis, and others offered an alternative to the Chicago-school imagery of cultural breakdown and social disorganization, highlighting the essential integrity and coherence of lower-class culture while emphasizing the systemic and institutional underpinnings of class inequality. On the other hand, in their eyes the lower class was incapable of forming anything but a culture of disadvantage, a way of life so limited by circumstance as to render poor people incapable of pleasure aside from immediate gratification, and devoid of moral or political agency.

It would be a mistake, though, to view the cultural and behavioral turn in poverty knowledge as a turn away from liberal reform. In many ways, the social anthropologists were playing out themes anticipated in Progressive political economy—of cultural difference, the need for uplift, even of psychological damage—albeit in a more self-consciously theoretical way. Nor did they see their emphasis on the autonomy, the psychological origins, the deviance of lower-class culture as a necessarily limiting factor in reform. "Cornerville people will fit in better with the society around them when they gain more opportunities to participate in society," Whyte wrote. "This involves providing them with greater economic opportunity and also giving them greater responsibility for their own destinies."[34] In this he captured the central theme of Depression-era and immediate postwar social anthropology: that the key to addressing lower-class cultural disadvantage was to recognize that lower-class culture would not change without prior changes in economic opportunity. Only later, in the much-altered context of prosperity and Cold War, would the "culture of poverty" begin to assume the aura of psychological determinism that, still later, would be used in conservative arguments about the futility of liberal antipoverty programs.

Moreover, in his study of unemployed workers in 1930s New Haven, sociologist E. Wight Bakke used cultural analysis to much different effect. Conducted under the auspices of Yale's Institute of Human Relations, Bakke's eight-year study combined the methods of more traditionally conceptualized economic, household, and social welfare agency surveys with family case studies, interviews, site visits, and, especially important, systematic observation over time. In two companion volumes published in 1940, Bakke followed first the economic and then the community and family strategies workers used to adjust to long-term unemployment—or, as he put it in the subtitle of the first volume, "the task of making a living without a job." Perhaps most remembered for documenting the great lengths workers would go to before resorting to cash relief, Bakke's study also stands out as an unusually sensitive study of the cultural and psychological impact of mass unemployment in a society with a deep cultural investment in work. Treating culture as a fluid array of beliefs, values, and coping strategies rather than as an all-encompassing system, Bakke told a story not of cultural lag or deprivation, but of flexibility, resilience, and change. Forced by the experience of unemployment to reexamine their notions of individualism and self-reliance, New Haven's workers were developing a distinctive working-class consciousness based on the value of collective action and their own growing awareness of the conflict of interest between employers and employees. Although gendered in its concept of employment—Bakke's "worker," despite the existing literature on female labor, was male—the study also offered a nuanced reading of how unemployment was transforming gender relations within the working-class family—often, in his eyes, with improved results. In what Bakke depicted as the most successfully "reconstructed" families, men had gotten over the initial impulse to reassert patriarchal authority in the household, and instead learned to establish more egalitarian, cooperative relations with their wives and children. None of this, to be sure, had occurred without trauma, as Bakke showed in case histories of several families. In an important sense, though, their continual cultural "adjustments" had put New Haven's unemployed workers in the advance rather than at the rear of reform: having come to accept the need for government assistance, having suffered the indignities of relief, their experiences could be used, Bakke thought, to construct a welfare state that would offer economic security while acknowledging the importance workers continued to place on self-support.[35]

POVERTY, PLACE, AND ECONOMIC DEVELOPMENT: THE SOUTHERN REGIONALISTS

Still a third approach to integrating culture with a critique of political economy emerged in the dominant sociological explanation for why, as a 1938 Report from FDR's National Emergency Council proclaimed, the South was "the Nation's number one economic problem." The NEC report, and the long-range program of federal investment and industrialization it helped to stimulate, would later come under criticism for concentrating too much on economic growth as the answer and ignoring the problems of income distribution, race, and political inequality that would continue to plague the postwar "New South."[36] In fact, though, the NEC recommendations were drawn from a far more comprehensive analysis of the South's economic problems that had been carefully built up over more than a decade by a group of sociologists at the University of North Carolina. Treating the South as a coherent cultural and geographic region, they argued that poverty was deeply imbedded in the South's culture as well as its political economy, a product of sectionalism and white supremacy as much as of low wages, inefficient land management, and the absence of an industrial base. Exploring the impact of this "culture complex" on the conditions of sharecroppers and mill workers throughout the South, they sought to shatter the then-prevailing mythology that economic backwardness could be blamed on the natural inferiority of the labor force. Their investigations provided the empirical basis for a "regionalist" program of economic and social modernization that would, they hoped, free the New South from the legacy of poverty and racial inequality it had inherited from the Old.

The intellectual home of Southern regionalism was the University of North Carolina's Institute for Research in Social Science, which under the leadership of sociologist Howard W. Odum had become the center of social scientific knowledge-gathering aimed at bringing the South into the twentieth century. Odum had started this ambitious enterprise in 1920, when he was invited to Chapel Hill to direct a new School of Public Welfare and to start what would be the first white department of sociology in the South. At the time, the University was beginning to emerge as a center of southern academic liberalism under President Harry W. Chase, a process Odum's arrival accelerated considerably. Within two years, he had founded the *Journal of Social Forces*, pitching it to a broad academic and (mostly southern) general readership with a combination of scholarly articles, investigative reports, editorials, and news of current events. Along with Chase, he was also one of the founders of the University of North Carolina Press, which within the next decade would make a name for itself as one of the leading university presses in the country. In 1924, Odum started the Institute for Research in Social Science as an interdisciplinary center for the study of contemporary southern issues.

The Institute, underwritten by the Laura Spelman Rockefeller Memorial, allowed Odum to construct the elements of a Chicago-like academic empire, complete with journal, press, and a sizable staff of full-time research assistantships. Working with young scholars such as Rupert B. Vance, Arthur F. Raper, Guy B. Johnson, Harriet L. Herring, Jennings S. Rhyne, Thomas J. Woofter, Jr., Margaret Hagood, and George S. Mitchell, Odum mounted a rigorously empirical research program that confronted issues few academics had been willing to take on: mill workers' conditions, farm tenancy, race relations, and—the subject of Vance's doctoral dissertation—the agricultural allegiance to "King Cotton." The Institute also helped propel Odum to national recognition. In 1929, he joined a handful of scholars as the only southerner on President Hoover's Research Committee on Social Trends, and in 1930 he became the first southerner to serve as president of the American Sociological Society. Meanwhile, he cultivated the philanthropic and policy connections that would establish the Institute as the major academic outpost for moderate white southern liberalism: hooked up with gradualist organizations such as the Atlanta-based Commission on Interracial Cooperation, the Institute renounced biological racism but remained unwilling to challenge the segregationist order. Only later, after World War II, did the Institute openly embrace racial integration. But the Institute's main goal, as Odum insisted, was not political but scientific: to develop a theoretical framework for analyzing the South's major problems, and with it to encourage a "reintegration" into the nation's political and economic mainstream.[37] That framework, known as regionalism, defined the South as a coherent geographic, ecological, cultural, and economic unit that, for reasons having more to do with its historical and cultural allegiances than with anything natural to the environment, was a veritable case study in poverty.[38]

The regionalist explanation for poverty rested on three central ideas, each based on a blend of cultural and political economic analysis, and each reflected in contemporary policy debates. One was the concept of the "cotton culture," first developed in Rupert Vance's dissertation, and a major part of the regionalist critique of the South's system of farm tenancy. For Vance and others, the "cotton culture" represented the legacy of slavery and the plantation system, now expressed in the complex of labor relations, land tenure practices, and feudal mythology that was keeping the system of sharecropping alive. Sharecropping, regionalists pointed out, was little better than slavery. Indeed, one of its tragedies was that it brought the landless white farmer into the same relationship of dependency that had tied blacks to the plantation: while presumably offered mobility and compensation for their labor, tenants remained in a state of "enforced arrested development," with no opportunities for accumulating property, skills, or a sense of "self direction." It was, as Arthur Raper so aptly described it in his book by that title, a "preface to peasantry" rather than the basis of an independent democratic yeomanry. What's more, it was terribly inefficient as a system of production, keeping the South mired in the kind of unmechanized, one-crop farming that depleted the soil, prevented diversification, put landlords and farmers at great risk of bankruptcy, and undermined the region's position in international markets. The most devastating impact of the "cotton culture," however, was on the attitudes and behavior of the tenants themselves. Cultivating the crop was particularly grueling, requiring extended periods of planting, chopping, and picking followed by shorter spans of seasonal slack. These demands had made an imprint on family habits, the regionalists thought, leaving tenants, for example, without a steady income and unpracticed in saving or thrift. The system virtually required tenants to have larger families, with plenty of hands to bring the crop in. And it encouraged them to be "shiftless" and mobile, offering little hope that the land they worked would ever be their own. Compounding these problems was a cheap but notoriously inadequate diet, virtually a recipe for the pellegra and listlessness that were routinely attributed to tenants' inborn ignorance. "Disinherited" from the land and "defenseless" against the landlord, the sharecropper had understandably become dependent and resigned—a "ready excuse," as one regionalist report concluded, "for keeping him under a stern paternalistic control."[39] The regionalists, though, had another agenda: reforming federal agricultural policy, which was overwhelmingly biased toward large growers, to recognize the needs of small and tenant farmers. In 1934, southern liberal and New Deal administrator Will Alexander enlisted Vance, Arthur Raper, and other regionalists in the federal lobbying campaign. Their research, summarized in a widely distributed pamphlet entitled *The Collapse of Cotton Tenancy* and later incorporated into the President's Special Commission on Farm Tenancy, served as the basis of important but short-lived programs of land reform, resettlement, tenant ownership, and rural cooperatives under the auspices of the New Deal's Resettlement and Farm Security Administrations.[40]

A second regionalist idea, the notion that the South was a "colonial" economy, proved even more consequential in shaping the New Deal response to southern poverty. First fully articulated in Vance's *Human Geography of the South* (1932), colonialism was a central theme in the National Emergency Council report, and from there became the chief justification for federally subsidized industrialization as the pathway to a more progressive, prosperous South. Vance's notion was couched in detached, scientific terms; by "colonial" economy he meant one that operated primarily to extract and export natural resources for manufacture outside the region—one, that is, that lacked the indigenous sources of capital or production to meet consumer demands. As the NEC Report suggests, however, the colonial analysis touched a raw political nerve, providing an air of regional victimization that Vance did not necessarily endorse. Colonialism helped to explain the "paradox," as the NEC report put it, that while the South was "blessed by Nature with immense wealth, its people on the whole are the poorest in the country. Lacking industries of its own, the South has been forced to trade the richness of its soil, its minerals and forests and the labor of its people for goods manufactured elsewhere." Reliant on the South as a source of natural resources and cheap labor, "outside" interests were eager to maintain its colonial status, and were opposed, by implication, to indigenous regional development. The NEC report went on to suggest that pro-northern federal policy was implicated in keeping the South behind. Correcting the "imbalance" would bring the South to its rightful position as an equal partner in the national economy.[41] Equally significant in this context was the part of Vance's analysis that the NEC Report left out: in order to modernize, he thought, the South needed to escape the myth of a "feudal" agrarian past. This called for a new social scientific realism that would help the region face up to its historical legacy of backwardness and poverty.[42]

In characterizing southern poverty for a national audience, the regionalists increasingly emphasized a third major theme, combining a familiar Malthusian logic with the emerging New Deal emphasis on the importance of purchasing power as the engine of economic recovery and growth: while reproducing far more than its share of the population, the South was not keeping up its share of consumer demand. Of course, these issues could be treated separately, and in the NEC Report they were. In its section on population, the Report warned that overpopulated rural districts were exporting their young—and poor—to cities in and outside of the South, putting a strain on services and creating competition in already depressed labor markets. In the section on purchasing power, in contrast, the southern population represented "the Nation's greatest untapped market," a threat to the northern economy not so much because of numbers but because it lacked the income to buy the goods.[43] In combination, however, high birth rates and low consumption posed a double threat to the national welfare. As Margaret Hagood warned in her study of farm tenant women, *Mothers of the South* (1939), rural mothers were producing children who, precisely because of chronic regional poverty, lacked the capacity to develop consumer tastes, or otherwise to reach the " 'quality' of population desired for American people." Hagood was quick to distance herself from "alarmist eugenicists" with their fears of white race suicide. The study itself was a rare and highly sympathetic look at the intelligence and "vitality" with which tenant farm women coped with the "triple role of mother, housekeeper, and field laborer," and tried to protect their children from the "pathology" of systemic poverty. And Hagood insisted that her findings offered evidence that whatever "quality" tenants lacked was due to environment and not biology. Nevertheless, her conclusions came with a clear-cut warning: as the source of an ever-growing proportion of the nation's people, the unreconstructed rural South posed a threat to its future welfare.[44]

Regionalism, then, provided a framework for understanding poverty as a product of the South's underdeveloped economy and its cultural lags—the latter of which included, Hagood thought, its ideological commitment to "patriarchy."[45] At the same time, in a strategy that would reemerge repeatedly in later poverty knowledge, regionalism also provided a framework not so much for avoiding but for downplaying the issue of race. White racism, to be sure, came under regionalist fire, principally for its role in perpetuating southern economic backwardness. The southern obsession with "keeping the Negro in his place," both Arthur Raper and Rupert Vance recognized, was keeping the sharecropping system alive; awakening to the reality of equality between the races would be the first step toward future development.[46] And yet, regionalism itself was the product of a segregated academic and social system that even self-professed racial egalitarians were unwilling to upset. Southern poverty, they maintained, could be addressed without directly confronting segregation, while economic restructuring would inevitably accrue to the benefit of blacks.

Certainly there was a degree of political strategy in their thinking—Raper in particular emphasized that black and white sharecroppers had a common interest in economic development. Nevertheless, by subsuming the race problem within the more generalized framework of regional poverty, they diminished the importance of racism as a source of poverty, while perpetuating an ultimately unsustainable logic that would subordinate racial justice to the goal of regional economic development.

Race was the central but not the only limitation in regionalist poverty knowledge. Margaret Hagood's criticism of farm tenant patriarchy notwithstanding, even her policy prescriptions were couched in the threat of overpopulation rather than gender inequality. Dedicated, as they were, to showing how farm tenants and mill workers had been caught up in the "pathology" of regional backwardness, regionalists were pessimistic, if not dismissive of the possibilities for grass roots organizing or unionization: the southern poor, like the region, were caught up in a culture of dependency. Nor, in characterizing the South as uniquely, peculiarly backwards, did the regionalist framework acknowledge the degree to which industrial capitalism had itself been a source of poverty—failing, that is, to anticipate the prospects of modernization without reform. This exceptionalism became especially problematic after World War II, when regionalists, caught up in the "growth psychology" championed by New South industrialists, gave structural reform the back seat to industrialization, full employment, and consumer markets.[47] In the context of postwar prosperity, concepts of economic colonialism appeared less applicable as an explanation for southern poverty. Not until the 1960s would the idea of internal colonialism reemerge as a prominent explanation for domestic poverty, and then, in the analysis of ghetto poverty offered by radical African American scholars, as an argument for separation from rather than reintegration within the mainstream economy. The American South, though, once brought into the mainstream economy and culture, would blame its poverty on the culture of the poor.[48]

Like so much in American society, poverty knowledge emerged from the Great Depression significantly, if not quite predictably, changed. Resurrecting and building on themes from Progressive political economy, social anthropologists and regionalist sociologists made culture the focal point for poverty knowledge, and its analysis the special province of academic social science. While challenging the antistatism and other aspects of Chicago-school ecology, they worked within the same basic frame of reference, in which "poverty" and "lower-class" were as much cultural as economic categories and the question was not whether but why and how the poor were culturally different from the middle and upper classes. Meanwhile, social science had continued to redefine its own role in the broader culture in ways that distinguished the new from the old poverty knowledge. Without necessarily denying—indeed, often embracing—the need for economic reform and cultural uplift, social scientific poverty knowledge would concern itself with chronicling the deeper cultural lags sustaining poverty and especially the cultural contradictions between economic reality and democratic ideal. In the process, they not only added to but shifted the vocabulary of Progressive poverty knowledge, with the now recognizably scientific terminology of cultural lag, deviance, and, especially for the southern regionalists, cultural pathology. During the Depression social scientists turned to culture in the spirit of professionalization, but equally in the spirit of social criticism and reform. The consequences of this turn, and its double-edged nature, were most dramatically played out in the sociology of race.

CHAPTER 3

From the Deep South to the Dark Ghetto:
Poverty Knowledge, Racial Liberalism,
and Cultural "Pathology"

IN *The Philadelphia Negro* (1899), W.E.B. DuBois had stretched the bound-aries of the Progressive social survey to provide an answer to a question Swed-ish economist Gunnar Myrdal was still asking nearly fifty years later: "Why is such an extraordinarily large proportion of the Negro people so poor?" Steeped though it was in the language of cultural deprivation, DuBois's explanation was primarily about political economy: Philadelphia Negroes, he showed, were systematically denied opportunities in the urban industrial economy because of racial discrimination and restriction. Moreover, discriminatory practices were not isolated or occasional, they were systemic and built into the everyday operations of the economy. And yet, despite DuBois's best efforts, not for another three decades—during black sociology's "golden age" in the 1930s and 1940s—would the overwhelmingly poor economic condition of African Americans be recognized in poverty knowledge as a legitimate, indeed a neces-sary, subject for research. Even then it was not cast, as DuBois had outlined, as a problem of political economy; it was cast, by Gunnar Myrdal among others, as a more encompassing problem of cultural pathology—the Negro's, and American society's writ large.[1]

Several developments contributed to this racial "breakthrough" in poverty knowledge, and to the particular form it took. Important among them was the surge of interest in the "Negro problem" coming from organized white philanthropy in response to the Great Migration, which drew unprecedented numbers of African Americans away from the rural South between 1910 and 1930 and prompted a shift in emphasis from Negro uplift to race relations research as a means of understanding and preventing racial conflict.[2] In the context of post–World War I immigration restriction, black migration also changed the "face" of urban poverty in social welfare agencies, as African Americans replaced European immigrants as the most visible, racially "other" urban newcomers. For social science, though, the "new" migration also repre-sented the equivalent of a natural experiment, and nowhere more so than in the city that Chicago-school sociologists had turned into a laboratory for scientific research. Chicago experienced a nearly sixfold increase in its black population in two decades and, like many cities before and after it, had been the site of a massive outburst of racial violence in 1919.[3] As the most renowned in a long tradition of post-riot research, *The Negro in Chicago* established a pattern of applied sociology that would shape popular perceptions not just about the roots of racial violence but about urban African Americans.[4] The focus on race relations was later given added momentum by the United States' entry into World War II, which not only provided chilling evidence of the consequences of racist ideology, but also gave the rising incidence of racial violence in Detroit, New York, and other urban areas new significance as a matter of international human rights.[5]

A second contributing factor was the growing number of African American social scientists who were eager to apply the latest sociological and anthropological theory to the study of a complex and changing Negro culture that, at least for some prominent scholars, was as much African as American in origin. Although operating within a highly segregated system, these scholars were beginning to gain the academic recognition that DuBois had been denied and even, from their outposts at Negro colleges and universities, to attract a sliver of the philanthropic research dollars that flowed mostly to white institutions. For them, and especially for E. Franklin Frazier, Charles S. Johnson, Allison Davis, and others who rose to social scientific prominence a generation after DuBois, embracing the standards of objectivity meant adopting—and adapting—the idioms of social ecology, human development, and personality and culture as analytic frames. At the same time, as part of a generation of "New Negro" intellectuals and activists coming of age in the 1920s and 1930s, they were keenly aware of the politics of culture not simply as an expression of class and racial identity, but as part of the understanding and argumentation that would advance the struggle for racial equality.[6]

Thus, a third factor bringing the Negro problem to the forefront of poverty knowledge was the transformation in scientific racial ideology that had been occurring since the early 1900s, and that ultimately provided liberals with a theoretical framework and justification for racial assimilation and egalitarianism. Building on the work of Franz Boas, W. I. Thomas, and Robert Park, racially liberal social scientists set out to shatter once-dominant theories of biological inferiority and to recast racial difference as a reflection of social environment, culture, and historical experience. The Negro, racial liberals argued, was fully capable of assimilating into modern industrial society—capable, that is, of assuming the cultural as well as the material living standards that social scientists specifically identified with the *white* majority. Culture, then, took on a special significance in social scientific racial liberalism and in what liberal social scientists hoped would be their signature contribution to the struggle for racial equality: unlike biology, culture was subject to change. Indeed, by learning to understand Negroes as fully human—as having a culture, a psychology, as subject to the same developmental laws shaping all human societies—Americans would come to understand that they were "essentially *white*," as Allison Davis and John Dollard put it, in their biological and mental traits.[7] Moreover, during decades when immigration was waning due to legislative restriction and economic depression, the concept of an American Negro culture took on the trappings of a new social scientific frontier. Studying the Negro was a part of "making our civilization . . . intelligible," wrote anthropologist Hortense Powdermaker, who like her colleague John Dollard conducted a community study of Indianola, Mississippi, while a fellow at Yale University's Institute of Human Relations. Dollard, a white sociologist trained at Chicago, was eager to apply what he was learning about psychoanalytic method in field research. Powdermaker, who was white as well but who was also aware that being Jewish identified her as "other" in the southern rural context, had just returned from fieldwork in the Southwest Pacific Islands for her book on the Lesu. Equipped with the methods earlier honed on "primitive" tribes and immigrant and native-born white communities, they and other white and African American scholars prepared to advance the cause of racial equality by exploring what they saw as unknown scientific territory.[8]

Together, these developments set the stage for an enormous outpouring of research on race relations and on black community and culture, much of it published in the late 1930s and 1940s, and all of it with the sponsorship and imprimatur of white social scientific philanthropy. The results are reflected in what are now recognized as classics from the "golden age" of black sociology, including E. Franklin Frazier's *The Negro Family in the United States* (1939); John Dollard's *Caste and Class in a Southern Town* (1937); Hortense Powdermaker's *After Freedom* (1939); *Deep South* (1941) by Allison Davis, Burleigh Gardner, and Mary Gardner; and *Black Metropolis* (1945) by St. Clair Drake and Horace Cayton. In these and other texts, drawn together in a sweeping synthesis in Gunnar Myrdal's *An American Dilemma* (1944), social scientists crystallized the elements of an emerging liberal orthodoxy on race. This new synthesis defined "the race problem" within a black/white paradigm, traced the roots of racial inequality to a wide range of social and cultural disadvantages rooted in white prejudice, and embraced integration and racial assimilation as desirable social goals.[9] Equally important from the perspective of poverty knowledge, these texts mapped out and diagnosed the elements of a distinctive and "pathological" black lower-class culture in the large, unassimilated poor populations of the deep South and the northern metropolis. It was in this form, as cultural pathology, that the "Negro problem" became part of poverty knowledge—and the source of what remains its most enduring, divisive debates.

For within the liberal orthodoxy, and very much part of its research literature, were several lingering unresolved tensions, best captured in an ongoing battle between Chicago-school sociology and W. Lloyd Warner's social anthropology. To some degree it was a variation of the broader debate about whether lower-class culture was a product of migration and temporary "disorganization," or a coherent, deviant, but organized response to structural inequality. But more fundamentally, it was a debate about the nature of American racism and, especially, about its significance in explaining the poverty that continued to engulf the majority of blacks in expanding urban ghettos. In social ecology, racial conflict was a natural and inevitable by-product of migration, an expression of temporary interethnic competition in a process that would lead to assimilation. For the Negro, as for all migrants, poverty and disorganization were part of the journey from rural village to modern, industrial society—and not, as such, a consequence of institutionalized racial discrimination. Social anthropology, in contrast, characterized American race relations as a system of caste, rooted in a deep psychological need among whites to maintain their supremacy, and imbedded in an airtight system of institutional, legal, and interpersonal relationships that conspired to keep the Negro poor and "in his place." The issue, in more contemporary terms, was about whether and how "race matters" in explaining the persistence of a black "underclass." As enduring as the debate, though, was a central premise both sides embraced: that black poverty was a form of cultural pathology and that its most visible expression could be found in the deviant behavior and values of the African American lower class.

There was one final factor, though, shaping the way poverty knowledge came to recognize the "Negro problem" as part of the "poverty problem," and that was the combination of racial and ideological barriers that relegated approaches that did not fit into the emerging liberal consensus to the margins of academic debate. Among them were critics of the "new orthodoxy" on American race relations, including Oliver Cromwell Cox, an influential Marxist sociologist who criticized the Chicago school, Warner, and Myrdal for "mystifying" and obfuscating the class exploitation underlying racial inequality in the United States.[10] Others, notably historian Carter Woodson, anthropologist Melville Herskovits, and W.E.B. DuBois, took issue with the orthodox characterization of black culture as a "distorted" product of white oppression, devoid of any African roots.[11] Still less did the liberal orthodoxy entertain any notion of cultural relativism that might have characterized black lower-class culture—and particularly the lower-class "matriarchal" family structure—as anything but poor, deviant, and undesirable. Instead, liberals consistently and insistently looked to this culture as pathological, a product of social isolation that would diminish as African Americans were given opportunities to advance and assimilate to the white mainstream.

RACE AND CLASS IN CHICAGO-SCHOOL SOCIOLOGY

Robert Park wrote about race relations throughout his career, but it was up to his students Charles S. Johnson and E. Franklin Frazier to apply Chicago-school theory in empirical research. In the process, they made important revisions to Park's naturalistic vision while remaining true to its spirit of optimism and gradualism in matters of race. The most prominent and influential black sociologists of their time, Johnson and Frazier provided scholarly justification for the view that equality would be achieved not through increased race consciousness and organizing but as a result of presumably race-neutral processes of urbanization, assimilation, and, especially, industrial unionization. The appearance of "the black industrial proletariat," as Frazier noted in the late 1940s, was the most "significant" and hopeful sign that all blacks were becoming absorbed into the mainstream of American life. Likewise, Johnson wrote in 1944, the interest of the southern Negro "is consistent with the overall trend of the national philosophy and the economic future of the Nation."[12] And yet, while looking to the industrial economy as the ultimate route out of poverty for blacks, both Johnson and Frazier accepted the Chicago-school characterization of poverty as a problem of cultural disorganization, and made what would be one of Chicago sociology's most enduring, and controversial, contributions to liberal poverty knowledge by writing about the matriarchal family structure of an unassimilated black lower class.

It was clear from early on that Chicago's naturalistic theories would at best sit uneasily with the social reality of race relations. As laid out by Park and Burgess in their *Introduction to Sociology*, the race relations cycle was essentially an extension of the more general model of human interaction: a staged process of competition, conflict, accommodation, and assimilation in which different racial groups gradually acquired a common language, social values, and way of life, and in which individuals would eventually compete freely as individuals rather than as members of a race or cultural group. But assimilation was not always the spontaneous process Park and Burgess envisioned as appropriate to a modern, democratic society. Slavery, as Park had pointed out in a 1913 essay, was a form of racial accommodation that involved the destruction of African culture and blacks' enforced incorporation as subordinates into the dominant culture of the master race.[13] Like all accommodations this one was temporary, however, and whatever degree of racial subordination remained was rapidly being undermined by the great black migration to the urban North. There, Park expected, the migration would be experienced as another in an ongoing series of "invasions" into the established ecological equilibrium, in turn setting off a cycle of reactions that would lead to a new equilibrium. Conflict would arise from competition over jobs and space, but would soon give way to a more stable accommodation. Race prejudice would be stimulated by black efforts to improve their social status, but would subside as the inevitable dynamic of residential mobility and industrial expansion took over. Over a period of time, blacks would become assimilated, this time as equals, into the urban environment.[14]

The limitations of this framework were evident even as Park and Burgess were writing their text. In the summer of 1919, following several years of mounting racial tension and violence, Chicago broke out into a five-day riot that ended in thirty-eight deaths, hundreds of injuries, mass homelessness, and thousands of dollars in property damage, the vast majority of it in the black community. In an effort to restore racial peace in the aftermath, Illinois Governor Frank O. Lowden appointed the Chicago Commission on Race Relations, a biracial group set up to study the incident and make recommendations. The result was what amounted to the first real encounter between Chicago-school theory and racial fact. Drafted principally by Charles S. Johnson, who had studied with Park and was then research director for the Chicago Urban League, *The Negro in Chicago* (1922) traced the origins of racial conflict to migration, and in particular to the intense competition for jobs, residential and recreational space between an expanding African American community and the white ethnic working class. Based on a thoroughgoing two-year investigation, it relied extensively on Chicago-school methods, combining interviews and other "subjective" documentation with more traditional census-based survey investigation. But the report also highlighted key factors missing from Park's theoretical scheme: discriminatory economic practices, deep-seated racial animosities, state-sanctioned segregation, and, especially, the politics of racial inequality. Thus, the Commission report concluded, blacks and whites had proved fully able to work side by side, but employers and labor unions routinely excluded blacks from industrial jobs. Government agencies sanctioned racial exclusion and upheld a cynical double-standard in enforcing the law. Politicians supported the roving white "athletic clubs" that had been found responsible for so much of the violence. And the resentments fueled by prejudice and extremism had created a dangerous level of "race consciousness" among blacks as well as whites. The race problem, then, was a product of policies, racial attitudes, and economic practices that the naturalistic "cycles" of urban growth and human interaction would not wipe away. The Commission's report concluded with fifty-nine recommendations to provide equal opportunities in employment, education, housing, services, and political representation, and to promote interracial understanding and cooperation.[15]

Clearly convinced that the race problem would not be resolved without public intervention, Johnson spent his early career directing advocacy research for the National Urban League in New York. As editor of the League's journal *Opportunity* he became fully engaged in the Harlem Renaissance and helped to further the movement's melding of social science realism and art.[16] Yet even as an advocate Johnson never strayed far from the principles of detachment and racial gradualism associated with the Chicago school. Damning as its findings were, the Commission report had been objective in tone and measured about assigning responsibility—enough so to draw criticism for its overly cautious point of view.[17] It also raised objections against efforts to stir race consciousness among blacks, warning that "thinking and talking too much in terms of race alone are calculated to promote separation of race interests and thereby to interfere with racial adjustment."[18] Black organizations would do better to promote interracial cooperation and help migrants adapt to urban demands, the Commission argued. Economic integration, not racial organization, would be the most effective avenue for advance.

Johnson continued to emphasize these themes after he went to Fisk University to head the department of social science in 1928. There he began a prolific career of academic research, publication, and institution-building that, along with his far-reaching foundation and government connections, put him at the top of his field. He also kept up the Chicago connection, luring Park to Fisk in 1936 and regularly recruiting department graduates and faculty for work on the continuing stream of research projects he was able to mount. Johnson's two major works, *Shadow of the Plantation* (1934) and *Growing Up in the Black Belt* (1941), applied the essentials of the Chicago-school framework to conditions among rural blacks in the South. In *Shadow* he gathered a wide range of statistical and personal material on six hundred rural families in Macon County, Alabama—essentially undertaking the kind of study Park and W. I. Thomas had first talked about twenty years earlier—painting a bleak portrait of an exploited, subservient peasantry enslaved by the cotton tenancy system and accommodated to its demands. Isolated from the influence of modern industrial society, the black tenants had developed a backward but organized folk culture, infused with traditional religion and sustained by the loose sexual norms and extended "matriarchal" family structure inherited from slavery. Johnson used the findings from this and related research to illustrate the depth of racial exploitation in the tenancy system, and to criticize the New Deal for ignoring the gross racial inequities in the rural South. But, like the southern regionalists, he put greater emphasis on the economic exploitation that affected white as well as black tenant farmers than on racism per se, and maintained that economic restructuring and urbanization held the key to change. Later on, in *Growing Up in the Black Belt* Johnson took the occasion of an American Council on Education-commissioned study of race and adolescent personality development to argue that economic development would lead to black cultural assimilation. Johnson drew his sample from eight different counties, observing that with the "movement from plantation to open rural settlement, to town and finally to city," rural blacks were gradually accumulating the signposts of modern culture: industrial employment, professional classes, and, most important, a "patriarchal" family structure.[19] Thus, while distinguishing himself from Park in his insistence on the need for government intervention, Johnson remained convinced that race relations operated within a moving dynamic of migration and economic development that would eventually result in assimilation.[20]

E. Franklin Frazier also focused on the themes of migration, economic development, and cultural assimilation in his two major studies of black family life, *The Negro Family in Chicago* (1932) and *The Negro Family in the United*

States (1939). Frazier was considerably more radical in his politics than either Park or Johnson, aligning himself with the movement for interracial unionization and socialist economic reorganization and occasionally showing sympathy for black nationalism in the 1920s and 1930s. But he also embraced the Chicago school's theoretical framework and commitment to scientific objectivity. This combination, of social democratic values and sociological naturalism, made for a curious blend in Frazier's approach to the problems of the black urban poor. Committed to the struggle against racism and discrimination, Frazier nevertheless brought an air of inevitability to his scholarly analysis of urban racial inequality, attributing it to the seemingly apolitical processes of migration, urban ecology, and the cultural "disorganization/reorganization" cycle. He produced a damning review of racist practices as research director of Mayor Laguardia's Commission on Conditions in Harlem, but in academic work wrote about poverty, delinquency, and family breakup as "natural consequences" of the impact of "modern civilization" on traditional peasant folkways.[21] He criticized the "black bourgeoisie" for its political quiescence and social climbing, but his scholarly analysis suggested that their assimilation was evidence of racial advance. And although strongly committed to furthering the cause of racial environmentalism, Frazier more than anyone was responsible for the "pathological" vision of black culture and family structure that was adopted by Myrdal and other liberal social scientists, and that has since haunted social policy with the specter of culturally inherited poverty. Central to that image was Frazier's analysis of the Negro "matriarchy" as an accommodation to slavery and black male joblessness, and as such a characteristic feature of lower-class culture and poverty.[22]

Frazier started to explore the relationship between poverty and family structure in his doctoral dissertation, published in 1932 as *The Negro Family in Chicago*. The study was thoroughly a product of Chicago-school ecology. Funded by the Laura Spelman Rockefeller Fund, the research drew on the considerable amount of community data collected in the department archives, relied on the department's cooperation with the Chicago Urban League, and was published in the Chicago Sociological Series with an introduction by Ernest Burgess. It also sought to distinguish itself from mere statistical social investigation, linking indicators of pathology and social disorganization to ecological theories of modernization and cultural change. Here Frazier was determined to dispel not only the claims of biological racists, but also the argument, made by anthropologist Melville Herskovits and others, that black family patterns could be traced to African traditions. According to Frazier, the black family was a reflection of a continuous process of "disorganization and reorganization" that had been occurring since slavery and was now under way in the cities of the North. Thus, he wrote, social disorganization was not "merely a pathological phenomenon for the care of social agencies but also represents a step towards a reorganization of life on a more intelligent basis."[23]

Frazier's Chicago research also combined the theoretical strands of ethnic assimilation and urban ecology as no other study had done. With Chicago as his laboratory for studying the black migration experience, Frazier plotted the processes of Thomas's disorganization/reorganization cycle on the organic urban landscape envisioned in Burgess's zonal map. Arriving as a peasant group accustomed to rural life, blacks settled in the "zone of deterioration," where some succumbed to the pressures of their new environment and adopted joblessness, delinquency, vice, and welfare dependency as a way of life. There were "others," however, "who prove[d] that the travail of urban life is a forerunner of new birth" and joined the ranks of the industrial working class. Moving south toward the "workingman's" zones, these migrants "pushed" more established black families further out into areas of residential stability—"invading" white neighborhoods as they went along. For Frazier, who minimized evidence of racially motivated resistance, this residential succession was inevitable, driven as it had been for other immigrants by population growth, upward mobility, and the natural "processes of selection and segregation." It also showed blacks becoming gradually assimilated to a modern, white, middle-class standard of living. To illustrate, Frazier drew up ecological maps showing the changes in wealth, occupation, social behavior, and culture that accompanied residential mobility—here again avoiding the issue of racial segregation. He paid closest attention to the map of black family structure, which showed steadily falling rates of female-headed households, single parenthood, marital instability, female employment, and family size in each successive zone. Blacks, he concluded, were reorganizing as a stable, class-differentiated urban population. This, of course, put the problem of social disorganization into an entirely different light; the poverty, crime, and family instability arising from urbanization were "the inevitable price which the Negro must pay for civilization." Social disorganization, as Burgess wrote in the book's introduction, was "not a matter so much of race as of geography."[24]

Frazier moved beyond the ecological and assimilationist framework in his far more ambitious survey *The Negro Family in the United States*. This study, an effort to tell the "natural history" of the black family, was also Frazier's most fully developed analysis to date of the origins and nature of the class differentiation he had begun to document in Chicago's black community. Here again Frazier sought to discredit both biological and Africanist interpretations, essentially treating blacks as an American ethnic group. He also maintained the hopeful outlines of the assimilationist narrative, finding evidence even in urban social disorganization of a "civilizing" process at work. But here more than in earlier work Frazier did acknowledge that blacks were distinguishable from other migrant groups—to some degree due to white racial prejudice but more importantly to their unique historical experience of slavery, post-emancipation subordination, and urbanization. The impact of that historical experience could be seen most clearly in the changing black family, and especially in its basic division into "patriarchal" and "matriarchal" forms. Originating in the disparities between free and enslaved blacks, that differentiation had been perpetuated through each stage of black experience, and could now be seen in the class-stratified urban social structure.

Contrary to subsequent characterizations of his work, Frazier did not see the matriarchal family as inherently disorganized. Like Charles Johnson, he understood it to be an adaptive response to the oppressive conditions of racial and economic subordination.[25] "Stripped" of their own cultural heritage by conscription into slavery, blacks had established a matrilineal family system as an "accommodation" to their own lack of autonomy in choosing and remaining with mates. Similarly, the matrilineal bond was the basis of the new accommodation that arose after the slave family had been undermined by the "crisis" of emancipation. Suddenly cut loose from the enclosed social system of the plantation, the vast majority of rural blacks were left rootless, and as men went "wandering" in search of work, a pattern of common-law liaisons and relaxed sexual attitudes prevailed. "Motherhood outside of institutional control was accepted by a large group of Negro women with an attitude of resignation as if it were nature's decree," Frazier wrote. "Benign" in the context of the rural countryside, this pattern was a disaster under the naturally "disorganizing" influence of the urban environment. The "simple rural family," forced into "deteriorated slum areas from which practically all institutional life has disappeared," inevitably fell prey to male desertion, beset now not just by joblessness, but by delinquency, crime, and welfare dependency.[26] The "crisis" of urbanization, then, was undermining what in the rural South had been an undesirable but stable family system, planting the seeds of what Frazier would later characterize as a pathological cycle of delinquency, crime, welfare dependency, and female-headed households. More than simply a holdover from the rural past, the disorganized urban family structure was sustained by the discrimination black men faced in the labor market, and compounded by the fact that black women could look to work—or welfare—as a means of support. "The real key to the organization of the Negro family today," as Charles Johnson wrote in 1941, "is found in the relative economic positions of men and women." Black women, it seemed, enjoyed an "independence" that was "complemented by 'irresponsibility' in the men."[27]

Despite their emphasis on economic factors, both Frazier and Johnson believed that family disorganization could play an independent role in perpetuating poverty as well. Thus, they concluded in separate studies on Negro youth commissioned by the American Council on Education, black children suffered from the burden of lower-class as much as racial status, and the socializing influence of the disorganized or matriarchal family was largely to blame. Lower-class children were exposed to instability, deviant "sex mores," and even violence from an early age. Equally important, they grew up isolated from the influences of middle-class culture and were taught to be resigned to their lot in life. Lacking the "security, affectational as well as economic, which children in the middle and upper classes enjoy," the lower-class youth sought "only the satisfaction of his individualistic impulses and wishes," as Frazier wrote. The lower-class family, then, was producing children who would have difficulty adjusting to the demands of modern life.[28]

Still, despite early premonitions to the contrary, Frazier remained convinced that, true to Chicago-school theory, family disorganization was not in and of itself a pathological development but a natural and temporary stage in the assimilation cycle. Nor was its eventual descent into a self-reproducing pathology a reason to conclude that the Negro lower-class family was, given the right economic opportunities, beyond repair. More than anything, and long before it was picked up and repackaged by Assistant Secretary of Labor Daniel P. Moynihan in 1965, Frazier's analysis of family disorganization was a brief for getting black men into industrial jobs, in part through cross-racial trade union organizing, in part through keeping foreign immigration at Depression-era lows. Only then would black men be in a position to take their rightful place at the head of a patriarchally organized family, he argued, in all confidence that the desired "reorganization" would occur. After all, the patriarchal family system that Frazier envisioned for the black industrial proletariat was already firmly established among the black middle and upper classes, who traced their own lineage to the comparatively privileged house slaves, the skilled artisans, the free landowning Negroes, and, more recently, the educated professionals who had absorbed the mores of the predominant white culture. "[I]n retrospect," he concluded after surveying the historic advance of the middle-class Negro family, "the waste of human life, the immorality, delinquency, desertions and broken homes which have been involved in the development of Negro family life in the United States . . . appear to have been the inevitable consequences of the attempt of a preliterate people, stripped of their cultural heritage, to adjust themselves to civilization."[29] In this context, Frazier's pathological designation was much more than a way of denying anything of worth, of African inheritance, or indeed of anything that could be described as a worthwhile cultural tradition, in the black lower-class matriarchy. It was also an essential part of the liberal case for assimilationism—and for opening up opportunities in the existing political economy, if not actually for political and economic reform.[30]

CASTE AND CLASS IN THE DEEP SOUTH

Frazier and Johnson did not ignore so much as minimize the importance of white prejudice as a force relegating blacks to lower-class status. Still less did they dwell on the structural or institutional underpinnings of racial subordination in urban labor and housing markets. Nor were they alone in emphasizing class more than racial dynamics as an explanation for black poverty. Eager to take advantage of the potential for heightened class consciousness during the Depression, Frazier and several of his colleagues at Howard University emphasized the common fate of white and black workers, and argued that class-based, interracial strategies were the key to advancing the race.[31] And yet, by heightening awareness of racial disparities in everything from employment to relief, the Depression also helped to foster a race-consciousness in social science. This sensibility was reflected, to some degree, in work by scholars such as DuBois, historian Carter G. Woodson, and anthropologist Melville Herskovits, who for years had been challenging the assumptions of the Chicago school by writing about the African roots of black American culture. By this time, DuBois was also defying liberal convention by advocating proposals to develop independent black economic and political cooperatives rather than taking a more strictly integrationist line. But it was another interpretation of race relations, coming from the white academic mainstream, that would come to prevail among racial liberals in the late 1930s. This was what became known as the "caste and class" school, and its leading academic spokesman was W. Lloyd Warner.

The notion that blacks could be considered an American caste did not originate with Warner, as critics were quick to point out, but it was Warner who first revived and elaborated on the theme as a way of understanding American race relations in a brief but very influential *American Journal of Sociology* article in 1937.[32] Fleshed out empirically in full-fledged community studies based in Natchez (*Deep South*) and Indianola, Mississippi (Dollard's *Caste and Class in a Southern Town*, Powdermaker's *After Freedom*), the caste and class framework traced the roots of black poverty to an all-pervasive system of racial subordination, aimed above all at maintaining white supremacy through interlocking mechanisms of economic, political, and legal control. But what made the system most powerful and enduring were its psychological and sexual controls. These were not temporary accommodations, as Frazier's model suggested, but rigid and absolute taboos that had become ingrained in black as well as in white culture and personality. "Endogamy," wrote Davis and Gardner in reference to the absolute ban on interracial marriage, "is the keystone of the caste system." It was the one "rule" that was never broken, presenting both an absolute barrier against social mobility and, as Dollard clinically noted, "exclusions from sexual contact of the lower-caste men." The taboo, which did not apply to extramarital relationships between black women and white men, allowed whites to fulfill their fantasies of complete subjugation while maintaining the idealized imagery of white female asexuality. This, a decided psycho-sexual "gain" for whites, was also a dimension of the gender imbalance that Johnson and Frazier had attributed to the economics of the black "matriarchy." "It appears, then, not only that the Negro man is subordinated in all his relations to the white but that his subordinate role weakens his relations with women of his own group," Davis and Gardner concluded. "If he marries, his wife may at least sometimes compare him with that potential ideal, a white lover." Powdermaker, noting that black women enjoyed these advantages over men in slavery as well as "after freedom," observed that they "furnished psychological support to the matriarchal family form."[33]

And yet the caste system was not without its psychological "gains" for the lower-class black man as well. For all the humiliations, he was compensated with greater freedom to act on his own psychological yearnings for sexual freedom, aggression, and dependence, according to Dollard. Unlike his middle-class counterparts, the lower-class black man could take out his frustrations in violent behavior (albeit aimed mostly at other blacks) and sexual promiscuity, while also maintaining the "luxury of his dependence relationship to the white caste." All of these represented "primitive biological values" that the white middle class had been socialized to repress. The result was behavior, Dollard wrote, that "draws and seems to deserve the low opinion of whites."[34]

Still, for the majority of blacks, who fell into the lower-class designation, the consequence of racial subordination was an inclination to accommodation, dependence, and "subservience" that, Dollard thought, "has been built into the personalities of individual Negroes," thereafter to be "culturally transmitted from one generation to the next."[35] And here the ambiguous implications of caste and class analysis were most apparent. For, while documenting and condemning the political, economic, and legal mechanisms southerners used to maintain and reinforce racial inequality throughout the generations, the caste and class analysis also introduced the possibility that the inferiority it generated could, through the mechanism of a specifically *lower-class* negro psychology and cultural inheritance, reproduce itself. Even though rooted in a system of racial oppression, that is, the subservience, dependence, and deviance social scientists associated with black lower-class culture might not need white oppression to survive.

Although more fully played out in later studies of a ghetto "culture of poverty," this theme was developed as early as the 1930s in a series of studies commissioned by the American Council on Education for the purpose of determining the impact of caste on personality development among black youth. The five-volume series, which emphasized the centrality of family structure and class-related cultural patterns in personality development, included contributions from Johnson, Frazier, and Warner. But of all the studies published in the series, the collaborative contribution from Allison Davis and John Dollard went furthest to suggest that personality development—and, by extension, learning problems—were more powerfully influenced by lower-class cultural practices than by racial subordination alone. Entitled, somewhat ironically, *Children of Bondage* (1940), the study was based on interviews and psychological case studies conducted in Natchez and New Orleans.[36] It focused on what

Davis and Dollard determined to be class-typed child rearing patterns, concluding that, in light of the combination of permissive impulse control and authoritarian discipline associated with the lower class, growing up poor was more
important in transmitting disadvantage than was growing up black. In contrast,
middle-class black children, though repressed and overly fearful of losing their
status, had been better equipped for success in school by the more puritanical
child rearing practiced by their parents.

Nor, despite their implicit condemnation of white supremacy, did the caste
and class studies question the notion that "white" and upper caste represented
the desirable cultural norm. Even while commenting on the psychological
damage (neurosis, frustration) suffered in black upper-class efforts to "acquire
the traits of the white caste," social scientists writing in the caste and class
tradition reaffirmed those traits—particularly, as Powdermaker described
it, a patriarchal family structure "with the man assuming chief economic responsibility and also chief authority"—as a sign of achievement and social
respectability.[37]

The psychological dimension of the caste and class analysis only reinforced
what was already a deeply pessimistic outlook on the possibilities for racial
change, adding to the note of psychological determinism just beginning to
creep into poverty knowledge more generally. The ACE series concluded with
a call for rehabilitative social engineering, aimed at changing lower-class child
rearing patterns, along with more aggressive federal antidiscrimination policies to improve black standards of living. The deep South community studies,
however, made little effort to disguise a more defeatist note. Presenting a static
picture of race relations, they suggested that there would be no basic improvement without a complete transformation of the southern social structure, a
prospect that, even with the presence of northern philanthropy and federal
government planning, did not appear to be anywhere on the horizon. For all
the economic reforms spurred by the Depression and New Deal, the view from
the ground up suggested that the caste system was too deeply entrenched in
southern culture and psychology to give way to interference from above. Incremental steps against any single "symptom" were also ineffectual, for the very
strength of the system was in how it operated as an integrated whole. So strong,
indeed, that its effect was to divide the society into two "self-perpetuating
groups of people, with extremely unequal privileges and opportunities," as
Warner and Davis wrote. "Once the strength of this system is perceived, only
the superficial observer, who must also be an incurable optimist, can argue
against the generalization that the Negroes form a lower caste in the South,
upon the sole ground that minor variations in the degree of their subordination
exist." Nor, internally stratified and racially "accommodated" as they were,
did southern blacks appear any more likely to organize themselves into a force
for change. Until the time when "basic changes" could be introduced, the

"lower class of Negroes," nearly three-fourths of the black population of the South, would continue to bear the brunt of the caste system, and, under its all-encompassing control, to reproduce the cultural deviance that had become a defining way of life.

THE SOUTH GOES NORTH: BLACK METROPOLIS

Warner's caste and class analysis represented a basic challenge to the assimilationist optimism of the Chicago school, offering in its stead a structural interpretation of race relations that left little room for incremental action and little hope for the poor. Frazier, who like Park had written about the castelike nature of race relations in the South, was somewhat dismissive of the caste and class "school," commending it for drawing attention to "the structural aspects of race relations" but criticizing its "static" and, he suggested, unoriginal analysis for failing to take account of the "changing conditions of urban living."[38] Despite this and other, more damning criticisms, the caste and class framework quickly became part of the social scientific mainstream, standing somewhat uneasily alongside Chicago-school theory as the leading liberal interpretation of America's race problem throughout the 1940s. Some even held out hope for reconciling and combining the two approaches, as Chicago-trained sociologists Elaine Ogden McNeil and Horace R. Cayton noted in an *American Journal of Sociology* research report published in 1941. Such a reconciliation was possible, they believed, with the recognition that the South and the North were two fundamentally different racial systems. In the South, the "fixed" and subordinate status of the Negro was "embodied in the structure of the society" and "necessary to its smooth functioning," making the structural analysis of the deep South community studies the most appropriate approach. In the more racially progressive North, however, the "rapid changes" in Negro status called for a more dynamic, process-oriented understanding of race relations, one that could capture the "free competition" that governed certain aspects of urban life for blacks and brought them into unregulated contact with whites. There was a duality in the black urban experience, when viewed as a whole, between the "fixed status" of the caste system and the "free competition" of the city. That duality became a central organizing idea in *Black Metropolis* by St. Clair Drake and Cayton, a book many consider to be a masterpiece of social scientific analysis for its blend of structural social anthropology, Chicago-school social ecology, and social survey techniques. It is also something of a landmark in poverty knowledge—a comprehensive formulation drawing at once on Frazier, Warner, and DuBois—that presents black poverty as the product of a racialized political economy, social disorganization, and a distinctive, culturally deviant lower-class way of life.[39]

Black Metropolis grew out of what was by far the largest of W. Lloyd Warner's research enterprises, a four-year WPA-funded research project set up
on Chicago's South side in the mid-1930s, nominally to study juvenile delinquency under the auspices of the University-affiliated Institute for Juvenile
Research. In reality, the project was a full-scale Warner-type investigation of
the internal workings and class-stratified social system of the black community,
carried out by a racially mixed staff that included 20 full-time graduate research assistants and some 150 WPA workers employed as interviewers and
clerical staff. Horace Cayton, an African American graduate student who
moved from Seattle to Chicago to study sociology with Park in the early 1930s,
was the project staff director under Warner. Later describing the experience as
a step toward becoming a recognized "race man" on Chicago's South Side,
Cayton noted that he was happy to be providing white collar jobs for black
community residents, but couldn't help but comment on the ironies of his
position. The staff, though purposely and consciously biracial, brought together a predominantly white group of graduate students and a majority black
staff of relief workers. It was also held up by local government officials as a
model of what the WPA was doing for blacks, even though, as Cayton knew,
blacks experienced widespread discrimination in relief work. Nevertheless,
and despite occasional labor disputes involving negotiations with the Communist Party–dominated WPA union, Cayton recalled the feeling on the project
as being "democratic" and interracial, infused with the hopeful spirit of the
New Deal.[40] And, with the arrival of St. Clair Drake shortly after the study got
underway, the project's intellectual leadership was in the hands of African
American scholars. A student of Allison Davis's at Dillard University and
fresh from his field work as part of the *Deep South* research team, Drake was
in Chicago to complete his Ph.D. in anthropology, and soon became recognized
as the "guiding force" in conceptualizing and organizing the research protocols
for the massive project.[41] After four years, Drake, Cayton, and Warner had
supervised an enormous compilation of personal interviews, ethnographic
field notes, newspaper files, institutional studies, and statistical data on the
black neighborhoods of the South Side, producing several graduate student
monographs and, equally important, keeping a large number of people steadily
employed.

It was not until the early 1940s, however, in an atmosphere of dramatic
racial change and heightened racial consciousness, that Drake and Cayton developed this vast compilation of scientific data into the synthetic, accessible,
and urgent community portrait that would become *Black Metropolis*. Some
sense of the changes at hand could be conveyed in the new census and survey
data the authors had begun to collect to bring their study up to date: more
than 60,000 black migrants arrived in Chicago between 1940 and 1944 alone,
attracted by the same promise of wartime job opportunities that was leading
millions of others to familiar destinations like Detroit, Pittsburgh, Philadelphia,

and New York, and, increasingly, to newer industrial labor markets in Los Angeles, San Francisco, and other western cities. Blacks were becoming a "city people," Drake and Cayton wrote, and it was "in the cities that the problem of the Negro in American life appears in its sharpest and most dramatic form." Less concrete, but equally powerful, was the change in consciousness they attributed to the impact of World War II, the growth of "race pride," and, more threatening, the intense and persistent frustration of black workers denied the opportunity for advance. The Negro problem had been transformed, "almost overnight," from a "chronic social difficulty" inspiring gradualist solutions to a national crisis requiring immediate action. White Chicago was beginning to sense the crisis—with the violent racial uprisings that had occurred in Detroit, New York, and several other cities in 1943 in mind, the newly created Mayor's Commission on Race Relations was eager to keep the racial peace. Mainstream social science had also taken notice: in 1944, Gunnar Myrdal's sweeping, scholarly indictment of American race relations was published to great acclaim. Responding to the changes in the racial climate, Drake and Cayton shifted their own sights from the methodological treatise commissioned in a grant from the Rosenwald Fund, and decided instead to write a book that would bring the scientific facts about race to a wider audience.[42]

Novelist Richard Wright captured the significance of the shift in his introduction to the original edition of *Black Metropolis*. "The dominant hallmark of the book is the combination throughout of the disciplines of both sociology and anthropology," Wright wrote. "The book examines the social structure as though it were frozen at a moment of time, which is the approach of anthropology; and it examines the processes and dynamics which take place in that structure, which is the approach of sociology." But for Wright the real power of *Black Metropolis*, going beyond the "mere facts," was in laying bare the social environment that had created "Bigger Thomas" and thousands of angry young black men like him. Bigger, the impulsive and violent character who murdered the white Chicago heiress in Wright's novel *Native Son* (1940), was a symbol of the irreparable psychological and cultural damage created by racial oppression, the kind of damage that, he warned, was the stuff not just of murderous rage but of fascist mass movements. *Black Metropolis* revealed the reality that "whites do not see and do not want to see": the Negro problem, a creation of the racism embedded in white American culture and institutions, could no longer be ignored.[43] Drake and Cayton, although considerably less "passionate" in their own rendering of Bigger Thomas's social environment, shared Wright's conviction that an immediate, perhaps violent racial crisis was at hand. Conscious of their own "role-bound obligation" to "discipline their feelings as they wrote," they attempted to tell the story of the Chicago Negro by integrating the established methods of liberal social science, and ended up, without fully intending to, revealing the internal contradictions of the science instead.[44]

Part 1 of *Black Metropolis* starts out with the "dynamic" tools of Chicago-school social ecology to present the history of blacks as a migrant group, mapping their experience along the immigrant trajectory of conflict, accommodation, and assimilation. Initially a miniscule presence in comparison to the masses of European immigrants, by the end of World War I and in the wake of the great "black diaspora" of 1914–18, blacks had "replaced" white European immigrants as "the primary source of unskilled and menial labor," and, like other newcomers before them, had "inherited the slums." Entering the urban economic and spatial order as the last in a long line of immigrants, they faced intense competition "for living space, economic goods, and prestige," and had not yet been fully "absorbed" into the "general population."[45] Things looked better during the extended "fat years" of the 1920s, when steady economic growth and immigration restrictions reduced intergroup competition, and the continued flow of southern blacks into the "promised land" helped to create a political strength in numbers. Even the rifts uncovered by the race riot of 1919 seemed to be healing, fueling hopes for the possibility of an egalitarian future. But the ecological model of competition and assimilation could only go so far to explain the fortunes of black Chicago, as even the experience of the "fat years" made clear. While showing the expected patterns of residential settlement, black migrants remained confined to a "black belt" that would sooner cut across residential zones than give way to racial mixing. Nor did the "fat years" leave blacks much beyond the margins of the urban economy, or any more welcome in the restaurants, stores, and nightclubs of the prosperous downtown. The "lean years" of the Depression and the dashed hopes of equal opportunity during World War II only reinforced what most in the growing black metropolis already knew: the story of the Negro in Chicago would be told not along the familiar immigrant line as rendered by Park and the Chicago school, but along the color-line, as anticipated by W.E.B. DuBois.[46]

Drake and Cayton devoted Part 2 of *Black Metropolis* to developing the concept of the color line in concrete detail. Drawing on social survey as well as ethnographic techniques, they shifted the analytic framework from social ecology to political economy and relied heavily on census data to document the forces keeping blacks in their socially segregated, economically marginal "place." The "job ceiling" was the strongest of the forces, in their view, elaborated brilliantly in charts reminiscent of DuBois's Philadelphia survey showing the racial distribution of employment, occupation, and job "types." Black men and women were disproportionately represented in unskilled, undesirable work and underrepresented in higher-paying managerial, clerical, and professional jobs. Nor could the discrepancy be explained away by differences in education, natural ability, or skill. The "job ceiling" was a tangible and institutionalized barrier, maintained by employer discrimination, labor union practices, and white racial prejudice, that purposely kept blacks from freely competing in the labor market. The black ghetto, too, hardly looked like a "natural" area of migrant settlement, in light of the real estate practices, racial covenants, city planning ordinances, and white resistance that kept it in place. The white immigrant could move, "once he gets on his feet," but "Negroes, regardless of their affluence or respectability, wear the badge of color. They are expected to stay in the Black Belt." Meanwhile, the widespread "ghetto conditions" that stemmed from poverty, overcrowding, and physical "blight" were used as a "convenient rationalization," by the University of Chicago among others, "for keeping Negroes segregated."[47] The combination of white prejudice, economic interest, and institutional practice that maintained the color line was formidable, then, and was operating to keep blacks both segregated and overwhelmingly poor. Still, as noted at the end of Part 2, the situation was not without hope: Chicago was not the South; the color line was not "static"; the job ceiling could be broken; and the "white folks" could be educated. Most important, in light of their growing numbers, the increased demand for labor, and the looming threat of a race riot, blacks in Chicago in the mid-1940s seemed to have political and economic expediency on their side.

This sense of tentative hope was quickly dampened by Part 3 of *Black Metropolis*, however, when Drake and Cayton once again shifted their analytic framework to present an anthropological view of life in Bronzeville, as Chicago's black South Side was known. The analysis was based on the Warner-Cayton fieldwork, conducted at the height of the Depression when most of black Chicago was either unemployed or on relief. It showed that the color line looked more castelike than not from inside the black ghetto, forming an "iron band" within which people lived "in a state of intense and perpetual awareness that they are a black minority in a white man's world." It also revealed Bronzeville to be deeply stratified as a community, divided by the gradations of color as well as by social class, and caught up in the elaborate apparatus of cliques, associations, social behavior, and cultural practices Warner had found in New England and the deep South. Finally, it revealed that Bronzeville harbored a large, culturally insulated lower class, isolated in a "world" bounded not by economic or spatial segregation so much as by deviant behavioral norms. To be sure, the lower-class world was complex and heterogeneous, encompassing "respectable," church-going, working-class families as well as the "denizens of the underworld." But at its core was the group of "disorganized and broken families" whose way of life was defined around pursuing pleasure, getting relief, and keeping the wheels of the illicit gambling industry known as "the policy" going rather than getting a job and getting ahead. An embarrassment to the socially ambitious middle classes who were forced to live among them, the lower classes were unconsciously acting out the frustrations of caste and class subordination in "[t]he vigor with which they shout or dance; the rapt attention that they fix on the policy wheel; the floods of liquor they consume," and the fundamentalist storefront religion in which they sought refuge. And yet, theirs could also be seen as the problem of migration, an expression of the "incomplete urbanization" of rural migrants from the South. This instability of lower-class family life had its origins, after all, in the tenuous sexual and economic "bargain" that E. Franklin Frazier had traced to the post-emancipation South, drawing "dependent," "wandering," marginally employed men to "dominant," economically independent women, who had nowhere else to turn for their own "affectational" needs. The high rates of illegitimacy and desertion that resulted from this "bargain," and the "wild children" and juvenile delinquents they in turn produced, reflected the impact not just of caste and class subordination, but of the internal disorganization of recent migrants from the South. Thus, drawing on the ecological concept of "disorganization" as well as the notion of psychological damage associated with caste and class, *Black Metropolis*'s anthropology of Bronzeville painted a portrait of a black lower-class majority that, just as much as the color line, seemed to exert a powerful force against its own advancement, by perpetuating a pathological way of life that even the most socially ambitious found hard to escape.[48]

Drake and Cayton's chapters on the lower classes of Bronzeville were descriptively riveting but intellectually jarring, presenting a bleak, almost determinist portrait that served more than anything to underscore the distance separating the observers from the observed. Clearly, the authors identified with the disdain and frustration of the black middle-class doctor who, in one illustrative vignette, was called upon to make a midnight house call to heal the knife wound "Baby Chile" had inflicted on her temporary lover "Mr. Ben." Powerful in rendering the doctor's inner conflict as he runs through the emotional gamut of obligation, compassion, cynicism, and disgust, the vignette treats the lower-class characters as one-dimensional stereotypes, setting the tone for the analysis to come. Relentlessly, even aggressively benighted, the majority class of Bronzeville appears more "accommodated" to its station than not, hardly capable of breaking through the barriers of caste and class deprivation—giving support to the idea, which Drake and Cayton later argued was a myth, that the black ghetto couldn't be organized. Even its most genuinely indigenous institution—the storefront church—was devoted to escapism and exploitation, acting as an impediment rather than an aid to advancing the race. The overpowering imagery of lower-class cultural dissolution also seemed to contradict Drake and Cayton's own predictions about racial advancement as they brought the Bronzeville section to a close: the same lower-class people they had characterized as pleasure-seeking, lazy, and apathetic, it turns out, were ready to demand access to jobs, better housing, desegregation, and equal rights. These very same lower classes had thrown their support behind all sorts of grass roots campaigns during the 1930s, ranging from the moderate "Spend Your Money Where You Can Work" campaign to any number of rent strikes and labor actions sponsored by the Left, and were likely to mobilize behind a " 'racial radicalism' of gigantic proportions . . . if Negroes feel that the Second World War liberated the world, but did not 'advance The Race.' "[49]

It was this more dynamic vision of the black masses that informed the fourth and concluding section of *Black Metropolis*, entitled "Of Things To Come." There, Drake and Cayton returned to the troubled but tentatively hopeful tone of parts 1 and 2, to the Chicago-school faith in the solvent of "free competition," tempered by the inescapable reality of DuBois's color line. The Job Ceiling and social segregation persisted, but they showed signs of "bending" and "breaking" precisely because Chicago was not ruled by a caste system like the deep South. The same duality—between "free competition" and "fixed status"—that caused conflict within the Negro personality presented a profound moral dilemma to the democratic urban North. Most importantly, though incapable of facing its moral dilemma, Chicago was gripped by the memory of 1919. White fear, combined with economic and political expediency, was opening the door to a relaxation of the color line and possibly even to a program of peaceful, informed social reform. The last section, then, suggested that it was not the lower-class or even the broader culture that needed to change; it was the political economy that propped up the color line. Perhaps that is why the fatalistic, psychologized view of lower-class culture in *Black Metropolis* was so jarring: it stood as stark testimony not so much to the need for as to the impossibility of reform.[50]

Even though Drake and Cayton did not manage to reconcile the tensions within liberal social science, *Black Metropolis* did show how pervasive—and problematic—the imagery of black lower-class culture had become in a social science that labeled it as at once pathological and adaptive, a product of internal social disorganization as well as external oppression, a transitional yet seemingly permanent feature of ghetto life. In this sense *Black Metropolis* was the most detailed and comprehensive statement to date of what liberal social science had to say about the black urban lower-class "world." But more than any single work it was Gunnar Myrdal's *An American Dilemma* that crystallized the idea of the black lower class as a cultural pathology in a double sense: as an expression of black lower-class deviance and of the broader cultural pathology of white racism.

THE "VICIOUS CIRCLE"

Drake and Cayton only briefly referred to racial inequality as a moral dilemma, but that particular formulation of the "Negro problem" was by then almost inescapable, brought home powerfully by Swedish economist and social democrat Gunnar Myrdal as the central thesis of *An American Dilemma* (1944). Commissioned by the Carnegie Corporation to conduct a comprehensive survey of scholarship on the American Negro, Myrdal used the occasion to chas-

tise American social science for its "value-free" pretensions as well as to uncover the morally intolerable contradiction between racial reality and
democratic ideal. It was from this vantage point, of empirical fact filtered
through moral "valuations," that he drew a portrait of black lower-class pathology and linked it to the pathology of white racism.[51] Drake and Cayton, along
with E. Franklin Frazier, W. Lloyd Warner, Allison Davis, John Dollard, and
dozens of other scholars had contributed to the vast body of background material Myrdal and his assistants compiled for the book. It was from their work
that Myrdal drew his portrait of the black lower class, relying on Frazier for
his discussion of the impact of slavery, migration, and poverty on the lower-
class Negro family, but otherwise adopting Warner's "caste and class" analysis,
with its emphasis on the persistence and rigidity of racial caste. Blacks' overwhelmingly lower-class status was not simply a reflection of poverty or ignorance, but of the "disabilities" and discrimination associated with race.[52]

Myrdal grounded his own "valuations" in a combination of Enlightenment
principles, liberal social science, and political pragmatism: the "American
Creed," defined as a belief in human equality, individual rights, and equal
opportunity for all; an environmentalist understanding of racial difference; a
belief in the functional, if not inherent, superiority of white cultural norms;
and racial assimilationism, based on the assumption "*that it is to the advantage
of American Negroes as individuals and as a group to become assimilated
into American culture, and to acquire the traits held in esteem by the dominant
white Americans.*" On the latter point Myrdal differentiated his assimilationist
premises from white cultural absolutism, noting that it was only in the
"pragmatic sense" that white culture was superior "*here, in America,*" where
it demanded "adherence . . . [from] any individual or group which is not strong
enough to change it." This somewhat qualified valuation also informed his
sweeping characterization of black cultural "divergences" as a "*distorted development, or a pathological condition, of the general American culture*" (em-
phases in original).[53] Because of the racism in the "general American culture,"
that is, the vast majority of blacks had not been allowed to assimilate as
other immigrants had, the price of which was to be found in the family instability, religious "emotionalism," high crime rates, "superstition," "provincial-
ism," "personality difficulties," and other "characteristic traits" of Negro culture. Of course, the black upper and middle classes were managing to escape
such cultural "peculiarities," gradually assimilating the family structure, ambition, morality, and manners of the dominant "national culture." The great
masses, however, remained isolated behind the walls of segregation, living
below the "American standard" of economic and cultural necessity and just
barely above the "mental servility" and dependence of the slave past. "Their
situation is not favorable for developing strong incentives to personal accomplishment and improvement. Standards of industry and honesty are generally
low," Myrdal wrote of the "large majority of Negroes everywhere."[54] "Negro"

culture was by definition a culture of poverty; the way to advance was to become culturally white.

Black culture was not the only "pathology" created by the caste system. The "economic situation of the Negroes in America" could also be described as "pathological" in much the same way, the product of low skills and lack of education but always and at each stage compounded by the fact of racial discrimination. Nor could the "extraordinary" poverty be explained only with the static, structural concept of caste. Instead, it was the product of a dynamic, cumulative "force, which, like gravitation, holds them down in the struggle for survival and economic advance," a "vicious circle" in which economic exploitation, low cultural status, and racial discrimination were "interdependent factors, mutually cumulative in their effects."[55]

The vicious circle of poverty had its origins in slavery and black economic exploitation, according to Myrdal, which in turn had confined blacks to low educational, moral, and cultural standards. Armed with an elaborate array of racist beliefs, whites then used black deprivation to justify further exploitation, rationalizing their actions with "evidence" that most blacks were incapable of rising to a higher station in life. Poverty could in this sense be seen as itself a breeder of poverty, for it triggered and justified the cumulative cycle of discrimination and exploitation that left blacks further and further behind. And yet, complex and intractable as it seemed, the vicious circle of poverty could in another sense be seen as a ray of hope: its same principles of interdependence and cumulation could be used to guide "practical planning" for programs to promote black economic advance. "[A] primary change, induced or unplanned, affecting *any one* of three bundles of interdependent causal factors— 1) the economic level; 2) standards of intelligence, ambition, health, education, decency, manners, and morals; and 3) discrimination by whites—will bring changes in the other two and, through mutual interaction, move the whole system along in one direction or the other," Myrdal wrote (emphasis added). Change did not have to be radical or all-encompassing to make a difference, he concluded, just targeted at "strategic" points in the circle that planners felt they could control. Identifying those points, of course, was the first step in social engineering, and a principal task for social scientists of race.[56]

The concept of the vicious circle did not originate with Myrdal, but *An American Dilemma* helped to make it the reigning metaphor in liberal social analysis for the next three decades. For one thing, it resolved a central tension between social ecology and anthropology by arguing that black poverty was not caused by cultural disorganization *or* racial oppression, but by both. For another, it offered reassurance to advocates of rationally planned, incremental change. It was also based on important revisions in caste theory that seemed to make American racism more readily susceptible to change. For the most part, Myrdal accepted the notion that there was a certain "rank order" to white racial discrimination, in which the absolute ban on intermarriage was at the top, followed, in descending order, by objections to social intermingling, integration, political participation, and access to economic opportunity. Similarly, picking up on a theme black writers had been sounding since DuBois, Myrdal pointed out that the rank order of black racial preferences was precisely the reverse, with the desire for jobs leading the way and the hope of intermarriage a distant last. And yet Myrdal, unlike Warner, Davis, and Dollard, did not accept this rank ordering as a reflection of the real motivations behind the caste system. In actuality, as suggested in the vicious circle dynamic, white people were more interested in maintaining their own higher status than in racial purity; the ban on intermarriage, in fact the whole array of anti-amalgamationist racial beliefs, was not based on a deep-seated psychological fear embedded in social personality, as Warner and Dollard had suggested. It was instead an elaborate rationalization, "an irrational escape on the part of whites from voicing an open demand for a difference in social status between the two groups for its own sake." Racism, then, was not a structural problem in either the psychological or the economic sense. It was a set of attitudes that could be proved to be irrational, subject to treatment and enlightened education, and, ultimately, would be defeated in the face of the American Creed.[57]

The vicious circle had much to offer liberal social analysts, but it created as many problems as it resolved. Even while recognizing the systemic interdependence of poverty and racial oppression, it defined them in the most individualized, least threatening possible way—as cultural deprivation, as discriminatory behavior, as irrational attitudes, and, most definitely, as deviations from the normal operations of an inherently democratic social and economic order. In some ways, then, Myrdal's analysis did precisely what he criticized "value-free" and "laissez-faire" sociologists for doing: in treating poverty and racism as social pathologies, he reified white cultural standards and economic capitalism as the democratic norm. Once the vicious circle was broken, inequality would be redressed through the normal workings of the system. Equally important, the imagery of poverty breeding poverty had the effect, however unintended, of severing the problem from a concern about systemic inequality, confining it to an isolated "other half" seen not as a part or a product of the mainstream but as outside a system otherwise devoted to equal opportunity. Widely deployed by liberals during the War on Poverty, the vicious circle offered reassurance that poverty could be eradicated by limited, "strategic" interventions, and without major changes in the economic status quo. Such imagery would very quickly come to haunt them, however, when the intractability of the vicious circle became an explanation for why liberal antipoverty intervention would not, and could not, work.

In its time and subsequently, *An American Dilemma* was rightly celebrated as a major achievement, a "triumph" for social scientific environmentalism and liberal assimilationism. It was also a repudiation of the disengaged, supposedly value-free social science Robert Park had come to represent. Myrdal himself did not shy away from making concrete policy recommendations, and looked forward to a substantially expanded role for the state in public education and in breaking down discriminatory barriers to "free competition." In these ways *An American Dilemma* was an affirmation of an older Progressive Era model of reform investigation. Indeed, having mapped the theoretical territory, it gave added reinforcement to the move toward applied social research exemplified by the ACE and other studies on race. And yet, Myrdal's study also showed just how thoroughly the ideas and categories of post-Progressive social science had come to dominate social problem, and now race relations, research. Myrdal himself was a political economist, but his American dilemma was formulated as a problem of culture and social psychology, and the solution as a job of social engineering and assimilation more than of political organizing and economic reform. The literature following in its wake reflected this "psychological and social psychological orientation," focusing heavily on prejudice, intergroup relations, and often, for policy and political purposes, on documenting the impact of racial subordination on the "Negro" personality.[58] Seen from this perspective, the golden age that culminated in *An American Dilemma* marked a turn away from rather than the culmination of the political economy of race that DuBois had mapped out years before, and opened the way for the racialization of poverty knowledge as in all senses a problem of cultural pathology.

Giving Birth to a "Culture of Poverty": Poverty Knowledge in Postwar Behavioral Science, Culture, and Ideology

THE IDEA of a lower-class culture was firmly entrenched in social problem research by the 1940s, although social scientists did not always agree on its source. Not until the two decades following World War II, however, did social scientists begin to engage in debate about the existence of an independent culture of *poverty* that could persist even without the immediate deprivations caused by modernization, class, and race. The distinction was more than semantic, reflecting important and interrelated postwar changes that profoundly affected social scientific thinking about the poor. One was the political economy of affluence, which lent superficial credence to the idea that America was becoming a "classless" society with a small, isolated substratum of people who were poor. A second was the postwar institutionalization of the behavioral sciences, which encouraged and redoubled the psychological emphasis that had earlier begun to emerge in research on class and, in particular, on race. A third was the resurgence of middle-class domesticity in Cold War ideology and culture, which reinforced the patriarchal family as a psychological and cultural norm, and treated deviations from it as a source of lifelong afflictions in the young. And a fourth was the rise of poverty as a global political issue, creating a whole new vista of research opportunities as the Cold War between the United States and the Soviet Union expanded to the "underdeveloped" world. All of these changes converged in the social scientific theory of the culture of poverty, developed by anthropologist Oscar Lewis in the late 1950s and more widely adopted as an explanation for the "paradox" of poverty in the affluent U.S. Thus, rooted though it was in the concepts and methods of an earlier generation, the culture of poverty was a distinctively postwar idea, and can be understood as an expression of the broader trends in postwar political economy, politics, and culture that reshaped liberalism as an ideology as well as its approach to social knowledge and to the poor.

THE CHANGING CONTEXT (I): PROSPERITY

The most prominent of these trends was the much-heralded phenomenon of mass prosperity, which helped to make economic inequality less visible as a political issue while creating an environment in which liberals would identify poverty as a "paradox" and "the poor" as a self-contained, culturally deprived social group. In reality, the "affluent society" was riddled with structural inequalities that made the experience of prosperity selective and that of poverty more concentrated among people—the elderly, racial minorities, women heading households, and low-skilled laborers in "depressed" areas of the economy—all of whom, as one report put it, affluence had "left behind."[1]

Nothing was more celebrated in postwar political economy than the widespread experience of affluence, symbolized in rising incomes, higher rates of home ownership, and especially in the ever-expanding acquisition of consumer goods.[2] Americans were a "people of plenty," as one prominent historian put it; affluence had become a characteristic fact of working- as well as middle- and upper-class life.[3] Less often recognized was the role of federal policy— higher defense spending, home mortgage subsidies, labor regulations, and social welfare benefits—in generating the growth and mass prosperity for which the U.S. economy was becoming renowned. Still less did the image of a "people of plenty" recognize the importance of organized social movements in broadening the distribution of national wealth. Instead, prosperity was greeted as a vindication of America's commitment to capitalism and free enterprise, an argument made with growing ideological fervor as the Cold War set in.

To be sure, the federal presence in the economy was more circumscribed than many liberals and activists had once envisioned, relying more heavily on growth than redistribution as a way to raise low incomes and avoiding efforts to achieve market reform. Liberals, for example, had lost legislative battles to sustain wartime levels of centralized economic planning, and to mandate full employment as a matter of law. By the late 1940s, with anticommunism on the rise, even once-militant labor leaders had been pushed into a more accommodating stance toward capitalism. The bargain they struck with private sector employers gained better union wages and social welfare benefits while diminishing the drive toward a more regulated economy and a more generous, universalistic federal welfare state.[4] Liberal intellectuals, too, came to an accommodation with capitalism that turned to celebration at the height of the Cold War. Affluence, they believed, had ushered in a new era of ideological "consensus," labor peace, and political stability—with no end in sight. The American standard of living was a triumph of the uniquely "mixed" (neither socialist nor "free market") capitalist economy and a limited welfare state.[5] The United States was close to achieving what the Soviets could only impose—a "classless" society—without recourse to violent, revolutionary force. The real revolutionary force was not Marxism but capitalism, and its impact could be measured in economic statistics: income was more equally distributed in the late 1940s than at any time since the start of federal income taxation in 1913.[6] Even the critics of "the affluent society" were more concerned with the consumerism and conformity it fostered than with the economic inequalities it reproduced. Poverty, to the extent that it was visible to social scientists at all, was at most a "residual" problem, relegated to isolated "pockets" of decline and cultural backwardness that an otherwise thriving economy had left behind.[7]

This is not to say that postwar prosperity put an end to the subject of social class. Judging from the steady stream of literature on the subject, both social scientists and the people they wrote about were more class and status conscious than ever. But class took on an entirely different connotation in postwar sociological writing, less an occasion for "muckraking" sociology than an opportunity for social scientists to make inroads into the fast-growing field of consumer market research. Writing under the auspices of Social Research Associates, Inc. (founded by *Deep South* coauthor Burleigh Gardner), W. Lloyd Warner showed advertisers how class analysis could be helpful in marketing their wares; Warner's students later put the message into practice, in a study of one of the most widely sought-after figures in consumer markets, *Working-man's Wife*, in which the point was not to learn whether she could manage the household on her husband's inadequate wages but to learn about her consumer "personality"—what she likes, where she shops, what clubs she joins—as the basis of a distinctive marketing niche. Nor was class analysis an occasion for criticizing capitalism; in the hands of the ever-popular Warner, it was testimony to the absence of rigid economic determinism that made the American way of life unique. In America, *Life* magazine quoted Warner as saying, anyone could climb the economic ladder, provided they had the attitude, psychological makeup, and determination to get ahead.[8] Besides, according to a prevalent argument in sociology, every complex society needed a system of stratification to help it function smoothly as a community, and to help individuals "adjust" to their appropriate stations in life. Even Warner's lower-lowers had a place in this functionalist hierarchy, provided society found a way of putting their penchant for brute force and unreflective pleasure to constructive use. If the lower-lowers displayed more than their share of social "pathology," it was from lack of personal adjustment mechanisms as much as from economic distress.[9]

And yet, much as prosperity may have reduced poverty among the masses, the postwar political economy also perpetuated structural inequities that left 25–30 percent of the population in poverty at any given time.[10] Talk of an inequality-reducing "social revolution" was highly exaggerated; income and wealth were less concentrated, but still unequal—and, after gaining ground in the early 1940s, the bottom 20 percent of earners did not add to their share of the growing economy at all.[11] Exaggerated, too, was the image of an economically secure, upwardly mobile working class. The 1950s brought slower growth and two major recessions, leading working-class families to rely more heavily than ever on women's wages and welfare benefits to stay out of poverty.[12] Automation, though speeding up agriculture, mining, and manufacturing production, displaced thousands of untrained laborers, continuing the flow of labor migration that had brought African American, Latino, and white workers to industrial cities during World War II. Several of those cities, however, were beginning to experience industrial decentralization and restructuring of their own, relegating especially the least skilled and nonwhite urban newcomers to unemployment or low-wage jobs.[13]

The image of mass prosperity also ignored the vast diversity and income disparities within the working class, a growing proportion of which was nonwhite and female, and employed not in the relatively well-paid, heavily unionized manufacturing sector but in low-wage, nonunion "pink collar" work.[14] Nor did the postwar boom come anywhere near closing the gender gap in earnings and employment, despite women's steadily increasing participation in the paid labor force. Indeed, having momentarily enjoyed access to higher-paying manufacturing jobs during World War II, women were shunted off into sex-segregated, lower-paying secretarial and clerical jobs, if not discouraged from working at all.[15] Most glaring, however, were the vast racial disparities— in wages, employment, education, housing, wealth, and income—that prevented the majority of African Americans and Latinos from achieving what amounted to a *white* American standard of living. "Bronzeville" had shared in the new postwar prosperity, wrote St. Clair Drake and Horace Cayton in a postscript to *Black Metropolis* in 1961, but the "job ceiling," the wage gap, and the color line persisted. Indeed, a generation of migration and federally sponsored urban renewal had left the racial boundaries of the black ghetto expanded, but very much intact.[16]

In income as in housing, the disparities of the market were only exacerbated by the unequal protections built into the structure of the welfare state. Farm laborers and "displaced" workers were among those left virtually without protection, while nonwhites could routinely expect separate and unequal treatment. Structured to keep women out of the paid labor force, the welfare system left single, nonwidowed mothers to rely on an increasingly unpopular, low-benefit Aid to Dependent Children program that, until the mid-1960s, allowed local administrators to cut them off on a whim. Significantly, these were the very groups—the rural poor, the long-term unemployed, the minority poor, female-headed households—singled out by social scientists as denizens of a "culture of poverty" in the affluent U.S. Poverty was a problem of low wages, unemployment, economic restructuring, and inadequate protections; but in affluent, Cold War America, liberal social scientists turned for explanations to the culture and psychology of the poor.

THE CHANGING CONTEXT (II):
THE BEHAVIORAL SCIENCES "REVOLUTION"

A second major trend shaping postwar poverty knowledge offers further insight into why: the quest for an interdisciplinary, methodologically rigorous science of human behavior, with the ability to predict as well as prescribe.

Spurred on by government agencies and private philanthropic funders, the behavioral emphasis in social science assumed the dimensions of an organized movement in the wake of World War II, leading to a vast expansion of the resources and institutional infrastructure for behavioral research.[17] Carnegie, Rockefeller, Russell Sage, and a newcomer, the richly endowed Ford Foundation, virtually invented the label "behavioral sciences" and proclaimed it the new frontier in social research.[18] Financially, they were dwarfed by the dollars for psychological and behavioral research flowing from the federal government under the auspices of the U.S. Department of Defense and two new postwar creations, the National Institute of Mental Health, and the National Science Foundation. Nevertheless, the private foundations infused the behavioral sciences with a special sense of mission that would have a lasting impact on the future of social research. The success of their efforts was soon reflected in the proliferating array of institutions devoted to interdisciplinary behavioral research, including university-based research centers such as the Institute for Social Research at the University of Michigan, Columbia University's Bureau of Applied Research, and Harvard's Department of Social Relations, as well as academic retreats such as the Center for Advanced Studies in the Behavioral Sciences in Palo Alto, established by the Ford Foundation in 1954.[19] The heyday of the University of Chicago and the local community study had passed. The future lay in the "multi-versity," in what C. Wright Mills called the "fetishism" of scientific method, and in the national sample survey, which gathered information on individual attitudes and behavior while leaving questions of social structure aside.[20]

At its loftiest, the movement behind the behavioral sciences aimed to reorganize social knowledge around individual and group behavior, professing the hope that better understanding of human motivation would allow enlightened leaders to bring control and rationality to a rapidly changing, war-torn world. More prosaically, it aimed to gain broader acceptance and legitimacy for disciplines that, for all their emphasis on objectivity and methodological rigor, were still considered "soft" by the scientific establishment and ideologically tainted by the political Right.[21] Two fundamental convictions lay behind these objectives, noted the Ford Foundation in announcing its Behavioral Sciences program: one that all problems—"from war to individual adjustment"—could be traced to individual behavior and human relationships; the other that methodologically rigorous research could uncover the "laws" of human behavior so that enlightened, democratic leaders might set society on a more rational course.[22] The possibility that these two convictions might involve a contradiction—that research into the recesses of human motivation might lead to a fatalism about the possibility of planned social change—did not prevent behaviorism from becoming a central article of postwar liberal faith. Nor did the antidemocratic implications of social engineering imposed from above. To the contrary, the liberal embrace of an individualized, psychologically oriented behavioral science grew out of and in turn reinforced the postwar "consensus" that major social problems could be resolved without recourse to political mobilization or conflict and without significant institutional or economic reform.

The postwar emphasis on individual psychology added momentum to the fascination with culture and personality that, while present, had remained relatively muted in the community studies during the Depression. But it marked a definitive break from the Progressive Era tradition of industrial and social survey research. Nowhere was this more evident than in the postwar transformation of the Russell Sage Foundation, which after 1948 would virtually drop its historic commitment to social work and industrial research to become the only national philanthropy specifically devoted to behavioral science research. Among the programs eliminated in the reorganization was the Department of Industrial Studies, run by Mary van Kleeck, a staff member since 1910. Van Kleeck, who had herself conducted pioneering research on women in industry, was renowned as a reform-minded knowledge broker, feminist, founder of the Women's Bureau in the Department of Labor and, in the 1930s, an outspoken advocate of Soviet-style national economic planning—the last prompting the foundation to place disclaimers on the policies if not the research methods advocated in the work she underwrote. But it was the foundation's postwar reorganization that finally eliminated her program, replacing what remained the most significant outpost of Progressive industrial investigation with programs to develop behavioral research as a science that would find applications in the study of law, medicine, and the military as well as in such traditional philanthropic areas as poverty and social work.[23] In this the transformed Russell Sage Foundation reflected a broader change in the political economy of knowledge that, just as much as the broader political economy of affluence, set the stage for individualizing poverty as a social problem, locating its origins in individual behavior rather than in economic and social arrangements, and tracing its "pathology" to individual personality.

Further evidence of the influence of the behavioral movement could be found in the substantive and methodological innovations it wrought. Among the earliest had been the integrative study of culture and personality, based on a melding of psychoanalytic, anthropological, and sociological techniques. Pioneered at Yale University's Institute of Human Relations in the 1930s, by the late 1940s the interdisciplinary focus on culture and personality had put individual psychological development at the center of anthropological and sociological research, making the use of Rorschach (ink blot), Thematic Apperception (image projection), and personal attitude surveys not only commonplace but *de rigueur* in postwar social research.[24] The culture and personality approach also shifted the emphasis in local studies from the community to the family, encouraging intensified scrutiny of its psychological as opposed to its social or economic functions in the life course. Studies of early childhood became something of a growth industry in postwar social science, extending from the question of individual development to cross-cultural comparisons of child rearing and its impact on differences in "national character" around the world.[25] Child-rearing patterns also assumed greater significance in the sociological study of class in the United States, redoubling the emphasis on the family as the source of deep-seated, class-typed personality differences that could in turn determine an individual's opportunities in life. The true methodological breakthrough in the behavioral sciences, however, came with the application of quantitative sampling, measurement, and predictive modeling techniques to surveys of personal attitudes and behavior, which finally brought the aura of "hard," data-rich, experimental science to behavioral research. These techniques had been cultivated in national opinion polling since the 1930s, but they got the full laboratory treatment in the U.S. Army's Research Branch during WWII. There, social scientists with training in psychology, sociology, and statistics conducted the most extensive research to date on the determinants of attitudes and behavior among a national sample of Americans, in this case to be used as a vital source of information for the recruitment, training, morale-building, and postwar reconversion of American GIs. Though explicitly set up, in the words of staff director Samuel A. Stouffer, "to do a practical engineering job, not a scientific job," these studies became standard-setters in social psychological theory and method once the war was over, in the process launching many an academic career. They subsequently became the basis of *The American Soldier*, a four-volume, multi-authored treatise produced under the imprimatur of the Social Science Research Council and written explicitly to advance the science of quantitative attitude measurement, social scientific prediction, mass communications experimentation, and social psychology more generally.[26] Its publication, underwritten by the Carnegie Corporation, held out the tantalizing prospect not only of observing the determinants of behavior with new, quantitative techniques, but of predicting and, ultimately, *engineering* human behavior with policies steeped in the latest scientific expertise.[27]

The changes that took social science in a more behavioral direction did not take place in a political vacuum. The demise of Mary van Kleeck's Industrial Development Department coincided with the political setbacks and rising anticommunism that put economic planning off the agenda and the labor movement on a more accommodationist course. Van Kleeck herself was subsequently subject to FBI surveillance and was called to appear before Senator Joseph McCarthy's committee in 1953.[28] No single factor contributed more to the rise of behaviorism, though, than its intimate association with America's wartime needs, needs that persisted well after the Allied victory over fascism had made the Cold War against communism the driving foreign policy force. Building on their research into culture and personality, anthropologist Margaret Mead, psychiatrist Erik Erickson, and specially formed committees of behavioral scientists gave the concept of "national character" both theoretical and strategic heft, pointing out its relevance in designing anti-enemy propaganda as well as in building civilian morale during World War II.[29] In *The Authoritarian Personality*, emigree sociologist Theodor Adorno developed a statistical method for linking personality traits, social attitudes, and political ideology, (known as the F-[fascism], A-S [anti-Semitism], and E-[ethnocentrism] scales), to determine the psychological roots of anti-Semitism, prejudice, and fascism and the social conditions under which authoritarianism could take hold.[30] *The American Soldier*, still recognized as a veritable founding document in experimental social psychological research, grew out of a vast military mobilization of social science behind the cause of winning the war. All of these studies were suffused with a sense of common commitment, not just to the scientific facts of human behavior, but to identifying, as Margaret Mead wrote, "the psychological equipment with which we can win the war."[31] All developed concepts and methods that would subsequently be applied to the ongoing fight against international communism, as they would to the understanding of racial prejudice, juvenile delinquency, and poverty at home.[32]

Few of the insights from this emerging, war-tinged behavioral science boded particularly well for the working class or the poor. Studies based on Adorno's F-scale measures, for example, traced fascism to a lower-class "anti-democratic personality structure," a theme later picked up by sociologist Seymour Martin Lipset, whose concept of "working-class authoritarianism" used the F-scale to designate lower-class character as a reactionary, racist, potentially dangerous political force. Such findings should provide fair warning for "intellectuals of the democratic left," Lipset wrote, reflecting his own postwar journey to the liberal center, "who once believed the proletariat necessarily to be a force for liberty, racial equality, and social progress."[33] The vision of American "national character" was equally, if indirectly, hostile in its implications for the poor. Americans had a fundamentally democratic personality, Margaret Mead claimed in her wartime morale work, and it had been nurtured in the upwardly mobile, white middle-class home. Achievement-oriented, acquisitive, individualistic, and fixed on the future, this personality type was not just the product of prosperity and democratic practice, Mead suggested, but the source of those virtues as well. Thus enshrined as the basis of what would later be known as the American "core culture," the middle-class personality embodied all the characteristics said to be missing in the lower class.[34] Even more troubling than the suggestion of lower-class un-Americanism, however, was what behavioral science had to say about its source. Once thought to be producing satisfied, if unambitious children with its over-indulgent, permissive ways, the working class was now said to be practicing rigid, "authoritarian," even "primitive" methods of child rearing associated with reactionary, racist politics as well as underachievement in life.[35] That was the conclusion reached by a team of Harvard social psychologists based on a comparison of middle- and working-class mothers in the early 1950s. Indeed, reversing findings reported by Allison Davis and Robert Havighurst less than a decade earlier, they concluded that middle-class mothers were not the strict, puritanical, impulse-denying figures they had been made out to be, but were "warmer," more loving, "more permissive and less punitive" toward their children than the mothers of the working class. The very notion of working-class permissiveness, they argued, was a romanticized vision from a politically distant past. Meanwhile, the sudden turnaround in the findings about middle-class child rearing had a more scientific, not to mention self-serving, explanation: the mothers were paying attention to expert advice.[36] Now considered quite literally to be a cradle of democracy, the middle-class family was tellingly compared by one sociologist to a "country which, having operated under an authoritarian form of government, has suddenly switched to a democratic form."[37] Whatever the source of the new permissiveness in child rearing, students of the middle-class family hardly hid the fact that they approved. Lower-class deviance, deprivations, and even political ideology, in contrast, were looking more and more like personality deficiencies inculcated by lower-class mothers in the young.

THE CHANGING CONTEXT (III): GENDER AND FAMILY IDEOLOGY

Even while reifying the image of an enlightened middle-class family norm, postwar social science showed signs of a broader cultural anxiety about the family that played an additionally powerful role in shaping knowledge about the poor. Sociologist Talcott Parsons captured something of this anxiety when he acknowledged that the family had lost its traditional economic and social "functions" in the face of the large bureaucracies, technological conveniences, and mass consumerism that characterized the modern age. He also tried to allay such concerns by arguing that the family was not in trouble but in "transition" toward a more "specialized" form. The new family form was more self-contained, less extended, and revolved exclusively around the *psychological* functions of socializing children and providing a stable social identity for adults—it was a "factory," that is, for producing human personalities. The modern family was also more dependent than ever on a sharp separation of "sex roles" between a socially dominant, breadwinning father and a nurturing, economically dependent mother to care for the children and the home. In this, its more modern, "nuclear" form, the family had actually risen in significance, according to Parsons, for it now had the awesome responsibility of maintaining the psychological conditions for social stability—a responsibility associated in Cold War America with no less than preserving democracy, capitalism, and the American way of life.[38] Whether or not this analysis proved reassuring to the few who could penetrate his prose, Parsons's streamlined, psychologized view of the modern family did offer the weight of scientific theory to the "domestic consensus" that emerged in postwar politics and popular culture as a response to the uncertainties of the Cold War and atomic age.[39] It also, as the prevailing norm in social scientific research, provided a new way of implicating the family—specifically, gender relations within the lower-class family— in the incidence and perpetuation of poverty across generational lines.

Concern about gender relations in the lower-class family was by no means new to postwar social science, but in the past much of that concern had been focused on the family as an economic unit, dependent on an often delicate balance of male and female work. Whether or not they accepted a "traditional," patriarchal norm, several studies recognized that this balance was of necessity a matter of negotiation and compromise within the working class. Thus, in W.E.B. DuBois's Philadelphia, black women had little choice but to become breadwinners on their own, especially in light of the low wages—hence the bad marriage prospects—of black men.[40] Some later social surveys used the prospect of married women's employment to make the case for a male "family wage," arguing that men would lose self-respect when their wives entered the paid labor force. Not that this diminished the economic role of the housewife; indeed, only the most "intelligent" and thrifty of housewives could translate industrial wages into an adequate standard of living. Others writing in the survey tradition, however, insisted that women were in the industrial work force to stay. In her study of female industrial workers conducted for the Pittsburgh Survey, Elizabeth Beardsley Butler claimed that improving *women's* wages and training would make for more "intelligent home making" and a more healthy family life.[41] In the 1930s Margaret Hagood's *Mothers of the South*, a survey of tenant farm wives, used the techniques of regionalist sociology to show how economic as well as family planning would allow lower-class women to negotiate the triple role of mother, housewife, and laborer they had to play.[42] Even the more psychological of the Depression-era studies maintained a focus on the family as an economic unit, couching gender relations within the framework of the balance between male and female work. Male unemployment set off a complex "cycle" of "readjustments" within the family, E. Wight Bakke wrote, as women and children took on greater responsibility for earning and managing household income while men accustomed to acting as sole providers found their authority diminished vis-à-vis their wives. Nor was the readjustment necessarily a bad thing; at least some of Bakke's families had emerged from unemployment with more tight-knit, cooperative, and less patriarchal bonds—and in this sense were better off for the ordeal.[43] In the sociological image of the black lower-class "matriarchy," on the other hand, the breadwinning female was definitely in charge, generating a combination of economic dependence and sexual irresponsibility in men. Still, as E. Franklin Frazier, Charles S. Johnson, and others insisted, the relationship was sustained not so much by the fact of female employment as by the economics of unemployment and racial discrimination against black men. The matriarchy was deviant, and less preferable than the middle-class patriarchal form, but it was also a cultural adaptation that would give way, Frazier believed, when black men were accepted into the industrial labor force and in a position to assume a position of authority in family life.[44] Thus from the Progressive Era through the 1930s the lower-class family, and particularly the position of women in it, continued to provide a perspective on the problems of wages, unemployment, and discrimination in the industrial capitalist economy.

In the postwar literature on the lower-class family, this emphasis on the economics of gender relations began to change. Social scientists, following the Cold War "domestic consensus" as much as the behaviorist "revolution," severed the family from its social and economic context and began to view it in a much more exclusively psychological light. Patriarchy, in this constricted, psychologized context, became more a necessity than a cultural norm, while lower-class gender relations were less significant as a *consequence* of low wages and unemployment than as the *cause* of personality damage in the young. Like so many other afflictions in the Cold War era, some of the damage would be associated directly with the faulty child rearing practices of mothers unenlightened by expert advice.[45] But analysts attributed the most deep-seated scars to the structural deficiencies of the lower-class family, and specifically to the sources that E. Franklin Frazier identified in a 1950 report on delinquency among black youths. Moving beyond the "social disorganization" framework that had informed his earlier work, Frazier explained delinquency as a reflection of the personality disorders wrought by the matriarchal household, in which children, and boys especially, had no one to meet their developmental and disciplinary needs. On the one hand there was the working mother who could not play her properly nurturing role; on the other, and more importantly, there was the absence of an authoritative breadwinning male.[46] Here again the contrast with earlier literature can underscore the significance of this change. First, in the streamlined psychologized view of the family the focus was no longer on external, social and economic conditions, but exclusively on the role of internal family characteristics in creating disadvantages for the young. From this perspective, women's labor force participation was not an asset or a necessity but a liability for the lower class, which is precisely how it would be treated (when not ignored altogether) in subsequent behavioral science research. Second, armed with an ever-expanding battery of psychological tests and developmental theories, social scientists were now "diagnosing" behaviors once viewed as cultural adaptations as deeply ingrained personality traits. The lower-class penchant for immediate gratification offers a case in point. Viewed by sympathetic anthropologists as a reasonable response to deprivation—why wait to enjoy what might not be there tomorrow?—by the 1950s the "inability to defer gratification" had been transformed into a certifiable personality disorder.[47] The cause? Not poverty, as the anthropological view suggested, but the absence of a father in the home.

This turn to diagnostics was greatly encouraged by the foundation-sponsored seminars, training fellowships, and research collaborations that, having gotten the personality and culture movement off the ground, then helped to make psychological training a regular part of the graduate curriculum in leading universities. There, anthropologists and sociologists would learn about a host of new diagnostic techniques, especially prominent among which was the Thematic Apperception Test (TAT). First developed by psychologist Henry A. Murray in the late 1930s, the TAT was designed to measure human motivation by asking respondents to create a story based on a suggestive picture. A trained interpreter would then "read" or "score" these stories to determine the unconscious needs motivating the respondent's behavior, and specifically to detect the presence of the need (n) for such hidden desires as dominance, dependence, punishment, and power. Applied in *The Authoritarian Personality*, the TAT was used to uncover the psychological needs being filled in the rise of fascism—and to create the scales that would implicate the lower class as a reactionary political force. Only in the 1950s, though, did it become a diagnostic tool to help explain differences in social class, when psychologist David McClelland developed TATs to measure what he called "achievement motivation"—or "n Achievement"—not as a component of culture but as a basic personality trait. McClelland himself was motivated by a desire to understand what he considered one of the most positive of personality traits and to see how it played out in human behavior. He was not disappointed. Dozens of TAT studies, most of them on white males, correlated high n Achievement with the revered American values of democracy, self-reliance, economic success, and the Protestant, capitalist ethic itself. Later on, McClelland identified n Achievement as the single most important factor in "the rise and fall of civilizations." Not surprisingly, considering that the test protocols were developed using white, middle-class college students, the studies consistently found high n Achievement in middle-class respondents, and low n Achievement in the lower class. Middle-class mothers, it seems, had learned a lesson that had been lost on the lower class: how, through proper weaning and toilet training, to cultivate a high-achieving personality in their sons.[48]

The research basis for these and other psychological diagnoses was contradictory, culturally biased, and remarkably simplistic at times. Different studies on the personality impact of father absence found sons who were overly dependent, passive, and showed homosexual or effeminate tendencies as well as sons who were aggressive and masculine-identified enough to join delinquent gangs. The consequences for daughters drew less psychological attention, though the conclusions followed the same theme in reverse: girls without fathers were more prone to independence, abstract thinking, and other "masculine" traits, rather than to the emotionalism appropriate to their sex.[49] In the growing literature on achievement motivation and social behavior, analysts interpreted TAT and attitude surveys based on scales using white, male middle-class respondents as the norm.[50] Psychologist Walter Mischel, a leading author-ity on the inability to defer gratification, used such "independent" scales in surveys of young black and East Indian respondents in Trinidad and Grenada, where he found that father-absence was principally to blame. But what truly convinced Mischel was an experiment that would later, often disparagingly, be referred to as the "candy bar test," which Mischel devised as a supplement to his attitude surveys. In this test the survey administrator would stand before a classroom full of children and offer them a choice of two rewards for having completed their surveys. Children who wanted the reward immediately (ImR) could have a small candy bar today; those who were willing to wait (DelR) would get a large candy bar the following week. For Mischel, this experiment did more than confirm the father-absence correlation, it identified the "DelR-ImR distinction" as the basis of an entire "cluster" of personality traits, later summarized in a survey of the literature to include social irresponsibility, low achievement motivation, delinquency, distorted time perspectives, and "imma-ture, criminal and neurotic behavior."[51] With such correlations, often backed up with quantitative attitude surveys, psychologically oriented researchers felt confident in tracing a whole host of social maladjustments to father-ab-sence and other examples of gender role confusion in the home. The authors of one study took great pride in their ability to use early childhood ego develop-ment to predict where on the socioeconomic spectrum their subjects would end up later in life.[52] The methods behind these findings would come under heavy criticism in the 1960s, but not before they had contributed to a harden-ing, if internally contradictory, profile of lower-class personality disorders as-sociated especially with the "broken" family and its violation of patriarchal gender norms.[53]

The damage was only compounded in the literature when the personality in question was black. For it was in the black "matriarchal" family that postwar psychology found its most pathological case.[54] There, in the eyes of psychia-trists Abram Kardiner and Lionel Ovesey, analysts would find powerful evi-dence of the deep "psychological scars" not just of poverty but of race. Kar-diner and Ovesey, both of whom were white, presented their own evidence in a study of twenty-five Harlem residents recruited for a six-month series of psychoanalytic interviews and psychological tests. Drawing from the marriage of anthropological and psychoanalytic theory, they determined there was a "basic Negro personality," and that its most fundamental characteristic was the self-hatred blacks had internalized from prevailing white racist beliefs. Though manifest in an assortment of upper and middle-class neuroses, the burden of racism had fallen heaviest on the black lower class, where it had triggered an "endless number of vicious circles . . . that can never end anywhere because they are self-perpetuating." The most damaging of the "vicious circles" origi-nated in the matriarchal family which, though itself a product of racism and black male unemployment, had taken on a separate psycho-sexual dynamic of its own. Stripped of the patriarchal authority accorded by conventional norms, the black man was further emasculated by the dominant black female, "first in the dominant mother and later in the dominant wife." Unable to escape this "confusion" in "sociosexual roles," he suffered not only a loss of esteem and personal efficacy, but sexual impotence as well. The matriarch, in the meantime, was too busy being the breadwinner to assume her naturally dependent, passive "maternal role," and she, too, suffered a distorted sexual identity that left her either "frigid" or promiscuous, but always incapable of conducting "normal" sexual relationships. What truly made this a self-perpetuating circle, however, was the distorted psychological development of the young. Left without a strong male figure to idealize, they turned to delinquency and all sorts of immediate gratification for compensation and release. In this way the matriarchal family had become not just the reflection but the actual vehicle of white racial oppression, and for reproducing its "mark" from one generation to the next.[55] Kardiner and Ovesey stopped short of concluding that black lower-class personality problems were inherited traits, instead insisting that each generation experienced the impact of racism anew. They also took care to distance themselves from racially conservative or even gradualist points of view. No amount of compensatory education, they argued, could undo the damage that racism had wrought. *"There is only one way that the products of oppression can be dissolved, and that is to stop the oppression,"* they wrote in the emphatic conclusion to their book (emphasis in original).[56] Nevertheless, by depicting the family as the immediate agent of oppression and emphasizing the permanence of childhood ego development in the course of later life, they had invested both class and racial deprivations with the almost biological quality that would later emerge in the more broadly encompassing concept of the culture of poverty.

Kardiner and Ovesey were hardly the only liberal social scientists to depict the black matriarchy as a source of psychological damage and of the social pathologies it bred. In the continuing battle against biological racism, both culture and psychology provided liberals with alternative, environmentalist explanations for high rates of poverty, illegitimacy, and delinquency among blacks.[57] And yet, inseparable though it was from the liberal psychology of race, Kardiner and Ovesey's vision of the matriarchy should also be understood as part of the same trends in postwar social science that made a psychological issue of class. Crucial to that analysis was an often unspoken consensus around a psychological as well as cultural ideal of the modern family that postwar social science had done a great deal to construct. Couched as it was in the values of patriarchy, female domesticity, and middle-class self-reliance, that ideal offered cold comfort to the millions of white and nonwhite Americans who, even if they aspired to achieve it, lacked access to the jobs, wages, social welfare protections, and educational opportunities that would enable them to sustain that way of life. Liberal social scientists, however, had turned away from political economy as a framework for analysis to focus more deeply than ever on the culture and psychology of the poor. By the 1950s, they had identified not only child rearing but "confused" or "disturbed" gender relations within the family as a means of transmitting low achievement, immediate gratification, and other traits defined as personality disorders from one generation to the next. In the process, they had adopted a framework that was incapable of recognizing a woman's productive labor while exaggerating the exclusivity of her reproductive role. No longer would the lower-class family, and the woman's place in it, be a window onto the problems and changing organization of work. Instead, it would be a window into the processes of personality formation and, in the case of the lower-class family, their part in creating the psychological conditions in which the "paradox" of "poverty amidst affluence" would persist.

THE CHANGING CONTEXT (IV): GLOBAL POVERTY AND THE COLD WAR

If World War II had opened the door to a behaviorist "revolution" in social science, it was the Cold War that truly paved the way for direct investigation of the culture and psychology of "the poor" as a distinguishable social group. For it was the Cold War that generated the need and the justification for opening up a whole new world—the "third world"—for technical assistance and applied behavioral research in the name of international aid to the poor. Global modernization, after all, was "our most effective counter-measure to Soviet propaganda," in the words of President Eisenhower, "and the best method by which to create the political and social stability essential to lasting peace."[58] It also created an unprecedented and continuous demand for knowledge of non-Western cultures and their people, reflected in government and foundation-funded expansion of "Area Studies" as a new interdisciplinary field. Few issues were more important than the question of what was keeping the countries of Asia, Africa, and Latin America from "developing" as industrial capitalist economies—in U.S. strategic thinking, the surest way to prevent them from falling into communist hands. Economists played a leading role in providing the answers, studying "development economics" in terms of the social and political preconditions for growth. But it was the answer from behavioral science, the culture of poverty, that would have most direct relevance for dealing with the "paradox" of poverty at home.

Anthropologists, of course, had been studying "primitive" or peasant cultures for years, but the goal of modernization put those cultures in an entirely different light. Viewed through the filter of U.S. policy, peasant or tribal communities were not "primitive" but "underdeveloped," their folkways not exotic but "backward," and their poverty a barrier to the necessary introduction of a more modern, democratic way of life. Accordingly, attracted by the opportunity to see their knowledge put into policy and practice, many anthropologists of the postwar generation joined up with the technicians of economic and social modernization in projects sponsored by an expanding network of public and private development agencies, led by the Ford and Rockefeller Foundations, the U.S. Agency for International Development (AID), and in some cases, as many locals suspected, the Central Intelligence Agency (CIA). Together, they sought to bring the amenities of Western technology, education, medicine, and economic development to the people they studied—and to find out what in traditional cultures might prevent modernization from taking hold. For many anthropologists and sociologists in the rising postwar generation, consulting on international development projects represented a first significant field experience. From a professional perspective, there was an air of coming of age about the prospect: anthropology, in line for at least a share in the growing research dollar, could expand the vistas of ethnographic field research. "Certainly the days of the anthropologist as a one man expedition must be over," Oscar Lewis wrote to his mentor, Ruth Benedict, from fieldwork in Mexico in 1944. The project he was working on, a joint U.S.-Mexican government effort combining development aid with research, was "an opportunity to observe behavior in a more or less controlled experimental situation," and had brought Lewis into contact with a wide assortment of government officials at a very early stage in his career.[59] It also signaled his willingness to embrace the values of modernization rather than, as Lewis criticized other anthropologists for doing, defending traditional ways of life "against the inroads of civilization."[60]

In their capacity as consultants and scholars, Lewis and other social scientific proponents of modernization launched a wholesale revision of what they considered to be a romanticized vision of traditional cultures in anthropological research. The first target for Lewis was no less an anthropological giant than the University of Chicago's Robert Redfield, who in a famous study of the Mexican village Tepoztlàn had bemoaned the loss of the villagers' harmonious, communal "folk" culture under the encroachments of more urban ways.[61] Much like his colleagues in the sociology department, Redfield looked at urbanization as a culturally disruptive, disorganizing force in a broader continuum between folk traditionalism and modern urban civilization. In *Life in a Mexican Village*, his 1951 "restudy" of Tepoztlàn, Lewis confronted this widely influential framework head on. Far from the "Rousseauean" idyll of integrated communalism that Redfield had made it out to be, Lewis wrote that Tepoztlàn was riddled with "violence, disruption, cruelty, disease, suffering and maladjustment" and an abject poverty from which only modernization could provide escape. Tradition in Tepoztlàn was little more than an obstacle to the necessary change; for all the modern conveniences that had penetrated its resistance, the village remained mired in a superstitious and primitive worldview.[62] Lewis was not alone in his revisionism; the Cold War made the problem of traditional culture a direct political concern. Political scientist Edward Banfield made this explicit in *The Moral Basis of a Backward Society*, his portrait of the Italian peasant village he called "Montegrano," published in 1958. Banfield spent a year among the villagers, never learning the language but acting as a self-described participant observer nonetheless. His observations led him to the deeply pessimistic prognosis that the villagers were culturally incapable of either political democracy or economic modernization—in his analysis, the two went hand in hand—because of what he termed their "amoral familism," an attachment to the nuclear family that kept the villagers fragmented, impoverished, and unable to work together toward "their common good." In a stunningly facile leap, Banfield generalized his conclusions to all "non-Western cultures of the world."[63] Others found the dangers of traditionalism closer to home. In studies of the rural coal towns and mill towns of the United States, social scientists portrayed a superstitious, often fundamentalist "pre-modern" worldview that left villagers passive, submissive, hostile to outsiders, and unable to share in the national wealth. The dead hand of tradition was not just a factor in rural poverty; liberals viewed it as a seedbed of reactionary politics as well.[64] Perhaps no one was more eager to revise the "myths" of traditionalism than U.S. historian Richard Hofstader, who not only rejected the idealized vision of populist agrarian democracy, but warned that it fed into a reactionary, racist, anti-Semitic streak in American politics.[65] The turn against traditionalism, then, was not confined to the movement for modernization in the "underdeveloped" third world. It also ran strikingly parallel to postwar revisionism in images of the American lower class. In the early 1960s, the two would run together, as the elements of rural traditionalism and lower-class urban culture became conflated into a single, undifferentiated concept of a culture of poverty that deviated from the American middle-class norm.

It is thus hardly surprising that social scientists found support for their conclusions about traditional or underdeveloped cultures in an ever-expanding arsenal of psychological tests exported from the United States. Social psychology and personality and culture, after all, had already been established as legitimate areas of policy concern during World War II. The demand for psychological knowledge continued in the major funding agencies during the Cold War, where it was used to uncover the secrets of stimulating economic development or to quell incipient revolution abroad. With the help of such easy-to-administer tests as the Rorschach, the TAT, and various picture-drawing tests, American social scientists set out to get even nonliterate people to reveal their innermost drives, in search of the psychological knowledge that would bring modernization and political stability to the third world.[66] Meanwhile, the study of child rearing practices was growing far more systematic and widespread, a development Margaret Mead attributed to breakthroughs in studying early child development and culture and personality, as well as to the growing ranks of professional women for whom research on children was a "natural choice."[67]

In the late 1950s psychologist David McClelland used all of these methods in an extravagently ambitious project to prove that a single personality trait— none other than the achievement motive (n Achievement)—was the engine behind *all* of the great civilizations in Western history and that measuring n Achievement "levels" in various societies could be used to *predict* the rate of GNP growth (or decline) over time. McClelland reported his results in *The Achieving Society* (1961), a sweeping historical and comparative analysis that encompassed ancient Greece, sixteenth-century Spain, the European Industrial Revolution, and the contemporary United States. Although he did draw from child rearing and personality studies, McClelland was primarily interested in making a quantitative case, and for this he relied chiefly on a method for "scoring" the number of achievement images in children's literature (and on ancient Greece vases as well). "It may come as something of a shock," McClelland wrote in *The Achieving Society*, "to realize that more could have been learned about the rate of future economic growth . . . by reading elementary school books than by studying such presumably more relevant matters as power politics, wars and depressions, economic statistics, or governmental policies governing international trade, taxation or public finance."[68] That was because n Achievement was cultivated in childhood—more precisely, in the way mothers raised their sons. Thus, he concluded from his masses of evidence, economic development in third world countries was not likely to happen without first bringing about psychological change. Fortunately, psychological research could offer guidance for this awesome task: McClelland urged development agencies to sponsor ideological campaigns for modernization, provide motivational training for budding entrepreneurs, and, above all, to teach mothers how to break with tradition and adopt more modern methods for raising their sons.[69]

Outlandish though it may seem in retrospect, McClelland's project was not much more than an extension of what was already happening in mainstream behavioral science research. Measuring achievement motivation had become a mini cottage industry for McClelland and his students at Harvard, where McClelland was affiliated with the prestigious Department of Social Relations. The project was also inspired by the broader movement to establish behavioral study as a quantitative, predictive, and policy relevant science. In the preface to *The Achieving Society* McClelland lavishly thanked the Ford Foundation's behavioral sciences program, not just for its "magnificent" patronage, but for the essential "spirit" that inspired the book: "hope and enthusiasm for the role that knowledge of human behavior might play in helping man control his destiny."[70] Most important, though, the project was grounded in a vision of social institutions and social change that had come to pervade the postwar behavioral sciences and that the behavioral sciences were beginning to impose on the non-

Western or "underdeveloped" world. It was a vision in which the individual personality, manufactured by the family, was the central driving force, and in which the family, reduced to its psychological function, was sharply divided into maternal child rearing and paternal breadwinning roles. Hence McClelland's remarkable disregard for the facts of political economy and for the economic agency of women and the family in the developing world. In this *The Achieving Society* was not at all a departure from the general direction of social problem research. It was also an example of the extraordinary hubris—not just of McClelland but of the postwar behavioral sciences—in their search for unifying theories of human psychology that could then be applied around the world. McClelland and his colleagues did in fact set up an enterprise for conducting achievement motivation seminars throughout the third world—an effort, incidentally, that AID and the Ford Foundation backed away from after critics in Congress stepped in.[71]

AFFLUENCE, BEHAVIORISM, MATRIARCHY, AND COLD WAR: THE CULTURE OF POVERTY IS BORN

In the idea of the culture of poverty Oscar Lewis extended a similar kind of logic across national, racial, and ethnic lines. Convinced that "anthropologists have a new function in the modern world," he wrote about the need to document the lives of the "great mass" of poor people in underdeveloped countries and to understand what they had in common with the lower classes all over the world. "It seems to me that the culture of poverty has some universal characteristics which transcend regional, rural-urban, and even national boundaries," he wrote when he first introduced the idea in 1959, and it could be found "in lower-class settlements in London, in Puerto Rico, in Mexico City slums and Mexican villages, and among lower class Negroes in the United States."[72] As a "cross-societal" concept, he later added, the culture of poverty offered a new way of thinking about race, allowing Americans "to see that many of the problems we think of as distinctively our own or distinctively Negro problems . . . also exist in countries where there are no distinct ethnic minority groups." From an extensive collection of life histories and psychological tests with families in Mexico and Puerto Rico, he distilled an ever-growing inventory of "traits," describing them as essential features of a "way of life, remarkably stable and persistent, passed down from generation to generation along family lines."[73] Economic "traits" formed a part of Lewis's inventory, including underemployment, low wages, and a "constant struggle for survival." So did the "mother-centered" or "matrifocal" family. But the crux of the list, which over the years expanded from thirty-six to seventy, were "traits" that are best characterized as behavioral and psychological: resignation, dependency, present-time orientation, lack of impulse control, weak ego structure, sexual confusion, and the inevitable inability to defer gratification, to name but a few.[74] In the recurrence of these traits Lewis saw something more than an adaptation to "objective social conditions." The culture of poverty was perpetuated by the family, passed on from generation to generation through its psychological impact on the children.[75]

There was a notable irony in Lewis's emphasis on psychology. The son of poor immigrants who grew up in and around New York City, Lewis (anglicized from Lefkowitz) joined many other working-class intellectuals of his generation in embracing Marxist theory while at the College of the City of New York (CCNY) in the 1930s.[76] This early influence, with its emphasis on the material basis of social identity and conflict, would continue to inform his thinking throughout his career, and, if anything, served as a kind of constant counterweight to the increasingly psychological direction in his own and, more generally, in anthropological, research. While a graduate student in anthropology at Columbia University, he was surrounded by such leading lights of the culture and personality movement as Margaret Mead, psychiatrist Abram Kardiner, and his own mentor Ruth Benedict. Lewis himself, however, was something of a latecomer to the field, focusing more heavily on economic organization and material culture than on psychological method in his course work. That his first book on Tepoztlàn included any psychological testing was not at all Lewis's choice. The project that employed him, funded by the U.S./Mexican Interamerican Indian Institute, had been designed explicitly to combine development activities with research on "the Indian personality," and came complete with a set of pre-designed psychological tests. Even then, Lewis relied on his wife (and lifelong collaborator) Ruth to administer and interpret the nearly overwhelming array of Rorschach, TAT, emotional response, moral judgment, and other tests.[77] Subsequently, he continued to turn to outside experts for psychological readings of his field material, frequently putting Lewis in the position of "defending" his informants against diagnoses of mental illness rendered by outside experts. "[T]he psychiatrists, clinical psychologists and social workers who have read the autobiographies and psychological tests of the people I have studied, have often found more negative elements and pathology than I am willing to grant," he wrote late in his career.[78] The arm's distance was already evident in his Tepoztlàn study, *Life in a Mexican Village*, which many consider to be his best work. Although he did devote attention to the question of personality development, the study put greater emphasis on the problems of economic stratification, land tenure, agricultural practices, and household economies—and provided a far more comprehensive community ethnography than any study Lewis subsequently did. In fact, as Lewis's biographer Susan Rigdon convincingly argues, Lewis's own strengths as a field researcher were much more in the area of material culture and household economies, reflected in a method for taking household inventories that was far more detailed than anything the Progressive-era budget surveyors had ever undertaken.[79] Nevertheless, after Tepoztlàn the community or any other kind of larger context all but disappeared from Lewis's analyses; he turned instead to a method he called "family studies," and to almost novelistic biographical and autobiographical expositions of his subjects' lives. It was out of this turn, to a more exclusive focus on individual personality as developed in the family, that Lewis developed the idea of the culture of poverty and offered it as a unifying concept for understanding poor people all over the world.

The culture of poverty did have its origins in political economy, according to Lewis's theory, even if it did perpetuate itself by psychological means. Found primarily in "class-stratified, highly individuated, capitalistic" societies, it arose out of the extreme isolation and marginality of poor people in modernizing societies. Thus, Lewis took care to distinguish between more "primitive" societies, in which poverty was an integral and near-universal part of life, and the subculture of poor people who were deprived of the benefits or a sense of belonging in modern industrial society. "The most likely candidates for a culture of poverty are the people who come from the lower strata of a rapidly changing society and are already partially alien from it," he wrote. Lewis was also convinced that the culture of poverty would not survive socialism: though still poor, the postrevolutionary slum dwellers he observed in Cuba "had a new sense of power and importance. They were armed and were given a doctrine which glorified the lower class as the hope of humanity." Most of the world's poor, however, were divorced from organized politics or social institutions of any kind; their passive, dependent, sometimes hedonistic culture was a "design for living" with the harsh realities of their own isolated lives. Only by making basic structural changes—developing the economy, redistributing wealth, organizing the poor, even staging a revolution—would the conditions that gave rise to the culture of poverty be changed. But that, Lewis warned, would not necessarily put an end to the culture of poverty itself. For once it was established as an adaptation to "objective" social conditions, the culture of poverty was absorbed and embraced by young children, who by the age of six or seven "are not psychologically geared to take full advantage of changing conditions of increased opportunities which may occur in their lifetime."[80]

The problem was that Lewis made very little attempt to provide direct evidence or analysis that actually linked behavioral and cultural patterns to the structure of political economy as experienced by the poor. Instead, he discussed political economy only in terms of the individualized "traits"—unemployment, low wages, constant shortage of cash—which he in turn described as part of the culture of the poor. Nor, despite what can only be described as an extensive and intrusive battery of psychological tests, did Lewis provide any systematic evidence or analysis to explain the "high incidence of maternal deprivation, of orality, of weak ego structure, confusion of sexual identification" and the "high tolerance of psychological pathology of all sorts" he identified as distinctive personality "traits."[81] His empirical evidence—presented in individual life sto-

ries, autobiographical narratives, and lengthy "day in the life of" vignettes—
hardly fit the theory of a patterned way of life that could be generalized across
or even within national boundaries. In *Five Families*, presented as Mexican
"case studies" in the culture of poverty, there is actually more diversity than
consistency reported across the lower class. *La Vida*, written in an attempt to
"test and refine the concept of a culture of poverty," was a collective biography
of a Puerto Rican family that even Lewis had to admit was unique, with a
"history of psychopathology," prostitution, and personalities that he described
as being "closer to the expression of an unbridled id than any other people I
have studied."[82] By then, Lewis's list of poverty traits had grown almost too
lengthy to be comprehensible, let alone coherent: the "matrifocal" culture of
poverty family, for example, was also part of "bi-lateral" culture of poverty
family form. Meanwhile, Lewis had done so little to contextualize the life
stories he presented that any connection to political economy or broader social
conditions was completely obscured. What was left were several detailed por-
traits of individual poor people and their families—most of them sympathetic
as characters, but all of them, in Lewis's presentation, deeply and perhaps
permanently damaged from the psychological suffering that poverty imposed
upon the poor.

The consequences are particularly evident in his Puerto Rico study, *La Vida*,
a controversial though influential study that dominated the scant social scientific imagery of Puerto Rico for many years. Published in 1966, it reflected an
important recent shift in social scientific thinking about postwar Puerto Rico:
rather than an exciting "social laboratory" for economic planning and modernization, the island was increasingly seen as a laboratory for studying the social
pathologies associated with "underdevelopment," and for understanding why
social intervention had not worked.[83] Lewis, himself skeptical of the images
of progress being promoted by Puerto Rico's controlling political party, raised
substantial funding from the U.S. Department of Health, Education and Welfare to prove that the culture of poverty cut across national boundaries—and
to take a "first step," as he put it, toward studying poverty in the United States.[84]
Building on the concept and methods he had developed in the *vecindades* of
Mexico City, Lewis assembled a portrait of multiple households within the
Rios family, extending from a notorious urban housing development called La
Esmeralda in San Juan to various run-down apartments in New York. All the
more notable, then, was the absence of any significant discussion of Puerto
Rican migration, of the active role of the Puerto Rican government in promoting it as part of its program of economic development and population control,
or even of migration's significance as a household strategy against poverty.
Lewis did report finding, albeit without describing the study, that "the precipi-
tating factor for leaving Puerto Rico" was not economic but "most often a
personal social-psychological crisis." He also reported that Puerto Rican migrants "formed small islands in the city and perpetuated their culture"—with-

out ever resolving whether these patterns reflected Puerto Rico, or the existence of a universal culture of poverty he had set out to prove.[85] Nevertheless,
the data he did present on a larger group of Puerto Ricans in New York suggested a very different story: their incomes were much higher, men and women
were steadily employed, and the majority of workers belonged to unions—
indicating, by Lewis's definition, that the culture of poverty did not survive
migration. Also conspicuously absent in this context was any discussion of
race, especially since the matriarch of the Rios family, Fernanda, was identified
as a Negro and her children as mulatto, or racially mixed. Here again Lewis
sidestepped an issue that, according to earlier research, made a profound difference in the fortunes and assimilation patterns of Puerto Rican migrants in New
York: how members of the Rios family negotiated their own racial identity in
the more racially polarized atmosphere of the mainland United States.[86] Nor,
in comparison to the chapter and verse on their sex lives, did Lewis offer any
insight into the wage-earning history of the Rios women, despite the fact that
among them they had worked as laundresses, prostitutes, factory laborers, and
migrant farm workers to provide for their families. The culture of poverty,
like the behavioral science tradition it grew out of, was blind to any but the
reproductive role of women, and narrowly fixated on the psychological dimensions of family life. In this and other ways, it was not only an incomplete, but
a distorting framework for understanding the nature of poverty and the lives
of the poor.

Despite or perhaps because of its many limitations, the culture of poverty was
greeted in the early 1960s as an important, and welcome, scientific idea. Certainly it established Oscar Lewis as something more than an anthropologist of
Mexico. Like McClelland's achievement motivation, it was exactly the kind
of universalistic concept that postwar behavioral science promoted: it could
be hypothesized, measured, and used to generate funding for research all over
the developing world. Unlike McClelland, Lewis had also captured an under-
current of the pessimism and psychological foreboding that often crept into
postwar behavioral research, and that served as a kind of corrective to the
optimistic assumptions about national prosperity and the mood of political
complacency it seemed to promote. By the early 1960s, some of that foreboding
was beginning to come through in social scientific explanations of the
"pockets" of poverty in the United States. Writing about Appalachia, and its
economic and cultural "lag," regionalist sociologist Rupert Vance suggested
that policy makers look beyond economic growth to include early childhood
development as a strategy for the future, while accepting the current reality of
a "lost generation of mountaineers."[87] Michael Harrington's best-selling *The
Other America* took the concept much further, helping to assure the future of
the culture of poverty as a popular as well as a scholarly idea. The poor in
America were like an "underdeveloped nation," Harrington wrote estimating

its size as some forty to fifty million strong. "They are a different kind of people. They think and feel differently; they look upon a different America than the middle class looks upon."[88] Lewis himself used the culture of poverty to puncture the "great publicity" Puerto Rico had been getting as a success story of modernization and economic growth.[89] For Harrington, Lewis, and others, then, the culture of poverty was more than an explanation for persistent disadvantage; it offered a dissent from postwar optimism about the solvent of economic growth, and a dire warning about the consequences of failing to act.

Most important to its public reception was the fact that the culture of poverty had widespread ideological appeal, especially to a generation of liberal and left-liberal reformers who, after years of Cold War, prosperity, and ideological "consensus," had grown more comfortable with the language of psychology, culture, and poverty than with that of political economy and class. To be sure, there were some who used cultural imagery to argue that intervention of any sort was both futile and wrong, but in the early 1960s those voices were few and scattered—the culture of poverty was an argument for reform. Rupert Vance used the mountaineers of Appalachia to make a case for a more truly comprehensive form of regional planning, combining economic development with educational and early childhood programs to break poverty's "vicious circle" before it could take hold. For others, including Oscar Lewis, the concept had more radical implications—at least in the context of the third world. There, the culture of poverty called for revolutionary action, as a means of eliminating the conditions of mass deprivation while giving the poor a sense of belonging and purpose in life. In much the same spirit, Michael Harrington called for a "vast social movement" to "empower the poor" in the United States.[90] And yet, by couching the analysis so exclusively in terms of behavior and psychology, the culture of poverty undercut its own radical potential and deflected attention away from any critique of capitalism implicit in the idea. Harrington's call for a vast social movement said more about the need for spiritual redemption and rehabilitation than it did about the redistribution of wealth. He also looked to the third world for metaphors, as if poverty were not indigenous to the American economy but somehow anomalous and "alien"—precisely the language Harrington used to characterize the world of the poor. Certainly this entailed political calculation—the culture of poverty, after all, would prove far more acceptable to a popular audience than would socialist critique. But it also played into a central tenet of the prevailing liberal consensus: that in the prosperous United States, as Oscar Lewis himself saw it, the problem of poverty could be resolved without significant political or economic restructuring; it called for rehabilitative programs to bring the poor into the social and economic mainstream.

In much the same way, the culture of poverty played into the liberal consensus by suggesting that the United States was no longer riven by the structural divides of class and race—and certainly not of gender—but faced a single, overarching problem of how to deal with the poor population in its midst. Isolated, maladjusted, and politically passive, this deprived population needed the galvanizing force of outside intervention to break what had become an internalized "vicious circle" of physical and cultural deprivation in order to benefit from the opportunities the affluent society could—and would—provide. It was very much in this spirit that the culture of poverty and other social scientific theories of cultural deprivation were taken up by liberal reformers in the late 1950s and early 1960s, first in a series of local community action experiments and then in the War on Poverty. Precisely because of their encounter with the structural problems of race, unemployment, and political power, however, both these experiments and the War on Poverty would reveal the limits of postwar poverty knowledge, and of the liberal "consensus" it helped to reaffirm.

CHAPTER 5

Community Action

IN THE self-consciously behavioral, psychological drift of postwar social science, poverty knowledge was becoming at once more global and more individualized. In many important respects, though, local communities, especially urban neighborhoods, remained essential venues for producing and applying poverty knowledge during the immediate postwar decades. There, with continuing support from national foundations and government agencies, social scientists trained in the methods and theories of urban ethnography resisted the individualizing drift of social problem research to insist that communities rather than individuals should be the units of analysis and reform. A series of community-based experiments sponsored during the 1950s and 1960s by the Ford Foundation, the National Institute of Mental Health (NIMH), and a new Kennedy administration agency, the President's Committee on Juvenile Delinquency (PCJD), illustrate the point. Drawing on more structural and ecological theories of human behavior, these experiments very specifically sought reform at the community and municipal levels to help prevent such problems as juvenile delinquency and inner-city neighborhood decline—eventually to conclude that the underlying problem was poverty and that the solution called for change at the federal as well as the local level of government. In those experiments social scientists reconnected with an earlier, more action-oriented view of knowledge to create what they saw as an alternative, less "psychiatric" theory of poverty that would later be acknowledged as the intellectual basis for an official program of Community Action in the federal government's War on Poverty.[1]

Very much like their Progressive-era counterparts, these later-model experiments in community action treated low-income neighborhoods as laboratories for research-based reform, and as vehicles not only for linking social science with official policy but also for garnering expert and "indigenous" cooperation in achieving community goals. Likewise, they looked upon poor communities as sites for creating a constant flow of new knowledge, understanding reform as an ongoing process of expert social learning and mutual understanding across the social divide. Also like their Progressive counterparts, the community action experiments accommodated a range of sometimes conflicting reform visions, alternating between resident uplift to promote assimilation and community empowerment to agitate for change. Equally important, they helped to solidify the personal networks and the institutional relationships, between local groups and national philanthropy, and between civil society and state agencies, that would help to translate poverty knowledge into policy reform.

And yet, the community-based poverty knowledge of the 1950s and 1960s differed from its Progressive Era counterpart in at least three significant ways. One was that to a far greater degree than the settlement-based reformers, the community action revivalists set themselves quite apart from and in strong opposition to social work practice, setting their sights instead on a concept of "systems reform" that would make individual casework obsolete. Second, they drew their expert leadership not from the ranks of female neighbors and reformers but from a cadre of predominantly male academic and foundation experts. As a result, their efforts were far more consciously and scientifically "experimental" than were Progressive Era studies, and were accompanied by stylized protocols for articulating theory, staging formal planning processes, and conducting evaluations—in the hope of serving as quasi-official "demonstrations" for interventions nationwide.[2] They were also accompanied by a rhetoric that was not only identifiably more scientific, but identifiably more masculine—most prominently the language of strategic intervention, of "guerilla" tactics, and of being out on the urban "firing line," that proponents used in positioning community action as the latest weapon in the war against poverty. Finally, as poverty knowledge, community action had far more to say about problems of cultural adjustment and social organization than about the issues of employment, wages, and work conditions that had absorbed the social surveyors—even though, as social scientists themselves were well aware, the communities they studied were being undermined by changes in the emerging postindustrial economy. Still, on the eve and throughout the early years of the War on Poverty, community action was very much a work-in-progress, part of an evolving concept both of poverty and of poverty research that would only later be overshadowed by an altogether different, more individualized and technocratic, but in its own way equally idealistic, research paradigm.

SOCIAL ECOLOGY REVISITED: THE INTELLECTUAL ROOTS OF COMMUNITY ACTION

At its core, community action was a combination of theory and practice, the former honed in a generation's worth of Chicago-school revisionism, the latter in foundation and government-sponsored efforts to codify and provide theoretical grounding for a type of community-based intervention that dated back to the settlement house. From Chicago-trained sociologists came the basic ecological framework for understanding social problems: as expressions of temporary cultural and social "disorganization" rather than as individual pathology, concentrated in the inner-city neighborhoods where urban newcomers gathered to gain an initial foothold on a trajectory toward assimilation and upward mobility. From various practitioners in the fields of juvenile delinquency and urban planning came a growing appreciation of the structural and systemic problems blocking this idealized vision of urban change. Refining and reshaping the ecological framework in subsequent research and action programs, an initially scattered network of sociologists and urban practitioners came together under the auspices of Ford, the NIMH, and the PCJD to cull the ideas that would later be absorbed into poverty knowledge, as an explanation and a set of action principles for responding to poverty.

One was a concept developed in the work of Chicago-trained sociologist Leonard S. Cottrell, following on an early suggestion by Robert E. Park, that urban neighborhoods lacked the "competence" to nurture and integrate individuals into the larger society. Cottrell, who had contributed to Clifford Shaw's massive study of *Delinquency Areas* in 1929, began developing the idea that only later became known as "community competence" in his subsequent social psychological research on families. In contrast to such Chicago contemporaries as Saul Alinsky, Cottrell took the notion of community reorganization in a more therapeutic than political direction: intervention, as he and coauthor Nelson Foote argued, should aim not so much at rehabilitating individuals as at restoring the family's overall "competence" to nurture individuals capable of functioning in a democracy. That meant a more holistic and "participatory" rather than individual and "passive" approach to healing—an approach Cottrell later developed into criteria for distributing agency funding for community-based antidelinquency demonstration projects when he was appointed as a key advisor to President Kennedy's Committee on Juvenile Delinquency in 1961.[3]

Indeed, Cottrell's role in the genesis of "community competence" from social psychology to delinquency to antipoverty intervention illustrates the importance of interlocking institutional networks in transforming community action, as filtered through Chicago-school social ecology and antidelinquency practice, into official poverty knowledge. Cottrell started his career right in the center of the behavioral science–policy nexus, having served in the U.S. Army's Research Branch as a staff researcher and contributor to Samuel Stouffer's massive survey of the American soldier during World War II. The soldier study was later picked up by the Social Science Research Council, which eventually landed Cottrell a staff position at the then-reorganizing Russell Sage Foundation in 1949, where he became a key research broker in the foundation's shift from "applied" social reform knowledge to "basic" but "mission-oriented" social research.[4] Now a frequently tapped member of SSRC and federal research committees, Cottrell was in a position to establish criteria for funding when the NIMH, in its own attempts to give the field of mental health a less psychiatric, more environmentalist spin, began to sponsor community-based antidelinquency experiments in the late 1950s and invited him to serve on the advisory and proposal review panel.[5] From there it was a natural step to the PCJD—itself an extension of social science and philanthropic networks, with a congressional mandate to make demonstration grants—where Cottrell endorsed what he considered to be the elements of "community competence" as standards for judging proposals: the efforts should be "indigenous," meaning that they were to involve local residents; they should be comprehensive, meaning that they should address the disorganization of community life as well as its individual manifestations; above all, they should aim to make the community more capable of dealing with its own problems—without, by implication, becoming dependent on the services of outside experts.[6] In the intense internal maneuvering for ideas that characterized the Kennedy administration's planning for the War on Poverty, the final link, from delinquency to poverty knowledge, came directly through the PCJD. The "competent community" concept, and its constituent parts, was absorbed into official Community Action Program guidelines.

Although greeted as a novel alternative to professionalized individual therapy, Cottrell's competent community was hardly radical—nor entirely new—as an approach to social reform. Nevertheless, it embodied two key notions—local participation and "indigenous" reform—that would later prove tremendously controversial when applied in the far more politicized context of the War on Poverty. Sociologist Lloyd Ohlin captured only a glimmer of this potential in a paper on urban community reform projects prepared for the Ford Foundation in 1961. On the one hand, Ohlin noted that "indigenous social movements" would serve "to redistribute and broaden the basis of social power and the exercise of authority" in the community. By respecting the subcultural norms and "life styles of the local community," they would also "furnish a buffer to the conformity demands of a mass society." On the other hand, he recognized that the ultimate success of the movements rested on their ability to "reduce pressures toward deviance" and to "heighten the personal investment of members in the established social order."[7] At least at this point indigenous participation—later and better known as "maximum feasible participation"—was attached to a basically amelioristic, culturally assimilative vision of reform.

By the early 1960s, the ideas of "indigenous participation" and building community competence had become firmly entrenched within the leading antidelinquency funding agencies. Meanwhile, Lloyd Ohlin and sociologist Richard Cloward were laying the groundwork for introducing a second key concept into community action and poverty knowledge: the idea that poverty and delinquency stemmed not simply from community "disorganization" but from the "systemic" barriers to legitimate opportunity that kept lower-class neighborhood residents from realizing their middle-class aspirations. Here again they were operating from a revised Chicago-school framework, this time moving in a more explicitly structural direction. Of the two, Ohlin was much more the product of the Chicago school, having learned from Chicago-influenced criminologist Edwin H. Sutherland and subsequently from Park and Burgess about applying theories of social disorganization to criminal behavior. After joining the faculty at the Columbia University School of Social Work in the mid-1950s, Ohlin began to work with Richard Cloward, then a sociology graduate student at the University's Teachers College, who had been heavily influenced by Columbia sociologist Robert K. Merton.[8] Cloward patterned his dissertation after Merton's vastly influential 1938 article entitled "Social Structure and Anomie," which laid out a theory explaining social deviance and criminal behavior as "normal" responses to the "inconsistency" between "culturally-induced success goals" and limited access to the "legitimate" institutional avenues for achieving them.[9] When Ohlin recruited his junior colleague to work on a Ford Foundation project, the stage was set for the integration of Chicago-school social disorganization theory with the Mertonian idea of blocked opportunity structures—and from there, via a major antidelinquency demonstration known as Mobilization for Youth, for its adoption into federally sponsored community action against poverty. The basic argument, as Cloward and Ohlin explained it in *Delinquency and Opportunity* (1960) was that lower-class boys had "differential access" to legitimate *and* illegitimate "structures of opportunity" depending upon the level of organization in the slum communities they lived in. The key to solving the delinquency problem, then, lay not in individuals or subcultures, but in the way the surrounding community was organized. "The target for preventive action," they concluded, "should be defined, not as the individual or group that exhibits the delinquent pattern, but as the social setting that gives rise to the delinquent." For that the starting point was an institutional "reorganization of slum communities," with the objective of providing lower-class youth with legitimate avenues to legitimate success.[10]

Although *Delinquency and Opportunity* never got much more specific about its implications for practice, by the time the book was published in 1960 the theory of differential opportunity structures had already gained wide circulation as *the* cutting-edge explanation for delinquency, with interlocking social science, philanthropic, and federal agency networks playing a key role.[11] Grantees and consultants to the Ford Foundation since 1957, Cloward and Ohlin were hooked into its earliest forays into community action, and by extension into the national obsession with finding a solution to the scourge of juvenile delinquency.[12] More recently, thanks in part to Leonard Cottrell, they had become part of Mobilization for Youth, an initiative started as a joint effort by New York City settlement houses to wage a " 'saturation' campaign against delinquency" on the Lower East Side. After approaching the NIMH for funds, the original settlement-house sponsors were informed that their proposal lacked a coherent theoretical framework. The review panel, chaired by Cottrell, encouraged the settlements to join forces with Cloward and Ohlin, eventually insisting, as a condition of an NIMH planning grant, that they give the sociologists a more prominent role. The result was a substantial overhaul of the original MFY proposal, placing opportunity theory at its center and expanding the original coalition well beyond the settlement house network to include the wide range of social agencies involved in the youth "opportunity system." Amidst considerable contention and internal struggle, the now-transformed MFY coalition proposed to reform the entire "system" for socializing low-income youth—education, vocational training, and social service institutions would have to change—through a combination of its own community-based services and local resident organizing to pressure city hall for institutional change.[13] Only later would MFY's organizing activities be used as evidence of communism, among other "subversive" activities; for now, with help from various Ford Foundation and NIMH supporters, MFY and opportunity theory had the endorsement of local, state, and federal officials, not to mention the liberal social science establishment.[14] In 1962, the reconstituted MFY received a total of $13 million in grants from the NIMH, the Ford Foundation, New York City, and the recently established President's Committee on Juvenile Delinquency to launch the federal government's first major community action demonstration. By then, Ohlin had agreed to join the PCJD as its chief research consultant, paving the way for making opportunity theory a part of the War on Poverty.

While delinquency networks were consolidating around opportunity theory, urban planners were working on a separate but parallel track to explore the possibilities of community action as a vehicle for a third concept that would be absorbed into poverty knowledge: comprehensive "systems reform." The reference point for their efforts went beyond delinquency and other manifestations of community "disorganization" to the social structural changes reshaping postwar American cities: industrial decentralization, white middle-class suburbanization, and, especially, the steady stream of Appalachian, African American, and Latino "new" migrants arriving to fill up "old" immigrant neighborhoods. Often unacknowledged in the behavioral sciences literature, these large-scale changes were a central preoccupation among big-city mayors, urban planners, and the handful of journalists who, like *Fortune* magazine's Charles A. Silberman, were regulars on the urban beat. While largely preoccupied with issues of metropolitan governance and the "bricks and mortar" of urban renewal, these urbanologists were also trying to come to grips with the "human face" of the new metropolitan reality with programs to help the new migrants assimilate. In community action, they saw an opportunity to achieve at least two goals at once: a comprehensive, integrated approach to providing services; and a platform for encouraging broader urban "systems reform."[15]

Informed though it was by Chicago-school concepts of the migration process, the postwar movement for urban systems reform rested on an important revision of the ecological model of urban growth. The product of newer and more applied disciplines such as urban planning and public administration, this revised vision emerged not in academic settings or urban "laboratories" but in the decidedly applied context of the postwar struggle for urban renewal and redevelopment. In the Chicago-school model, urban growth was a story of industrial development, which began in the innermost loop of the city and radiated outward in the inevitable process of industrial expansion. While destructive in its impact on residential neighborhoods, industrial expansion in the larger scheme of things was an essential component of the city's vitality and made the inner city itself the center of a growing economy. In contrast, the revised understanding of urban change was grounded in the accelerating processes of economic restructuring and technological change that were taking industrial growth centers outside the city core, which was itself shifting its base to information and financial services. In the new, decidedly more pessimistic understanding, the central city faced a future not of growth but of economic and social "obsolescence": abandoned by industrial manufactures, middle-class suburbanites, and upwardly mobile immigrants alike, those old Chicago-school "zones of transition" were becoming dead ends for the host of black, brown, and "white ethnic" migrants streaming in from the South. In a phrase coined by economist Raymond Vernon and later picked up by the Ford Foundation, they became known—with veiled reference to their racial composition—as the "gray areas" of the inner city. It was in the hope of restoring the "gray areas" to their original "ecological" or assimilative function that Ford and other funding agencies sought to make community action a kind of catalyst for more wholesale urban governance and social welfare systems reform. The first step, they determined, was to modernize outdated social service institutions in light of the "new" migrants' needs. Now, more than ever, social agencies needed to work as an integrated, comprehensive system for addressing a whole complex of interrelated problems, ranging from education to mental health, suffered by a population both poor and culturally deprived.[16]

The NIMH played an early and pivotal role in mobilizing intellectual energy behind the blend of community action and urban systems reform, in this instance under the auspices of its long-range planning division, directed by physician, psychiatrist, and former Public Health Services worker Dr. Leonard Duhl. Critical of the drift in mental health toward psychiatry and individual psychotherapy, Duhl's division was at the forefront of a more "environmentalist" approach in the field. Through it and other more specifically focused research programs, the NIMH was becoming an important source of funding for research on the urban lower class—most notably, aside from the work on delinquency, in exploring the sociological and social psychological impact of urban renewal and of large-scale public housing.[17] In May 1956, Duhl hosted the initial meeting of what was to become an eleven-year consultation with an interdisciplinary group of research consultants who called themselves the "Space Cadets" (in a tongue-in-cheek comparison between theirs and the mission of Soviet astronauts aboard Sputnik), joining biologists, physicists, city planners, and social scientists into a kind of "invisible college" for the agency planning division, and a scientific sounding board for emerging NIMH policy initiatives in juvenile delinquency, housing, urban renewal, and, later, poverty. As a culmination of their communal enterprise, the Space Cadets produced an edited volume entitled *The Urban Condition* in the early 1960s, in which Duhl laid out the core assumptions and implications of a view that linked the new understanding of urban change to an ecological understanding of social problems. Issues traditionally defined as behavioral problems could no longer be thought of as individual matters, Duhl noted in his introduction to the volume, but instead should be understood in terms of their community of origin, with their own "community of solution." Looked at within the "vast complexity" of the "total urban environment," delinquency, poverty, and related problems were part of a larger systems failure that kept cities bogged down in the old fragmented way of doing things. Equally important, Duhl presented the need for rational planning and "systems change" as a demand for the more interdisciplinary, politically engaged, action-oriented, and what he saw as the potentially more democratic, form of research that both the NIMH, and the community action experiments more generally, were in a position to cultivate.[18]

More visible as a practical program for urban systems reform was the Ford Foundation's enormously ambitious Gray Areas program, officially launched in 1961–62 with a series of community planning and action grants to five midsize cities and the state of North Carolina.[19] Several years in the making, the Gray Areas program was steeped in the fundamentals of community action, but it also differed from its counterpart in the field of juvenile delinquency in important ways. Committed, at least nominally, to indigenous participation, Gray Areas was actually far more concerned about making services more comprehensive and efficient than about involving community residents in bringing about the reforms. Like the "executive-centered" urban mayoralties it funded, the program adopted an unapologetically top-down approach—in which the foundation, and other elite institutions established for the purpose, would act as outside "catalysts" to spark systemwide change.[20] By all accounts its most successful program was New Haven's, which under the directorship of local labor organizer Mitchell Sviridoff had set up an impressive array of education, youth, and legal services programs and, through the operations of a private, nonprofit organization known as Community Progress, Inc., was managing to goad the established services bureaucracy into better coordination. New Haven was much less successful, though, when it came to citizen participation; community organizing was simply not a priority. Moreover, while basically compatible with opportunity theory, the Gray Areas program looked elsewhere for its theoretical frame. In its view of the community residents as unassimilated migrants, Gray Areas was pure Chicago school. Himself impatient with detached academic theorizing, Gray Areas program director Paul Ylvisaker had come to this less as an application of theory than as a rationale for the foundation's urban and "youth development" programs. The underlying problem in poor urban neighborhoods, Ylvisaker thought, was the city's failure to assimilate its "backwoods" migrants into the urban mainstream. Minimizing—in part due to internal foundation politics—the structural and racial barriers they faced, Gray Areas played up cultural deprivation as an overriding common denominator in poor communities—at one point organizing special workshops for urban law enforcement and social service professionals to tour the deprived southern communities whence their new clientele had embarked.

Despite occasional tensions within the emerging community action movement, on several key points the various experimental programs were very much in sync: about the need for new or dramatically reformed social service "systems"; about social science as an agent of reform; about neighborhood participation as a form of consensus-building if not actual organizing; and, about the collective nature of the learning-by-demonstration process—a commitment that prevented too much hardening of positions at the outset. So, too, were the NIMH, the Ford Foundation, and the PCJD convergent in their institutional stance: as newcomers to social service provision (the Ford Foundation, having gone national with its huge Ford Motor Company endowment just after World War II, had none of the connections to old charitable philanthropy that Russell Sage, Rockefeller, and even Carnegie had) they positioned themselves as "change agents" in the field. With this in mind, and with the help of an ever-expanding network of social scientists, urban planners, local citizens groups, a few good government politicians, and federal agency bureaucrats, Ylvisaker, Duhl, Cottrell, and other "idea brokers" worked assiduously to put community action—in all its variations—on the federal policy map. They also looked around in the federal bureaucracy to find and shake loose the scattered resources that, they argued, would be far more effective in the hands of knowledgeable community leaders prepared to administer them comprehensively. Most important, from the standpoint of poverty knowledge, they committed substantial resources to building and creating the norms for what they saw as a new kind of knowledge—hands-on, activist, practical as well as theoretical, and, more often than not, produced as part of the ongoing process of community action rather than in more traditional academic venues. It was in the course of this ongoing process, of community action as political as well as social learning, that community action began to shift its own language and frame of reference, from delinquency and Gray Areas to poverty.

LEARNING FROM COMMUNITY ACTION: THE LIMITS OF SOCIAL SCIENCE AND REFORM

Bold though it may have been in its vision of social science as a "change agent," community action rested on what, within the liberal social scientific tradition, was a fairly conventional idea of the poor—based on community and environmental rather than individual analysis; on concepts of cultural deprivation, social "disorganization," and the inadequacy of social service systems rather than of structural inequalities. True to its (however much revised) Chicago-school origins, community action continued to absorb race and class differences within this conceptual scheme, while embracing assimilation to the existing social and economic order as its ultimate goal for the poor. Nor was community action especially, or inherently, radical as a process for bringing about change. Even the most "bottom-up" of the experiments started out with a somewhat apolitical idea of rational, comprehensive planning as the essential community action approach. These, indeed, were the very features that made community action pass political muster—first within the ranks of funding agencies and then among liberal but cautious bureaucratic planners within the Kennedy and Johnson administrations.

And yet, these were also the very features of community action that came under challenge during the first stages of social and political learning in 1961–63, when the experiments actually got off the ground. The experience did not so much change as sharpen and politicize the underlying analysis—including the tensions within it—while anticipating the issues that eventually would confound community action as a strategy and a knowledge base for addressing poverty.

The most immediate and obvious "lessons" community action evaluators remarked on had to do with the enormous degree of political and bureaucratic resistance to rational systems reform.[21] Some of this had to do with resentment of the outside "change agents," but for evaluators the real culprit was a combination of bureaucratic inertia and interagency rivalry. Indeed, having been mandated by Congress to fund local demonstration and action programs, the President's Committee on Juvenile Delinquency review board was so struck by the apparent lack of local interagency cooperation that it risked disapproval from Congress and sent all of its initial grant applicants back to the drawing board with one-year planning grants instead.[22] Nor, despite its close affiliation with Attorney General Robert F. Kennedy, did the PCJD have the leverage to get much coordination, cooperation, or program funding from the more established federal agencies, putting the committee in the politically uncomfortable position of having money to fund no more than four or five of the sixteen communities that had earlier won planning grants.[23] The experience left PCJD executive director David Hackett intensely frustrated—and eventually provided ammunition for the argument that none of the existing "old line" federal agencies was capable of directing the War on Poverty.

The issue of "indigenous" or resident participation raised a second dilemma for community action, stemming on the one hand from vagueness and ambivalence about its purpose, and on the other from community action's underlying view of the poor. Despite their belief in the value and importance of "indigenous" participation, community action theorists had not been specific about how it was to be achieved. For Leonard Cottrell, coming from the mental health perspective, resident or indigenous participation meant breaking down the distinctions between expert and client in the therapeutic process of building community competence, beginning with a cooperative effort to identify problems and arrive at consensus on goals. For the "executive-centered" mayors and planning experts engaged in urban renewal and systems reform, however, participation was primarily a mechanism for gaining consent for centralized redevelopment plans. Meanwhile, local organizers, including those associated with community action projects, were looking elsewhere for models and advice. Many turned to Saul Alinsky, who earlier had broken off from the Chicago-school affiliated Chicago Area Project to establish the Back of the Yards neighborhood council and, not long after, the Industrial Areas Foundation. For Alinsky, resident participation meant political organizing and genuinely local autonomy—not, as was so often the case, control "by outside groups whose basic interests are, in the final analysis, either not identified with or opposed to the objectives sought by the people 'back of the yards.' "[24] Alinsky's approach also acknowledged the conflicting interests among class and ethnic groups and sought to exploit those acknowledged differences in the process of building stronger community organization. Of all the prevailing models Alinsky's most forcefully challenged the notion that neighborhood residents were culturally deprived. Nothing proved more powerful as an immediate source of inspiration and tactics, though, than the unstoppable momentum of the civil rights movement in the South, with its language of rights and brilliant use of public demonstration to provoke official action. Like Alinsky, the civil rights movement appealed to emerging notions of neighborhood empowerment that were beginning to sharpen internal tensions within and between the different community action experiments. At Mobilization For Youth, the program to "Organize the Unaffiliated" caused a rift within the founding coalition by confronting city hall and the social welfare establishment with tactics such as rent strikes, sit-ins, school boycotts, and mass demonstrations beginning in 1963. The basic tensions—between "top-down" and "bottom-up," cultural rehabilitation and empowerment, resident involvement and resident control— were to continue throughout the history of community action, with important repercussions for poverty knowledge: for while Alinsky-style organizing drew tremendous political fire during the War on Poverty, so, too, from a different direction, would the social scientific concept of a culture of poverty.

Complicating and inextricably tied to the problems of participation and empowerment in community action was the deeply divisive issue of race. But race posed an even more fundamental challenge, for while continually raised within the context of racial in- or ex-clusion, the encounter with race in the demonstration projects revealed a basic conceptual flaw in community action and its sociological roots.[25] The problem was obliquely captured in the language of "Gray Areas" itself, which Paul Ylvisaker and others recognized as a way of maneuvering around rather than confronting directly the problems of racial conflict and discrimination. At the time, Ylvisaker recalled, he was operating under a strict but unspoken racial "embargo" imposed by the controversy-shy Ford Foundation trustees. But on a more basic level the problem was built into the assimilation framework community action embraced, as captured by journalist and *Fortune* magazine editor Charles Silberman in his book *Crisis in Black and White* (1964). Silberman wrote about the exclusion of African Americans from community action planning, pointing out that the "academicians, government officials, and 'civic leaders' " who drew up the plans routinely failed to consult "the people being planned for . . . as if the residents of a Negro slum needed to be told what their problems are!" Calling the Gray Areas program a "grandiose fusion of paternalism and bureaucracy," he criticized the Ford Foundation for ignoring the basic conflicts of economic and political interest as well as the deep-seated racism separating blacks, working-class whites, and well-endowed white institutions. But Silberman's book—written, as he acknowledged, with funding and cooperation from the Ford Foundation—was equally damning in its analysis of the "white liberal" assumptions underlying Gray Areas, and above all the analysis that "makes no distinction between the problems faced by Negroes and those faced by other contemporary migrants." The expectation that blacks would be assimilated just like past and current generations of white ethnics ignored "the central fact," Silberman wrote, that "the Negro is unlike any other immigrant group in one crucial regard: he is colored." For Silberman, the failure to confront this "central fact"—not only of racism but of its structural dimensions—was "white liberal" community action's fatal flaw.[26] This, too, was a flaw that would continue to haunt both community action and poverty knowledge, as the concepts of social "disorganization" and cultural deprivation became increasingly racialized.

   Community action's experimental phase also presented a direct challenge to the actual practice of social science, as knowledge demands expanded from conceptualization and planning to evaluation. To some degree the challenge was methodological: how to arrive at concrete, measurable indicators of success for programs that were by definition interactive, process-oriented, and most likely subject to unanticipated changes?[27] Despite the investments they made in evaluation, neither the Ford Foundation nor the PCJD were of much help in the matter. Ford's ever-widening network of outside evaluators, paid consultants, and informal observers remained essentially without guidance with regard to the criteria for success, and efforts to develop a systematic evaluative framework for Gray Areas programs were sporadic. The real barriers to evaluation were more political than methodological, however, as it became increasingly clear that social scientists and practitioners were pursuing different, if not conflicting, interests. "The action-oriented professional has regularly lambasted the ivory tower, whose inhabitants supposedly spend all their time gathering data aimed not at solving concrete human problems, but at building bigger and better theories to be discussed at stuffy conferences and debated in unreadable journals," wrote North Carolina Fund director Michael P. Brooks in an article reflecting on the tension. "The researcher, for his part, is often heard belittling the action-oriented practitioner for his failure to conceptualize clearly, for his inability to think in terms of systems; for his tendency to act on the basis of subjective whims or impressions; . . . and for his apparent fear of evaluation on the grounds that it might call his own actions into question."[28] Even had the demonstration projects been subjected to the most scientifically rigorous type of evaluation, however, it is doubtful whether their sponsors had the capacity to absorb and act on the lessons. For one thing the time frame was far too short—no community-based project could reasonably be expected to produce "results" within two years. Nevertheless, and more importantly, the political demand was for quick and visible results, and the emphasis on gaining notice in Washington. Under these circumstances, community action's early success would be measured more on its degree of innovation than on its capacity—or incapacity—to effect change.

Even at this early stage, then, the local demonstration projects highlighted the limitations of community action as a conceptual as well as a practical social scientific frame. Visions of cooperative, rational planning ran up against the realities of political infighting and bureaucratic resistance. Resident participation brought notions of cultural deprivation under scrutiny and political challenge, but it also raised the question of whether community action could happen without a challenge to authority. The belief that race could be understood or addressed within the "neutral" context of migration was quickly shattered by the experience of racial conflict and resistance, while structural economic conditions raised the question of whether systems reform alone was enough to change the "opportunity structures" in increasingly nonwhite, urban, working-class neighborhoods. Finally, community action's experimental idealism—its belief that change could be achieved in a scientific process of planning, experimentation, assessment, and knowledge application—was itself being challenged by the incompatibilities between the scientific objectives of research and the political demands upon action. Meanwhile, community action proponents were faced with the political pressures of sustaining support for their efforts and attracting more resources for the experimental programs. It was in this context, of experience, bureaucratic frustration, and political need, that they began to search for a more powerful institutional base from which to launch community action as an instrument of social policy and social reform, and to revise their conceptual framework to focus on the root causes of urban social problems. They found what they were looking for in 1963, when officials in the Kennedy and Johnson administrations started to gear up for a war on poverty.

PART TWO

CHAPTER 6

In the Midst of Plenty: The Political Economy
of Poverty in the Affluent Society

"THE WORDS 'poverty' and 'poor,' although on the threshold of revival, were not parts of the public language," wrote sociologist Hylan Lewis of the years immediately preceding the War on Poverty. The problems were there, he went on to say, "but society chose not to see them—or at least not to call them that."[1] In sociological and anthropological literature the poor were referred to as the "lower-lower classes," the "culturally deprived," urban "newcomers," and only more recently as victims of a "culture of poverty." In economics, poverty was barely recognized as a subject worthy of study; it had been lost, as economist Theodore Schultz wrote in 1964, "for want of a theory."[2] Even in applied research the poor were more likely to be recognized—if at all—as part of some broader economic or social problem, as were the "low-income" families featured in hearings sponsored by Congressman John Sparkman in 1949, the residents of "depressed areas" in the drive for the Area Redevelopment Act of 1961, and the "structurally unemployed" in analyses behind the Manpower Development and Training Act of 1962.[3] "Poverty," as such, was not yet seen as a distinctive social problem, much less as the target of a concerted government attack.

It was thus with a tone of outrage and discovery, and no small degree of political calculation, that social scientists and social critics began to draw attention to the problem of poverty in the early 1960s. Within the Kennedy administration, it was economists, led by Chairman of the Council of Economic Advisers (CEA) Walter Heller, who were leading the charge. Heller and his CEA colleagues were the chief spokesmen in favor of an "attack on poverty" as a central component of a Kennedy domestic policy for the upcoming election year of 1964.[4] But they were also engaged in a struggle to define the poverty problem on their own terms—as a problem, that is, that could be addressed within the boundaries, indeed, as a constituent part, of the broader economic agenda they had been pursuing since 1961. The aims of this agenda—faster growth and full employment—were to be achieved by means of a massive individual and corporate tax cut. Growth, economists reasoned, would be the single most effective weapon against poverty. Meanwhile, an added, more targeted set of programs for the poor would help to deflect the critics of the growth agenda, who pointed to evidence of a presumably new form of poverty that would not respond to growth alone. Thus, it was in a process of political, social scientific, and interagency negotiation that administration economists, uncomfortable with psychological renditions of a problem they sought to remedy with economic measures, nevertheless came to incorporate the notion of a culture of poverty and a set of remedies for it—community action—within the blueprint for the War on Poverty in 1964. In the process, they laid out the basic elements of a new political economy of poverty which, in looking to individuals as the source of the poverty problem, had more in common with the culture of poverty than with the political economy of Progressive reform.

POVERTY KNOWLEDGE AND THE "NEW ECONOMICS": KENNEDY'S CEA

Although dubbed the "new economics" in the press, the ideas Kennedy's CEA brought to Washington were actually rooted in developments that had been reshaping the field since the 1930s and that lay behind the articulation of a new political economy of poverty in the 1960s.[5] The most prominent trend was the "Keynesian Revolution" that had swept the discipline in the wake of the Depression and World War II. Keynes had revolutionized economic policy thinking in several ways, in particular by paving the way for such controversial policy measures as deficit spending—a virtual guarantee that Keynesianism would meet with considerable resistance in Washington—while at the same time shifting the emphasis of liberal economic reform from monopoly and market regulation to increased consumer capacity, full employment, and above all, growth, as mechanisms for maintaining a stable economy. Never a single "school" of thought, American Keynesianism had shifted from an initial, New Deal emphasis on expanded redistributive public spending and aggressive full employment guarantees to a heavier reliance on market-driven growth and "compensatory" social welfare policy during the immediate postwar years. Though reined in from the initial New Deal reform vision, this "commercial Keynesianism" still marked a significant departure from older economic orthodoxies.[6] Enough so that, despite its sweeping success in most of the postwar academic world, the "new economics" had a much harder time penetrating Washington policy making circles in the 1940s and 1950s. Kennedy's CEA arrived in Washington determined to win acceptance for their ideas, and especially determined to use government policy to stimulate faster economic growth and full employment—in their minds, the most powerful weapons against poverty.[7]

A second trend shaping the thinking of Kennedy's CEA was the postwar "revival" of neoclassical labor market theory, which by the late 1950s had largely displaced the once-dominant institutionalist tradition in the field of labor economics. The neoclassical revival marked an attempt to return labor studies to its earlier grounding in the theory of competitive markets developed in the late nineteenth century by British economist Alfred Marshall, posing a challenge to the institutionalist tradition and to its central premise that laws, social policy, firm practices, and trade unions were more important in determining wages and productivity than were the naturalistic laws of supply and demand.[8] By the 1930s, the neoclassical revival was gaining momentum in the U.S., embraced first by a generation of economists who accepted the basic market framework but sought to refine it with a greater sense of "realism" about the constraints that prevented workers from acting as rationally "maximizing" free agents, and then by a group of hard-liners who put market forces at the very center of human activity.[9] By the mid to late 1950s, the more hard-line group, including Milton Friedman, Jacob Mincer, Gary Becker, and Theodore Schultz at the University of Chicago, was establishing itself at the forefront of labor economics. Critical of the institutionalists and the labor market "realists" for their failure to develop alternative theories, this Chicago school used the neoclassical market model to explain, and, more important, to predict, all aspects of labor market behavior and outcomes. The result was a simplified, streamlined view of labor market operations that, in sharp contrast to the institutionalist view, attributed wage rates and workforce behavior to the immutable laws of supply and demand, assumed conditions of perfect competition, and regarded trade unions and other regulatory agencies as barriers to the ultimate goal of market efficiency. By highlighting market forces, neoclassical theorists diminished the importance of institutional practices and politics as factors in shaping economic outcomes. At the same time, they exaggerated the role of rational choice, individual behavior, and the level playing field by assuming that workers should be viewed in the same light as their profit-maximizing employers, as rational actors operating without constraints to maximize their own individual self-interest. This rational, individualized worldview was at the heart of human capital theory, which was a hallmark of the neoclassical revival, and its major link to the study of poverty in the 1960s.

In its emphasis on competitive markets, human capital theory complemented the direction taken by postwar Keynesians in the U.S. While "commercial Keynesianism" suggested that economists could manipulate "demand side" factors without too much direct interference in the private market, human capital theory showed liberals how market principles could be applied on the "supply side" to expand opportunity without massive redistribution. Individuals in the labor market operated along the same principles as physical capital, according to the theory, making rational choices to invest in their own education and training for the greater returns it would bring in the future. Such personal investments had become increasingly important to national wealth as well as individual well-being, they argued, adding not just to individual earnings but, by improving productivity, to overall economic growth. The gains made by American workers, that is to say, should be understood not as the product of institutional factors such as unions, government policy, or firm practices, but as market returns to individual investments. Similarly, individual skills and behavior, not institutional practices or sociological factors, could explain both differences in earnings and why people were poor. Conservative though it may have been in its implications, human capital theory caused greatest intellectual excitement among liberals, as a justification for social investment in education and training as the key to individual mobility and to higher aggregate productivity.[10] Most important, it made fighting poverty, through human capital investments, compatible with economic growth.

Accompanying the Keynesian and human capital "revolutions" was a third development in postwar economics that also shaped the character of poverty knowledge in Kennedy's CEA: an increasing emphasis on mathematical theory and quantification, spurred along by expanding computer capacity and by sophisticated econometric methodology, which promised to make economics a more precise science. This rising "scientism" had a profound impact on academic economics in general, as later reflected in the almost complete turn to quantification as a language of mathematical equations—as itself the stuff of analysis—rather than as one means of presenting documentary evidence. Along with the movement to revive neoclassical theory, this approach to quantification put a premium on large secondary data sources such as the census and on a certain type of analysis, one very different from the historical, hands-on, and case study approaches favored in institutionalist economics and in the social survey. In contrast, "scientific" economic analysis would revolve around market-driven models and quantitatively "testable" hypotheses—in turn fueling a demand for more and better data suited to the specifications of neoclassical models.[11] The impact of such modeling was equally important in the policy realm, for it heightened the confidence of economic policy practitioners in their own ability to predict economic performance and to translate complex social and economic processes into quantifiable, achievable policy goals—4 percent unemployment and, within a generation, 0 percent poverty.[12] And they would use it in arriving at a "scientific" definition of poverty that could similarly translate into a realizable policy goal.

Kennedy's first CEA appointees, Walter Heller, Kermit Gordon, and James Tobin, were also caught up in the political and institutional changes that would have a profound impact on poverty knowledge by giving economics greater prominence in shaping the postwar social and economic policy world. Having entered the profession during the Depression and World War II, Heller and his colleagues had a firsthand appreciation of the significance of the Employment Act of 1946 to their profession: By establishing the Council of Economic Advisors and the Joint Economic Committee of Congress, the Employment Act opened the door to a more central and institutionalized role for professional economists in articulating and adhering to national economic goals.[13] They were also convinced that their predecessors had failed to realize the CEA's full policy potential.[14] Armed, then, with the theories and methods that had been incubating in academe for two decades, they were determined to make the "new economics" the basis of a more informed, activist policy regime.[15]

In the new economics, then, liberals found a powerful analytic and institutional platform from which to wage a national campaign against poverty. The impact on the subsequent trajectory of poverty knowledge was immense. First and foremost, the new economics made the struggle against poverty compatible with lightly managed, if not free-market, capitalist growth. The new economics also provided a central theoretical framework—neoclassical labor market theory—from which economists and, later, sociologists, began in the mid-1960s to generate "testable hypotheses" and to build an expanding program of poverty research.[16] The ubiquity of the neoclassical model as a way of explaining the causes and consequences of poverty—alternately labeled human capital, social capital, or cultural capital—indicates the extent to which that central theoretical framework still prevails. So, too, does the overwhelming emphasis on individual-level attributes as "causes" of poverty, an emphasis that avoids recognition of politics, institutions, or structural inequality. Poverty is "transmitted," in this approach, when individuals "inherit" traits from their parents; it "persists" when individuals and families remain poor for a long time; it is a characteristic of poor people, not of the economy, and is reproduced through individual behavior, not through policies or institutions or social relationships that perpetuate inequality over time. The new economics also introduced a particular mode of analysis to the study of poverty, one based on model-building and hypothesis-testing, on quantitative and secondary rather than ethnographic and case study research, and on the individual rather than the community as the unit of analysis. This new political economy, presumably more neutral, scientific, and nonideological than the old, was eventually embraced by administration policy makers as an alternative to the increasingly action-oriented direction being taken by community-based sociological research. This reversal of fortunes was not, however, the simple triumph of objective "science" over partisan "ideology"—after all, Chicago-school sociology had not long before used the mantle of objectivity to establish its claim as a superior form of social knowledge. It was the result of an extended, highly contested, inherently political process of problem-definition, policy planning, and what became known as "social R&D" in the Great Society welfare state—beginning with the CEA's own efforts to gain acceptance for its Keynesian program for achieving universal prosperity and perpetual growth.

THE CEA, POVERTY, AND THE GROWTH AGENDA

The starting point for the CEA's analysis of poverty was the problem of growth: slow growth and high aggregate unemployment during the Eisenhower administration, they argued, were the chief culprits behind poverty; faster growth would provide the key to wiping it out. Indeed, the fight against poverty was announced as only one, somewhat belated part of the overall plan to "restore momentum" to Eisenhower's slack economy and to revive full employment and government-stimulated growth as chief policy goals.[17] To achieve this Keynesian, growth-centered agenda, the economists first had to reinvigorate the CEA itself as a policymaking institution following its eight-year slumber under the Republicans. Most of all, as Heller recalled, "we had to sell modern fiscal policy to an unbelieving and highly suspicious public."[18] The new way of thinking about the economy, they promised, held the key to a future of managed prosperity and to the goal of reducing, if not eliminating, poverty as well.

Heller and his colleagues faced a number of early barriers to achieving their growth-centered agenda, not the least of which was Kennedy's own conservatism when it came to deficits and spending as ways of stimulating the economy. Much to the dismay of his economic advisors, Kennedy pledged to balance the budget in his 1961 State of the Union address, leaving them with little room to mount what they'd hoped would be an aggressive antirecession spending and tax cut program—and still less for the growth measures required to "lift all boats"—as the saying goes—out of poverty.[19]

The CEA encountered a second, more lasting barrier in the form of competing economic ideas, most notably in an alternative analysis of unemployment that threatened to stop the high-growth agenda before it got off the ground. This analysis, increasingly popular among economic conservatives as well as left-liberals in the labor movement, held that unemployment was a "structural" rather than an aggregate growth problem and hence would not respond to the simple solvent of more growth. The conservative version of the argument was largely based in concerns about inflation, and insisted that there was a certain, relatively high plateau of unemployment—5–6 percent—below which inflation would begin to rise too far and too fast. Labor's version of the argument, on the other hand, arose out of concerns about the impact of automation on employment levels, and came to the opposite policy conclusion. Structural change, technology, and, especially, automation were responsible for persistently high unemployment rates, the argument went, and threatened to render industrial, low-skilled, and, especially, minority workers unwanted and obsolete. In a debate that would continually resurface over the future course of antipoverty policy, the left-liberal analysts called for more aggressive job creation, retraining, direct labor market interventions, and minimum income guarantees in response to poverty and unemployment—proposals that went well beyond the CEA's aggregate growth strategy.[20] The immediate challenge in 1961, as the CEA saw it, was to disprove the structural unemployment analysis altogether, quashing the idea that it was impossible or undesirable to reduce unemployment without a direct government role in creating new jobs.

Heller and his colleagues countered these barriers with a combination of statistical analysis, education, public relations, and political compromise that would have important consequences for the future course of poverty knowledge and policy. They were willing, for example, to give up on "the expenditure route" to stimulating growth, acknowledging a history of "unsuccessful efforts to get expenditure increases out of Congress" and nodding to the "political constraints of the day." Instead, they concentrated on drumming up support for a major, unprecedented series of tax cuts as a way to stimulate growth. "The real choice," as CEA economist Arthur Okun later put it, "was between tax cuts and no fiscal stimulus at all."[21] The CEA economists also worked quickly to establish their credibility as analysts, backing their positions with an impressive array of statistical tables and quickly outflanking their counterparts in the administration as a ready source of reliable information. Here the CEA had two distinct advantages: access to the latest available government data; and, especially important, a staff of recruits from top academic departments who were schooled in the latest econometric techniques. Staff economist (later Nobel laureate) Robert Solow constructed a detailed statistical refutation of the structural unemployment concept for the CEA's 1961 Economic Report, which was updated annually for the next several years. Arthur Okun published what is widely considered to be a groundbreaking article on the concept of "potential GNP" while a CEA staff member, in which he measured the "gap" between actual and potential economic output by calculating what the economy could produce at full employment. Such analyses provided the intellectual—and statistical—justification for a more activist approach to economic growth, while minimizing the necessity of structural measures to combat long-term unemployment and poverty. They were also important in linking poverty to the achievement of concrete, numerical policy goals—4 rather than 5 percent employment, and 4 rather than 2 or 3 percent economic growth.[22]

Public relations was another part of the CEA strategy, extending within and outside the administration. An especially able "policy entrepreneur," Heller proved adept at briefing the President on CEA analyses and positions in a steady stream of concise, readable memos. Heller's CEA was also adept at packaging old Keynesian ideas in appealing "new" concepts like "constructive deficit," "fiscal drag," "full employment surplus" and the "output gap." Reversing the removed stance taken by his Republican predecessors, Heller made frequent appearances in Congress and was active on the public speaking circuit. Skeptical at first, the press soon got caught up in the spirit, coining the "new economics" appellation in 1962 and serving, as Okun recalled, "as the textbook for the biggest course in elementary macroeconomics ever presented." The upshot of all this activity was a virtual "tutorial" in the new economics, with the public, the Congress, corporate America, and the Cabinet as pupils, and the president himself at the head of the class.[23]

By 1962, the CEA was beginning to make significant progress, and to build support for the $10 billion personal and corporate tax cut that had become the centerpiece of its growth agenda. In June, Kennedy officially abandoned his attachment to balanced budget orthodoxy when he delivered the commencement speech at Yale University. In July, *Newsweek* reported growing momentum behind the tax cut idea, listing the Chamber of Commerce labor leader Walter Reuther, and several business figures among its backers and even acknowledging its origins in the "new economics." In August, the president announced that he would propose the CEA's tax cut in 1963.[24] The new economics was on its way to becoming the new economic orthodoxy in Washington. Thus far, though, the CEA had taken little time to develop a full-fledged analysis and program for addressing the issue that was beginning to crop up with greater frequency among critics of the CEA's growth-oriented policy: the problem of poverty.

POVERTY AND THE LIMITS OF GROWTH

The nation's "discovery" of poverty owed a great deal to the journalistic depictions of mass deprivation that began to appear in the early 1960s, but it can also be traced to a debate about liberal political economy—and specifically about the limits of growth—that took place largely outside the realm of the popular media.

The first traces of the relevant debate could be seen in John Kenneth Galbraith's *The Affluent Society* (1958), a hugely popular book that started out as a project to explain "why people are poor" and developed into a penetrating critique of the excesses of growth, the materialism of American consumer culture, and of the liberal mindset that helped to bring them about. In the end, "poverty" per se received scant mention in a lengthy manuscript. Nevertheless, what Galbraith had to say set off a series of responses that would eventually develop into a debate among liberals about the potential and the limits of growth as a strategy against poverty.

Galbraith himself was no stranger to the Kennedy policy establishment. One of a number of intellectuals who had actively advised and supported Adlai Stevenson for president in 1956, Galbraith had been among the first to endorse Kennedy's candidacy in the 1960 primary, and he remained a close advisor after the election. As Kennedy's ambassador to India, he was on the fringes of economic policy decision making, however, and could generally be relied upon to articulate a position to the left of the CEA. His opposition to the proposed tax cut should have come as no surprise; he had been arguing in favor of increased government spending and redistribution for years.

In fact, Galbraith's main target in *The Affluent Society* was precisely the liberal political economy that the CEA espoused. Specifically, he criticized the "conventional wisdom" that had led postwar liberals to give up on redistribution in favor of continuous growth as the solution to "all the social problems of the day."[25] The single-minded pursuit of growth had created a whole litany of new problems, according to Galbraith, including inflation, excessive consumer debt, the corporate concentration of power, the rise of the military-industrial complex, and a starved public sector. There was a "curious unevenness" to American life, captured brilliantly in Galbraith's imagery of the well-fed (on convenience food) American family driving a cadillac on badly paved roads, alongside "blighted" inner cities, through a polluted environment. But nowhere was the unevenness more evident than in what he called the "new position" of poverty in this affluent society. Aggregate growth had not brought "an end to poverty and privation for all," as the conventional wisdom held. Instead, growth had produced something new: "a self-perpetuating margin of poverty at the very base of the income pyramid." For the first time in history, poverty was a characteristic of a few rather than the many; what was once a "general affliction" was now a "residual" problem, an "afterthought" affecting a "voiceless minority" who had proved immune to the benefits of economic growth.[26]

In a manner befitting such an "afterthought," Galbraith buried his discussion of the "new" poverty near the back of his book and offered a somewhat dismissive analysis. Using a poverty line of $1,000—one-half the amount used by a congressional subcommittee a decade earlier—he estimated that less than 10 percent of the population could be categorized as poor.[27] Underscoring the gap between the poor minority and the prosperous majority, Galbraith cast the poor in familiar stereotypical terms: the "case poor" as the "farm family with the junk-filled yard and the dirty children playing in the bare dirt," there because of "mental deficiency, bad health, inability to adapt to the discipline of industrial life, uncontrollable procreation, alcohol" or other personal deficiencies; or the "insular" poor stuck in "islands" of deprivation such as Appalachia, unable to get out because of inadequate education, racial discrimination, or the absence of support services.[28] Neither group would benefit from the general rise in income promised by growth advocates, since "[t]o spend income requires a minimum of character and intelligence." And yet Galbraith was less concerned about poor people's behavior than about the political economy that left them marginalized in the first place. An attack on poverty, according to Galbraith, would require a complete reordering of economic priorities, away from growth for its own sake and towards redistribution for the sake of "social balance."[29]

Galbraith's contention that the poor would not benefit from economic growth stimulated an immediate rejoinder from the Joint Economic Committee of Congress—then chaired by a highly regarded economist, Illinois Senator Paul Douglas—which in 1959 commissioned economist Robert J. Lampman to examine postwar trends in low income. Lampman's analysis stood in stark contrast to Galbraith's: it was based on careful, if dry, statistical analysis; it estimated poverty rates at the substantial level of nearly 20 percent (based on a $2,000 poverty line); it attributed postwar reductions in poverty almost entirely to economic growth; and it blamed inadequate growth for the poverty that remained. Calculating from rates of reduction when the economy was at its peak, Lampman also projected that poverty could be cut dramatically in the future with more aggressive efforts to sustain growth.[30] This 1959 analysis was circulated by the Joint Economic Committee, and drew the attention of Walter Heller, who at the time was acting as an advisor to Hubert Humphrey's campaign for the 1960 Democratic presidential primary. It was not until three years later, though, that the differences between Galbraith and Lampman entered into the policy debate. By then, Heller was chairman of President Kennedy's Council of Economic Advisers and had hired Lampman as his staff "expert on poverty." By then, too, proponents of an alternative, "structuralist" view of poverty began to criticize the CEA's growth-centered economic agenda for its failure to do anything for the poor.

Picking up on themes from Galbraith, "structuralist" views of poverty in the early 1960s started with two related observations: first, growing affluence had fundamentally changed the nature of America's poverty problem, transforming it from a "mass" phenomenon to the experience of a smaller, isolated minority. Once traceable to the widespread unemployment and low wages that were to be expected of a less developed economy, poverty was now a "paradox" that lingered despite growth and prosperity. Second, despite expanding opportunity for the working- and middle-class majority, American society was still fundamentally unequal. Poverty was in this sense a selective experience affecting specific "underprivileged" groups—those structurally disadvantaged by age, geography, racial discrimination, and family structure—rendering them incapable of benefiting from the "general" economic growth policies being promoted by the CEA. The structuralists argued that the poor were *qualitatively* different from the rest of American society, and the difference had to do with more than just the absence of jobs or income. True antipoverty policies, they believed, would have to acknowledge the structural economic, social, and political problems underlying the new poverty and address stratification at its source.

The structuralist position was hardly based on a single, coherent set of arguments, however, and in fact it appeared in many different and scattered guises. One version of the argument emphasized underlying economic forces, building primarily on the structural unemployment analysis that still held sway within labor and civil rights circles as an alternative to human capital explanations of wage inequality and unemployment. In his 1962 book *Challenge to Affluence*, Swedish economist Gunnar Myrdal attributed persistent poverty to structural economic forces—automation, changing skill requirements, and the "historic inequalities" of labor exploitation and racial discrimination. With overtones of his earlier missive on American race relations, *An American Dilemma*, Myrdal warned ominously of a growing "underclass" of unskilled "unemployables" that could prove "fatal for democracy." Myrdal's "Marshall Plan to eradicate poverty" acknowledged the importance of aggregate growth, but argued that growth without "social justice" would only deepen existing inequalities. Myrdal proposed extensive labor market restructuring to increase demand for low-skilled labor, including direct job creation and retraining, along with minimum wage improvements, "large-scale redistribution," and public investment in depressed areas.[31] Similar arguments had earlier cropped up in the extended debate over "depressed areas" legislation that finally resulted in the passage of the Area Redevelopment Act (ARA) of 1961. A much-circumscribed version of earlier proposals for direct federal investment and regional economic planning, the ARA offered modest assistance to high-unemployment communities in the form of loan guarantees, training grants, and technical advice.[32] Even in this watered-down version, however, "depressed area" legislation reflected persistent concerns about the impact of structural economic change—and the inadequacy of policies that relied on growth alone as the answer.

Similarly focusing on automation, labor market exclusion, and racial exploitation as primary causes of poverty, influential leaders within the civil rights movement were also articulating a more structural concept of poverty in the early 1960s, building toward their own version of a "domestic Marshall Plan" that would come to include job creation and income guarantees as well as more specifically race-targeted measures to combat segregation, discrimination, and the absence of capital in black urban communities.[33] Such proposals were becoming especially worrisome to the White House in the spring and summer of 1963, as the movement prepared for its historic March on Washington in August, with jobs and freedom as the core demands.[34] The National Farmer's Union, too, was beginning to focus on the impact of structural economic change on groups disadvantaged by race and occupation, and particularly on rural farm families. In 1961, the NFU established the National Policy Committee on Pockets of Poverty, which three years later issued a report calling for measures to address "underlying economic trends" and recognizing, as Galbraith had said in a speech to the group a few months earlier, that the task of eliminating poverty "won't be accomplished simply by stepping up the growth rate any more than it will be accomplished by incantation or ritualistic washing of the feet."[35]

But the structuralist interpretation of poverty was not always couched in such obviously structural terms. The Pockets of Poverty Committee Report relied in part on an analysis by Oscar Ornati, an economist at the New School for Social Research who, while acknowledging structural economic change as a key underlying cause of poverty, focused more narrowly on documenting the characteristics of the population in poverty—specifically, on the demographic characteristics that differentiated the "new" poor from everyone else. The resulting analysis left ambiguous policy implications, indicating that there might be a double edge to the structural interpretation of poverty. In a study he began conducting for the Twentieth Century Fund in 1961, Ornati argued that the elderly, southern farm families, nonwhites, female-headed households, and low-education achievers formed an "underdog" or "pariah" class that was "disembodied from the economy" and outside the mainstream altogether. Ornati's policy proposals similarly concentrated not on reforming broader economic and social conditions but on group and individual rehabilitation. "Policies aimed at the economic development of the total society . . . are of very limited use in the fight against poverty," the study concluded, calling instead for policies that would target groups with "multiple poverty-linked characteristics." Labeling these as "structurally oriented" solutions, Ornati's suggestions were actually confined to personal rehabilitative measures, stressing education, skill development, expanded mental health services, and other interventions aimed at changing the characteristics of the poor.[36]

The structuralist critique of growth was also beginning to appear in more popular formats in the early 1960s, and nowhere more forcefully than in Michael Harrington's *The Other America*. Aiming to shock where the academics had merely analyzed, Harrington introduced affluent America to the invisible "underworld" of the poor and took structuralist interpretation in the somewhat unlikely direction of the culture of poverty.[37]

Like other structuralist authors, Harrington used the novelty of contemporary poverty as his starting point, writing of "the first minority poor in history, the first poor not to be seen, the first poor whom the politicians could leave alone." Playing on the ironic theme that had been cultivated in the literature since Galbraith, Harrington described how this "new poverty" had emerged from the American postwar success story: economic growth that reduced unemployment and poverty from "the decisive social experience of the entire society" to the experience of a hidden minority; a labor movement that organized the "majority poor" but left those in "unorganizable jobs" behind; and a welfare state that had worked brilliantly for the "middle third" but ignored the millions who desperately needed it. But when it came time to discuss the contemporary forces sustaining poverty, Harrington seemed to leave political economy behind, focusing instead, and at length, on the self-perpetuating "vicious cycle" of deprivation and psychological isolation that entrapped society's "rejects" and threatened to capture their children as well. A "culture of poverty" had emerged out of the structural changes of the past thirty years, a culture "radically different from the one that dominates the society," with a language, a psychology, a "world view" characterized by hopelessness and "personal chaos." This all-pervasive culture rendered the poor immune to economic progress and beyond the reach of the existing welfare state. Most "deadly" of all, it was "increasingly associated with the accident of birth."[38]

For Harrington, as for others in the early 1960s, the existence of this culture of poverty only strengthened the case for more comprehensive structural solutions. Lampman's projections to the contrary, economic growth would not "automatically" reduce poverty rates, Harrington argued, for growth alone could not begin to penetrate the barriers of racial discrimination, community deterioration, and the culture of poverty that oppressed the "other Americans." The poor needed better housing, health care, antidiscrimination legislation, jobs, and, most of all, measures "to destroy the pessimism and fatalism that flourish in the other America." Such a "vast and comprehensive program attacking the culture of poverty" would come only through an equally vast political and spiritual transformation in the affluent society, a "vision" to enable "[t]he nation of the well-off . . . to see through the wall of affluence and recognize the alien citizens on the other side," a "passion to end poverty, for nothing less than that will do." The call to arms, Harrington was convinced, could only come from the federal government.[39]

The "new poverty" depicted in *The Other America* evidently struck a chord where more academic analyses could not. With the help of a laudatory review by *New Yorker* writer Dwight Macdonald that is said to have drawn the president's attention, Harrington became required reading among Washington liberals, and eventually appeared on the best seller lists.[40] But for all its rhetorical radicalism, Harrington's book actually presented structural analysis in its most narrow and politically benign form, as the culture of poverty. By focusing on the socially deviant characteristics of the poor, Harrington's version of the structuralist analysis could—and would—be used to justify a strategy based on individual remediation rather than political and economic change, in effect undermining the premises upon which the structuralist analysis of poverty had been built in the first place. Despite the attention the structuralists drew to labor market restructuring and social stratification, this literature was focused not on inequality but on deprivation, for the most part leaving unchallenged and unspoken the premise that postwar economic growth had, by itself, created a vast majority of prosperous middle-class Americans. "Inequality of wealth is not necessarily a major social problem per se," wrote Dwight Macdonald in the *New Yorker* review essay, "Poverty is." Even in the short time span separating Galbraith's *Affluent Society* from Harrington, a subtle but important shift had taken place.[41] In the structuralist literature, the analysis of poverty was becoming less about the political economy of affluence, and more about the demographic and psychological traits that distinguished the poor from everyone else. And it was in this form that the structuralist interpretation of poverty would eventually be adopted by the CEA economists and absorbed into the existing liberal growth agenda as a justification for more government spending on behalf of the poor.[42]

THE POLITICAL CONSTRUCTION OF POVERTY

By early 1963, the poverty issue was becoming hard for the administration to ignore, as pressure mounted from sporadic but compelling media reports and from left-liberal criticism of its proposed tax cut. When a February 1963 television documentary lit up the White House switchboard with inquiries about what was being done for the poor, Heller's CEA took the lead in constructing an official analysis of poverty that would affect research and policy agendas for years to come. Based though it was on social scientific analysis, it was also shaped by Heller's sharp awareness of political interest and need—most immediately, to defend CEA growth policies against the structuralist critique that they would bypass the poor, but also to establish the CEA and the administration as the locus of expertise on poverty. In late spring 1963, Heller began his own campaign to "launch a Kennedy offensive against poverty," envisioning it as the next step in realizing the CEA's broader growth and prosperity agenda, while providing the president with a powerful campaign theme.[43]

This combination of politics and social science would guide the construction of poverty through its various stages within the administration over the next several months, culminating in the odd, or at least uneasy, combination of "new economics" and old "culture of poverty" analysis that the CEA's 1964 Economic Report to the President—the blueprint for the War on Poverty—embraced. The first priority for Heller was to elaborate upon a concept of poverty consistent with the CEA's vision of economic growth, and to get it onto the administration's domestic policy agenda as such. That in itself required some delicate maneuvering, for among the CEA's structuralist critics were members of the Kennedy cabinet, including Secretary of Labor Willard Wirtz, who were skeptical about the prospect of an across-the-board tax cut and convinced that the growth package would not work for labor without more intensive efforts to respond to structural unemployment. More important, the CEA itself had adopted elements of the structuralist analysis, acknowledging, in its 1962 Economic Report, that there were some groups—"[families] headed by women, the elderly, nonwhites, migratory workers, and the physically or mentally handicapped—who are shortchanged even in times of prosperity."[44] The key, then, was to acknowledge this substratum of the "poorest families" without making too sharp a distinction between poverty and the problems of unemployment and slow growth. Too sharp a distinction, growth-oriented economists worried, could lead to mere "casework solutions." More important, according to calculations by CEA poverty expert Robert Lampman, drawing too sharp a distinction would be wrong. The poor for the most part "are not Negro or old or rural," Lampman noted in a harsh critique of preliminary reports from Oscar Ornati's structuralist report, but "are in consumer units headed by male-urban-whites under 65 years of age." Besides, he added, "I just can't accept the idea that at some particular date in history we passed a sound barrier beyond which the historical relationship between rising per capita income and reduction of poverty ceased to function." Growth and full employment remained "the two measures which can have the greatest effect in reducing poverty in the future."[45]

As a CEA staff member in 1963, Lampman was in a position to deflect even as he incorporated elements of the structuralist perspective on poverty, and Heller relied heavily on him for background analysis in preparing to propose a Kennedy antipoverty initiative. Heller and Lampman had first come together on the poverty issue indirectly in 1959, when Heller was identifying themes for Hubert Humphrey's presidential campaign and took note of Lampman's study for the Joint Economic Committee. But the two economists shared more than an interest in poverty. Both had their degrees from the University of Wisconsin, and were committed to the "Wisconsin Idea" of applying economic expertise in service to government. Both careers also exemplified the transitions taking place in postwar economics. Like Heller, Lampman combined the distributional concerns of a Wisconsin-School institutionalist with the theoretical and methodological revelations of the "Keynesian revolution."[46] He made his first professional mark with his work on wealth inequality, in the mid-1950s publishing a critique of the then-prevailing notion that an "income revolution" had dramatically reduced the degree of inequality in the U.S. Eventually, he would become better known for his contributions to the economics of poverty, as an early spokesman for the link between poverty and sluggish economic growth.[47] In his 1959 paper on poverty for the Joint Economic Committee, Lampman criticized Galbraith's contention that more growth would not make a dent in the new poverty, and predicted that maintaining growth rates at their high postwar levels would by itself reduce poverty rates from roughly 20 percent, where they stood in 1956, to 12 percent by 1976.[48]

By 1963, though, Lampman and Heller were beginning to look seriously beyond the growth strategy for a more specifically targeted approach, both to address the problems of those who would not automatically benefit from growth and to preempt critics on the left who claimed that Kennedy's policies were not doing enough for poor and minority groups.[49] While retaining the CEA's signature emphasis on aggregate growth as the central engine of progress against poverty, they began to put greater stress on structuralist proposals such as expansions in the existing social welfare system, retraining and, for the next generation, intensive human capital investments "to improve the health, education, attitudes and motivations of children of the present poor," and prevent the spread of "intergenerational" poverty. Like a disease, poverty was "subject to control if not eradication," Lampman wrote in an internal memo laying out the basics of the CEA's conceptual framework. The solution was to "promote exits" from poverty and to "prevent retreats" into what Lampman now characterized as a separate "world" of the poor.[50]

With the outlines of a growth-and-structuralist framework established, Lampman turned to what he recognized as a second political and conceptual task: arriving at a "politically workable definition or concept of poverty," as he told Heller, that would focus the program on absolute deprivation, and quite consciously avoid defining poverty as a problem of inequality. "Most people see no political dynamite in the fact that our income distribution at the low end is about the same as it has always been," Lampman noted, setting aside the concern over persistent income disparities that he himself had been writing about since the 1950s.[51] "Probably a politically acceptable program must avoid completely any use of the term 'inequality' or of the term '*redistribution* of income or wealth.' "[52] Lampman and his CEA colleagues were also wary of psychological and cultural definitions of poverty, concerned about the social work solutions they implied. Instead, they insisted that poverty be defined narrowly, as income that fell below a certain minimum standard rather than as an expression of inequality, social disadvantage, or a state of mind. Such an income-based definition, they reasoned, would lend itself to the growth-centered strategy they were proposing. It would avoid stigmatizing distinctions between the "deserving" and the "undeserving" poor. Above all, the narrow, absolute income definition had practicality on its side. It had "the great merit of being something we had some numbers on," Lampman recalled, offering a yardstick for assessing the country's progress against poverty and a numerical basis for setting policy goals. "Relative" poverty was difficult to grasp and would always be with us; "absolute" poverty was easy to measure and could actually be wiped out.[53]

There was more than the politics of practicality at stake, though, as Heller, Lampman, and their CEA colleagues were well aware. For while income was, at least on the surface, an amoral, measurable, and inclusive criterion, maintaining a narrow, income-based definition of the poverty problem would also allow officials to skirt the question of what structural inequalities lay behind the poverty numbers, and in particular to avoid explicit mention of racial subordination and discrimination as dimensions of poverty. Gender, as such, did not even enter the framework as a category of analysis. Thus, while the numbers pointed to "female-headed families" as among those who "proved quite immune to economic growth," the CEA offered no analysis of female wages or employment opportunities as one possible explanation; nor did female wages enter into the picture—as it had for earlier social surveys—of male-headed family income and poverty. More consciously, though, and with awareness of the political repercussions, the CEA analysis did not ignore but it did minimize the necessity of taking steps to combat racism as part of a program against poverty. Indeed, Lampman took care to note that nonwhites were *not* to be listed among the groups who proved "immune to growth"—even though they did suffer disproportionately high poverty rates. Instead, he pointed out how much nonwhites, having "shared in growth" during past boom times, could be expected to benefit from the CEA tax cut. If anything, Lampman argued, going a step further, tight labor markets would push employers to "break down the barriers of discrimination and overlook handicaps in a frenzy to hire any and all workers." An attack on poverty, then, while in this sense an answer to mounting civil rights demands for jobs and economic justice, could be constructed as color-blind in actual content. With those concerns in mind, Heller proposed to fold civil rights, along with a wide panoply of education, training, and welfare proposals, into a more "general framework . . . within which public responsibilities for achieving 'widening participation in prosperity' can be viewed"—taking care, in a balancing act that poverty knowledge would increasingly be called upon to pull off, not to racialize the issue of poverty while recognizing it as a non–race-specific way to target African Americans for economic advance.[54]

Politics came even more explicitly into the construction of poverty when the CEA established itself at the helm of an interagency task force to hammer out the conceptual and policy framework that was eventually adopted for the War on Poverty. Playing on his position as the administration's guardian of economic health, Heller set the tone for cabinet-level discussion, while Lampman and other CEA staff members worked closely with economists at the Bureau of the Budget to provide statistical data, cost estimates, and, most important, to act as gatekeepers for proposals coming in from other agencies. Thus assured dominance in conceptualizing the program, the CEA economists were also in a position to distance themselves from old-line agencies such as HEW and Labor, which routinely came in with what looked to be self-serving proposals for expanded social welfare and labor market policies. Also at issue, though, in what the CEA routinely portrayed as the politics of bureaucratic self-interest, was the skepticism expressed by agency heads about the wisdom of a specifically designated "poverty program": better, they argued, to build on programs with a potentially more universal appeal.[55] Convinced that these arguments were a cover for agency expansionism, CEA antipoverty planners began to look elsewhere for proposals. It was in this context that economists came to embrace community action as a genuinely new idea, with special appeal as a way of cutting through the old allegiances and rivalries between existing agencies.

Throughout, but especially in the final, legislative stages of planning, presidential style and campaign politics played a part in the administration's construction of poverty as well. With an eye to the upcoming presidential election year, Heller began trying out various slogans and themes for the poverty initiative—the generic, broad-gauged "Widening Participation in Prosperity" later gave way to a proposed focus on youth and opportunity—most, up to the last minute, trying to avoid using the downbeat, stigmatizing term "poverty." Having gotten a tentative go-ahead from President Kennedy in early November 1963, Heller laid out the political parameters the proposed legislative package should meet: a focus not on poverty as a structural or systemic problem but on individuals and groups in poverty; on "self-help" and access to opportunity rather than "passive acceptance of handouts"; and, in recognition of "inevitable budgetary constraints," on "a relatively *few groups and areas* where problems are most severe and solutions most feasible" (emphasis in original).[56] Then, in the weeks following President Kennedy's assassination, the emotionally numbed task force found itself in search of a way to appeal to the bold "Johnsonian" style—while remaining within budgetary constraints established by Kennedy and Heller. Complicating matters was the fact that no one, not even Lampman, felt that the CEA or the task force had much more than a superficial understanding of the poverty problem—let alone a repertoire of bold, "Johnsonian" ideas that would work. Here again, with time running short to prepare a 1964 legislative package for the new president, community action had a special appeal. In fact, it seemed to offer solutions to several dilemmas at once: limited to a small number of community-based demonstrations, the approach would be targeted, it would buy time to gather more knowledge about poverty, it would not require major new funding, and, in a legislative package made up principally of repackaged existing proposals, it would be innovative. "This may be the way to really make something of this poverty program," one task force member told Heller in mid-December; community action was on its way to becoming *the* poverty program.[57]

With the idea that would become the community action program still in embryonic form, Heller presented the broad outlines of a "major 'Attack on Poverty' " in a White House meeting with presidential advisor Theodore Sorenson and several other cabinet members in late December. Most of the legislative details remained unresolved, the program had not met with full approval from the other agencies, and nobody liked the stigmatizing "poverty" label. Nevertheless, the CEA had mapped out the central themes of a presidential appeal to Congress, to be delivered in the State of the Union, the Economic Report, and a special message early in the session. The program would feature a major emphasis on youth, "significant redirection of previously proposed but not yet enacted legislation," and a series of coordinated local demonstration programs as its main components. The new budget request would be modest, presented as the first step in a ten-year attack on poverty.[58] To these would be added an appeal to the country's sense of affluence and altruism, playing up the theme of poverty in the midst of plenty or, as one memo-writer had put it several weeks earlier, "the obligations which a prosperous majority owes to a submerged and desperately poor minority."[59]

Thus it was that in a six-month period of intensive planning and interagency negotiation the CEA economists had expanded their initial emphasis on employment and growth to incorporate, first, the structuralist notion of a segregated population with the trappings of a culture of poverty, and then, for entirely pragmatic purposes, the sociological concept of community action.

These changes were reflected in chapter 2 of *The Economic Report to the President* of 1964, entitled "The Problem of Poverty in America." Written "to provide some understanding of the enemy and to outline the main features of a strategy of attack," the chapter was presented as a synthesis of existing poverty expertise, drawing chiefly on the CEA's statistical analysis and the small body of literature produced since the late 1950s. For Lampman, who had been commuting from Madison to assist the poverty task force, it was "maybe the best sort of applied scholarship I've ever been involved in."[60]

The overall Economic Report was, as usual, a political brief for the new economics, and specifically for the CEA's formula for expanding prosperity and employment without resort to structural economic change. Unemployment, then measured at 5½ percent, was "the country's number one economic problem," the CEA reported in chapter 1, and faster growth through the too-long delayed tax cut was the number one solution.[61] Automation might be causing some structural displacement, according to chapter 3, but nothing that could not be addressed through added growth and human capital investments.[62] Poverty, measured according to an income cutoff of $3,000, would be substantially reduced by the growth and employment that would be stimulated by the tax cut.

But then the report moved on to the "human face" of poverty, to the millions who were beyond the reach of economic growth. "The poor inhabit a world scarcely recognizable, and rarely recognized, by the majority of their fellow Americans," the chapter began in Harrington-like language. "It is a world apart, whose inhabitants are isolated from the mainstream of American life and alienated from its values. . . . Worst of all, the poverty of the fathers is visited upon the children."[63] Separating the poor from the rest of America were not structural barriers but "certain characteristics"—low education, race, single parenthood, old age—that were themselves the causes of poverty. Complicating matters further, the *composition* of the poverty population had changed in recent decades, as growth lifted two-parent families, working-age men, and others out of poverty and left those with "special handicaps" behind to form a larger share. Thus, "in the future economic growth alone will provide relatively fewer escapes from poverty. Policy will have to focus more sharply on the handicaps that deny the poor fair access to the expanding incomes of a growing economy."[64] While tax reduction remained "the first requisite of a concerted attack on poverty," the administration would offer a more "comprehensive" package of existing and new legislation, under the rubric of a "common target—poverty," and a common theme—enabling poor Americans "to *earn* the American standard of living by their own efforts and contributions."[65]

Although it was premised on the essential compatibility between the objectives of economic growth and antipoverty ("Humanity compels our action, but it is sound economics as well"), the CEA report's characterization of the poverty problem was an important step in the official government definition of the poor and poverty as problems cut off from the mainstream, a "world apart."[66] Economic growth would not be enough to break the "vicious circle" entrapping a significant minority of the poor. And yet, the CEA report did not call for the "Marshall Plan" Gunnar Myrdal had envisioned, nor for the explicitly redistributional economic and political reforms suggested by Galbraith and Harrington as a response to the new poverty. Instead, policy would take the human capital approach, in an attempt to overcome the handicaps of the poor themselves. Research, following suit, would focus narrowly on the characteristics of the population in poverty—to the near exclusion of larger problems of social and economic inequality which had given rise to the idea of "poverty amidst affluence" in the first place.

The 1964 Economic Report represented the first concerted effort to bring the analytic tools of the "new economics" to the problem of poverty, but the economists had not had the last word. For in the process of negotiating what amounted to a hybrid, internally conflicted but politically acceptable concept of poverty, they had opened the door to another, quite different kind of poverty expertise—attached to the sociological idea of community action—only later to find out just how incompatible the new economics and the old sociology could be.

ENTER COMMUNITY ACTION

Community action came to the CEA task force relatively late in the planning process, with a great deal to recommend it: in contrast to most things being suggested by the old-line agencies, the idea was new, it was low-cost, it offered a way to overcome the fragmentation of services in the existing system, and, when implemented in the form of a few limited demonstration projects as initially proposed, it afforded policy planners much-needed time to experiment and to learn more about poverty conditions around the country. The proposal for community action was "based on the view," CEA staff member William Capron wrote, "that we have not had adequate time to develop a carefully thought out program."[67] Above all, community action could be seen to fit in with the overall conceptual framework devised by the CEA task force for the War on Poverty: with tax-cut-induced economic growth as the weapon of choice for the bulk of the problem, these local community-based experiments would offer comprehensive remediation for those who were trapped in the "cycle of poverty," all by way, as historian James Patterson describes it, of a "hand up, not a hand out."[68]

In actuality, as the economists were soon to discover, community action was not so easily contained. For one, there was the immediate problem of selling the idea to a president who was about to declare "unconditional war on poverty" and who wanted an impressive national program to accompany the rhetoric. Just before presenting their proposal to Johnson, the planners upped the community action allocation from $100 to $500 million, absorbing all of the funds allocated for the poverty initiative. "In the course of a single week, in mid-December," James L. Sundquist later wrote, "aid to community organizations was transformed from an incidental idea in the War on Poverty into the entire war."[69] More important, community action was caught up in the gradually building momentum of the movement for social reform that had originated in the experimental demonstration programs launched in the late 1950s and early 1960s in response to juvenile delinquency and other expressions of social "disorganization" in declining inner-city neighborhoods. The architects of these community action experiments were themselves in search of an overarching framework for their varied efforts, a "unified program" that would get to the "root causes" of these interconnected social problems. For them, news that the Kennedy administration was contemplating an "attack" on poverty came at an opportune moment, just as they themselves were shifting their sights.

The odyssey of community action in planning for the War on Poverty created a legacy that was as controversial as it was complex. In some ways, its absorption into the War on Poverty changed the community action idea, channeling what for some had been a broader vision of community reorganization and institutional reform into the narrower effort to break the "cycle of poverty" with comprehensive services to rehabilitate the poor. Indeed, the War on Poverty heightened and exaggerated the latent conflicts within community action, ultimately contributing to its political demise. At the same time, community action proponents threatened to transform what the economists had proposed as the conceptual framework for the administration's antipoverty initiative, taking a strategy based on economic growth, human capital, and improved social services and introducing several unexpected elements: one was the "sociological" view of poverty as a cultural and psychological condition; a second was the notion that the federal government would act as a catalyst for change and local community "empowerment"; and third was a view of social science research as an instrument for participatory planning, program evaluation, and decision making at the community level—and as such itself an instrument of social change. No sooner had CEA economists adopted community action as an idea for the War on Poverty, than they found themselves working, with only partial success, to keep its more radical potential in check.

In the months leading up to LBJ's declaration of war on poverty, proponents of community action had been adapting and refining their goals. In June 1963, just when the Council of Economic Advisers was establishing its first interagency task force on poverty, the flagship antidelinquency experiment Mobilization For Youth issued a new mission statement that effectively reordered its priorities. Reducing poverty would be the first order of business, the statement announced, with MFY working to "change social conditions so that new economic opportunities are created."[70] In September, Paul Ylvisaker announced that "poverty, and the vicious cycle of poverty" would become the "label" for the "essential concerns" of the Ford Foundation's Public Affairs program, albeit qualifying the announcement with a caution against a retreat to "the one-way street of charity and the hand-out."[71] But the immediate connection between community action and the administration's nascent antipoverty initiative came at the hands of David Hackett, Executive Director of the President's Committee on Juvenile Delinquency, who mobilized the juvenile delinquency and urban reform networks to put the idea into the policy pipeline, eventually leaving both community action and the poverty initiative significantly changed.

Like many others doing antidelinquency work, Hackett was frustrated with the limitations the PCJD was encountering in its efforts to create better opportunities for low-income youth, and particularly with his difficulties in persuading old-line federal agencies to coordinate and concentrate their resources in the experimental communities. Hoping to galvanize a core of supporters within the federal bureaucracy, he began in late spring 1963 to gather a number of sympathetic agency staffers in a series of weekly meetings held in Attorney General Robert Kennedy's office. The initial purpose of the meetings was to discuss the need for a stronger federal coordinating mechanism, but the agenda turned to the PCJD's conceptual limitations as well. "If the work of the President's Committee is to affect more than a few demonstration cities and if these demonstrations are to succeed, comprehensive local planning must be supported by more effective coordination at the Federal level," Hackett explained to Robert Kennedy later that fall. And, he added, the PCJD programs needed to aim at a different target: "poverty and its effects."[72]

The interagency group, self-styled as "Hackett's guerillas" in reference to its aim to shake up the bureaucracy, drew heavily from the networks that had been forming around juvenile delinquency and urban reform since the late 1950s, counting NIMH program officer Leonard Duhl, Housing and Home Finance Administration official Frederick O'R Hayes, and PCJD staff members Richard Boone and Sanford Kravitz among its regulars. Several of the "guerillas" had already come together earlier, to help plan the president's proposed National Service Corps—an effort that eventually found its way into the War on Poverty as the "domestic peace corps," or VISTA.[73] The National Service Corps experience had also played a role in moving community action proponents to broader ambitions, featuring among its activities a tour, arranged by Richard Boone, of poverty "pockets" around the country not at all unlike those visited by LBJ, Robert Kennedy, and President Bill Clinton in future "poverty tours."[74] Hackett was prepared, then, when Budget Bureau staff member William B. Cannon invited him to submit some proposals to the CEA/Budget poverty task force in the fall of 1963. At the time, faced with a "laundry list" of lackluster ideas from old-line agencies and a fast-approaching deadline for a new poverty plan, Cannon and his colleagues were in serious need of some new thinking.[75]

Hackett responded with memos directed to Robert Kennedy and CEA Chair Walter Heller in early November, in which he outlined a plan that took community action's new found focus on poverty and combined it with the recent experiences of the PCJD demonstrations and the National Service Corps. "From our work on the National Service Corps we know of competent people in the Federal government who can be brought together to develop a comprehensive attack on poverty," he told the Attorney General. "What we are proposing is continuous planning on a national scale to make better use of Federal resources in programs which more effectively serve the poor."[76] For Heller, Hackett sketched out an elaborate plan "that would encourage a dramatic approach to the problems," based on a kind of research that would more directly involve the poor. The plan would create a series of task forces "to study the large pockets of poverty in the nation . . . and to approach the problems of the poor first by consulting the people themselves, examining their life conditions, then looking through them at the institutions which are attempting to assist them." After reviewing these community-based inquiries, the task forces would make recommendations for legislation, for new "administrative arrangements in the Federal Executive departments," and for a few—no more than five—comprehensive demonstration projects with interdepartmental support. After reporting their findings to a cabinet-level committee on poverty, the investigative task forces would continue to evaluate the demonstrations and continue research and planning. The "central focus" of all this activity would be "on that poverty which is passed on from one generation to the next."[77]

Hackett's memos made the rounds among the CEA and Budget Bureau planners, complete with a list of suggested task force members that included the PCJD and Gray Areas regulars. At that point the CEA initiative was shaping up as little more than a series of existing legislative proposals—the tax cut, plus increased funding for education and training programs. Here, at last, was something concrete to tie it all together, a way to make the scattershot array of federal interventions more coordinated and efficient—without major new spending. In late December community action, minus Hackett's elaborate task forces, appeared on White House aide Theodore Sorenson's desk as the core of the CEA's antipoverty proposal. In his January 1964 State of the Union address, President Johnson announced that he would soon be presenting a major new package of legislation to lead an attack on poverty.[78]

Suddenly community action, only recently a relatively obscure and experimental concept harbored by Ford and PCJD, was caught up in the constant whirlwind of politics and planning that led to the passage of the Economic Opportunity Act in August 1964. That was when the selling of community action started in earnest, for the man LBJ put in charge of yet another new antipoverty task force—Peace Corps director and Kennedy in-law Sargent

Shriver—was skeptical to say the least. Following a Sunday afternoon meeting to brief the new team on plans to date, William Cannon and other members of the original CEA task force feared they were back to square one. "The whole aim of the meeting was to sell Sarge on what we'd been doing and particularly Community action," Cannon recalled. "Sarge hardly heard us, to be frank." Seeking to repeat the success of the Peace Corps, Shriver was looking for "something glamorous, easily understood, apparent in its workings," and immediate in its effects.[79] Community action was none of those things. Nor were its chances improved by the ideas competing for a place on the legislative agenda. With the slate wiped clean, agency officials who had been opposed to community action from the start had a chance to resurrect their original proposals. Calling community action a "band-aid," Secretary of Labor Willard Wirtz mounted a second effort to put large-scale job creation at the center of the poverty strategy. Representing that position on the task force was a strong contingent from the Department of Labor, led by Assistant Secretary Daniel Patrick Moynihan.

Soon, however, community action was back in the antipoverty package, with the help of Cannon and other well-placed advocates at the Budget Bureau, and persuasive, reassuring spokesmen like Paul Ylvisaker and New Haven Gray Areas director Mitchell Sviridoff, who came in to consult with the task force. Shriver also learned very quickly that a major jobs program was out of the question; the decision had already been made to keep poverty spending to a minimum, and LBJ flatly rejected the task force proposal to finance job creation with a cigarette tax. To Robert Lampman, the original CEA poverty analyst called in from Wisconsin to assist the new task force, it was all somewhat mystifying. The Shriver task force was like "a campaign train," he recalled, referring to the "extraordinarily chaotic atmosphere" and changing cast of characters surrounding the endeavor. "Every time I would get there there would be a different car on the train, a different sort of company." Most surprising from his point of view was "the importance of this community action idea."[80]

By then community action was beginning to take on a momentum of its own. When Lampman had last been closely involved in the poverty planning, drafting the CEA Economic Report in December 1963, the growth-stimulating tax cut held the key to the drive against poverty, supplemented by expansions in existing educational and employment and training programs. Community action, at that point very new, was primarily a way to bring it all together more effectively. Now, community action was positioned to become much more. Firmly established as one among several new initiatives that would be created by the legislation (Job Corps, VISTA, and loans to poor farmers were among the others), community action was being shaped for federal adoption not by economists interested in better service delivery but by the people who thought of themselves as having been in the trenches from the start: Richard Boone, Sanford Kravitz, and Frederick O'R Hayes—three of Hackett's "guerillas"—working under the direction of UAW labor organizer Jack Conway. For most of the spring and summer of 1964, they made up the core of an Urban Areas Task Force designated to develop a plan for setting up a national community action program in anticipation of legislative approval. In their hands, community action would become much more than a federally sponsored services coordinating mechanism; it would become an instrument of social reform. The proposed Economic Opportunity Act laid the groundwork. Local organizations would get federal money to develop comprehensive, coordinated antipoverty plans. Research and demonstration would be continuous and community-based, yielding the kind of knowledge that local practitioners could put into action. Most important, in a requirement that had never appeared to date in community action criteria, local community action plans would be "developed, conducted and administered with the maximum feasible participation of the residents of areas and members of the groups served," enforcing the principle of "indigenous participation" that, while present in community action from the start, had only recently emerged as a dominant concern.

For the existing community action experiments, the impact of all this federal-level planning was immediate and unexpected. From the start, it brought them instant star status, along with an "influx" of federal site visitors eager to witness the new idea in action. New Haven, the Gray Area showcase, even established a separate public information office to handle the attention. Local directors were much in demand, as were their foundation sponsors. Paul Ylvisaker had something to boast about to the trustees. "[T]he community action section of the poverty program builds heavily on the experiments of the Gray Areas project," he reported, noting that New Haven's Mitchell Sviridoff and North Carolina's George Esser "had quite a hand in drafting and shaping it." Passage of the Economic Opportunity Act of 1964, and the Foundation's role in it, was the program's "proudest achievement."[81] Indeed, from the perspective of all of its institutional sponsors, community action's triumph was complete: a new kind of social science, a new kind of philanthropy, and a new approach to urban reform.

And yet it was also with a slight sense of loss, and trepidation, that those most directly engaged in the local community action experiments saw it become caught up in the momentum of the antipoverty program. For in the process of being discovered and taken up as the latest weapon against poverty, the local projects had lost both the shield of experimentation and the luxury of testing their assumptions about the possibility of rationally informed social change. David Hackett's initial proposal to the contrary, community action was not to be regarded—or judged—as experimentation but as action. "In a sense, the promoters of community action had succeeded too well," wrote evaluators

Peter Marris and Martin Rein a few years later. "Their ideas became fashionable before they were proved."[82] Suddenly subject to an influx of federal dollars, Ford Foundation consultant Clark Campbell warned, the local projects were also apt to lose sight of their original goals. The foundation would need a "continuing interest in maintaining for posterity the integrity of programs already launched," he wrote not long after the poverty program had been started. Such were the concerns raised at a foundation-sponsored conference held in Puerto Rico in December 1964, at which OEO officials joined Gray Area grantees to discuss "the kinds of problems and questions that arise in organizing and executing community action programs of the type contemplated by the new Economic Opportunity Act." Little attention was given to a more basic question: just how community action, unproved as a method for combating juvenile delinquency or promoting urban systems reform, was going to "break the cycle of poverty."[83]

The political triumph of community action also carried another price. For even as they provided the institutional means for community action's swift rise to prominence, the Ford Foundation, the PCJD, and the administration's Poverty Task Force were continually drawing and redrawing the boundaries of political and ideological acceptability within which the initiatives would have to operate. For all its potential radicalism as an idea of empowerment and neighborhood control, as of late 1964 community action had consistently steered clear of policies that would entail direct government intervention in local economies, and remained tentative in addressing the problem of race. Aware of the transformations that were reshaping inner-city neighborhoods, community action was nevertheless principally aimed at what appeared to be a more tractable and ideologically acceptable target for change: the cultural deficiencies of the poor. Like the social scientific concepts of social "disorganization" and community breakdown that informed it, community action was based on a fundamentally limited idea, the culture of poverty, that effectively skirted the systemic nature of social inequality and economic change. In disconnecting the poverty problem from urban restructuring and urban politics, the early community action experiments had created a setting within which poverty could be defined as a problem of individual deprivation—precisely the feature that made them acceptable to poverty planners in the first place. As Office of Economic Opportunity official John Wofford later concluded, "community action . . . was attempting to reach community consensus at a time when race, politics and poverty were pulling communities and the nation apart."[84]

What emerged, then, from community action's abbreviated episode of experimentation was a view of poverty that, at least on the surface, was very much in line with what the new economics proposed: a problem that could be addressed without recourse to structural measures such as targeted job creation, without seriously upsetting the political status quo, and without explicit mention of race. Added to that was a view of social change as an orderly process of informed, consensus-based, and above all rational planning, in which social scientists would play a central role, and the poor would participate as equal partners. Within months of the official start of the War on Poverty, this conceptualization of the poverty problem, and certainly of how peacefully the battle against it could be waged, had itself come under fire from a chorus of voices on the front lines.

CHAPTER 7

Fighting Poverty with Knowledge:
The Office of Economic Opportunity and the
Analytic Revolution in Government

THERE WAS NO official definition of poverty when Lyndon B. Johnson made his declaration of war on poverty in 1964. Even the poverty warriors at the newly established Office of Economic Opportunity (OEO) were struck by how little they knew about the problem they had been conscripted to combat. Taking their mandate seriously, they quickly set out to gather—or, to continue the metaphor, to mobilize—the kind of knowledge they needed to win the war: it would be statistically rigorous, methodologically sophisticated, based on nationally representative data, and, most significantly, it would be explicitly modeled on an approach to policy analysis that was said to have revolutionized decision making at the Department of Defense.[1] Thus, in all the haste, idealism, confidence, and no small amount of confusion that accompanied LBJ's war on poverty, a new phase in the history of poverty knowledge began. Liberal government, through a constellation of sometimes-competing agencies, would develop the most elaborate, far-reaching apparatus for measuring, tracking, and experimenting with programs for poor people in the world.

Almost overnight, or so it appeared, the study of poverty was transformed—from an uncertainly connected bundle of university-based sociological and anthropological community studies, into a precise, federally funded analytic science with national-level data sets and neoclassical economic models at its core. Reestablished as a legitimate subject for academic inquiry, it was also becoming the basis of a substantial, government- and foundation-subsidized, public/private enterprise in applied economic research, an enterprise devoted to the singular proposition that, as economist James Tobin put it, "It Can Be Done!" Poverty, according to the new economic experts, could be "conquered" within nearly a decade of launching the war.[2]

In actuality, the transformation of poverty knowledge was not accomplished easily, and not without both political struggle and political consequence. After all, the analytic approach favored by economists stood in sharp contrast to the increasingly, and more explicitly, politicized research tradition that had brought community action to the fore. The differences, of course, went well beyond discipline, data, and methods. They touched on very different notions of how the War on Poverty should be fought: with an emphasis on local organizing for direct, transformative action; or through rational, "top-down" planning toward readily achievable national goals. For the first part of the OEO's seven-year life span, the two approaches sat uneasily side by side, their differences institutionalized in an intra-agency division between the volatile, politically controversial Community Action Program (CAP) and the division for Research, Programming, Planning and Evaluation (RPP&E). Only with the political demise of community action did the analytic model come clearly to dominate OEO-sponsored poverty research. Indeed, for a brief time, at its earliest inception, the OEO cultivated a more overtly political, if only very loosely conceptualized, brand of action research.

KNOWLEDGE FOR ACTION

The vision of OEO as an action agency was in fact a departure from the conceptualization outlined by the administration's original poverty task force, which had adopted community action as a way of coordinating existing government services and proposed a new federal agency to rise above the "bureaucratic morass" that social welfare programs had become.[3] That conceptualization abruptly changed, however, as soon as Sargent Shriver took over as LBJ's "Chief of Staff for the War on Poverty" in February 1964. Almost immediately, Shriver began to push hard to make OEO an operating as well as a planning agency, recognizing that the new operation would have a much greater chance of political survival if it actually had something besides planning to deliver.[4] He fought for and won control of new programs like the Job Corps, and then threw his considerable energies into a strategy of fast growth and immediate, visible action once agency operations got under way. "We knew that we had to get the funds out fast," CAP administrator John G. Wofford later wrote, because "the anti-poverty program had to 'prove itself' quickly in the eyes of Congress, the White House, and the country at large."[5]

The emphasis on quick action was also very much ingrained in Shriver's personal and administrative style. Brother-in-law and political operative to the Kennedys, Shriver had truly come into his own as director of the Peace Corps in 1961, which he ran with a Kennedy-esque combination of visionary idealism and the competitive, bottom-line instincts of a corporate CEO. "Nice guys finish last," and "Good guys don't win ball games," read the signs on his wall.[6] Surrounding himself with an intelligent, hard-working, and loyal inner circle of "young turks," Shriver had managed, with little time and lots of public relations, to turn the idealism of the Peace Corps idea into a force for large-scale mobilization of volunteer service around the world. Seeking to replicate his success, Shriver set the same standards for performance in the new poverty agency. "Shriver drives himself and his staff relentlessly," one loyal aide wrote, referring to the seven-day work weeks and late-night hours that quickly became the norm at OEO.[7] He also replicated his idiosyncratic administrative approach, which combined an openness to new, creative thinking with an insistence on maintaining personal control over all levels of decision making. This approach was epitomized in the famous Shriver staff meeting. Described by one frequent participant as a virtual marathon of "verbal mayhem," staff meetings became the ultimate test of toughness for the predominantly male OEO leadership, where individual presentations would be subjected to "the roughest tests of imaginativeness, feasibility, efficiency, practicality, and political salability that his closest associates could devise." For Shriver, sharpest of all in the cross-examination, the meetings were also essential tools for planning, generating new ideas, and making major policy decisions.[8]

Despite his early skepticism about the program, Shriver attracted a staff top-heavy with community action experts and enthusiasts. Among them were four of "Hackett's guerillas," Jack Conway, Richard Boone, Sanford Kravitz, and Fred O'R Hayes. Together these four had conceptualized and developed the legislative provisions for the new community action program, including the language requiring "maximum feasible participation" of the poor.[9] Conway, a trade union organizer "on loan" to the task force from the AFL-CIO, became the first director of CAP. Boone, whose career had taken him from Chicago-area police captain to the Ford Foundation's Youth Program and the President's Committee on Juvenile Delinquency (PCJD), was appointed associate director for planning. Kravitz, a social work and community planning professional who had staffed the PCJD, was Boone's deputy for research and development. And Hayes, a budget officer with the Housing and Home Finance Administration at the height of urban renewal, was in charge of CAP operations. As a group, the new CAP leadership had little experience with running major government programs. What they did have was a history of engagement in community-based reform and a growing conviction that no meaningful change would occur without basic political as well as administrative changes in the local status quo. The poor need access to power as well as resources, Boone wrote in the agency's controversial Community Action Workbook in March 1965.[10] Still, the CAP staff remained committed to consensus-building as the key to change: the ideal community action agency, as Conway spelled it out, would operate like a "three-legged stool," joining public officials, private agencies, and the poor in a process of cooperative planning.[11] Only after their work had gotten substantially under way did OEO officials begin to confront some of the internal contradictions imbedded in this framework. "There was a gnawing question about the capacity of a structure based on 'consensus' to work effectively for broad social change," Kravitz wrote a few years later, "but none of us, in our euphoria over the opportunity to mount the program at a nationwide level, were really prepared to raise openly that question."[12]

CAP administrators were prepared, though, to jettison community action's time-consuming research, planning, and program development requirements in the interest of getting funds out to applicant communities, a mission to which they were spurred on even further by Shriver's campaign of "maximum feasible public relations."[13] OEO announced its first round of grants just six weeks after operations started in October 1964, in a strategically timed Thanksgiving press release touting them as the beginning of a "major assault on ignorance, want and deprivation on six different fronts" involving "119 separate anti-poverty projects in two-thirds of the states in the nation." CAP grants were spread out over nine states, twelve cities, six rural areas, and an Indian reservation, the press release boasted, and funds had also been made available for fourteen Neighborhood Youth Corporation programs and the construction of several new Job Corps Centers. Regular press releases in the weeks to follow kept the numbers coming. Nothing seemed too small or too preliminary to report: 150 new trainees for the VISTA program; $82.6 million in new projects, including "a $6,000 small business loan to a former Pittsburgh steelworker to expand his 12-seat luncheonette"; agreements from governors to build 18 new Job Corps Centers in 15 states, along with projections of 100,000 enrollees within the first year. By mid-January, OEO had announced more than $200 million in new spending in 33 states and Puerto Rico, giving President Johnson occasion to proclaim that the agency had provided "nearly 400 transfusions of new opportunity to disadvantaged Americans in every part of this land" in its first 101 days.[14]

The political reaction to OEO's activist stance and fast growth, high-visibility strategy was immediate, and, as the poverty warriors quickly discovered, the most negative came from the local powers that be. The major source of trouble was community action, where the politics proved more vicious than even the most seasoned of the activists had anticipated.[15] The first line of attack began when OEO said no to city halls, holding up funds for community action agencies in Philadelphia, San Francisco, Los Angeles, Cleveland, and New York on the grounds that they were controlled by the mayors and insufficiently representative of the poor.[16] Despite pressure from local congressional delegations and other well-connected lobbyists, Shriver held firm. In January, the White House got a warning from Baltimore Mayor Theodore McKeldin that the Mayor's Conference, a traditional Democratic Party stronghold, was about to revolt—a threat it would follow up with later that year.[17] Still, Shriver responded with a "singularly liberal and activist" stance, as one OEO administrator saw it, vigorously defending both the principles of community action and the independence of his staff.[18] But by then other sources of protest had set in, as the grants that were approved stimulated an "avalanche of telegrams" from groups left out of the "official" coalition. "In effect," a *New York Times* reporter concluded, "Mr. Shriver and his Office of Economic Opportunity have inherited a thousand local political fights."[19]

OEO's emphasis on activism and growth also made a mark on its formal research activities, here again leaving little room for the deliberative processes of planning, theory development, expert consultation, or evaluative "social learning" that had been such a central feature of earlier community-based reform. Nowhere was the impact more evident than in OEO's demonstration research program, which came to symbolize the agency at its most innovative and politically controversial, and which, in its efforts to bring the core concepts of community action to fruition, effectively transformed the very notion of demonstration research from a mechanism for small-scale experimentation into an instrument for direct, and in some cases immediate and large-scale, action.

The CAP demonstration research program was authorized by section 207 of the Economic Opportunity Act, which reserved 15 percent of CAP's annual allocation for experimental programs that could be funded directly from Washington without going through local community action agencies. Modeled on the idea of demonstration research embraced by the President's Committee on Juvenile Delinquency and in the Ford Foundation's Gray Areas Program, these grants were meant to be a testing ground for innovative programs that might not well up from the community level but that, ideally after a period of experimentation and evaluation, might provide models that could be replicated elsewhere.[20] Sanford Kravitz, the former PCJD staff member who was directly in charge of the "R&D" effort, developed plans for the program with a PCJD-like operation in mind. Research staff would be organized into substantive specialties, work closely with grantees to develop theoretically informed proposals, and then submit the proposals to independent experts for review. Kravitz changed his plans, however, in his first meeting with the new OEO director just after the agency opened. Shriver wanted no part of outside review committees. "You're supposed to be smart, you have a Ph.D, you bring me the proposals and I'll make the decisions," he told Kravitz. Two weeks later, "the word came down that Shriver wanted grants ready for funding before Thanksgiving," Kravitz recalled, setting off a "whirlwind effort to get proposals in." The program's first funded project was a South Bronx program for training paraprofessionals in community mental health centers—based on a proposal written in a Washington hotel room over a weekend.[21] Head Start, too, started out as a hastily assembled CAP demonstration project, this one originating from a Shriver idea for a "kiddie corps." Against the advice of early education experts, who predicted it could not be done (new experts were soon brought in) by the end of the summer of 1965, the Head Start program had enrolled two hundred thousand children, and was well on its way to becoming the most popular of all OEO programs.[22] CAP administrators also used demonstration projects to push past the limits of standard social service reform, establishing neighborhood-based health centers, paraprofessional programs to train community residents as providers, and educational programs to draw community residents more directly into school governance.[23] Some of these programs, including Neighborhood Health Centers, Upward Bound, Foster

Grandparents, and, of course, Head Start, would come to be considered the most successful of the OEO demonstration programs, and several were earmarked for special funding from Congress in future amendments to the Economic Opportunity Act.

For the most part, however, the ideas for demonstration projects originated from the theories and the frankly ideological convictions of the CAP R&D staff. Unencumbered by the usual sign-offs and other requirements of the larger operating program, the demonstrations became a vehicle for stretching the limits of "maximum feasible participation" beyond social services to political empowerment. In this case the popularity of a few of its projects could not insulate the OEO demonstration research program from political attack. For what the program became best known for, where it "left its deepest mark," were the projects funded as experiments in organizing the poor politically.[24] A grant to the Syracuse University Community Action Training Center provided the funds for training community organizers in the methods advocated by Chicago organizer and OEO critic Saul Alinsky, with the idea that they would then "fan out" into the community to mobilize the poor to advocate on their own behalf. The group's first target was none other than the OEO-approved local community action agency, which had the support of Syracuse Mayor William F. Walsh. Responding to the rent strikes, demonstrations, sit-ins, voter registration drives, and city-hall protests organized by the renegade group, Walsh accused the organizers—and the OEO—with fomenting "class warfare." A second organizing grant, in Richmond, California, took a somewhat different tack and focused on strengthening already-existing poor people's organizations to demand better services and job opportunities. A third, to the California Center for Community Development in Del Ray, was aimed at training the rural poor as organizers, and got in immediate trouble when members of the local congressional delegation accused the Center of trying to organize a strike among migrant farmworkers.[25] Most notorious in its long-term repercussions for OEO was the "high-risk," nearly $1 million R&D grant to Chicago's Alinsky-inspired The Woodlawn Organization (TWO) for a youth development project involving the Blackstone Rangers and the East Side Disciples, two of the most notorious street gangs in the country. The project drew a steady stream of sensational charges, ranging from gun running and drug smuggling to revolutionary plots, leading up to a congressional investigation and suspension of the project, but no evidence that TWO could be faulted for much beyond lapses in judgment in the way it managed the grant.[26]

By the end of 1965, and well before the TWO scandal, the CAP demonstration program had been permanently labeled a hotbed of radicalism by critics on the outside and as a lightning rod for unwelcome controversy within the agency. Shriver himself had always blown "hot and cold" on the demonstration program, on the one hand thrilled with the success of programs like Head Start, and on the other visibly annoyed at the negative publicity and controversy associated with the program. He took to calling Kravitz "Dr. Strangegrant," and frequently made the R&D program the object of barbs at staff meetings. "Well, what have you nuts got cooked up for me now? In which funny papers am I going to land now?" he would say when new grant requests came up for consideration.[27] Shriver also took steps to tighten the relatively free rein the R&D program had enjoyed, and retained final sign-off on all demonstration grants even after approval for other CAP applications had been devolved to the regional offices. By the end of the year, OEO had curtailed or ended funding altogether for the most controversial of its community organizing activities. The combination of public attack and congressional action dealt the much deeper blow to the community action R&D program. In 1966, the legislative allocation for experimental demonstration programs was slashed to a fraction of what it had been, as a clear punishment for its most confrontational projects. In effect, the idea of action-oriented demonstration research was cut off before it could do much more than get started.

By then, though, the administration had deemed the entire community action program a political embarrassment, and was taking active steps to curtail its organizing activities. In September 1965, Budget Director Charles Schultze wrote a memo to LBJ criticizing CAP for "organizing the poor politically" and got the president's agreement to direct administrators to restrict their focus to local coordination and comprehensive planning.[28] Shifting away from its earlier emphasis on local autonomy, OEO also began to encourage prepackaged "national emphasis programs" such as Head Start.[29] The most activist of the CAP leadership began to leave the agency. Richard Boone, convinced that the OEO was no longer a vehicle for social change, organized the Citizens Crusade Against Poverty as an alternative grass-roots voice of the poor. As a portent of things to come for poverty knowledge, he was eventually replaced by a former Department of Defense official, Donald Hess.

The political fate of the Community Action Program spelled the beginning of the end for the idea of community-based action research within OEO. As the federal commitment to community action began to wane—eventually to disappear altogether—so, too, did the political demand for the theories, methods, and practitioners of the research that had helped to bring it about. Nor, despite its own ongoing program of research and demonstration, had CAP done much to establish a sustained and credible program of actual research. Under pressure to grow quickly and to prove its muster as an action program, CAP had set aside many of its social scientific aspects—the planning, the theorizing, the evaluative emphasis on social learning—leaving itself without fully developed alternatives to its earlier, increasingly discredited, concepts of social disorganization and cultural deprivation. Meanwhile, controversy was raging over precisely those concepts, most pointedly, as discussed in chapter 8, in reaction to the Moynihan Report on the Negro Family. With community action on the defensive, and its sociological tradition under fire, the stage was set for what in contrast appeared to be a more politically neutral kind of poverty knowledge, which would carry out the OEO's commitment to bringing the full powers of research to bear in the War on Poverty with an approach that could hardly have been more starkly different from the action research sponsored by CAP.

LEARNING FROM DEFENSE: THE OFFICE OF RESEARCH, PLANS, PROGRAMS, AND EVALUATION

While the transformation of poverty knowledge was tied to the demise of community action, it also represented a significant political achievement in its own right: it put the OEO at the forefront of a larger movement to spread the gospel of a new kind of policy analysis throughout the federal bureaucracy, to put public decision making on a more scientific footing—to export, that is, the so-called "analytic revolution" from defense to domestic use. Leading the way in the revolution was the OEO's office of Research, Plans, Programs and Evaluation (RPP&E), a clone of the Department of Defense Office of Systems Analysis, then the main government outpost of an approach to policy decision making developed at the RAND Corporation just after World War II.[30] Systems analysis was a highly advanced form of operations research, that relied heavily on econometric modeling to choose among different kinds and combinations of weapons and to gauge their effectiveness in meeting broader strategic objectives. Systems analysis put a premium on conceptualizing strategic objectives in concrete, quantitative terms, on weighing alternatives in terms of measurable costs and benefits, and, above all, on a rational way of thinking about defense policy alternatives.[31] Systems analysis also suggested new criteria for assessing the performance of particular weapons systems, focusing on how they contributed to overarching objectives rather than just on immediate target efficiency. Finally, systems analysis promised to introduce a sense of fairness into the patronage-ridden world of weapons procurement. In the hands of the systems analysts, noted the economist and RAND-trained Pentagon analyst Alain Enthoven, weapons decisions would be based "on explicit criteria of the public interest" rather than "compromise among institutional, parochial or other vested interests."[32]

The RAND analysts had been evolving and applying their new techniques in government contract work throughout the 1940s and 1950s, but it was not until the 1960s, during the Kennedy and Johnson administrations, that systems analysis would really begin to penetrate the government defense bureaucracy. The person most directly responsible was Robert McNamara, the rising star of the automobile industry who was recruited from his new position as president of the Ford Motor Company to head the Department of Defense in 1961. McNamara was well acquainted with the basic principles of systems analysis, having served on an Air Force operations research team and having subsequently followed the techniques being developed at RAND in his own efforts to shake up the management procedures at Ford. When he took over as Secretary of Defense in 1961, McNamara brought in a group of systems analysts recruited directly from RAND.[33] Together, the Secretary and his "whiz kids" proceeded to shake up the Pentagon bureaucracy from within, beginning with a new, more centralized planning structure that had been developed at RAND, designed to strengthen the link between budget making and policy objectives. Its purpose, as one close observer later wrote, "was to recast federal budgeting from a repetitive process for financing permanent bureaucracies into an instrument for deciding the purposes and programs of government."[34] Not surprisingly, the new Programming, Planning and Budgeting System (PPBS) would prove highly controversial among military bureaucrats. Nevertheless, it was credited with revolutionizing management at the Pentagon, at considerable cost saving, and won accolades for McNamara within the administration.[35] In 1965, the Johnson administration announced that it planned to institute PPBS throughout the government.

PPBS was promoted with great fanfare in official government announcements. The system was "very new and very revolutionary," President Johnson said in a press conference in August. At his direction, agency heads would set up "a very special staff of experts" equipped with "the most modern methods of program analysis," to find "new ways to do jobs faster, to do jobs better, and to do jobs less expensively." The new system would make decision making "as up-to-date . . . as our space exploring programs," Johnson added, offering "the full promise of a finer life" for Americans "at the lowest possible cost."[36] A later Budget Bureau directive, though a good deal more prosaic, also held forth the prospect of considerable change in the way policy and budget decisions would be made at the agency level. Current practice lacked the "formalized planning and systems analysis" that should go into budget decisions, the directive complained, leaving agency goals vague, existing programs unevaluated, and top management uninformed by a sense of the costs and benefits of alternative approaches. The new PPB system would change all that, making the budget a framework for "setting goals, defining objectives and developing planned programs for meeting those objectives." It would begin with a new way of conceptualizing objectives, as a set of concretely stated "outputs" against which analysts would judge program performance, and assess the costs and benefits of alternative approaches. Henceforth, sound policy would depend on the existence of "permanent specialized staffs," trained in "systems analysis, operations research and other pertinent techniques," and equipped with "concrete and specific data" about how "inputs" and "outputs" could be most efficiently matched.[37]

In practice, the PPB system proved a good deal less revolutionary—and much harder to implement—than planned.[38] As the defense intellectuals themselves came to realize early on, systems analysis was no substitute for political judgment, and more often than not, its rational calculations were but a small factor in the ultimately political process of decision making. Moreover, in order to work the new budget system would require a strong commitment from top agency leadership and at least a modicum of receptivity from program staff.[39] For most agencies, however, PPBS was an imposition from the outside, which ignored historically established institutional cultures and practices and, by centralizing policy making in the agency head, threatened to upset the existing balance of power between program managers and central administrators within agencies. Nor was it easy to implement. PPBS created massive demands for appropriate data and analytically trained personnel—both in short supply in 1960s Washington—generating "a rush," as one observer noted, to convert "the small band of military analysts in the Department of Defense, RAND, and other defense-oriented organizations" into instant social policy analysts.[40] But even the most experienced analysts found it difficult to translate complex social policies into "outputs-oriented" program categories.[41] By 1968, a congressional study found that only three of sixteen agencies had made "substantial progress" towards implementing the system. Within a few years, close observers were sounding the death knell of PPBS. Nevertheless, the brief era of PPB had one lasting legacy. Systematic policy analysis was alive and firmly entrenched in key areas of domestic policy making, and nowhere more firmly than in the two government institutions that would play the most central role in shaping the course of poverty research: OEO's office of RPP&E and HEW's office of the Assistant Secretary for Planning and Evaluation (ASPE). For economist Alice Rivlin, who succeeded defense analyst William Gorham as the director of ASPE, PPB's "most important effect was the creation of an analytical staff at the department level, which brought into the Secretary's office a group of people who were trained to think analytically and whose job it was to improve the process of decisionmaking."[42] These were the very people who as part of an expanding federal research bureaucracy, would introduce the protocols of systems analysis to poverty research.

POVERTY ANALYSTS

As it turns out, the OEO did not need the Budget Bureau to instruct it in the basics of the new budgeting system. By the time the PPBS directive was issued in October 1965, the RPP&E office, headed by economist and former RAND research director Joseph Kershaw, was already prepared to submit its first long-range planning budget. "For once I think we are ahead of the game," Shriver wrote on the initial White House memo announcing that PPB was soon to be a requirement.[43] Shriver himself could take at least partial credit for this accomplishment. Like other members of the Kennedy and Johnson administrations, he was very impressed with what Robert McNamara was doing at the Defense Department, and, in his search for the "best and the brightest" for the new agency, actively sought to bring the defense analysts into the War on Poverty. His earliest recruit was Pentagon "whiz kid" Adam Yarmolinsky, who, as Shriver's deputy on the antipoverty task force, was effectively in charge of packaging the Economic Opportunity Act of 1964. Shriver and Yarmolinsky had first met during Kennedy's presidential campaign, when Yarmolinsky was a practicing lawyer and foundation urban affairs consultant, counting among his clients Paul Ylvisaker at the Ford Foundation. While not himself trained as an analyst, he soon gained a reputation as one of the brightest and most acerbic of the defense "whiz kids" when he became special assistant to Secretary of Defense Robert McNamara to help restructure policy making at the Pentagon. In the eyes of conservatives within the military establishment, he had also come to symbolize everything that was wrong with the new order at the Pentagon: he was an outsider, a graduate of Harvard and Yale, an urbanist, and he had taken a strong stand on the enforcement of civil rights guidelines in personnel and training practices. At Shriver's behest, Yarmolinsky took a Pentagon leave to join the poverty task force in 1964, with full White House assurance that he would be appointed OEO's deputy director once the poverty legislation was passed.[44] Yarmolinsky was sacrificed, however, in an eleventh-hour deal with the North Carolina congressional delegation: in exchange for their support, Yarmolinsky, the ivy league intellectual and civil rights enforcer, would have to go.[45] Despite what many of the poverty planners considered a great and probably unnecessary loss, an essential connection had been made. In one instance at least, Shriver set up the new agency much the way Yarmolinsky might have, with a policy and planning office modeled on the Office of Systems Analysis at DOD. To run it, he chose Joseph Kershaw, formerly of RAND and then Provost at Williams College, who in turn recruited a RAND analyst, economist Robert Levine, to be his deputy in charge of research and planning. Neither had substantial knowledge of the poverty problem. What they did have was training and experience as systems analysts—and a strong conviction that their skills could be applied to this "very new and very exciting" poverty initiative.[46]

Both Kershaw and Levine spent the initial months of 1965 commuting to Washington while finishing up other obligations. When they arrived to set up the policy and planning shop in early summer, then, they were already several steps behind the action programs. OEO had grown "very big very fast," as Levine saw it, and without any visible signs of planning. The fast growth strategy was beginning to exact a price. Nowhere was this more evident than in the troubled Job Corps program, which since the spring had been reeling from a barrage of highly publicized mishaps and criticisms coming from all quarters. Corpsmen were reportedly disillusioned by the combination of administrative unpreparedness, lack of curricular materials, and unfamiliar surroundings that greeted them at several of the new centers. Media reports of high dropout rates, overpaid staff, and isolated incidents of violence, drinking, or local vandalism involving trainees added scandal to the mix. The program also suffered from the all-too-familiar consequences of overpromise. Having pledged to enroll one hundred thousand trainees by the end of its first fiscal year, the Job Corps was having trouble meeting even 10 percent of this goal. To make matters worse, OEO had raised expectations among the some three hundred thousand potential enrollees who had responded to a large-scale post-card recruitment scheme that had emerged out of one of Shriver's brainstorming sessions. Rather than focusing on how to develop the capacity to respond to this unexpectedly vast demand, it seemed, the "dominant problems for the Job Corps were keeping the Corpsmen from dropping out in large numbers and maintaining control over those who stayed in."[47]

Amidst the administrative "chaos" and overextended promises, Kershaw and Levine nevertheless held out great hope for the role of systematic planning and program analysis, if not to tackle the day-to-day problems of running OEO, then to set the agency, and the larger War on Poverty, on a more orderly and rational overall course of action. For despite the criticisms and local crises that were keeping the action programs in a seemingly constant state of embattlement, June 1965 was still a time of great optimism at the OEO. The agency had the talent, the president's commitment, and—or so the planners assumed—the promise that resources would be available to win the war.[48]

The first step for Kershaw and Levine was to fill out the "skeleton staff of planners" that they found in the RPP&E office upon arrival in Washington. In contrast to the career bureaucrats who then populated the office, Kershaw and Levine were looking for people with the disciplinary and practical background required for analysis: for the most part, this meant economists or sociologists with quantitative, empirical research skills, but above all it meant the ability to think in rational systemwide terms.[49] Hoping to bring "new blood" into the agency, the RPP&E heads looked outside the usual government channels, relying on their own academic, professional, and think tank networks for recruits. Economist Harold Watts was a skilled young econometrician who, like Levine, had done his graduate work under James Tobin at Yale. Walter Williams, a recent Indiana Ph.D., came via Budget Bureau Director Charles Schultze.[50] Robinson Hollister, a Stanford-trained economist who had taught with Kershaw at Williams, was just returning from a stint in Paris working on a manpower training study for the OECD. Those who did come from government agencies had proven capabilities in systems review. Myron Lefkowitz, who became RPP&E's health specialist, was a sociologist and for several years had been working in the Office of Research at the NIMH. Alvin Schorr, a social work Ph.D., trained caseworker, and special assistant to the Commissioner of Social Security, had put himself at odds with program administrators and much of the social work profession by calling for a family allowance that would reduce the reliance on social work rehabilitation in AFDC.[51] By mid-summer, RPP&E had enough of a staff to get to work on its first, and in many ways defining, major project: putting together what, absent a sense of irony or any reference whatsoever to Soviet-style planning, was known in systems analytic parlance as a Five Year Plan for the entire War on Poverty.[52]

Following the PPB methodology (presented in stylized input/output flow charts accompanying the document), the planners began by outlining two defining policy goals in as concrete, time-limited terms as they could: one, referring to the recent OEO decision to adopt an official, income-based poverty line was to eradicate income poverty by the year 1976; the other, admittedly long-term, was to "make permanent changes in those social and economic factors that limit poor people's access to opportunity."[53] Relating these goals to existing programs and cost/benefit analyses, the plan then offered a three-pronged strategy that combined job training and public service employment; a "massive" but more targeted and social service-oriented community action program; and the favored and most enduring of all analytic reform proposals, a universal income guarantee delivered in the form of a negative income tax. Budget projections for the five-year plan were tremendously ambitious: nearly $10 billion in additional government expenditures against poverty, including $4 billion in new OEO spending, bringing the overall level of antipoverty spending to $30 billion.[54]

The Five Year Plan generated considerable interest both within and outside of OEO when it was sent to the Budget Bureau in October 1965. As the planners never failed to point out, it was "the first such submission by any civilian agency of the Government."[55] The plan also followed through on a promise made in a report sent to Congress earlier that spring: "to develop a cost effectiveness system modeled on the Pentagon's method of choosing between rival weapons."[56] In a "command performance" before top White House and Budget Bureau officials, Kershaw made as strong a pitch for the new "OEO system" as he did for the budget itself. "The OEO system 1. Provides a framework for systematic program decisions. 2. Identifies costs and benefits of program alternatives. 3. Focuses staff effort on central program issues and 4. Consolidates planning, programing and budgeting systems," according to the accompanying materials. It was also a system for rational decision making at the program level. In OEO's new "program change system," program proposals would be informed by "poverty profile analysis," "research studies," "cost effectiveness studies," and "program evaluation,"—all weighed, of course, against the existing five year antipoverty plan. Planning, in other words, promised to transform the programs, as well as the decision making processes at OEO. Especially striking was just how much the Five Year Plan departed from current, politically vetted antipoverty practices: resurrecting strategies that had already been rejected by the administration, the plan called for major expansion of income maintenance and government job creation. There was also at least one notable absence: the political and local organizing role envisioned by Community Action administrators at OEO was not even mentioned in the Five Year Plan. "[T]he economists of the planning division did not argue against the political power and community organization dicta of Shriver's social theorists," Levine later recalled with no small hint of disdain, "they didn't understand the concepts and ignored them. Community Action was to be a deliverer and coordinator of services; organization of the poor was not readily assimilable into the model."[57] By then fed up with the political controversies aroused by community action "theorists," Shriver endorsed the Five Year Plan enthusiastically.

The 1965 National Anti-Poverty Plan could only have been created in a moment of high expectation, both about the promise of rational decision making and about the level of funding that would be available for the War on Poverty. "In retrospect," Levine wrote in 1970, "the fascinating thing about these [budget] figures were [sic] that we really thought they were possible."[58] The moment passed quickly. In late August 1965 even before the first Five Year Plan was officially presented, word came down that escalating costs for the crisis in Vietnam would crowd out almost all additional domestic spending, and a Budget Bureau circular asked all agencies to take "aggressive efforts . . . to identify savings which can be considered with your budget submissions."[59] Not long before, a violent uprising in the impoverished Watts section of Los Angeles had precipitated a rash of renewed charges that CAP was fomenting class and race warfare, and rebellion in the streets—making the possibility of any expansion in community action impossibly remote. Besides, President Johnson remained resistant to the major growth of income maintenance envisioned in the negative income tax idea, and both the CEA and Labor (in a reversal of its earlier position) opposed public employment in favor of faster growth and vastly expanded manpower and training programs. The combined result was a flat-out rejection of the first Five Year Plan and its budget projections. The administration cut the poverty budget back from the $10 billion originally requested to $1.75 billion, leaving OEO with only a very modest increment in existing funding levels and ignoring RPP&E's big new proposals altogether.

The drastic scaling back of the budget request came as a rude awakening for the planners as well as for Shriver, and signaled the beginning of a more general, administration-led retrenchment of expectation and activism at the OEO. CAP, by then transformed from "what was to have been the keystone of the federal antipoverty program into a less central but politically embarrassing force on both the local and national scene," was the most visible target.[60] But the mood of retrenchment had an effect on RPP&E as well, which "consolidated its grandiose ideas and began to live in the real world rather than the exciting dream world of 1965," Levine recalled.[61] In June 1966, RPP&E submitted its second Five Year Plan, indicating how, primarily by pulling back from its jobs and community action proposals, it would adjust to the new programmatic austerity. In part responding to the tighter economy brought about by increased expenditures for the Vietnam War, the analysts' proposed employment strategy would shift from job creation to growth and training, reducing the public employment program to a contingency plan in case of unexpected downturn. Adjustments in the CAP request reflected a more explicit response to political and budgetary constraints. Community Action, still a "major weapon" in the antipoverty arsenal, would now operate on the principle of "catalysis": rather than providing services directly, community action agencies would be used to concentrate funds from other government agencies on poor areas, a move budget planners could not refrain from attributing to "our experience in proposing a large fiscal 1967 budget for direct CAP delivery of services and our failure to obtain this budget." The new Plan also put more emphasis on "individual improvement," building on the popular success of Head Start to call for increased investments in early childhood education, and greater attention to parental involvement. The planners were less willing to compromise on the negative income tax, which they continued to promote as an economist's dream come true. The proposed NIT would complement employment and opportunity programs, they argued, while producing a simplified "substitute for the demeaning programs now lumped together under the head of Public Assistance." The NIT would also be compatible with free market principles—giving individuals more choice in labor market decisions and eliminating the need for the minimum wage once implemented, the document argued. Most of all, it was "well within our financial capacity," at a cost that would rise from $2.9 to a total of $17 billion by 1976. "We believe that the time is coming . . . when American people will accept . . . a guaranteed minimum income at the poverty level as a right in a wealthy country and we propose to start moving in this direction now." In combination with the opportunity programs, the NIT would "end poverty in the United States as we define it today by 1976, 200 years from the declaration that the pursuit of happiness is among the inalienable rights of Americans."[62]

While administrative restrictions left the analysts with a limited range of antipoverty weapons, in some ways retrenchment actually enhanced the position of RPP&E within the agency, and particularly by establishing budget planning as a form of political advocacy in Shriver's annual struggle to keep the War on Poverty alive. With ammunition prepared by the planners, Shriver attacked budget cutbacks not only as a calculable "retreat" from existing levels of commitment, but also as "an explicit abandonment of systematic budgetary and program analysis in favor of classical number juggling aimed at equalizing the agony." Moreover, it would represent a "reversal" of the government's commitment to the poor that would lead to alienation, or more "dangerous" outcomes, and would only reinforce the impression that "the poor must bear the burden of defense."[63] Shriver got reinforcement in these arguments from former CEA chairman Walter Heller, at that point back at Minnesota, who wrote to Johnson in December with a "hardheaded economic and fiscal case" for increased spending on Great Society programs. "A billion or two next year could spell the difference between progress and stagnation," he said, adding that it was "peanuts when compared with GNP, previous tax cuts, and the recent rise in personal income and profits," and could "do a lot of good in strengthening the economic and political base for Vietnam." The case was "airtight," he told the President: "a Headstart for poor children" would have a far bigger payoff "than a headstart to Mars."[64]

RPP&E was becoming more influential within the agency in other ways as well, as Shriver came increasingly to rely on the analysts as a source of policy advice and assistance in the effort to bring more order to OEO activities. In 1966, they absorbed responsibility for the annual as well as long-range budget planning, bringing them more centrally into the day-to-day operations of the agency. Shriver also gave RPP&E "sign-off" authority on CAP R&D proposals, and proved quite supportive when the analysts made bids for CAP funds to finance research projects of their own.[65] At the same time, the analysts became more tempered in their own expectations of what rational analysis could deliver. By the time they submitted their second Five Year Plan, the RPP&E staff was well aware that their long-range budgets would never be actual blueprints for administration policy; by the time of the third submission, "OEO admitted frankly that the resources, necessary for the success of the plan, were not readily available" and presented it almost as testament of what, given the political will, would be possible. They were also prepared to concede that, as Levine said in a 1968 congressional statement on the role of analysis at OEO, "decisionmaking is not an analytic process, it is a political one."[66] At most, analysis would be "an influence . . . that's all" on policy decisions, and at times that influence would be overlooked entirely.[67] To illustrate his point, Levine used the example of the 1967 amendments to the Economic Opportunity Act which, contrary to economic thinking and all the empirical evidence, prohibited OEO from encouraging the rural poor to migrate to urban areas in the belief that migration had contributed to overcrowding and rioting in the cities. He might just as well have pointed to a much earlier episode in which RPP&E, under direct orders from Shriver following his meeting with powerful Catholic Church leaders, severely curtailed its original recommendation for vastly expanded family planning services in the first Five Year Plan. Nevertheless, on balance the Five Year Plans represented a limited but important victory for the planners in RPP&E. By applying the tools of systems analysis, the planners had brought a sense of coherence and structure to the inchoate array of programs under the umbrella of the War on Poverty while establishing OEO itself as a cutting edge research and planning agency. In the process, they articulated a vision for OEO that was more compatible with the administration's and that would take the agency far away from its troubled career as an agency representing political empowerment and action at the local level. It was a vision that emphasized planning, not direct political action, as the agent of change; efficiency, not local empowerment, as the standard for judging program priorities; service delivery, not "maximum feasible participation," as the objective behind CAP. It preserved the idea that poverty, defined as an income deficit, could be eliminated without resorting to major political or economic restructuring. And it established analysis as a model for the kind of poverty knowledge that would be required to fight, if not to win, what the analysts assumed would be an ongoing war against poverty.

THE ANALYTIC RESEARCH AGENDA

Three issues dominated RPP&E's research agenda, as befit the needs of analytical policy planning: poverty measurement; cost/benefit program evaluation; and quantifiable, controlled experiments to test out new approaches to helping the poor. Although recognizing these as thorny, ultimately political problems, the RPP&E planners also had faith in the tools of analysis to provide an unassailable scientific basis for the antipoverty plan.

Preceding all else on the agenda was the need for statistical data, which at the time was a sorely lacking but essential ingredient in the effort to understand, as noted in one OEO report to Congress, "the strength of the enemy" as well as "the nation's ability to do battle at any given time and place."[68] Stimulated also by the prospect of developing predictive models for assessing program costs and benefits, OEO analysts set out to gather ever more precise information on the demographic characteristics of poor people, their income, household structure, and program use, and on their likely behavior over time. This they accomplished by funding a series of national surveys (including an oversample of poor households in annual census data and the longitudinal Panel Study of Income Dynamics) that have since become the essential data of poverty research—easily replacing the far more time-consuming methods of primary data collection and participant observation in community-based research. Like the Keynesian Revolution and its impact on aggregate income data, the War on Poverty led the way to a "microdata" (household and individual-level) revolution that itself would have a tremendous influence on the scientific understanding of the "nature and causes" of poverty.

In addition to immediate policy needs, the seemingly technical task of gathering more and better data was also shaped by a series of political decisions dating back to the original CEA task force on poverty. One was the decision, favored by the economists who dominated the early task force discussions, to define the poverty problem as lack of income, reflecting their assumption not only that income offered a universalistic and straightforward measure of need, but also their confidence that they had the means—through an economic growth-centered strategy—to win a war against poverty so defined. Second, and related, was the decision to use an absolute definition of poverty, on the grounds that any effort to target inequality through explicitly redistributional means would be both politically unacceptable and technically infeasible; absolute poverty could actually be eliminated; relative poverty, by definition, would always be with us. Third, and most recent, was OEO's decision, announced in May 1965, to use the poverty thresholds developed by Social Security Commission analyst Mollie Orshansky in measuring the size and composition of the poor population.

Orshansky had first developed her poverty measure as part of a highly significant development in the research program of the Social Security Administration: taking note of the rising proportion of divorced or never-married as opposed to widowed mothers on AFDC, the Social Security Administration research division had determined to end what had been an ongoing statistical series on AFDC widows and to investigate the changing situation of all poor families with children instead.[69] Orshansky volunteered for the assignment and, in the absence of an official poverty standard, did what most social surveyors before her had done: combined survey data on household need and household spending patterns to come up with a measure of her own. She was also continuing a tradition that distinguished her as one among the "ladies of the federal government," as economist Eugene Smolensky called them, who were in the business of estimating need well before the War on Poverty was declared, as part of the regular course of agency activity.[70] A lifelong public servant who, with a B.A. in math and statistics, had moved from research positions in the Children's Bureau and the Department of Agriculture to the Social Security Administration in 1958, Orshansky was one of a respected but mostly invisible cadre of women research professionals based at SSA and other government agencies during the postwar years. Often trained in economics or, like Margaret Hagood, in sociology, these women found job opportunities in federal government and other "applied" endeavors when university jobs were largely closed off to them, although within government they were often clustered in research bureaus focusing on such traditional "women's" concerns as social welfare, female labor force participation, families and children, and home economics.[71] That experience as a career government statistician, a far cry from systems analysis, was what gave Orshansky the wholly unexpected designation as author of the government's official poverty line. That, and the political pressure mounting on OEO analysts when, several months after the start of the War on Poverty, they still had no official measure of their own.

Critics, including a group gathered by the national Chamber of Commerce, were starting to take notice of the fact that the agency was still operating with the admittedly arbitrary across-the-board cutoff of $3,000 the CEA had identified in its 1964 Economic Report, leading to the "odd result," as Orshansky would later point out, that an elderly couple with $2,900 income for the year would be considered poor, but a family with a husband, wife, and 4 little children with $3,100 income would not be."[72] Building on her earlier work on children in poor families, Orshansky herself came up with a set of meticulously calculated poverty thresholds for no fewer than 124 different family types—classified according to age, sex, race, size, workforce participation levels, and divided evenly between farm and nonfarm units—based on what nutritional and budget surveys said it would cost to feed a family on a minimalistic "economy food plan," multiplied by three to allow for other subsistence needs.[73] The results were published in a Social Security Bulletin article, aptly entitled "Counting the Poor," which, under the gun to fix the poverty line in response to their critics, OEO analysts gave wide circulation within the administration as the breakthrough they had been looking for. Before long, and evidently without consulting the Budget Bureau or the Council of Economic Advisers, OEO issued a press release announcing that a new, more precise way of calculating the official poverty line had been found. Fellow economists, including CEA staff member James Bonnen, had serious doubts, complaining that the new "Orshansky measure" was just as arbitrary as the old $3,000 cutoff, and infinitely more complicated.[74] No one was more surprised, though, than Orshansky herself, who had never meant her measures as official government standards. Concerned primarily with suggesting a way to vary the measure for family size, Orshansky took pains to recognize that her work was at best an "interim standard," "arbitrary, but not unreasonable," and minimalistic at best.[75]

The official poverty line would be subject to ongoing criticism over the next several years, much of it focused on matters of both technical and political importance, such as its failure to include either assets or in-kind benefits, and its inadequacy in accounting for rising costs and standards of living.[76] Easily lost in these disputes were certain more basic political and conceptual realities. By all estimations, the poverty line—any poverty line—was an arbitrary cutoff point, and yet it would determine who was classified as poor, and who not, who would be eligible for program benefits, and, perhaps most important, the demographic profile of the group on whose behalf a major new set of policy initiatives was about to be implemented. As even the most preliminary of analyses made clear, what might appear to be small changes in measurement standards could make an enormous difference in the profile of the poor. Indeed, a 1995 proposal for revising the poverty standard, offered by a National Academy of Sciences panel, would raise the number of employed people classified as poor and decrease the number of "non-working" poor.[77] The new poverty line also gave official sanction, and then added the weight of numbers, to the idea that poverty was chiefly a problem of income deprivation, and that it was a problem people experienced as individuals. Once entrenched in government agency business, this way of measuring poverty virtually closed off efforts to introduce more relativistic or nonincome alternatives—measuring poverty, for example, in relation to median income, or according to broader indicators of inclusion and opportunity such as access to education, adequate health care, transportation, and housing, or other amenities considered basic to social citizenship. The new poverty line also helped to establish the poor as a separate, easily definable social group.

Nevertheless, and despite all its recognized flaws, in the minds of OEO's architects and supporters, the adoption of an official poverty line achieved important political aims. "It enabled a quantification . . . of the changing number of poor people and hence of progress toward the goal of eliminating poverty," wrote economist Robert J. Lampman, presenting the possibility as well of confronting new policy proposals "with the rude and restrictive challenge, 'what does it do for the poor?' " Future administrations would be "judged by their success or failure in reducing the officially measured prevalence of poverty," James Tobin predicted.[78] At the same time, the adoption of the poverty line also represented an official step in defining the parameters of poverty knowledge, for it made counting the poor—once carried out primarily by social reformers and the invisible "ladies of the federal government"—the business of more visible, professionally trained economists. Although proponents of the "narrow income" definition thought it practical and morally neutral, they also used it as part of a politically neutered conceptualization of the poverty problem: one that routinely shunned class as a conceptual category and reduced race and gender to demographic indicators divorced from social context. Most important in terms of the new poverty knowledge, the official poverty line confined poverty to a problem of individuals—measurable in the characteristics and traits of poor people rather than in some more expansive index defined to include measurable traits—income and wage distribution, unemployment rates—of the political economy. In this sense the official poverty line was itself an indicator of a larger, more problematic development in social policy and research: the separation, in economic as well as social knowledge, of the problem of poverty from the problems of employment and growth with which the "new" economists had started their inquiry.

RPP&E laid the groundwork for what would soon become an equally substantial part of the new poverty knowledge by stimulating demand and setting standards for the evaluation of social action programs in the 1960s. Once again, PPBS doctrine and political pressures combined to exert new demands on the knowledge that would be produced for policy purposes, and to impose new standards on practices that had for the most part been conducted unsystematically, and sporadically, in government social policy. In the new approach, evaluation would be a central component of systematic policy decision making, conducted by a separate analytically trained staff; it would assess programs according to concrete outcomes, and against measurable policy objectives; it would be conducted with the tools of rational analysis and the methods of economics. It would also create a new research specialization out of a practice that, until that point, had little academic self-consciousness. Indeed, according to one contemporary text, the field was in a "sorry state" of affairs—enough so, as Joseph Kershaw soon learned, to make it hard to *give* academics the money to develop the theory for measuring "inputs and outputs in community and social action projects." In an effort to engage "the best minds," Kershaw approached Yale University President Kingman Brewster with an offer of OEO support in early 1965—only to be refused, politely, when Brewster could not find the faculty willing to take the project on. Sargent Shriver summed up the situation with characteristic impatience. The academics were distinguished, he told Kershaw, but "they gave birth to a mouse." He went on, in an equally characteristic show of pressure, to remind Kershaw that Congress was sure to start asking questions about what concrete research RPP&E had produced.[79]

More than any other component of the RPP&E program, evaluation research brought the OEO analysts in direct conflict with the "social theorists" in the Community Action Program, in this case over what should constitute—and who should determine—the standards for judging program success. Evaluation, for analysts, required concrete measures of goals, outcomes, and costs, and, ideally, control group comparisons to assess what would have happened if the program had never existed at all. The problem, of course, was that community action did not lend itself to such measures at all: it was about process as much as product—intangibles (or, at least, unquantifiables) such as empowerment, self-determination, and quality of life. For program administrators and community residents, the "input and output" indicators imposed by outside evaluators were anathema to what the idea of community action was all about. For this reason and others, CAP was not willing to cede jurisdiction for evaluation to the analysts in RPP&E. Adding to the tension was the fact that Kershaw and Levine were feeling pressure, from Congress as well as from Shriver, to produce "concrete performance data" in order to justify the agency's budget requests, even demanding, by 1967, control-group evaluations for OEO programs. In response to such demands, RPP&E created a separate, beefed-up evaluation division with responsibility for determining whether or not OEO programs were meeting measurable antipoverty objectives. The resulting tensions, which one staff member likened to the "East/West missile situation," set the stage for a major dispute within the agency and the larger research community over a controversial, unfavorable evaluation of the already enormously popular Head Start program.[80] Prominently aired in the media and carried over into the Nixon administration, the dispute brought the deeper divisions between RPP&E and CAP to the surface, and became a struggle over the value of analytic vs. community-based research in fighting the War on Poverty.

From its inception as Shriver's idea for an OEO "kiddie corps," Head Start had violated almost every principle of rational planning and systematic decision making associated with systems analysis. One of the earliest and most visible of the OEO's new initiatives, the program was planned, organized, and up and running as a summer demonstration project within a span of about six months, accompanied by a massive publicity campaign that quickly swelled enrollments from the initial target of 100,000 in a select number of "competent" communities to more than a half-million children in 3,300 communities nationwide. By fall 1965 Head Start had been designated a phenomenal success, a "landmark in the maturity of our democracy," as President Johnson said, and by 1967 it was enrolling 2 million children year round. The problem, according to emerging and widely reported evaluation evidence, was that the program didn't work—at least by one key indicator of success: this was the so-called "fade-out" phenomenon, which showed Head Start children starting the regular school year with an initial boost in cognitive ability but quickly losing the edge as their classmates caught up during the year. The findings were hardly fatal—indeed, early childhood educators used them to promote a continuation program, known as Project Follow-Through. Nor were they exactly rigorous, as developmental psychologist Urie Bronfenbrenner complained in response to the prominent coverage about the "fade-out" in the *New York Times* and the *Washington Post*. Nevertheless, the misnamed "fade-out" (the absolute gains made by Head Start children did not diminish; their relative gains got smaller as their peers caught up) was quickly becoming the conventional wisdom, leaving RPP&E analysts skeptical about any further expansion of Head Start.[81] Robert Levine, based on his own review of evaluations through 1967, arrived at the "admittedly unpopular conclusion that within a highly limited anti-poverty budget, Head Start should not be overstressed." He advised Shriver to maintain the "far cheaper" summer programs at steady state, but to hold the line on expanding the full-year effort until more definitive proof of its effectiveness came in.[82]

Controversy exploded, however, when RPP&E's new evaluation division announced its plans for a national control-group review which, over the objections of Head Start administrators, would ignore alternative measures of health, nutrition, motivation, and family functioning to focus exclusively on whether the program raised children's test scores. The study, conducted under contract by the Westinghouse Learning Corporation and Ohio University, was to take place over a one-year period beginning in June, 1968.[83] Months before its release, with a Republican administration in office, the political stakes suddenly escalated. In his Economic Opportunity message to Congress in January 1969, President Richard M. Nixon reported on preliminary findings recently made available to the OEO, saying that the still-unfinished study confirmed "what many have feared: the long-term effect of Head Start appears to be extremely weak." Nixon also noted that the findings came from "a major national evaluation" that would "be available this spring."[84] Fearful that the administration planned to use the evaluation to cut back or eliminate Head Start, advocates launched a very effective campaign to discredit the Westinghouse report—drawing front page headlines in the *New York Times* repeating allegations that the report was "full of holes" and a "potential political disaster."[85] Several days later the *Times* reported that the White House was "beginning to retaliate" against the study's critics "in part because the report is crucial to several policy decisions that Mr. Nixon has already made."[86] As it turned out, the worst fears of Head Start supporters were unfounded. While Nixon cautioned that the program remained an "experiment," its political popularity assured continued support, although to this day not at a level of funding sufficient to cover all children who are eligible.

Neither "side" turned out to be a "winner" in the ongoing debate over Head Start evaluation. The program indeed survived, but its benefits had been called seriously, and publicly, into question and it would continue, in the eyes of the Nixon administration, to be treated as an " 'experimental' rather than as an established program."[87] Although generally acquitted by reviewers consulted by RPP&E, the Westinghouse Study also came under heavy criticism from influential evaluation and early childhood experts, raising equally serious questions about the validity of an evaluative science that could produce very different results under alternative methodological approaches. The controversies over Head Start evaluation also underscored the methodological and political limitations of analytic techniques as an approach to assessing early education and other social action interventions. With its reliance on "concrete" indicators and fixation on quantifiable outcomes, impact evaluation confined itself to variables it could easily measure as evidence of program success, and ignored or devalued more subtle, less easily quantifiable program objectives. Invariably, this meant the programs would be judged according to the measures of individual gains—such as cognitive ability or raised income—rather than more elusive indicators of community-level change. The cost/benefit framework also turned out to be a rather blunt instrument for policy decision making, in some instances creating an artificial "bottom line" performance standard that not only established inappropriate expectations but also made impact evaluations particularly vulnerable to political abuse. Easily lost in the debate over whether Head Start was a "success" in these terms was a more fundamental question about what the program—as a time-limited and modest intervention amidst poverty, inadequate school systems, and restricted opportunity—should have been expected to achieve in the first place. Moreover, in reality it was the strength and organization of a political constituency, not cost-effectiveness, that would determine the fate of Head Start or other social programs.

But if it highlighted some of the limitations of analytic evaluation, the controversy over Head Start hardly ended in defeat for the RPP&E Evaluation Division. As the White House defense of the Westinghouse study indicated, analytic, cost/benefit evaluation was, if anything, the wave of the future in the Nixon administration. In February 1969, the president's newly created Council for Urban Affairs began to develop proposals for restructuring OEO with a greatly enhanced role for research, planning, and evaluation.[88] In March, the

General Accounting Office issued an independent assessment of OEO evaluation practices that offered strong vindication for the RPP&E vision of what evaluation should be all about. Likening the ideal evaluation technique to "the framework within which business investment decisions are made," the report envisioned a methodology which would "remove judgment from the process and, in essence, permit the public authorities to settle society's problems by computation."[89] It concluded by calling for a much greater investment in quantitative, cost/benefit studies of program impact. When the Nixon administration announced the restructuring of OEO later that year, it followed up on that recommendation, and substantially expanded the agency's evaluation staff and capacity.[90]

Having begun on an uncertain and hotly contested note, then, systematic, outcomes-oriented evaluation became the norm for assessing social action programs at the OEO, where it met the standards not only of the analytic research office but the increasing demand for scientific evidence of program performance from the administration and in Congress more generally. By the late 1960s, it had become standard legislative practice to require and in some instances to earmark funds for impact evaluation in authorizing legislation for educational, manpower, antipoverty, health, and other social welfare programs, and by 1972, one study reported, expenditures had reached nearly $100 million for evaluation in only four of the largest social welfare agencies. A decade later, a General Accounting Office survey reported 228 non-Defense evaluation operations within the federal government.[91] One of the mainstays of the burgeoning field of poverty research, the huge demand for systematic evaluation was also the basis of a new research profession, which rapidly spawned specialized training programs, professional associations, journals, and nonprofit contract organizations of its own.[92] As the first of its kind in a domestic federal agency, RPP&E's Evaluation Division would continue to play a major role in shaping the standards for that profession. At the same time, in the increasingly uncertain politics of antipoverty policy, the capacity to evaluate would also go a long way toward assuring the continued viability of analytic research at OEO, and elsewhere in federal government; cost/benefit evaluation, among other dimensions of the analytic revolution, was a legacy of the War on Poverty that would survive, and thrive, in the post–Great Society years.

So, too, would a third feature of the RPP&E research agenda, which aimed to introduce a new standard in social experimentation to poverty research. This was melded, once again, with an effort to rein in and redefine what had come under the rubric of Community Action demonstration research. In contrast to the politically charged CAP demonstrations, RPP&E proposed demonstrations that could be conducted under "reasonably controlled conditions," replicated in several sites, and based on experimental—i.e., randomly assigned control group—design. After all, demonstrations were only worthwhile if they could provide statistical evidence of measurable antipoverty effects.[93]

RPP&E was not especially successful in its efforts to control CAP demonstration funds. It did, however, score by far its most impressive success with an experimental demonstration program of its own. In 1967, OEO launched the New Jersey Graduated Income Maintenance Experiment, a large-scale, three-year controlled experiment designed to test the feasibility of the negative income tax idea—quite specifically, to find out whether the government could institute a guaranteed minimum income without causing a huge dropout from the labor force. More than simply a test of the economists' favorite antipoverty measure, the New Jersey project was widely regarded as a breakthrough in social science and a major step forward in the use of systematic experimentation for policy purposes. As discussed more fully in chapter 9, it heralded the emergence of a network of nongovernmental analytic research organizations dedicated to poverty research and policy—a poverty research industry—and helped to usher in a brief but heady period of large-scale social experimentation in domestic federal agencies. Over the next several years, and with the full support of the Nixon administration, analytic research offices funded large-scale demonstration experiments in the areas of income maintenance, housing, health care financing, and education. By then, and largely as a result of RPP&E's early efforts, demonstration research had taken on an entirely different meaning from the one it had acquired as a component of community action: no longer a system of "random innovation," as economist Alice Rivlin called the projects funded earlier in the 1960s, demonstration research would be less overtly political, and more systematically planned.[94] It would strive for experimental conditions complete with control groups and random assignment. It would be conducted by academically trained researchers, who more and more would be affiliated with specialized research institutions. And it would be designed not as a test of theories of political empowerment and systems change, but as a test of the impact of policy changes on individual behavior.

RESTRUCTURING OEO: THE TRIUMPH OF ANALYSIS AND THE DEMISE OF COMMUNITY ACTION

The OEO of 1968 was a much different agency than what it had started out as in 1964. Shriver resigned in late 1967, leaving OEO in the hands of career government official Bertrand Harding. CAP had settled in to become the "service deliverer" some hoped it would be, having been tamed first by administrative measures and then by the 1967 Green Amendments to the Economic Opportunity Act (proposed by moderate Republican Edith Green) giving local officials effective control over the community action agencies. The bulk of OEO funds were congressionally earmarked for politically safe national emphasis programs, including Head Start, Legal Services, Neighborhood Health Centers, and—Shriver's early caution notwithstanding—Family Planning. The major new initiative for the year was the Job Opportunities in the Business Sector (JOBS) program, an effort sponsored by the newly created National Alliance of Business, headed by Henry Ford, to train and locate private sector jobs for the "hard-core" unemployed.[95] And, while the stream of accusations, congressional investigations, and threats of funding cuts would continue unabated, the agency itself had become largely absorbed with the day-to-day administration of the some one thousand local community action agencies and other programs it had spawned. For organizers of the 1968 Poor People's March, the Citizens Crusade Against Poverty, and other grass roots groups, the real problem was that OEO had become part of the establishment.

After November 1968 things at OEO changed even more fundamentally. At first thrust into uncertainty over whether Nixon would follow through on his campaign threats against the War on Poverty, agency staff soon found the new administration moving in surprising directions. Two major announcements boded particularly well for the future of analytic research. One was Nixon's endorsement of the analysts' most cherished policy proposal, the negative income tax, in the form of his proposed Family Assistance Plan. The other was the announcement of a fundamental redefinition in the "purposes, structure and programs of OEO," that would make it a major R&D arm for the whole of domestic policy.[96]

The driving force behind these moves was the new Council for Urban Affairs, created by executive order in January 1969 to develop a national urban policy and to provide the president with a new "domestic policy and priority-setting machinery" as a counterpart to the National Security Council.[97] The Urban Council was staffed by Daniel Patrick Moynihan, a Democrat, former Labor Department official, and political science professor who had a few years earlier written in praise of the "professionalization of reform" represented by the War on Poverty and the "profound advance in knowledge" that had helped to make it possible. Reserving particular praise for the "econometric revolution" that had taught "men . . . how to make an industrial economy work," Moynihan predicted an equally dazzling breakthrough in "the simulation of social processes" and "a still wider expansion of knowledge available to government as to how people behave."[98] By early 1969, Moynihan had tempered his views considerably, calling them "overly optimistic," as he wrote with some despair of the failure of social science to develop either the understanding or the policy framework for a coherent strategy against poverty.[99] He was also about to publish *Maximum Feasible Misunderstanding*, his idiosyncratic attack on community action which alleged, among other things, that a small group of social scientists had used the movement to impose their own ideological agenda on unsuspecting localities. While critical of the community action "theorists," Moynihan remained a strong believer in analysis, and advocated a continuing role for social science in evaluating program effects. He was also becoming increasingly convinced of the need for an income guarantee in the form of a European-style family allowance, which brought him close to the negative income tax promoted by the RPP&E analysts since 1965. With the help of Moynihan's persuasive skills and analysis provided by some of the RPP&E holdovers from the Johnson administration, the Council had overcome strong opposition from leading presidential advisors to persuade Nixon of the political as well as the policy merits of proposing the basic income guarantee with a work requirement attached. Nixon's Family Assistance Plan (FAP) was presented as a bold and dramatic pledge to move forward against poverty and, more importantly, as a way to follow through on the promise of welfare reform that had been a central part of the campaign platform.

Clearly impressed with the whole analytic approach as well as with one of its central policy ideas, the Urban Council also looked to the RPP&E operation in its broader effort to strengthen the president's domestic policy making capacity. In one early proposal, the Council's Subcommittee on the Future of the Poverty Program outlined a plan to designate RPP&E as a separate staff unit, with a broader range of programmatic responsibilities, within the Executive Office.[100] The eventual reorganization plan kept RPP&E, now renamed the Office of Planning, Research and Evaluation (PR&E) within the OEO, doubled the size of its professional staff, and reallocated operating funds to expand its budget for evaluation and experimentation. It also proposed a sharp curtailment of OEO's operating functions, beginning with immediate "spin-offs" of Head Start, Job Corps, Neighborhood Health Centers, and other "proven" programs to other agencies, while leaving CAP as a much smaller program dedicated to the support of "innovative self-help" initiatives in communities. A new Office of Program Development would significantly expand CAP planning and evaluation capacities, and would be positioned to create an even and steady "flow from the research stage to the development stage to the program stage." Thus "streamlined," the new OEO would no longer be an action agency, would become less of an operating agency, and would be tapped instead as a source of innovation, experimentation, and analytic knowledge—an in-house "think tank" for domestic policy making.[101]

The restructured OEO signaled the Nixon administration's more general intention to use an expanded analytic capacity for its own policy objectives and, with its emphasis on innovation and experimentation, suggested a bright future for what Alice Rivlin referred to as "systematic thinking" in federal decision making. Valued for their "neutral competence," RPP&E analysts also found their services in continued demand.[102] While Levine left OEO to go briefly to the newly established Urban Institute and eventually back to RAND, the transition to the new PR&E was smoothed by considerable staff continuity, and by the undeniably inbred nature of the analytic profession. Heading up the new research office were economists John Wilson and Thomas Glennan, the latter once a RAND staffer who had, with OEO funds, begun to develop RAND's work in the area of domestic manpower and training. They were soon joined by economist Edward Gramlich, a Yale graduate and classmate of Levine's who had been working on macroeconomic policy at the Federal Reserve Board since the mid-1960s. Wilson and Glennan were Republicans, Gramlich and several of the RPP&E staff holdovers Democrats. Without universally embracing the professed goals and commitments of the Great Society, they did share a common commitment to putting existing and prospective social programs on a more rational footing, and the analytic skills to make it happen. They even shared a certain academic style that made for continued tension with the Nixon administration's counterpart to CAP R&D, the new Office of Program Development (OPD). While hardly the "activists" or "ideologues" of CAP's early days, "OPD's people were considered 'unanalytical.' They had a broad social science orientation and relied on knowledge of social problems rather than technical skill." In contrast, the economists and mathematically trained PR&E analysts were known as "high-level academics" and "pipe-smoking types" within the agency; for some, they came to symbolize OEO's growing distance from the poor, and from the more hands-on, operational concerns of making programs work. Like the new OEO director Donald Rumsfeld, the analysts also enjoyed the confidence of the White House, and were themselves attracted to the prospect of having a central role in domestic policy decision making.[103] Rumsfeld, a moderate Republican and Illinois congressman who was a strong believer in research and scientific experimentation, was given a dual appointment as OEO director and assistant to the president, presumably giving the agency a direct pipeline to the White House. During his tenure, the PR&E research budget rose to $23 million in fiscal year 1971, more than triple its size in the last year of the Johnson administration, and the staff expanded from twenty to more than fifty professionals.[104]

The new PR&E office was not simply an expanded RPP&E, however. Once the signature product and a major preoccupation for RPP&E analysts, the annual Five Year Plans were much shorter, less detailed, and less important in the overall scheme of things in PR&E—in part a reflection of the demise of the PPBS system itself.[105] PR&E also vowed to put much greater emphasis on determining "program efficiency" by measuring "the extent to which antipoverty programs are meeting basic objectives," and above all on the use of scientifically designed field experiments to test policy innovations. Roughly two-thirds of the OEO research budget went to such experiments, according to one estimation, including the New Jersey and a second, rural negative income tax experiment, along with educational vouchers, health insurance, and performance contracting experiments.[106] Most important, PR&E was working chiefly in the service not of OEO as an antipoverty agency but of the White House and the President's new Domestic Council. And for the Nixon administration, welfare, not poverty, was taking center stage as domestic enemy number one.

Despite its brief day in the sun as "a presidential think tank," PR&E did not survive much longer as an independent analytic office. Nor could it control the political fate of the OEO or the War on Poverty. In early 1973, OEO staff was informed that "[i]n view of the overall budgetary situation facing the President in fiscal 1974," and "in accordance with the President's 'New Federalism' proposals returning both responsibility and resources to States and localities, no funds will be provided to continue the Office of Economic Opportunity after June 30, 1973." The operating programs that had not been spun off in the initial restructuring—Legal Services, various health and nutrition programs, migrant farmworker programs, and others—would be transferred to other agencies. PR&E activities—and staff—would similarly be absorbed, for the most part by the Office of the Assistant Secretary for Planning and Evaluation (ASPE) in HEW. Community Action operations would be shut down entirely.[107] Poverty research and analysis would survive, and flourish, but the federal government's political and institutional commitment to ending poverty had officially come to an end.

There is no doubt that the OEO analysts accomplished a great deal of what they set out to achieve in 1964. By the end of the decade they had inscribed poverty research with a greater degree of precision, quantification, and methodological innovation than it had ever before achieved. They had stimulated a steady and ongoing expansion of research in academic and applied institutes, and were helping to establish poverty as a recognized specialization in economics. They had also put the agency, and poverty research more generally, in the recognized vanguard of a still-burgeoning analytic revolution that brought new standards to the policy making process in social welfare agencies. OEO analysts were also bringing new knowledge to the poverty debate, challenging, for example, age-old ideas about the culture of poverty with statistical evidence that far more people were temporarily than chronically poor. Their negative income tax experiments were similarly yielding what they thought to be heartening results—providing scientific evidence, for all the skeptics, that most people would keep on working even with a modest income guarantee.

But these very same accomplishments had also done a good deal to undermine knowledge as a force for political change: for one thing by making poverty research a more specialized, and enclosed, profession; for another, by neutralizing poverty as a political problem by reducing it to quantifiable, individualized variables; most importantly by keeping the focus on the characteristics of poor people rather than on the economy, politics, and society more broadly construed. As we shall see, the analytic ethos of neutrality undermined the ability to mobilize knowledge either for or against scientifically evaluated reform—an incapacity that would come to haunt poverty experts in the 1980s and 1990s when several new, more explicitly ideological and conservative think tanks began to use the very same techniques and knowledge analysts had perfected, this time to undermine the welfare state. This is not to say that analytic knowledge was ever politically neutral—after all, it was almost entirely dependent on the good graces of the administration in charge. And although born in an extraordinarily expansive mood of liberal idealism, it proved equally- if not better-suited to the post-liberal era of diminished expectations and policy retreat. For then, with the welfare rolls "exploding" and the affluent economy in decline, there was greater demand than ever for the precise, bottom-line standards analysts brought to poverty research. Before long, and without visible or organized protest, the impressive apparatus poverty analysts had developed was almost entirely devoted not to ending poverty but to the growing political obsession with welfare reform.

CHAPTER 8

Poverty's Culture Wars

OEO's POLITICAL and organizational infighting was by no means the only battle shaping the future course of poverty research. If anything, it was overshadowed by a series of far more public, increasingly polarized battles over what liberal social science had to say about the culture of poor people and what government could or should do in response. Most public of all was the outcry and extended controversy that greeted Assistant Secretary of Labor Daniel P. Moynihan's report on the "crisis" of the Negro family in 1965. Released to the public in the aftermath of the Watts riot, when the Civil Rights movement was internally divided over growing black militancy, Moynihan's analysis of the internal "pathology" gripping the lower-class black family sparked a wide-ranging reaction that served to question if not undermine the much older, liberal sociological tradition it drew from. To appreciate its impact on the course of poverty knowledge, though, it is useful to start by considering the long-standing tensions within that liberal sociological tradition—over concepts of class, race, and culture in particular—that the Moynihan Report brought to the fore.

The academic version of poverty's culture wars took place in the relative calm of a year-long seminar on poverty that began several months after the Moynihan Report was first released. Convened by the American Academy of Arts and Sciences in 1966, the seminar was attended by several of the War on Poverty's leading intellectual lights and chaired by Moynihan himself, then on what would turn out to be a brief academic hiatus between the Kennedy/Johnson Department of Labor and Nixon's domestic policy staff. The gathering included more sociologists and anthropologists than economists, reflecting the then-current state of academic poverty expertise. Also in attendance were a number of OEO poverty warriors from both Community Action and RPP&E. Whatever their disagreements, this was decidedly a gathering among liberals, dedicated to the tasks set out in the seminar's companion volumes, *On Understanding Poverty* (edited by Moynihan) and *On Fighting Poverty* (edited by James Sundquist of the Brookings Institution).[1] And yet, as Moynihan put it, "something, somewhere had gone wrong" with any intellectual consensus they once might have shared. *There was no common understanding as to the nature of poverty or the process of deliberate social change*" (emphasis in original). Put more starkly by economist Harold Watts, the social scientists were divided over "two radically different" concepts of poverty: the "narrow economic" definition, which focused on income deprivation, and the "culture of poverty," which focused on behavior, attitudes, and a distinctive way of life.[2]

To some degree Watts's formulation was an exaggeration: in either version, the object of research was poor people and the question was what distinguished them—money or culture—from everyone else. Seminar members were fond, it seems, of the legendary (probably apocryphal) exchange between Ernest Hemingway and F. Scott Fitzgerald: "The rich are different from you and me," says Fitzgerald; "Yes, they have more money," says Hemingway in return. It also glossed over the nuances in academic debate over poverty, including widespread disagreements, all aired at the AAAS seminar, over the meaning of culture, the limitations of using narrow income measures, and the significance of race.[3] But in another way the juxtaposition that Watts posed is illuminating, for it points to the intellectual context for understanding the subsequent, albeit temporary, dominance of what he called the "narrow economic" point of view. While OEO analysts were remaking poverty as an applied, economic science, the idea of the culture of poverty, in all its variations, came under attack from within the academy as well as from organized political groups. It was an attack that went to the heart of the liberal sociological tradition, calling into question not only its ideas about the nature of poverty but also the assimilationist ideology that informed those ideas. It was an attack, too, that targeted not just the concept but the political hazards of the culture of poverty. In these ways, the "culture wars" undermined what had been the central conceptual framework for sociological poverty knowledge since the 1920s—the idea of poverty as a cultural problem—although they did not, as became evident in the 1980s, lay it to rest.[4]

Within the confines of the AAAS seminar, the debate over the culture of poverty could be seen as a distillation of much older academic debates: over the origins and nature of lower-class culture; over whether and how that culture should be changed; and, when the discussion turned to black lower-class culture, whether it was principally a reflection of class or racial disadvantage. But it is also worth pointing out where the protagonists did *not* disagree, and that was about the existence of a distinctive subculture separating the poor from everyone else. Indeed, based on an exhaustive review of the social science literature, sociologists Peter Rossi and Zahava Blum found an impressive "descriptive" consensus on what distinguished this poverty subculture from the cultural mainstream. Drawing mostly from community studies, child rearing literature, and attitude surveys, Rossi and Blum came up with a composite that read very much like an Oscar Lewis inventory, with weak or maternal family structure, illegitimacy, apathy, low self-esteem, political authoritarianism, religious fundamentalism, and the ubiquitous inability to defer gratification topping the list.[5]

The lines of debate, then, were not over *whether* but *why* the poor were culturally different and, by implication, whether policy could do anything to make them more like everyone else. Here there was a split that had been simmering in the class literature for more than a decade, but that had grown especially heated in response to Oscar Lewis and in the politicized context of the War on Poverty. Lewis, charged critics, had an essentialist, almost genetic, idea of culture, equating it with deep-seated behavioral and psychological patterns and treating it, in his own words, as "a way of life that is passed down from generation to generation along family lines."[6] Like anthropologist Walter B. Miller, a prominent student of juvenile gangs who also attended the AAAS seminar, Lewis emphasized the autonomy of culture and its imperviousness to change. That, of course, begged the question of whether lower-class culture *should* be subject to reform efforts, a proposition Miller rejected on the grounds that it was not only futile, but wrong, threatening to rob the country of the "positive functions" of a culture that had supplied "the vast army of woodsmen, construction workers, cattlemen, Indian fighters, frontier women," and others who had been doing brute work for centuries.[7] Oscar Lewis, in contrast, saw little redeeming about the culture of the poor, save perhaps "a capacity for spontaneity" that was far outweighed by its brutality and despair. Lewis's answer, at least for underdeveloped countries, was nothing short of social revolution to redistribute resources and power to the poor. In the U.S., though, where the problem of poverty lay in small and isolated "pockets," the poor needed intensive psychological and social work interventions before they could be expected to benefit from improvements in the opportunities and material conditions they faced.[8]

The sharpest criticism of the culture of poverty came from proponents of a more "situational" approach to culture who, following the earlier lead of social anthropologist Allison Davis, treated culture as a kind of coping strategy for dealing with the changing vicissitudes of life. Davis's "situational" interpretation was later applied and developed further by sociologists Herbert Gans and Lee Rainwater, who took the occasion of the AAAS seminar to distance themselves from culture of poverty theorists and their psychologically deterministic views. Gans criticized Oscar Lewis and Walter Miller for equating culture with behavior and for treating it as a semipermanent, inherited trait. The poor might lack aspirations and behave badly, Gans argued, but not because of deviant values or deeply imbedded psychological flaws; their cultural patterns might persist from generation to generation, but not because culture was an inherited trait. Gans himself had even written about a "pathological" subculture among unemployed men raised in welfare-dependent, "female-based families," worrying in particular that the men raised in such families seemed to be incapable of adjusting to the work demands of a modern, more automated world.[9] The answer, Gans and other situationalists insisted, lay not in trying to fix the pathology but in addressing the long-term unemployment from which it stemmed. Meanwhile, lower-class culture was a reflection of the limited opportunities society offered, and would persist within families only as each succeeding generation faced the same deprived conditions as the last. Indeed, the vast majority of lower-class families did accept mainstream, middle-class values even as they adopted more relaxed or unconventional behavioral norms. This was what anthropologist Hyman Rodman called the lower-class "value stretch," a mechanism, he argued, through which poor people adjusted to their own relative deprivation.[10]

The academic culture wars also touched on several long-standing tensions within the literature on black lower-class culture, here again turning less on the question of whether this was anything but a "poor" culture than on the question of whether to treat it as inherited or entirely situational. Was lower-class culture a legacy of slavery—perpetuated by the matriarchal family—or the product of persistent racial oppression from a society dominated by whites? Anthropologist Hylan Lewis, arguing from a strictly "situational" view, had written about an "evolving national subculture" in his 1955 community study *Blackways of Kent*, but denied that it had slavery as its source. Black lower-class culture was sustained by persistent and repeated racism and by the "adjustment devices" racism brought forth.[11] These views were later echoed in an influential study by his student Eliot Liebow, whose classic urban ethnography *Tally's Corner* argued that the street corner men of Washington, D.C., were not operating in an independent cultural tradition but had adapted their tough, blatantly disreputable habits as a cover for their inability, due to discrimination and unemployment, to achieve conventional work and family goals.

And yet, even the most hard-nosed situationalists continued to point to a hard core of pathology that could become self-perpetuating if left unchecked. To some extent this reflected the enormous influence of postwar race psychology, which without denying the situationalist interpretation had added a somewhat contradictory twist. Black culture was an adaptive response to continuing white racism, but the damaged, self-hating black personality was as well.[12] Writing about the damage in *The Mark of Oppression*, psychiatrists Abram Kardiner and Lionel Ovesey had earlier implicated the "Negro" personality and culture in a kind of internalized self-reinforcing "vicious circle" of self-hatred, low achievement, and sexual dysfunction that displayed itself in lower-class "matriarchal" families—and the children raised in them—in visibly "pathological" ways. Thus, while locating its origins in ongoing racial oppression, Kardiner and Ovesey were essentially treating lower-class pathology as an inherited psychological trait.[13]

From there it was easy to make the leap to the legacy of slavery, even while blaming persistent racism for playing a reinforcing role. This was the interpretation offered by Harvard psychologist Thomas Pettigrew, whose 1964 *Profile of the American Negro* was considered a definitive work in the field.[14] After surveying some 565 studies of black culture and personality, Pettigrew concluded that blacks as a group showed high rates of weak ego identity, low self-esteem, and "serious sex role conflicts," and that the experience of racial subordination was the main reason why. Significantly, this put Pettigrew at odds with a similarly synthetic review study, published just a few years before, which had concluded that the problems Pettigrew linked to a distinctly "Negro" psychology were actually problems of social class.[15] But Pettigrew thought the black poor suffered a double psychological burden, that could be traced back to slavery in two major ways. One was that ever since slavery blacks had been forced to succumb to a subordinate social and economic role, which historian Stanley Elkins had identified as the source of a "servile" or "Sambo" personality, based on his controversial analogy between African American slaves and victims of Nazi concentration camps. The second, and more important, was the "matrifocal" family, which caused resentment and role reversal between men and women and left children unable to defer gratification and sexually "confused." Here Pettigrew cited a slew of studies on the impact of father-absence in the home, including the famous candy bar tests done by psychologist Walter Mischel, who found that fatherless boys preferred to have a small candy bar immediately, rather than waiting for the promise of a larger candy bar within a week.[16] Further proof lay in the tendency of black mothers to encourage unnaturally dominant, achieving behavior among black lower-class girls, Pettigrew reported, while their male counterparts were more passive and, according to one prominent attitude survey, "agreed more often [than white boys] with such 'feminine' choices as 'I would like to be a singer' and 'I feel more intensely than most people do.' "[17] Together, then, the subordinate personality and the matrifocal family represented the "special burden" slavery had placed on subsequent African American generations, and particularly on the poor. Pettigrew used this evidence of psychological damage to argue that the fight against racial discrimination was important, but nowhere near enough: dealing with the Negro problem would require a full-scale attack on the poverty that was keeping the matriarchal family alive, while incorporating such psychologically rehabilitative measures as military training for fatherless boys.

As Pettigrew's policy directives suggest, race psychology was not the only influence behind the growing emphasis on pathology among the black poor. So, too, was an effort among liberal social scientists to dramatize the need for action against racism *and* poverty as the next phase in the struggle for equal rights.[18] But also at work was an undeniable sense of racial menace that, especially in the wake of the massive urban migration, black "ghettoization" and interracial violence of the postwar years, made the black lower-class subculture seem more concentrated and dangerous than in the past. In the early 1960s, even before the most visible racial uprisings of the decade began, social scientists brought the themes of persistent poverty, political urgency, and racial menace together in studies of impoverished "dark ghettos" and of the lower-class subculture and "pathologies" they bred. Conducted in the ethnographic, community studies tradition, several of these studies grew out of federally funded research and action programs of the kind that large-scale, survey-based quantitative analysis would soon overshadow. Such was the genesis of social psychologist Kenneth Clark's 1965 study of Harlem, *Dark Ghetto: Dilemmas of Social Power*. Clark started the study as the research director of Harlem Youth Opportunities Unlimited (HARYOU), a community action project originally funded by the President's Committee on Juvenile Delinquency. His HARYOU report, "Youth in the Ghetto," was a passionate plea for a redistribution of political and economic power, envisioning a massive organizing effort within the ghetto to demand and take control of the external resources for change. Issued just before the Harlem riots of July 1964, the report's subtitle—"A Study of the Consequences of Powerlessness"—was eerily borne out by events. After internal battles that pushed him off the HARYOU board, Clark used his report as the basis of a more complete picture of the "pathologies of American ghettoes," with an emphasis on "what happens to human beings who are confined to depressed areas and whose access to the normal channels of economic mobility and opportunity is blocked."[19] A second influential study, Lee Rainwater's *Behind Ghetto Walls*, grew out of an HEW/Public Housing Administration demonstration project to improve social services in one of the nation's most notoriously segregated, badly designed, and ill-kept housing projects, Pruitt-Igoe in St. Louis. (Pruitt-Igoe was later immortalized in documentary footage of its implosion after officials condemned it in the early 1970s.) Commissioned by the NIMH to evaluate the demonstration, Rainwater put more emphasis on studying the community, turning the "study of problems in a public housing project" into "a study of the dynamics of socioeconomic inequality."[20] Together, these studies illustrate how, through a blend of cultural theory and race psychology, liberal social scientists were using black lower-class pathology as a premise for an expanded program of social and economic reform.

Thus, both Clark and Rainwater treated ghetto culture as an adaptive mechanism rather than an inherited way of life. Selling drugs, playing "the dozens," having babies out of wedlock, and other unconventional behaviors were lower-class ways of adjusting to what Rainwater called the "world of the disinherited," cultural mechanisms for negotiating between mainstream norms and an impoverished social reality. But the real pathology of the ghetto did not derive from the punishments of class alone. Its source was the institutionalized racism that the ghetto symbolized, as expressed in the "Negro's complex and debilitating prejudice against himself." This core aversion to blackness, once physically embodied in slavery and caste, had since become internalized within lower-class black culture, and nowhere more thoroughly than in the lower-class family, for Rainwater the "crucible of identity" through which black children learned that they were "essentially bad." Those first crucial lessons were subsequently reinforced by ghetto walls, to the point where whites could count on blacks "to do the dirty work of caste victimization for them."[21] The result, as Clark wrote, was a form of "institutionalized pathology," expressed in crime, drug addiction, illegitimacy, family instability, and in patterns of sexual deviance that resulted from the "imbalance" of economic and sexual power between women and men.[22] That this pathology had become "self-perpetuating" did not absolve white society of blame. Indeed, without comprehensive efforts to open up economic and social opportunities, Clark's Harlem neighborhood would not be able to sustain the cultural rehabilitation he hoped to undertake. Likewise, Rainwater concluded, social policy should not treat the family "as the main villain of the piece," with "an army of social workers" sent in to fix the pathology. He joined Clark in calling for a comprehensive program of job creation, income guarantees, desegregation, and local empowerment as a necessary precursor to the cultural rehabilitation that he was confident would follow in its wake.[23]

The concept of a self-perpetuating pathology—transmitted by a "vicious circle" connecting racism, male unemployment, female-headed families, and deviant social behavior—had thus become a key component of the social scientific case for a more aggressive attack on poverty as an integral part of the wider struggle for equal rights. Informing this argument was a blend of situationalist cultural analysis, race psychology, racial liberalism, and a commitment to government action to reverse racism's effects. But equally important to the argument was a commitment to a largely unquestioned cultural ideal that even at the time had come under some criticism for being overly individualistic, achievement-oriented, mired in the materialism of consumer capitalism, and, although couched in terms of a color-blind society, essentially white. That this ideal was based on a patriarchal vision of gender relations was nowhere more evident than in the powerful sense of "sociosexual" threat emanating from the literature on the black lower-class family. This sense of threat was not only expressed in the sexualized anxieties over the impact of the "matriarchy" on men, but also in the complete blindness of the literature to the problems black women faced in their own wage-earning roles. Instead, as more than one study noted, the very fact of significant female participation in the labor force could be cited as further evidence of how pathological the lower-class black family had become.[24] This gender bias was also reflected in the policy proposals liberal social science endorsed, which repeatedly ignored the wage and employment discrimination suffered by black women while calling for targeting jobs and employment programs on men. In this, as in its growing emphasis on pathology and psychological damage, the liberal, "situationalist" interpretation of black lower-class culture was entirely consistent with Oscar Lewis's culture of poverty. And it was in this form, as a blend of situationalist, psychological,

and racial theory, that the cultural tradition in sociology came into th
light of public and political scrutiny, in the controversy started in 19
still raging while the AAAS seminar met, over Daniel P. Moynihan's
on the Negro family.

In the spring of 1965, then Assistant Secretary of Labor for Policy Pla
and Research Moynihan began working on an internal planning docume
the hope of persuading the administration of the need for a new, more conc
government effort to push the "Negro Revolution" from legal equalit
"equality of results." Entitled *The Negro Family: The Case for National
tion*, the report relied heavily on three decades' worth of liberal social scie
to present "the evidence—not final, but powerfully persuasive—that the Ne
family in the urban ghetto is crumbling." In light of this evidence, Moynil
advocated a "new approach" to policy which would take government beyo
the commitment to civil rights embodied in the landmark Civil and Voti
Rights Acts of 1964–1965. Although deeply rooted in the legacy of racism
the issue was not racial discrimination but poverty, and in particular the "diso
ganization among the lower-class group." Fundamental to that disorganizatio
was "the deterioration of the Negro family." With this the nation was "con
fronted with a new kind of problem. Measures that have worked in the past
or would work for most groups in the present, will not work here. A national
effort is required that will give unity of purpose to the many activities of the
federal government in this area, directed to a new kind of goal: the establishment of a stable Negro family structure."[25]

Strictly speaking, the Moynihan Report was not meant as a scholarly contribution to poverty knowledge; its main purpose was to influence the administration's policy agenda on race. Significantly, it was produced outside the established bureaucratic channels for poverty knowledge, and outside the analytic
networks being established at OEO. Seen in this light it can be, and has been,
understood as a strategic document—one in a long line of social scientific
analyses that turned to cultural pathology to dramatize and enhance the case
for structural reform.[26] For some, indeed, this has been reason enough to overlook, or ignore, Moynihan's more incendiary pathologizing to praise the Report for its bravery and foresight in drawing attention to the gravity of racism
and of soon-to-worsen black unemployment, welfare, and single parent rates—
despite the fact that, as the Report's reception indicates, Moynihan's strategic
turn to pathology failed. The reality of the Report, though, is both more complicated and less instrumental than that. For although it was written as a policy
paper, and in this sense as a strategic document, it was also distinguished by
several other features that make it of particular importance in understanding
why subsequent poverty knowledge took the direction it did.

First was the fact that it was a distillation of the major themes from three
decades of sociological literature on lower-class black subculture—including

its invocation of cultural pathology to make a case for more concerted government action against poverty and racism. Second was what the Report and its aftermath revealed to be a growing disjuncture between the psycho-cultural diagnoses of liberal social science and the political economic agenda it professed to support—raising the specter of a culture so tangled in pathology that it was incapable of responding to expanded opportunity. Contributing to this sense of disjuncture was the fact that Moynihan's report merely called for national policy, opening the door for widely ranging speculation on what that policy should be. Equally important was its attempt to bypass the political networks of the civil rights movement, presumably to set a more "scientifically" based agenda for policy reform. Third was the fact that it was written, released, and debated during an enormously tumultuous period in the politics of both race and poverty, when organized minorities were struggling against the local white establishment for access to Community Action funds, when the Watts riots transformed the public image of the race issue, when civil rights leaders were internally divided over a turn to radical tactics in their ranks, and when poverty warriors within the administration were being instructed to curtail their expectations in light of the escalating war in Vietnam. Finally, for all of these reasons, the public release of the Moynihan Report sparked a political and an intellectual crisis for what up until that point was still the dominant, cultural tradition in liberal social scientific poverty research.

The Moynihan Report was not distinctive for its findings, which simply "reflected what we saw as a consensus among social scientists writing in that generation or the previous one," as Moynihan later recalled. Even such attention-grabbing language as the "tangle of pathology" was borrowed from existing scholarly reports.[27] The footnotes and text are crowded with references to the work of such well-known social scientists as E. Franklin Frazier, Kenneth Clark, Thomas Pettigrew, Nathan Glazer, and Moynihan himself, and Frazier, in a passage on the problem of family disorganization, got the last word in the Report. Most important, the basic analysis followed a familiar path in tracing the causes of black lower-class pathology, essentially combining Frazier's sociology of disorganization with the postwar psychology of race. Thus, the Report traced the historical causes of the pathology to the psychological as well as the cultural damage of slavery, citing Stanley Elkins for evidence of the submissive "Sambo" personality and Frazier for the emergence of the dominant matriarch. The initial impact of slavery was compounded by segregation, urbanization, persistent poverty, and, especially, male unemployment rates of "catastrophic" proportions. The cumulative effect of this history of subordination had been especially hard on black men, who, when "forced into a matriarchal structure" by racial subordination, had been denied their natural role as breadwinners and authority figures in a predominantly patriarchal society. ("The very essence of the male animal," Moynihan explained in the Report's most infamous passage, "is to strut.") In recent times, however, the pa-

thology had become self-perpetuating, as indicated in social psychological research linking matriarchy and the absence of a dominant male figure to sex-role confusion, a "hunger for immediate gratification," delinquency, and even to neurotic behavior among boys.[28] Thus, the tangle of pathology was now being passed from generation to generation through the family's psychological impact as well as the matriarch's inherent inability to socialize the young. All of this pointed to the urgency of "restoring the Negro American Family" with, as Frazier had put it, "those changes in the Negro and American society which will enable the Negro father to play the role required of him."[29]

The Moynihan Report did distinguish itself from past literature in two important respects. One was its prolific use of government statistics to dramatize the tangle of pathology. The tables and graphs started out with a story of family disintegration, then followed up with statistics on the "failure of youth," as measured alarmingly in 30 percent unemployment, delinquency, school drop-out, and in "the ultimate mark of inadequate preparation for life," a failure rate of 56 percent on the Armed Forces mental test.[30] No attempt was made to explain or contextualize these statistics; they were merely presented as evidence of the tangle of pathology at work. More important, though, was the Report's attempt to make direct correlations between economic trend data and what Moynihan referred to as "indicators of social dysfunction," illustrating, for example, the high correlation between black unemployment rates and marital breakup.[31] By far the most significant of these statistical correlations points to the second distinguishing feature of Moynihan's report, and that is its repeated and relentless emphasis on the matriarchal family as the "fundamental source of the weakness of the Negro community at the present time." Much as subsequent commentators have pointed to Moynihan's emphasis on unemployment as a causal factor, the Report itself continually underscores the theme that the contemporary crisis cannot be understood "in terms of the visible manifestations of discrimination and poverty" alone.[32] And here is where Moynihan reported his most striking statistical "find." The number of AFDC cases opened, once statistically correlated with black male unemployment rates, was now (as of 1962) rising *despite* measured unemployment decline. With this one statistical correlation, by far the most highly publicized in the Report, Moynihan sealed the argument that the "pathology" had become self-perpetuating: pathology, here measured as welfare "dependency," was no longer correlated with the unemployment rate; it was going up on its own.

The fact is that the statistical correlation "proved" nothing of the sort. As studies at the time and subsequently indicated, unemployment and economic recession were never more than partial explanations for changes in welfare enrollment rates. Equally important were changes in and variations among local administrative practices, eligibility rules, welfare law amendments—including those passed in 1962, and, for blacks especially, migration from the South to less restrictive northern cities. And while rising rates of single-parent families were certainly contributing to expanding welfare rolls, those trends were hardly confined to African Americans, and, according to information available at the time, had been gradually growing for well over a decade before 1962. Besides, as research later confirmed, case load expansions were hardly an appropriate measure of "dependency," since people use welfare for a wide variety of reasons, most of them for a relatively short period of time.[33] More problems in the correlation could be found in the statistics themselves. Hardest to explain is the fact that the graph mapped *nonwhite* male employment against the *total* number of welfare cases opened. More understandable, in light of the Report's overarching argument, is the absence of any correlation between caseloads and employment rates among nonwhite *women*. Indeed, in the Moynihan Report, as elsewhere, female employment was reported only as a sign of pathology; otherwise, statistics on black women were confined to illegitimacy, female-headship, and welfare receipt. In contrast, Drake and Cayton's *Black Metropolis*, not cited in the Report, had included detailed information on women as part of the discussion of the employment and labor market prospects facing *all* blacks.[34] Finally, as critics at the time and subsequent research have shown, the *total* nonwhite employment statistics mask at least two important developments that indicated a much worse job situation for nonwhite men at the time. One was the much higher rate of unemployment for young nonwhite men; the other was the steady decline in any sort of labor force participation among African American men, a development not measured in the unemployment statistics at all. This unmeasured decline in labor force participation, William J. Wilson and Kathryn Neckerman later argued, helped to explain both patterns of AFDC enrollment and lower marriage rates among blacks. In other words, welfare and unemployment had not, as the Moynihan Report suggested, somehow become "unglued."[35]

What, then, given this emphasis on a self-perpetuating pathology, would a national policy to strengthen the Negro family be? Moynihan himself favored large-scale employment programs, reflecting a position he and other Department of Labor officials had been taking since planning for the War on Poverty began. In future months he would become a more vociferous advocate of a European-style family allowance, another of his long-favored ideas. The Report also hinted at military training for boys, a solution Moynihan had flirted with in an earlier Department of Labor investigation, where he had first learned of the racial differences in Armed Forces mental tests.[36] For the most part, however, the Report offered no specific policy recommendations. Nevertheless, it did provide the intellectual backing for Lyndon B. Johnson's landmark civil rights address, coauthored by Moynihan and delivered at Howard University on June 4, 1965. In it, LBJ recognized the "special nature of Negro poverty," caused by unemployment and the "breakdown of the Negro family structure." He also pledged unspecified government action to move to the next stage of the struggle for black equality—"not just equality as a right and a theory but equality as a fact and as a result."[37] Toward this end, he promised a special White House conference in the fall. It was this speech, and the impending conference, that drew public attention to the existence of the Moynihan Report, although its actual contents were kept under cover until August—as it happens, just about a week before the outbreak of riots in Watts. In the meantime, press reports and rumors had leaked the Report's most sensationalistic claims about family breakdown, creating an atmosphere of intense speculation and built-up resentment, especially among civil rights activists who felt the administration and its experts were trying to co-opt or distract from their own social agenda. By the time the Report officially became public, what everyone knew about what one critic called this "two-month wonder, over publicized before it was released," was that it focused on family deterioration and was being touted by some as a call for Negro "self-help."[38] Reactions to Watts hardly helped matters; both the press and a desperate White House used the Report as a kind of semiofficial explanation, once presidential press secretary Bill Moyers distributed copies a week after the violence began. The next day brought a highly provocative column from conservative columnists Rowland Evans and Robert Novack, calling the Report a "much-suppressed, much leaked Labor Department document which strips away usual equivocations and exposes the ugly truth about the big-city Negro's plight"—not unemployment but "broken homes, illegitimacy, and female-oriented homes." Meanwhile, Moynihan became something of an instant expert on riots, with figures on illegitimacy rates in Watts to back him up.[39]

It is hardly surprising, then, that the reaction to the Moynihan Report came primarily in the form of a "revolt."[40] Civil rights groups objected to its rhetorical implication that there was one, pathological form of Negro family, as well as to its overwhelming emphasis on family breakdown as a cause rather than a consequence of poverty and community distress. Though exonerating Moynihan himself from charges of personal racism, several commentators saw the Report as the basis of a "new racism," couched in scientific logic and designed to distract attention from the structural nature of poverty and institutionalized racism.[41] Most of all, though, civil rights leaders tried to steer the conversation back to where they thought it belonged: jobs, income, housing, health, and central city decline. All of these issues had, in fact, been on the civil rights agenda for years, and were to make up the central components of the movement's "Freedom Budget" officially released in October 1966.[42] Indeed, the Moynihan Report stirred both resentment and suspicion among advocates who had long been warning about the consequences of neglecting the problems of employment and economic inequality, only then to have them presented as issues of social pathology by a government expert claiming to act on their behalf.[43] But civil rights concern also focused on the content of the Report, in part because of what public reaction had already revealed. The idea of a self-perpetuating pathology, no matter how rooted in structural inequality, did not make a "case" for social and economic reform. "The prescription," as one commentator wrote, "is to change the deviants, not the system."[44]

Civil rights leaders were by no means the only ones critical of the Moynihan Report. Anthropologist Hylan Lewis, in a background paper prepared for the White House Conference, offered an alternative, much less "alarmist" and nonpathological view, explaining single-parent families as a consequence of poverty, and emphasizing the diversity among low-income families. Economist Mary Keyserling, then the director of the Department of Labor Women's Bureau, took strong issue with the notion that black women were "overemployed," pointing out black women's contributions to household income, as well as the then much more rapidly rising rate of labor force participation among white women.[45] Herbert Gans wrote that the matriarchal family "has not yet been proven pathological," citing studies on the extended kinship networks that brought stability to black families and had been shown to raise many a "successfully" adapted boy.[46] While overshadowed by the intense political reaction to the Report, these critiques anticipated a more extensive literature, much of it directly or indirectly stimulated by the Moynihan Report, that challenged its social scientific premises. Historical and anthropological research was especially important in this regard, showing, for example, that the slave and post-slavery family was neither matriarchal nor disorganized, that in the process of urban migration blacks established a stable working class, that the feminized kin networks of low-income black families provided what would today be called "social capital" in poor neighborhoods, and that black lower-class culture has been a good deal more conscious, alternative, and creative than images of cultural pathology could possibly convey.[47] Such criticism hardly prevented the Moynihan Report from maintaining a respectable life of its own. During the 1980s, Moynihan was hailed as a prophet of the underclass. More important, his key statistical correlation—the mythical "break" in the correlation between unemployment and welfare rates—was very soon revived when, now as domestic advisor to Richard M. Nixon, he made it the centerpiece of his analysis of a new, but related "crisis" in welfare dependency.[48]

It would be a mistake, then, to regard the Moynihan Report as principally a matter of liberal strategy gone awry—the familiar strategy, that is, of using cultural pathology to make a dramatic case for structural reform. For even though the Report was a strategic policy document, Moynihan was writing as a social scientist as well, synthesizing themes that, if anything, would grow more pronounced in his work, and especially the theme that pathology, including the dreaded welfare dependency, was a consequence of the absence of males from their rightful place as heads of families.[49] In this sense, as critics at the time recognized, Moynihan's was far more than a flawed strategy for a good cause; it was an expression of a deeply flawed, and for a time anyway, a shared social scientific vision of the dynamics of gender, race, and poverty in the black lower-class family.

The more immediate impact of the Moynihan Report was to politicize the idea of culture and to shatter any sense of consensus that cultural theorists might have had. In its aftermath, many social scientists began to question their own use of the cultural framework, believing that it had been hopelessly corrupted in what had degenerated into a debate over the "undeserving poor." Hylan Lewis, one of the first to break from the separate culture idea, urged social scientists to pay more attention to the tremendous diversity among families in poor neighborhoods, while warning against the political misuse of findings based on oversimplified and sensationalistic generalizations about their "presumably . . . preferred or chosen way of life."[50] Herbert Gans called on social scientists to shift the focus of research away from the poor, noting that "if the prime purpose of research is the elimination of poverty, studies of the poor are not the first order of business at all." Much more important were "studies of the economy that relegates many people to underemployment and unemployment and of the society which leaves teenagers and old people without viable economic and social functions." Gans eventually distanced himself from his own earlier analysis of lower-class culture, remarking that economics, not cultural pathology, was what separated the poor from the more stable working class.[51] Even Oscar Lewis became ambivalent, according to his biographer, and in responding to his harshest critics called the theory "simply a challenging hypothesis which would be tested by empirical research." The response was somewhat disingenuous, considering that Lewis had earlier proposed that the culture of poverty was virtually a worldwide phenomenon, transcending national boundaries.[52]

Nevertheless, Lewis's retreat does suggest just how thoroughly discredited his culture of poverty theory was by the end of the 1960s. Two separate volumes were devoted to anthropological criticism of the idea, as were dozens of journal articles and scholarly panels.[53] Oscar Lewis was the most prominent target of this criticism, but the broader literature on lower-class culture came under scrutiny as well. Adding to the numerous academic criticisms, which focused on methodology, use of evidence, and psychological determinism, was the inescapable fact that the culture of poverty was a thoroughly political idea, a device, in critics' eyes, for "blaming the victim," "neutralizing the disinherited," distracting from the real issues of structural inequality and, as one government researcher who once embraced it wrote, "an example of how we social scientists misled the architects of the War on Poverty by putting forth notions which turned out to be spurious."[54] Such concerns were only confirmed when political scientist Edward Banfield, drawing on studies written by Gans, Walter Miller, and Allison Davis, among others, published *The Unheavenly City* (1970), a scathing attack that used the concept of lower-class culture to argue that nothing, short of extreme authoritarian measures, could be done to help the urban poor.[55] Still, it is even more important to recall the origins of the pathological idea of lower-class culture in liberal sociology—because it is within that tradition that it would be resurrected in the 1980s, when William Julius Wilson, invoking Moynihan, wrote about the emergence of an urban "underclass."[56]

Poverty researchers did not entirely abandon the issues of race, family instability, and illegitimacy in response to the Moynihan Report, as some have suggested, but they did begin to approach them from the safer distance of quantitative data and rationalistic models that treated race and class as demographic variables rather than as either cultural or political economic facts. To be sure, this was not simply a by-product of the "culture wars" alone. The reality is that by the late 1960s the ethnographic, community-studies tradition that had given shape to the culture of poverty and its variants was rapidly being eclipsed by a more quantitative, technocratic model-building impulse in the social sciences more generally. Within that framework, the newer political economy of poverty, based on neoclassical economic assumptions and dominated by human capital theory, became the basis of a research industry built and maintained by foundations and government analysts eager to maintain a more neutral scientific veneer. As we shall see, this new, more "scientific" poverty knowledge shared more in common with the cultural tradition than its practitioners cared to admit: both were inquiries devoted principally to documenting the characteristics and behavior of the poor.

PART THREE

CHAPTER 9

The Poverty Research Industry

THE POLARIZED debates of the late 1960s may have tarnished the reputation of academic social science, but they did not impede the steady expansion of federally funded poverty research over the next decade and a half. From 1965 to 1980, federal funding for poverty research rose from nearly $3 million to just under $200 million, most designated for the "applied" purposes of measurement, program evaluation, and policy analysis.[1] Federal research dollars also underwrote the development of new and elaborate methodologies for carrying out these tasks, leaving poverty research with a sophisticated array of survey, experimental, and modeling techniques that were virtually unmatched in any other field of social research.[2] Nor, despite Richard M. Nixon's avowed determination to dismantle the War on Poverty, did government demand for analytic poverty knowledge show signs of slowing down. Amidst the economic stagnation, unemployment, and inflation that plagued the 1970s, social spending rose steadily—particularly for social insurance and "in-kind" transfer programs such as Food Stamps—and with it the demand for better numbers on who was being served, how, and how efficiently.[3]

Feeding the federal demand for social knowledge was a corresponding "explosion" in the field of policy analysis, heralded by the creation of formal professional associations, specialized journals, and, especially, the rapid expansion of graduate training programs at major universities nationwide. "Policy sciences" represented a "new study field," announced the *New York Times* in 1970, citing the founding of new graduate programs and a journal by that name. The field, like the academic curriculum, was more and more based on "the problem-solving, decision-making, and forecasting techniques pioneered by the nation's 'think tank' research institutions," noted the *Times*.[4] It was also very much tied to the increased emphasis on rational planning, budgeting, and evaluation within government bureaucracies, and to the attendant, rapidly growing market for government contract research. So, too, paradoxically, did policy analysis stand to benefit from growing skepticism about government institutions in the 1970s, which generated efforts to remodel government bureaucracies for greater administrative efficiency while also intensifying competition among existing bureaucratic players to develop their own independent sources of analysis.[5] By the end of the decade, the field was sufficiently well established to have generated a budding literature of contra-analytic critique: Policy analysis would "speak truth to power," to cite the title of a prominent text in the field, but it spoke very much from the inside.[6] Thus, as sociologists and anthropologists watched both community action and cultural theory get pummeled in the political fray, analysts were well positioned to continue the transformation of poverty knowledge, begun during the War on Poverty, into a highly pragmatic, technical subfield of applied microeconomics.

It would be a mistake, however, to view this transformation only in terms of the demise of sociological theory or the laws of supply and demand. The analytic turn in poverty research grew out of a positive and proactive ideological commitment as well—generally speaking, to Progressive-era ideals of expert statecraft, but more specifically to a particular *kind* of knowledge, based on methods derived from economics, and steeped in a market-oriented worldview. Reflecting these values, poverty analysts showed a preference for certain kinds of solutions to the poverty problem—emphasizing income over services, targeting individuals rather than empowering communities, and favoring interventions that worked outside the market over attempts to achieve market reform. Equally important, the market orientation extended to the production of knowledge, as analytic research brokers, in search of truly "objective," nonpartisan, and disinterested research, turned to the mechanisms of market competition to generate policy expertise.[7] Here, too, the analysts tapped into an older American tradition, of trusting to private sector institutions what Europeans looked to governments and political parties to do. But the poverty analysts looked to a more recent and immediate example for inspiration. They set out, and succeeded, in creating a research industry like the one that produced knowledge for the Department of Defense.

By the 1970s, the number of trained analysts in all branches of government had grown tremendously, as had the prominence of the poverty agencies for housing top-notch research and policy "shops." While analysts had little control over actual policy decisions, they were in a position to define the problems and the policy choices, and to determine how policies should be assessed. They also had control over substantial research budgets, which, with the cooperation of private foundations, helped to finance an expanding and interlocking institutional network of think tanks, university institutes, and both non- and for-profit research corporations devoted to analytic social research. These institutions, and the analysts who circulated easily in and between them, nurtured a distinctive subculture in public policy and government, held together by a shared language if not always a consensual understanding of social problems, and by a shared appreciation for the possibilities of scientifically controlled social experimentation, econometric modeling, and outcomes evaluation as tools—and, more and more, as requirements—of the policy making trade. This analytic subculture, or "subgovernment" as it has sometimes been called, effectively colonized poverty knowledge by creating and then subsidizing several newer research organizations expressly created as extensions of policy analytic thought.[8] Three of these organizations—the Institute for Research on Poverty at the University of Wisconsin, the Urban Institute in Washington, D.C., and the Manpower Demonstration Research Corporation in New York—were especially important in generating the new poverty expertise. Each carved out a particular niche within the growing market for policy-related social knowledge, and each, in its own way, lobbied extensively for particular standards of technical proficiency and professional legitimacy in the field. In the process, they helped to make poverty at once bigger—as in "big science"—and more specialized, more prominent but more exclusive and enclosed, more "public" in its association with public policy but more privatized as a subsidized, extra-governmental enterprise.

Despite its own claims to nonpartisanship, the poverty research industry owed its success as much to the changing political climate as to its disinterested technical proficiency. One reason, no doubt, was its tendency to reduce the most volatile of social problems into quantifiable, individualized, variables—while leaving questions of politics and power unasked. Class, race, and gender were absent as real categories in poverty analysis, their "effects" instead measured as individual characteristics related to demography, education level, and personal behavior. This individualized approach became especially compelling to philanthropic and government knowledge brokers in the late 1960s and 1970s, for it had a way of neutralizing—and neutering—the issue of poverty at precisely the moment when the politics of class, race, and gender were growing more visible in electoral coalitions. This does not mean, however, that poverty knowledge was not gendered and racialized in its own right. From its origins in the defense research industry, the analytic world was predominantly white and predominantly male. More important, its analytic categories were replete with widely understood, if unspoken, references to gender and race, as was especially evident in Richard Nixon's appeal to "forgotten" (white, male-headed) "working poor" Americans—squeezed out by the (black, female-headed) "welfare dependent" poor—in announcing his ill-fated Family Assistance Plan.[9]

A second reason for its success in a changing political climate was that analytic poverty research was much better equipped to serve than to influence the political agenda of whatever administration was in power; after all, its very existence was almost entirely dependent on federal government largesse. By the mid-1970s, most of what was recognized as scientific poverty knowledge was being produced either by staff analysts working directly for government agencies or within the tightly knit network of nongovernmental research organizations that relied on government contracts for support. The poverty research industry was well established, and its endeavors were beginning to produce a substantial body of analytic expertise. But, especially when it came to welfare policy, politics still drove the decisions and, ultimately, the agenda for research.[10]

Working within the political and institutional parameters of a heavily contract-driven research industry, poverty analysis in the 1970s did achieve some of what they had set out to accomplish in the headier days of the War on Poverty. One aim was to establish standards and techniques for assessing America's progress against poverty—standards and techniques that, for all they may have left out in terms of political empowerment and social justice, remain widely accepted benchmarks of economic well-being and of the distribution of social welfare benefits. By these measures, the federal government in the mid-1970s could be credited with at least one significant advance: thanks largely to an enormous growth in federal social welfare spending, the poverty rate was at an all-time low of 11 percent as opposed to 20 percent in 1964—a great deal of it due to the impact of Social Security and other programs in reducing elderly poverty rates. A second aim was to bring more precision to the picture of poor people that informed policy makers if not the public at large, leading poverty analysts to conclude, based on data that tracked family income over time, that a far more diverse group of Americans fell into poverty than popular imagery would suggest. A third aim was to use scientific and, especially, experimental study to improve and, in at least the notable instance of the negative income tax experiments, dramatically to expand the scope of policies for poor people. To this as to other aspects of the knowledge-building enterprise, poverty analysts brought values of fairness and equity as well as scientific objectivity; analytic knowledge, they believed, would lead to better programs for the poor.

There remained, however, the uncomfortable, unexamined question of whether this new knowledge did or could serve the interests of the poor: for by far the most consequential development in poverty knowledge during the 1970s was its retreat from the goal of ending poverty and its subsequent subordination to the imperatives of welfare reform. Here poverty research reflected not just a change in national politics but the even more fundamental impact of economic decline, and the gradual unraveling of the Keynesian consensus that had injected Great Society poverty knowledge with such confidence and hope. Now, perplexed by the combination of unemployment, wage stagnation, and runaway price inflation, liberal economists were no longer confident that they could achieve the combination of fast growth, high employment, and rising wages that was once their most trusted antipoverty weapon. But neither, at least not within the boundaries of poverty knowledge, could or would they try to explain why. Instead, more than any other single factor, and certainly more than bringing poverty to an end, it was the political obsession with welfare that gave poverty knowledge its rationale, its relevance, and, ultimately, shaped its meaning as the Great Society came to an end.

"THINK TANK" FOR THE POOR

"A think tank that thinks for the poor," was *Business Week's* headline in a 1968 report on the University of Wisconsin's Institute for Research on Poverty (IRP). It was founded, in the words of the reporter, "to play the same role on behalf of the war on poverty that more conventional think tanks play on behalf of more conventional wars."[11] Certainly this was the view of its original instigators in the OEO office of Research, Planning, Policy and Evaluation (RPP&E). As RPP&E's Robert Levine told an initially skeptical Sargent Shriver, the IRP was slated to be a kind of academic RAND Corporation, set up to produce "fundamental knowledge" while also responding to the agency's more "applied" research and policy needs. When the IRP was established, in 1966, RPP&E was defining those needs around three basic, very ambitious, goals: to find out who was poor and why; to determine whether programs were meeting their objectives; and to find the best way of eliminating income poverty by 1976.[12]

The search for an academic RAND had been initiated by former RAND defense analyst Joseph Kershaw very soon after his appointment as OEO's research director. He fairly quickly settled on Wisconsin as the natural site, playing especially on the "Wisconsin Idea" of the socially engaged academic that had made the university a training ground for applied social science beginning in the late nineteenth and early twentieth centuries. The Wisconsin economics department could lay claim to a long lineage of institutionalist economists—Richard T. Ely, Henry C. Taylor, John R. Commons, Edmund Witte—who had made major contributions to agricultural planning, workers' compensation law, unemployment insurance, and Social Security, among other policy areas.[13] More recently, the department had shown a willingness to break somewhat with the institutionalist tradition and to embrace newer, more mathematical, neoclassically oriented and econometric trends.[14] Most important, Wisconsin had Robert Lampman, "the man," as *Business Week* reported, "who has done most to force economists to think about poverty," and widely considered the nation's leading expert on the poor. What RPP&E wanted, Levine noted after visiting the Madison campus in March 1965, was "a chance to affect the next generation of projects carried on by these people," and a "continual relationship in which they criticize what we are doing . . . and initiate ideas to be put into operating programs and planning."[15]

The idea of such an arrangement appealed to the department economists, although the University was, as Lampman later put it, "cool" to the idea of being treated as "an outpost for a government agency."[16] There was also the worry that Washington would cool to its own commitment to poverty research, leaving the University with a center on a politically sensitive issue, with no guaranteed funding to keep it alive. After assurances from Kershaw and an endorsement from the Ford Foundation, a deal both sides could live with was struck: IRP would have at least five years of funding, while the University would make a "moderate effort" to create "an institutional research capability which could react rapidly to requests of the Assistant Director for research at OEO."[17]

The Institute for Research on Poverty was officially announced in March 1966, with Lampman as its temporary director and $1.7 million to cover the next twenty-one months. Those were "flush times" in Madison, as a later government report put it, with the relatively unrestricted budget devoted to a broad range of individual faculty projects in economics, sociology, anthropology, psychology, and law.[18] The reception was hardly smooth in Washington, however, where IRP became caught up in the running intra-agency battle between the Community Action Program and RPP&E.[19] "The crux of the controversy has been the *carte blanche* given the University of Wisconsin," noted a U.S. Office of Inspection report in 1968, highlighted in what one OEO lawyer called the "total emasculation of the government from having any influence on the Institute's line of research."[20] The real heart of the contention, though, was an issue that had divided RPP&E and CAP from the start: what kind of knowledge did it take to fight a war on poverty, who should define it, and, increasingly pertinent as budgets grew tighter, should it be academic at all? On this front, IRP staff members were not exactly reassuring to Washington. Director Harold Watts, an economist who had worked on the RPP&E staff, believed that the IRP's main contribution would be to "long-range research," while Robert Lampman endorsed the Institute's "non-spectacular" style of operations, preferring to be deliberative and cautious rather than trying to make a big splash.[21] IRP's backers in Washington offered a more vigorous defense, noting that the Institute was attracting "top-notch" economists to contribute to "the nation's understanding of the nature, causes and cures of poverty," an important achievement even if their research was not always immediately relevant to OEO concerns. Equally important, the IRP was testament to OEO's "courage" in being the only agency willing to establish a truly "independent, intellectual, objective organization . . . following the facts and the truth as they became available no matter where they might lead."[22] For Community Action Program staff members, that was precisely the problem with IRP: the preponderance of economists, their hostility toward community action, and the sinister uses to which their work might be put. To CAP, as the Inspector's report pointed out, IRP appeared as the "cosa nostra" of evaluation—and it just so happened to have four former RPP&E employees on its staff. "It's kind of nice," one person quipped prophetically. "If OEO goes out of business the Institute for Research on Poverty will be around to study why it died."[23]

Such talk of conspiracy was, to say the least, greatly exaggerated. In fact, at the beginning IRP research was fairly eclectic, not exclusively economic, and generally more ignorant than hostile toward the social action aims of OEO.

But the IRP disputes did underscore the growing rift between RPP&E and Community Action in their ideas about "policy-relevant" knowledge, and the institute in Wisconsin was decidedly on the analytic side. IRP had a special relationship with the OEO research office, a National Academy of Sciences panel later noted, smoothed by a mutual appreciation for its economic research and by the "personal acquaintances" that tied the two.[24] The Institute, "while not entirely of the economics discipline, is disciplined by economics," the NAS panel observed, and its research was beginning to show signs of a "collective point of view." IRP also got high marks for the quality of its research, the "hallmark" of which was "competent and sophisticated quantitative analysis of income distribution and its determinants with a policy focus on transfer payments and in particular the negative income tax." What it did not include, as the panel acknowledged, was much questioning of the political economy or social relations beyond the characteristics of the poor.[25] In the era of post–Great Society politics, these were precisely the features that would help the IRP, and analytic poverty knowledge more generally, to prevail. Nowhere was this better illustrated than in the widely heralded social experiment that would truly put the IRP on the map: the New Jersey Income Maintenance Experiment, a hugely ambitious, multimillion dollar test of the RPP&E's sure fire weapon for eliminating poverty, the negative income tax.

New Jersey's was actually the first of four federally funded experiments conducted from the late 1960s through the 1970s, to demonstrate the efficacy of what for many, and especially economists, was an idea whose time had come: a federal minimum income guarantee.[26] Equally important, it was by far the most ambitious federal attempt at controlled social experimentation to date, and in that sense a test of a powerful new policy analytic "tool." Planned by OEO starting in 1966, the New Jersey experiment already had a strong coalition of subscribers when the IRP became part of the research team. Foremost among them were the OEO economists who had been actively promoting the idea of a negative income tax (NIT) since 1965. The NIT was one of many possible approaches to a guaranteed minimum income, but to a growing number of economists it was the fairest and most efficient, not in the least because it would emphasize cash rather than services, it would work through the tax rather than the social welfare system, and it would not intervene directly in the market. The basic idea was to offer families below a certain level of income a kind of refundable tax credit, that would be gradually reduced until they reached a "break-even" point, and that could be used to supplement income from work. Thus, in its simplest version, a family with no other income might receive a flat-out grant of $3,000 while those with low earnings would receive varying subsidies until their earnings totaled $6,000.

NIT adherents ranged across the political spectrum, but for the economists at OEO it held particular promise on two major counts: first, as a quick way of eliminating income poverty at a reasonable added cost; and second, as a way of providing cash assistance to a group commonly referred to as the "working poor"—stereotypically white, two-parent, with a male breadwinner—who for the most part were categorically ineligible for welfare support.[27] Eventually, supporters urged, the proposed NIT should be expanded to replace the complicated array of categorical welfare programs altogether.[28] Despite growing support from within his administration, the idea was a nonstarter with LBJ, who preferred hand-"ups" to hand-"outs" in his War on Poverty and who in any case was keeping a lid on antipoverty spending as he escalated the war in Vietnam. Meanwhile, despite their confident-sounding projections, OEO proponents were themselves uncertain about how and at what cost the NIT would actually work. The key issue, in their minds, was a variant on the age-old question in poor law reform: would able-bodied men stop working when presented with income from the state? Economists assumed there would be some fall-off in work effort; the question was how much. If the NIT were to pass muster in politics, proponents needed hard evidence that the work disincentive—and the cost—wouldn't be unacceptably high.

After several attempts to estimate this "labor market effect" with conventional econometric methods, OEO analysts got wind of an innovative, if "breathtakingly simple" idea: the NIT could be tested by running a live social experiment, complete with "experimental" subjects (who would receive the "treatment," or payments) and a "control group" (who would not).[29] The idea came in the form of a proposal that was making the rounds in foundations and government agencies in 1966, submitted by an MIT graduate student named Heather Ross. Ross originally proposed to run a small-scale experiment working with the United Planning Organization, a Washington, D.C., community action agency funded by OEO. With OEO's encouragement, she instead teamed up with more established researchers at Mathematica, a relatively new, for-profit research firm founded by Princeton University economists to take advantage of a growing market for defense as well as domestic policy research. By the spring of 1967, her original idea had grown into a far more ambitious plan for a three-year experiment, involving nearly fourteen hundred families all told, at a cost that would eventually total just under $8 million. It had also taken on something of a bandwagon effect for an expanding constituency of academic researchers, policy analysts, and government research bureaucrats with sometimes competing interests in mind. Academics were heavily vested in the scientific integrity of the experiment, and in its possibilities for generating data for theoretical models of labor supply. NIT advocates wanted evidence that the idea was effective and politically acceptable, hoping to lay the groundwork for future reform. OEO also wanted to promote controlled social experimentation as a major new tool for rational planning, thereby showing that the agency was in the vanguard as "an important innovative force in the Federal establishment," as Robert Levine wrote to Sargent Shriver.[30] Besides, a successful experiment, even three to five years down the line, could be a major step towards OEO's stated goal of eliminating income poverty by 1976.

Despite warnings from his own political advisors, Shriver was persuaded to garner an initial $1.5 million from OEO's community action budget for the project, and in the process found a way to put Wisconsin's Institute for Research on Poverty to good use. Wary of awarding funds directly to a for-profit research firm, Shriver told his staff to make the grant to "those eggheads in Wisconsin" and to have them subcontract with Mathematica to run the experiment itself.[31] In fact, IRP economists became centrally involved in designing and supervising the experiment, which proved an important turning point in the Institute's as yet undistinguished career. For Director Harold Watts, the NIT experiment was IRP's "salvation," proving its policy relevance while providing a central research focus and, just as important, cultivating its expertise in what was quickly becoming the hottest issue in poverty research. The groundswell for a simplified, consolidated, if not guaranteed federal income maintenance system was growing even outside Johnson administration circles, with endorsements ranging from the Chamber of Commerce in the name of simplicity, to welfare and civil rights advocates in the name of better, less stigmatized benefits. In response, LBJ agreed to appoint business executive Benjamin Heineman to head up a prestigious blue ribbon study panel, successfully stalling action, but adding luster to the NIT and providing added rationale for the experiment. Even before the experiment was launched, the Ford Foundation was looking to the IRP for advice on how to spend the $3 million it had set aside for income maintenance research, much of which eventually went to a second, rural, NIT experiment.[32]

The combination of academic and political interest that led to the NIT experiment was reflected in key aspects of the design as well, beginning with its deliberately narrow focus on issues of labor supply or work disincentive rather than on the broader array of social, political, and psychological impacts an income guarantee might have. To some degree, this reflected a pragmatic concern to avoid overcomplicating the experiment, but it involved theoretical and political decisions as well. The experiment was restricted to two-parent, male-headed "working poor" families, reflecting economists' assumptions about the labor market as well as the greater political and social value OEO assigned to labor force participation among men. Female-headed families, in the experimental logic, were already eligible for welfare and therefore not apt to be affected in their workforce behavior by the prospect of an income guarantee. Besides, as a relatively small percentage of the officially recognized labor force in the first place, the designers assumed, single mothers were not likely to have a big impact even if they did drop out. Following much the same reasoning, the sample population was restricted to "poor and near poor" families—up to 150 percent of the poverty line, or $5,000 for a family of four—both to focus on where the costs would be greatest and to avoid appearance of subsidizing the nonpoor. Finally, the experiment was conducted in urban New Jersey, which at the time did not offer AFDC benefits to two-parent families, was conveniently close to Mathematica, and, most important, had a social services administration—headed by ex–Ford Foundation program officer Paul Ylvisaker—that was sympathetic and willing to cooperate.[33]

Equally significant, though, were the political and social realities that were ignored, avoided, or simply unanticipated in the experimental design. By subjecting the sample population to a low income cutoff, for example, the experiment included only a small sample of working wives—then, as now, often the key to raising family income above the poverty line. A second unanticipated factor brought the experiment planners face-to-face with the changing social geography of race. In each of the New Jersey cities selected—Trenton, Paterson-Passaic, and Jersey City—researchers were surprised to find that the income eligible population was overwhelmingly black or Puerto Rican. In search of racial balance—i.e., a sufficient number of sufficiently poor whites—researchers had to go outside the study area altogether to add the predominantly white city of Scranton, Pennsylvania, to the experiment.[34] Clearly, however, such immediate contextual factors were of little interest in the researchers' minds. Despite the fact that their site decisions were being made in the wake of a third consecutive summer of urban riots, the research design made no attempt to assess the significance or potential impact of this obvious racial divide.[35] Nor, for that matter, was the research designed to take the peculiarities of local labor markets into account; this was to be a study of labor *supply*. But perhaps the most conspicuous absence goes back to the exclusion of female-headed families from the experiment, at the very moment when Congress, with a 1967 welfare reform known as the WIN (for work incentives) amendments, was changing welfare law to get welfare mothers to work. At least in its original genesis and planning, the NIT experiment was removed from what were fast becoming the central issues in the politics of welfare reform: not fairness, adequacy, and efficiency in reducing poverty—the economists' standards—but the soon-to-be ubiquitous trio "waste, fraud, and abuse."

Then again, antiwelfare backlash did not seem to be threatening support for the experiment—at least, not at first. Instead, in 1969, the just-launched New Jersey experiment and the IRP got a wholly unexpected endorsement from a most unlikely source, when the recently installed Nixon administration embraced not just the guaranteed income but the broader analytic movement that had helped to bring the experiment about. Following several months of task force planning that kept the future of poverty research unclear, President Nixon announced plans for a comprehensive package of social policy changes, in which "revamping" OEO as a domestic policy think tank was only the start. His ambition was no less than to reverse the post–New Deal trend towards federal government responsibility, by introducing revenue-sharing, a "new federalism," and, especially consequential for poverty experts, abolition of the "failed" welfare system in favor of a national minimum income, later to be known as the Family Assistance Plan.[36]

Nixon's domestic policy was more pragmatic than ideological, but it did have at least two consistent themes: distancing itself, without wholly retreating, from Great Society commitments, and breaking up the political power of the interest-laden New Deal bureaucracy.[37] The reorganized OEO seemed indeed to be in sync with those goals. Very much in the forefront of the analytic revolution, PR&E, as the reorganized policy shop was known, was prepared to judge government programs by the outcomes they produced rather than the allegiances they protected. By 1970, it had already launched or was playing a central role in planning several large experiments in areas the administration had targeted for change, including housing and education vouchers, performance contracting in service delivery, and health insurance reform. It was also preparing a comprehensive evaluation of community action programs across the country, with the intention, as the IRP researchers contracted to do the work soon realized, of drafting legislation to replace CAP altogether.[38] The agency intended to take a broader view of poverty than in the previous administration, OEO Director Donald Rumsfeld reported to the IRP advisory committee, in an attempt to play down the connection between Nixon's antipoverty agenda and the racialized perception of the War on Poverty that Nixon himself had helped to promote—measures like FAP would be for everyone, but especially for Nixon's "forgotten" white working class. In all these ways, the Nixon years promised to be a good and exciting time for analysts in government, and especially for the kind of sophisticated economic research the IRP and the New Jersey income experiment could provide.[39]

In fact, though, the New Jersey experiment was fundamentally redirected by the antiwelfare politics Nixon sought to encourage and unleash, which transformed the political meaning if not the design of the experiments—from ending poverty to welfare reform. Not long after the experiment was up and running in early 1969, zealous New Jersey prosecutors began a series of investigations to rout out experiment participants they suspected of engaging in welfare fraud. The charges actually stemmed from a recent change in New Jersey policy that made poor two-parent families eligible for AFDC—a change, coincidentally, that undermined part of the rationale for excluding one-parent families from the experiment, but that proved especially damaging to the families identified in the local press as welfare cheats.[40] And yet, this local reaction must be understood not just as traditional antiwelfare backlash, but as part of the broader changes in national politics that were reshaping the political meaning of the New Jersey experiment, and subsequent poverty research. Welfare had become much more of a major national issue between the time the experiment was conceived and the time it was in the field, thanks in part to the growth in size and changed racial makeup of AFDC, but more importantly thanks to the deeper racial and ideological backlash that Nixon and others

exploited in making the so-called "welfare crisis" an issue of national concern.[41] Rising costs and swelling rolls were the immediate signposts of the
crisis, as White House analysts saw it, but its deeper causes were growing
"dependency" among unmarried black women and the self-interested behavior
of New Deal/Great Society welfare state bureaucrats.[42] The Family Assistance
Plan would be a strike for independence and against "welfarism," Nixon declared when he first announced the reform, by abolishing AFDC altogether
and offering a minimum federal income for *all*, including two-parent working
poor families, in its place. Nixon proposed a variation—albeit less generous
and with an added work requirement—on the negative income tax idea that
liberal analysts had been endorsing for years. In doing so he attached the NIT,
and the New Jersey experiment, to a reform movement that aimed more to
prevent welfare dependency and monitor behavior than to find a way of bringing income poverty to an end.

Initially encouraged by their newfound political immediacy, researchers
soon found it to be a curse. After all, they were still in the early stages of the
three-year experiment when FAP was before Congress, and reluctant to make
any conjectures about results. In reality, they had little choice. The White
House—in the person of Daniel P. Moynihan—knew about the experiment and
wanted hard scientific evidence that would help FAP legislation along. "The
future of social experimentation is on the line," OEO official John Wilson
reportedly told researchers at IRP; they were given three days to come up
with something concrete.[43] Their report to Congress, feverishly assembled in
a weekend of hand-coding data, was almost too good to be true: the experiment
had so far produced no evidence of work disincentive; low administrative
costs; no impact on family stability; and, based on attitude surveys, a ringing
endorsement for poor people's motivation to work. "We believe that these
preliminary data suggest that fears that a Family Assistance Program would
result in extreme, unusual, or unanticipated responses are unfounded," the report concluded, in measured, scientific style.[44] Such timely results may have
helped with the House Ways and Means Committee, and earned favorable
coverage in the press, but they drew a completely different, unwanted kind of
attention once FAP made its way to the Senate Finance Committee—where it
ultimately met defeat. Seeking to discredit the experiment as well as the FAP,
Delaware Senator John Williams dispatched the General Accounting Office to
investigate the New Jersey operation and later demanded access to all family
records in a thinly veiled effort to dig up evidence of welfare fraud. Williams
had been gunning for the experiment ever since it was first announced, calling
it a test of a "socialistic idea." Eventually, he and the GAO backed down from
their more extreme demands, but not without first occupying and turning the
New Jersey field office into a kind of armed encampment, leading researchers
to guard the family files under lock and key. [45] In the end, neither the favorable
evidence nor the investigations made much difference in the political fight.

FAP drew opposition from among key political constituencies, prominent among them southern Democrats and the welfare rights movement.[46] But the brush with politics had made a difference for the experiment, channeling its findings within the central concerns of the welfare reform debate.

By the time the New Jersey results were final, in December 1973, a second try at FAP legislation had been rejected and the political moment for negative income taxation had passed. Nevertheless, from an analytic perspective the experiment was highly successful, laying the groundwork for a future of NIT experimentation that increasingly followed a logic and momentum of its own.[47] By the early 1970s, plans for three additional income maintenance experiments were well under way, each more ambitious, expensive, and, in the minds of their sponsors, better designed than the last. Although still planned for the long-term rather than for the immediate legislative schedule, the experiments were more and more geared toward key issues in the ongoing welfare debate. One would test the idea in two rural areas; a second among blacks in the ghettos of Gary, Indiana—with a specific emphasis, reflecting where concern about "welfare dependency" was highest, on black female-headed families; a third, run simultaneously in Seattle and Denver, would include a manpower training component while paying closer attention to the experiment's impact on family structure.[48] New Jersey also provided vindication for what is known in analytic shorthand as "experimental design"—in which eligible participants are assigned randomly to "treatment" and "control" groups—which was rapidly becoming the analytic standard while shunting less "scientific" research models aside.[49]

Moreover, the New Jersey experiment had also proved an important institutionalizing force for the emerging poverty research industry, gaining kudos for the OEO, launching the IRP as a nationally recognized research institution, and providing Mathematica with the basis of a new subdivision that would eventually grow into a separate, 500-staff enterprise devoted to evaluation, experimentation, and social policy research. Despite the inevitable tensions, the experiment helped to reinforce the personal and informational ties that linked these institutions together, while highlighting their mutual interdependence as well. These ties in turn helped to cultivate a distinctive, if highly circumscribed, political culture in analytic networks: based on sophisticated research, a shared economic language, concerned with research method as much as substance, and conducted principally through the journal articles, agency task forces, conferences, and behind-the-scenes staff meetings that constitute a kind of enclosed, analytic public sphere. The New Jersey experiment may not have swayed Congress, but it surely strengthened analytic support for the NIT, and subsequent experiments helped to keep the idea alive in government circles long after FAP was defeated. The fact remains, however, that support, even awareness of the NIT was largely confined to a small group of economists and policy planners within the analytic subgovernment and the private sector research organizations it funded, who shared an increasingly specialized, technical body of knowledge, but who ignored the kind of broadly based public education and organizing that would be necessary to mobilize political support for the idea. Indeed, it can be argued that this was precisely what made social experimentation acceptable as a form of policy advocacy, giving knowledge the appearance of political neutrality, when in fact it was politics by other means.

Meanwhile, the success of the New Jersey experiment put the IRP—and its sponsors—in good standing to weather yet another Nixon administration "reorganization"—this one, in early 1973, spelling the final demise of the Office of Economic Opportunity. What remained of Community Action was pretty well decimated, while less controversial programs were dispersed within the federal bureaucracy. PR&E analysts expressed surprise and disappointment, and many of them left government in response. But they left assured that the basic commitment to analytic research would continue in what was slated as PR&E's new home: the much larger Office of the Assistant Secretary for Policy and Evaluation (ASPE) at the Department of Health, Education and Welfare.[50] After all, ASPE had been founded, in 1965, on the same rationalistic convictions and by the same kind of people who had first brought analytic thinking to the OEO. Its first director, William C. Gorham, had been dispatched from the Defense Department Office of Systems Analysis to help bring the large and unwieldy HEW bureaucracy into the analytic age. Under Republican leadership analysis had, if anything, become more entrenched. At the time of the transfer, ASPE's analytic staff had grown to well over one hundred from the thirty it started with in the early Nixon years, and it would continue to grow steadily until reaching its peak of three hundred in 1978. William Morrill, the new Assistant Secretary also recruited from defense analyst ranks, was said to enjoy an unprecedented degree of influence with HEW Secretary Caspar Weinberger.[51] Besides, ASPE had already launched a program of analytic welfare research, including two ambitious NIT experiments of its own. This research would now become part of its expanded income security division, based largely, as one staff member put it, on "people, projects and the policy research budget inherited from OEO." New ASPE research guidelines showed basic continuity with the priorities the OEO analysts had pursued—including continued funding for the IRP.[52]

And yet, easy as the transition to ASPE may have been it also signaled changes in the political economy of research funding that would have implications for the ongoing production of poverty knowledge. Now lodged within a larger, if more stable, bureaucracy, poverty would not only have to compete with other program areas for research dollars; it would also be attached to the way HEW conceptualized its central program and policy concerns. These, of course, included a wide array of programs to help poor people, but not the singular mandate to end poverty that had defined OEO at the start. Poverty research at ASPE would not only become more analytic than ever; it would also become more absorbed into the singular, ongoing fixation among agency analysts on someday achieving their own NIT-like version of comprehensive welfare reform. No sooner had Nixon's FAP fallen by the political wayside than ASPE, with Secretary Weinberger's approval, mounted a major analytic campaign behind a new version of the simplified guaranteed income—this one known as the Income Supplement Program and very explicitly designed with the goals of welfare replacement, social service "devolution" (to the states), administrative efficiency, and preservation of work incentives in mind.[53] As we shall see, the push for this kind of comprehensive welfare overhaul in turn became a driving force behind the development of new and more elaborate research technologies for estimating program costs and benefits as well as behavioral patterns among the poor.

The loss of OEO as the central government poverty agency also created a second kind of competitive pressure, this one attached to the diffusion of federal funding sources for poverty research. In fiscal year 1977 ASPE, still the largest single source, was spending $20 million on poverty research, but other agencies were close behind. The Department of Housing and Urban Development (HUD) alone was spending $19.9 million, and the Department of Labor $4.5 million, according to a National Academy of Sciences report.[54] This was not simply a product of the decentralization of program responsibilities; each of these agencies was politically vested in cultivating its own network of scholars and organizations—that is, in backing up the agency position with the agency analysis—as well. Nor was this proliferation confined to the executive branch. As part of its Vietnam- and Watergate-era challenge to the "imperial presidency," Congress created its own independent analytic resources, most notably by establishing the Congressional Budget Office (CBO) in 1974.[55] These moves to expand analytic capacity did not necessarily reflect a simple faith in systems analysis—its mystique had long since been shattered by the debacle of Vietnam. If anything, the analytic explosion was driven by a more knowing view of the importance of analytic expertise in the political process, an awareness that "the numbers" should not be taken at face value even as, in an era of waning affluence, they were becoming more weighty in social policy debates. At the same time, again reflecting a more "knowing" attitude towards research, government agencies were stepping up efforts to make federally subsidized research more directly accountable, or "relevant" to their policy and program needs. As a result, various agencies were relying more heavily on task-oriented contracts than grants in their support for research on social problems, in turn encouraging the expansion of private sector enterprises set up expressly to meet those demands.[56] On the whole, then, the market for poverty research was certainly growing, but it was becoming more competitive in all sorts of ways. As demand grew more diffuse, organizations like the IRP could no longer expect to rely on a single funding agency, no matter how large the grant. And yet as the number of private research contractors expanded, mere technical expertise was no longer enough; analytic organizations needed to establish what is known in foundation circles as their "comparative advantage" in order to win contracts for the big-ticket research projects that would allow them to survive. In this environment, the IRP could position itself as uniquely academic, while continuing to look for new opportunities to get involved in large-scale multi-investigator research projects like the New Jersey NIT experiment.[57] The Urban Institute cultivated a different market strategy, and in the process played a central role in developing yet another highly technical research technique that promised to transform the welfare policy debate.

THE URBAN INSTITUTE AND MICROSIMULATION MODELS

The Urban Institute had already proven itself adept at responding to market forces. After all, it was founded on the principle that the discipline of the market—in this case, the government contract market—was the best antidote to academic irrelevance or, worse, the bureaucratic biases of "in-house" agency research.[58] That was in 1968, during the waning months of the Johnson administration, when several defense research industry incumbents joined together to create their version of a "domestic RAND," a free-standing, government-financed think tank that would help to solve the nation's toughest urban problems, from ghetto poverty to suburban sprawl.[59] Significantly, it was this very logic that took the Urban Institute away from its early focus on urban America and more in the direction, as one evaluator put it, of "where the money was": among other issues, poverty and welfare reform.[60]

The idea for an urban institute had been germinating in Johnson administration task forces since 1964, but by the late 1960s it was imbued with increasing urgency after three summers of ghetto uprising left urban policy in disarray. White House aide Joseph A. Califano made no secret of his frustration: there were plenty of academic urbanologists to call on, but no place with the kind of data and analysis that would really help in policy debate—the kind of information, that is, that he was familiar with from his days as Robert McNamara's assistant at the Department of Defense.[61] And so, when LBJ sidestepped HUD's network of urbanologists and told Califano to take charge, Califano recruited a group of high-powered private-sector incorporators with visible ties to the defense establishment—and no visible urban expertise. Ford Foundation President (and Kennedy/Johnson National Security Advisor) McGeorge Bundy was prominent among them, pledging $1 million in initial support, as was Robert McNamara, who at the time was about to take on the presidency of the World Bank.[62] Hastily dispatching with the idea of a HUD-led, university-based enterprise ("It's doomed," McNamara reportedly said, "because it'll never get the visibility and attractiveness it needs to get funding and people"), the board used its influence to get pledges of $15 million in total contract support from OEO, HEW, and the Departments of Labor and Transportation as well as HUD.[63] They also went outside established urban networks for the Institute's first director, appointing William C. Gorham, the former RAND-then-Defense Department analyst who as the first director of ASPE was already credited with bringing systems analysis to HEW.[64] But it was not its founding alone that gave the Urban Institute more of an analytic than an urban stamp. Just months after the urban think tank was incorporated, it was operating within a Republican government contract market, in which demand for analysis was growing, but support for what Gorham referred to as "mission-oriented" (vs. "task oriented") research was a much harder sell. Despite more than $12 million in general support from the Ford Foundation, the Urban Institute in the 1970s was built up around the compartmentalized categories and political priorities of the policy world it was set up to serve.[65]

The Republican years in fact produced something of a windfall for the Institute, as the federal bureaucracy became suffused with research officials who could appreciate the technical proficiency of its research. Federal contracts were responsible for nearly 80 percent of an annual expenditure that had grown to $10.2 million by 1977, when the Institute staff reached a peak of 277 members.[66] And it was during this period of heavy federal dependency that the Urban Institute found its own distinctive niche in poverty research, by marketing a technique known as microsimulation modeling expressly, though not exclusively, for the purposes of welfare reform. Microsimulation modeling was still a rather arcane research specialty in the late 1960s, but like social experimentation its potential impact on policy making seemed immense. The basic idea was to adapt techniques used in economic forecasting to build computer models capable of simulating the benefits and costs of proposed policy changes—all in the promise of achieving a degree of precision unheard of in previous social policy debate.[67] To do this, analysts need three key ingredients: detailed information about the eligible population; agencies willing to invest in and use the technique; and a clear-cut policy application. By the late 1960s, poverty analysts had all three: the first microsimulation model was developed by analysts on the staff of the Heineman Commission (appointed by LBJ to assess the pros and cons of the negative income tax) using a survey commissioned by the OEO. This model, known as RIM (for Reforms in Income Maintenance) was then taken up by ASPE to help make the case for Nixon's Family Assistance Plan, drawing attention and support for the model if not for the actual reform. The RIM model had created "a situation probably without precedent in the development of social legislation," Daniel P. Moynihan later recalled, referring to the accuracy and budgetary "discipline" it brought to the debate.[68] Of course, since FAP itself failed there was no way of really testing what the model predicted about program costs, but it did give a more concrete picture of who stood to benefit and who to lose. Equally important, it gave administration projections an aura of exactitude that no others in the debate could claim. Like social experimentation, then, microsimulation modeling had become closely intertwined with the analytic drive for welfare reform. And, like the IRP, the Urban Institute was ideally positioned to gain: all of the original RIM model-builders were on staff, where they were working on a new and better version that would in turn be used for estimating the impact of ASPE's new and better version of welfare reform. That new model, known as TRIM (for Transfer Income Model), gave ASPE a tool that no other policy shop had, and established the Urban Institute as Washington's premier center for applied microsimulation, which appeared to be a growth industry in its own right.[69]

By the mid-1970s microsimulation modeling was clearly coming of age, especially judging from the amount of funding and the proliferation of acronyms it inspired. With government grants and general research funds totaling $8.4 million, the Urban Institute had adapted TRIM for use in housing and health as well as income maintenance policy research, and was at work on another breakthrough in modeling, called DYNASIM, for projecting economic and demographic trends over time.[70] There was even competition stirring in the once contained and tight-knit field. Breaking away from the Urban Institute, a small group of researchers established a for-profit Washington-based office of Mathematica Policy Research that was aggressively marketing a model called MATH to rival TRIM as an even better tool for simulating social policy reforms—effectively taking advantage of interagency rivalries to create a demand for bigger, better, and more up-to-date policy tools.[71] Moreover, however bewildering the constant succession of acronyms, they were in fact becoming common currency in social policy debates. The MATH model had a feature role in debates over food stamps in the mid 1970s, which quickly bogged down under the weight of competing cost/benefit estimates. The "countermodeling" grew even fiercer in the interagency squabbles over welfare reform, when MATH, TRIM, and a newer model known as the KGB (named after its authors Kasten, Greenberg, and Betson—albeit in an atmosphere heated enough to inspire thoughts of the Soviet spy agency) became weapons in an embarrassing and all-too-public fight between ASPE and the analysts at the Department of Labor over which agency would have the upper hand in President Carter's Program for Better Jobs and Income (PBJI).[72]

The significance of microsimulation modeling lay less in the particulars of these squabbles than in what it revealed about what poverty knowledge had become: technical, insular, driven by the imperatives of the research industry and its emerging technology, and accessible to only a few. Heavily subsidized by government funding, the industry could even be said to be taking on certain culture-of-poverty–like features: dependency, social isolation, a self-perpetuating "cycle" of models to test and data to generate. The appearance of the hi-tech models—and their impact on policy—exemplified all of these problems, and more. For one thing they were enormously expensive to develop, to maintain, and, at an estimated $1,000 per use, even to run.[73] They were also based on built-in but hidden assumptions—about unemployment, economic growth rates, and inflation, for example—that could make an enormous difference in what the simulations would predict. For this very reason they could easily be manipulated, as agency model-users were clearly aware, and yet they managed to endow the inherently political act of cost/benefit analysis with an aura of impartiality that nonexperts were ill-prepared to challenge. At least when it came to formulating and debating various options, the growing emphasis on modeling helped to put power in the hands of the people who had the numbers and made poverty policy making less accessible to those who did not. Moreover, despite their adoption in several policy areas, in reality the models were uniquely suited to a certain kind of reform, in which the main "variables" were income, incentives, individual and/or household behavior, and measurable program costs. Still, one is hard put to find examples in which these models actually furthered, as opposed to slowing down, delaying, or even preventing, the cause of analytic reform.

Even granting that microsimulation could make a contribution to estimating program benefits and costs, it absorbed an enormous amount of resources and attention that could and should have been devoted to other questions. By the late 1970s, the Urban Institute had a broad research portfolio indeed, including research on housing, transportation, health, income maintenance, social services, and public finance. But it was notably silent on the most important issues affecting cities and the urban poor. Deindustrialization, race, and central city ghettoization received only glancing attention at the Institute, and none were the central focus of major research programs. Revenue-sharing, President Nixon's sweeping overhaul of urban public finance, inspired only the narrowest research to monitor how the localities were spending federal funds.[74] Even its research on poverty—more appropriately characterized as research on the poor—was almost completely detached from any sort of political and economic context, let alone that of urban decline. In a triumph of technique, the Urban Institute had built its reputation for reliability and objectivity on the analytic methods rather than the substance of its research, precisely the methods that enabled it and other Great Society research institutions to flourish in an era of post–Great Society politics.

MANAGING RESEARCH FOR FEDERAL POLICY: MDRC

In much the same way, it was an important victory for analytic knowledge when the Manpower Demonstration Research Corporation (MDRC) was established to sell the employment and training field on the concept of experimental design in demonstration research. But the story of MDRC is significant for another, more important reason, for it shows how poverty research networks, following the lead of post-Great society policy, engaged the issue of work: not, as principally, as a problem of structural declines in employment and wages, but as social rehabilitation, the road to self-sufficiency, for the most recalcitrant of the poor.

MDRC's story once again sounds the themes of opportunity and bureaucratic need: it was created specifically to run a large-scale employment and demonstration project sponsored jointly by the Ford Foundation and the Department of Labor in 1974. But MDRC also grew out of decisions made by the Ford Foundation and other key nongovernmental knowledge brokers in their attempts to moderate the liberal agenda for the post–Great Society age. One was to withdraw from the vaunted aspirations with which so many Great Society programs, including the new social research institutions, had started out. Thus, while the IRP was dedicated to no less than finding the "causes, consequences, and cures" for poverty, MDRC very consciously claimed the more limited objective of testing out incremental policy changes with modest, precisely delineated goals. A second decision was to conduct demonstration projects in direct and carefully orchestrated partnerships with federal government agencies, rather than using them, as in the case of Gray Areas and Community Action, as outside catalysts for change. Indeed, in the view of Ford Foundation vice president and Gray Areas veteran Mitchell Sviridoff, with whom the idea for MDRC began, the "activist experimentation" of the 1960s had gone "too far, too fast." The new way of conducting demonstrations during the 1970s, in contrast, would concentrate on the unglamorous work of implementing, managing, and evaluating social interventions, while requiring "prior evidence" not only that the foundation and the government would act as "*bona fide* partners rather than competitors or adversaries," but that government agencies would be willing to foot most of the bill.[75]

A third decision aimed at moderating the liberal agenda was to avoid direct confrontation with the issue of race in antipoverty funding, a decision, as we have seen, that had been made over and over again in the Ford foundation's past. But in contrast to the days in which focusing on race was simply "*verboten*," playing down race in the 1970s signaled more of a selective, if strategic, retreat. It was based on the belief, expressed by Sviridoff in the foundation's 1969 Annual Report, that 1960s social programs had been too narrowly targeted on the minority poor—a belief many liberals felt had been corroborated by Richard Nixon's successful appeal to the "silent majority" at the polls. While admitting that such beliefs could be exaggerated, Sviridoff's critique of the Great Society agenda was very much couched in racial terms. "[T]he deprived black has hope," he wrote of the impact of 1960s social reform, "the near-poor white does not." Worse, the most "visible" of the civil rights and social change programs at least appeared to have come at the expense of the over-taxed white lower and lower-middle class. "The task for the seventies," then, was not to abandon but to "recast" the antipoverty agenda, in a way "that will reduce polarization . . . yet still meet pressing needs for social reform."[76] In reality, with the exception of a relatively small, short-lived "working-class program," the foundation did not reduce its principal focus on the minority poor. But it did couch its antipoverty agenda in self-consciously race-neutral, problem-specific terms—distressed communities, teen pregnancy, disadvantaged workers—which could be addressed as issues of behavioral and social pathology apart from race.[77]

Sviridoff himself figured prominently in getting MDRC started, as did the research and policy networks he could mobilize as the Ford Foundation's vice president for National Affairs. A former labor organizer for the UAW, Sviridoff first gained attention in national antipoverty circles as the director of New Haven's model Gray Areas/Community Action Program, moving from there to a brief stint heading up New York City Mayor John Lindsay's Human Resource Administration, and then to the Ford position—a job Paul Ylvisaker had been passed over for—in 1967. By then his ties to labor were more policy- than movement-oriented, putting him in ongoing touch with the leading voices in manpower policy and research. Such was also the case with his community development connections, where Sviridoff was consistently a voice of moderation and practicality, of the "executive-centered" rather than the "participatory" style, and of judging local organizations by their "managerial abilities and technical proficiency rather than by their proneness to shake a fist or lead a picket line." It was very much in this spirit that Sviridoff put the Ford Foundation at the forefront in creating a new class of private nonprofit "intermediary" organizations designed specifically to handle the complexities of management, supervision, technical support, and evaluation that neither large government funding agencies nor small local program operators could handle on their own.[78] Although steadfast in their claims to political neutrality, such intermediaries were also safe vehicles for the kind of indirect, expertise-based advocacy the nonprofit tax laws would allow. One of the earliest intermediaries, the Vera Institute of Justice, had been created by Ford in the early 1960s as a voice, albeit neutral, for criminal justice reform. It was a Vera project known as "Wildcat," a work/training program for recovering drug addicts and criminal offenders started in 1969, that Sviridoff and others in the manpower and poverty networks parlayed into the National Supported Work Demonstration that the MDRC was created to run.

Modeled on the European concept of sheltered employment—heavily supervised and subsidized jobs created for disadvantaged workers—Vera's Wildcat project had two features that touched on growing preoccupations in the federal administration of both manpower and poverty programs.[79] The first was its focus on the least trained and socially outcast workers, a group known in manpower as the "disadvantaged" or "hard-core" unemployed. While the designation wasn't new, it had changed considerably since the Manpower Development and Training Act of 1962, which had defined disadvantage in reference to blue collar male workers displaced by automation. The War on Poverty had brought a different, narrower focus to federal manpower programs, emphasizing the most marginalized and least skilled workers, and particularly poor, unemployed minority youth. This emphasis was indirectly heightened during the Nixon and Ford administrations, when the decentralization of employment and training responsibilities left federal administrators concerned that localities would simply leave minority youth in the cold.[80] But it was the changing politics of welfare that made the administrative transformation complete, as the combination of rising costs, fears of "dependency," and the growing proportion of black, unmarried AFDC recipients increased political pressure to get welfare mothers off the dole. The 1967 WIN amendments had already written this objective into welfare law, giving HEW and the Department of Labor joint responsibility for training AFDC recipients to work. Adding to this were reports from social science linking welfare and single motherhood to a whole cycle of social pathologies, including crime, addiction, and intergenerational poverty, that work training could presumably break. Thus, by the early 1970s, the interests of manpower and welfare bureaucrats were beginning to converge on a highly stigmatized, predominantly nonwhite subgroup of the poor population, a subgroup defined not just as unemployed, but as antisocial, and definitely considered hard, if not impossible to serve. It was on this common ground that Sviridoff and his collaborators at the Department of Labor persuaded HEW/ASPE, along with five other federal agencies, to become part of the funding consortium behind Supported Work.[81] When the national demonstration got under way in 1975, it defined young high school dropouts and welfare mothers along with criminals and drug addicts as its key target groups. Together, in the shorthand used in Supported Work and Ford Foundation communications, this "chronically unemployed" population made up the core of a new "underclass."[82]

Of course, these shifts in the administrative meaning of the "disadvantaged worker" resulted from very real changes in American culture and political economy as well. One was the steady rise in married women's participation in the paid labor force, which helped to give bipartisan political legitimacy to the idea that welfare mothers should not only be expected but required to work. A second was the dramatic economic decline and racial polarization in older industrial cities, most visible in the inner-city neighborhoods where African Americans and Latinos had become increasingly concentrated after two decades of industrial decentralization and white suburbanization. Both of these developments were related to broader economic deindustrialization, which in combination with ongoing racial segregation in housing and jobs had indeed created the conditions for what Gunnar Myrdal referred to as an economic "underclass" cut off from the mainstream labor market opportunities. But Supported Work and other programs like it did not treat the underclass as a problem of labor markets and political economy; they concentrated on changing individual behavior instead. Thus, Supported Work departed from its European counterpart in at least one significant way: rather than creating a new category of *jobs* that were permanent and "sheltered" from ordinary market demands, Supported Work explicitly provided transitional (usually one year) employment to help its clients "acquire the habits and discipline of work."[83]

Supported Work had a second feature that appealed to manpower and poverty administrators, and that was its commitment to the analytic idea of rigorous, unbiased, policy-relevant research. Nowhere was this commitment more explicit, or controversial, than in the insistence upon using experimental methods to evaluate the project's results—methods, that is, that called for the random assignment of eligible program applicants into "treatment" and "control" groups. By then fairly well entrenched among poverty researchers, this "pure" experimental method had met with wide resistance from practitioners in the manpower field, some who insisted that the "real world" of labor markets simply could not come close to the laboratory ideal and others who objected to the idea of denying people services for the purpose of social research.[84] But the proponents of the experimental method had several key advantages on their side. One was that manpower administrators felt intense pressure to produce concrete, scientific evidence of success, especially in light of its nearly $30 billion worth of less-than-successful programming that, many thought, had produced no useful knowledge of what worked.[85] A second was the presence of analysts in the Department of Labor and ASPE, who insisted that Supported Work should have a strong experimental research component, and who were willing to put up the funds. A third was the by-then well-established network of institutions with the analytic expertise to conduct research on the scale Supported Work envisioned: after an intense competition that involved both the Urban Institute and RAND, the research contract for evaluating Supported Work was awarded to Mathematica and the Institute for Research on Poverty— which hoped to replicate the collaborative relationship they had established during the New Jersey negative income tax experiment. Finally and most important was the presence of a high-powered research advisory group, composed almost entirely of economists and created specifically to lend scientific credibility to the Supported Work demonstration design. This group, recruited by Sviridoff and later constituted as the MDRC board, was heavily invested in the analytic technique. Among its most important functions was to establish the criteria for choosing which of the many local program operators submitting applications would qualify as demonstration sites.[86] A commitment to upholding these standards in turn became a crucial part of the culture and ethos of the MDRC staff, which was responsible for managing what had grown into a fifteen-site, multimillion dollar test: not just of supported work for the disadvantaged, but of a new analytic standard in demonstration research.

On at least the second of these tests, MDRC was more successful than even its founders expected. Within four years of its official incorporation, it was running as many large-scale demonstration projects, all principally financed by federal government contracts and all focused on addressing some problem—public housing, work and welfare, youth unemployment, and, later, teen pregnancy—associated with the most disadvantaged of the poor. Although still heavily reliant on the Ford Foundation and the Department of Labor, it had a solid reputation throughout the domestic federal bureaucracy and was an established presence in the nonprofit analytic world. So impressive was MDRC's performance that Ford and the Department of Labor were collaborating on a second intermediary, Public Private Ventures, for the growing market in youth employment demonstration research.[87] Perhaps most important to its longevity, MDRC was a standard-setter in social policy demonstration and, more generally, for policy-related research.

And yet, this very success also underscores the degree to which poverty knowledge could be seen as an increasingly conservative force, for MDRC research was not only confined to the boundaries of existing federal policy; it played a role in defining those boundaries as well. As the requisites for demonstration research became more strictly experimental so, too, did they become less associated with activist reform. Head Start, to cite the most prominent example, had started out as a decidedly un-"scientific" demonstration and had become national policy without adequate tests of whether and how it would work. The new style of demonstration, in contrast, promised to replace the kind of political conviction that Head Start was based on with neutral expertise. In reality, it imposed standards that made the policy development more inaccessible to those without *analytic* expertise. Equally important, MDRC's style of demonstration research was not apolitical in actuality. It merely devoted itself to what was already politically sanctioned—and to what lent itself to testing with quantitative, analytic techniques. Neither of these criteria left much room for demonstration projects aimed at institutional, labor market, community action, or other innovations in which the individual was not the target of reform. Just as problematic in its political implications was the very principle at the heart of the MDRC enterprise: that social policies should—and could—be tried and proven effective under small "laboratory" conditions before being adopted nationwide. This principle may have justified the use of costly scientific demonstrations in developing policies for the poor, but it had the effect of subjecting antipoverty proposals to a test of effectiveness rarely imposed on programs for the middle and upper classes. Nor did it result in the adoption of experimentally "proven" programs except, as in the notable case of welfare reform, when the results could be used to justify existing political preferences. The Supported Work Demonstration offers a case in point. The evaluation concluded that the programs showed promise, especially for AFDC mothers, and should be adopted as part of a stronger national commitment to integrating the disadvantaged into the mainstream labor force. Those recommendations were ignored, though, when the report came out in late 1979; by then, the Carter administration had already introduced the kinds of austerity measures that would eventually eviscerate employment and training programs once the Reagan administration stepped in. Nevertheless, the Supported Work findings did not go entirely unnoticed: they helped to provide, for those who wanted it, scientific legitimacy for the concept of work-based approaches to welfare reform.

Of course, MDRC had little reason at the experiment's outset to anticipate that the Supported Work findings would be hijacked by an increasingly punitive and exclusionary welfare reform debate. After all, including welfare mothers in the experiment had come as an add-on, an afterthought; Supported Work, like the then-ongoing negative income tax experiments, was mounted as an effort to expand the range of policies to help people deemed hard to employ. All the more ironic, then, that Supported Work did have one other lasting, unanticipated and unintended impact: At the hand of journalist Ken Auletta, who wrote a series of articles about participants in the program, Supported Work gave visibility to the idea, captured in his title, of *The Underclass*.[88] Borrowing from the experiment to give scientific credence to his impressionistic report, Auletta used MDRC's disparate target groups—criminals, drug addicts, long-term welfare recipients, high school dropouts—as the defining features of an undifferentiated group of poor people in what was rapidly becoming the new terminology for the undeserving poor.

THE FAILURE OF ANALYTIC REFORM

What happened with Supported Work could be extended to poverty research in general: by the end of the 1970s, it was thriving as an industry and had several analytic achievements to its name, but even its most seasoned practitioners had to question whether it was making any difference in policy at all. At times it appeared that analytic research was hurting the antipoverty cause. Such was the case of welfare reform.

In an ideal analytic world, welfare would have been the apotheosis rather than the bane of analytic reform, for by the late 1970s it had been subject to every possible research and policy planning technique—basic cost/benefit analysis, social experimentation, microsimulation, and a work training demonstration project run by the MDRC. A clear-cut analytic consensus informed and was continually reinforced by this research: welfare was complicated, inefficient, inadequate, and extremely unfair, especially to the two-parent working poor. And it was primarily on these grounds, rather than the more politically charged problem of "dependency," that poverty analysts had been working through the channels of the analytic subgovernment to sustain a movement for reform. ASPE was very much at the center of this analytic movement, which throughout the 1970s remained devoted to replacing the whole income maintenance system with some form of negative income tax. The idea was still very much alive, despite the failure of Nixon's Family Assistance Plan, and had since survived a chilly reception from President Gerald Ford, who had instituted a cost-saving crackdown on bureaucratic waste, administrative errors, and absent fathers instead.[89] Arguing in its favor were the ever-accumulating results of analytic research, indicating first of all that the vast majority of poor people were not long-term welfare dependents and were not even poor (by official measures) for long periods of time. Better still were the findings from the several NIT experiments, showing what economists interpreted as a relatively small decline in work effort and mostly positive social effects. With all this evidence on how people would react to a guaranteed income, moreover, analysts were hoping to incorporate behavioral projections into their micro-simulation models to predict more accurately than ever what a guaranteed income proposal would cost. Thus, when a newly elected President Jimmy Carter promised a complete welfare overhaul as part of a broader package of domestic policy reforms (national health insurance was a second piece, anticipating Bill Clinton in 1992), ASPE was at the ready with the data, the models, and the experimental findings to make the case for a guaranteed income as the reform of choice.

The problem was, to paraphrase an oft-quoted line from analyst Henry Aaron, that not all of the "witch doctors" agreed.[90] Aaron, the Brookings Institution economist who headed up ASPE during the Carter years, represented one side—the negative income tax side—in what is best described as the analytic warfare that erupted within the administration over welfare reform. The other side was the analytic office at the Department of Labor, which had been built up to rival ASPE in strength if not in size, and which was advocating stepped-up government job creation as part of a broader effort to combat unemployment and pursue labor market reform.[91] The dispute over welfare actually resurrected a debate the Department of Labor had lost during the War on Poverty, when CEA economists had argued that job creation would be unnecessary with faster aggregate growth. But that was when unemployment was running between 4 and 5 percent, and the Department of Labor was outflanked by the more powerful CEA. This time, with recent memories of 9–10 percent unemployment and an analytic office of its own, the Department of Labor was determined to make job creation an integral part of the welfare reform proposal, and to establish the provision of guaranteed jobs as a cardinal principle in federal programs for the working poor. For this reason, Labor analysts harbored no small resentment toward the negative income tax advocates at ASPE, who had always been skeptical of job-creation approaches and who seemed more concerned with efficiency than with keeping the "working poor" off the dole. Assigned to collaborate on the welfare reform proposal, Labor and HEW analysts instead became embroiled in an often bitter battle over rival proposals, in which the weapons were none other than the microsimulation models developed at the Urban Institute, Mathematica, and ASPE to inject technical accuracy and analytic discipline into the policy debate. Using competing models as well as diverging economic assumptions, it turns out, analysts could produce widely differing estimates of what their proposals would cost.[92] In the end, the two sides did manage to compromise, producing an elaborate reform package that combined guaranteed incomes and government jobs, known as the Program for Better Jobs and Income (PBJI). They even agreed to test the proposal with the advanced KGB microsimulation model. But not before the "modeling wars" had become public knowledge and not without continuing, highly embarrassing controversy over what the Carter reform package would cost: using the very same KGB model, the Congressional Budget Office forced the administration to revise its $2.8 billion price tag when it calculated a cost of $17.4 billion instead.[93]

By then, analytic research had already struck another, entirely unexpected blow, when analyses of the negative income tax experiment in Seattle concluded that it had caused marriages to break up. Although those findings have since been disputed, the political impact was immediate, and widely publicized. Senate hearings on the research drew coverage in the press and featured negative income tax proponent Daniel Moynihan's humble reversal. "We must now be prepared to entertain the possibility that we were wrong," Moynihan said, citing the new findings as reason to withdraw his support for the income guarantee.[94] The fallout from the experiments was to continue, when income guarantee opponents determined that the work reduction reported in the findings was not, as analysts claimed, a modest or acceptable price to pay. Indeed, in the hands of conservative critics, the experiments have since been used as proof that welfare causes people to stop working and marriages to break up.[95]

Analytic disputes did not "kill" Carter's welfare reform proposal; political problems did. But the episode did reveal crucial elements on which, for all its technical know-how, analytic knowledge had failed. The preponderance of competing models complicated rather than resolving the inter-agency debate, making it more inaccessible to nonexperts than ever, and providing fuel for popular sentiment that insulated government "experts" were not responsive to public concerns. On a deeper level, though, the PBJI episode reveals how completely the energies of the poverty research industry, with all its advanced technology, were being channeled into a very narrowly defined set of issues revolving around the characteristics, behavior, and attitudes of poor people, and the programs and benefits they received. That this should be *a* focus in poverty knowledge was not necessarily problematic in itself. If anything, what was coming through in the research was just how widespread was the experience of poverty and how "mainstream" in behavior and values were the poor. Poverty research was developing a much more precise statistical picture of the poor population, while drawing attention to important demographic changes, such as dramatic declines in elderly poverty, and growth among families headed by women, over time. So, too, could analysts trace the "target efficiency" of the complicated array of federal income transfer programs with measurements, in Robert Lampman's terminology, of "what they do for the poor."[96] Such research documented essential facts that no one involved in the continuing struggle against poverty would want to be without: among them, that Social Security was the government's most powerful antipoverty program; that the vast majority of federal income transfers went to people considered nonpoor; and that, nevertheless, the huge increase in federal spending—from $37 to $140 billion in the decade after 1965—had reduced officially measured income poverty from 20 percent to 11 percent, its all-time mid-1970s low.[97] In their own way, poverty analysts had become advocates for better poor people's programs earning the wrath of a then little-known think tank called the Heritage Foundation as a "$2 billion a year growth industry" devoting itself to the "cause" of the negative income tax.[98]

The problem was with what was being left out. Poverty analysts rarely incorporated institutional practices, political decisions, or structural economic changes into their research; the focus was on individuals and families, not society—in economists' terminology, on the side of "supply," not "demand." Sociologists built enormously elaborate models to study class stratification (though not often calling it that), including individual characteristics such as family background, income, skill-level, and race, calculating how much family "inheritance" versus schooling explained the "variance," while paying little attention to the social and political settings within which inequality is produced.[99] Race was generally not a subject for direct inquiry, and then more often as a demographic, as opposed to a social and political, fact. Research on race was itself largely segregated from the mainstream of poverty analysis, often at the behest of the funding agencies rather than the researchers themselves.[100] When female analysts began, in the early 1970s, to put gender issues on the agenda, funding agencies framed their interests in the narrowest way: the growth in the number of minority female-headed households, and the question of whether welfare was causing families to break up. The Ford Foundation was less concerned about research on all single mothers, as one program officer indicated to a grantee, than in the poor and minority women implicated in the "Moynihan type argument relating these families to social pathology."[101] At the same time, the poverty analytic network was in danger of replicating the very inequalities that remained marginalized in its own research. A handful of women were beginning to gain prominence in analytic research, but the same could not be said for nonwhite scholars. Criticized by outside reviewers and the small number of minority researchers on its own staff, the IRP raised outside funding to recruit minority fellows in the late 1970s, but continued to feel plagued by charges that it was inhospitable to minorities and remote from nonwhite research networks.[102] Complicating this was the overwhelming turn to quantitative and model-building methods, mirroring trends in the social sciences writ large, which required training, access to large databases and computing facilities, and a certain kind of academic socialization that were simply not available outside elite, predominantly white institutions.

On the whole, then, research on the "causes and consequences" of poverty pointed to the characteristics of poor people, while research on its "cures" concentrated on the most efficient, equitable way to get government income to the poor. In this narrow focus, poverty knowledge was to some extent simply following the government lead. But the new poverty knowledge was shaped by the assumptions and ideological convictions of the analysts who were producing it as well, notably by the rationalistic, market-centered worldview that lay at the heart of their science and by a growing conviction, heightened by sobering findings from cost/benefit program evaluation, that as a strategy against poverty income maintenance was far cheaper, more efficient, and politically safer than economic and social reform. Equally notable, though, was the way the poverty issue was—or was not—being framed as an economic problem: in the face of high unemployment and chronic inflation, analysts failed to concentrate the energies of poverty knowledge on explaining the underlying shifts in the economy that had brought the postwar era of steady growth and rising wages to an end. Likewise, they lavished far more attention on reforming welfare than on envisioning more equitable economic policies—an approach that, however expedient amidst the uncertainties of the 1970s, made it easier to think about poverty as a failure of individuals or of the welfare system, rather than of an economy in which middle- and working-class as well as officially poor Americans faced diminishing opportunities.

Dependency, the "Underclass," and a New Welfare "Consensus": Poverty Knowledge for a Post-Liberal, Postindustrial Era

DESPITE THE DEBACLE of the Program for Better Jobs and Income, in 1980 the future for poverty research looked secure. Poverty rates were rising, but analysts felt they had better tools than ever to identify the "causes, consequences, and cures." If the research of the past decade had shown anything, it was that government was a necessary force in the fight against poverty—and that the myth of an intractable culture of poverty could be laid to rest. As an industry poverty research was thriving, even after some enforced belt-tightening during the late Carter years. Federal agency funding was in the hands of trusted research brokers, heavily concentrated in the Department of Health and Human Services (formerly HEW) Office of the Assistant Secretary for Planning and Evaluation (ASPE), who were schooled in and appreciated the value of analytic research.[1] In 1980, ASPE announced that funding for a national poverty research center would now be open to outside bidders—the Institute for Research on Poverty would be asked to compete with others for multi-year core funds. The competition caused no small amount of consternation at the fifteen-year-old Institute; thanks in part to IRP efforts, poverty expertise—and the field of potential institutional challengers—had proliferated since 1965. Still, director Eugene Smolensky had reason to feel assured on at least one point: the IRP would win "if we write the best proposal." The ASPE leadership, after all, showed "a fine appreciation for academic research."[2]

And then, with Ronald Reagan's election in November, came the "revolution" in social policy that promised to undermine the liberal welfare state, and with it the institutional networks, the federal contract market, and the ideological underpinnings of poverty research.

The new administration struck its first major blow with OBRA, or the Omnibus Budget Reconciliation Act of 1981, which slashed federal antipoverty budgets and severely restricted eligibility rules to eliminate aid for all but the "truly needy." Then, in a far more radical version of Nixon's "new federalism," the administration sought to devolve, privatize, or altogether eliminate the very government programs that had kept up a continuing demand for poverty research. Meanwhile, the huge deficits fueled by Reagan's defense spending and supply-side economics rapidly transformed the policy debate, crippling the prospects for any but the most minimalist efforts to shore up what was left of the social "safety net." With the Keynesian consensus a shambles, policy analysts increasingly gave in to the draconian logic of making trade-offs within an already diminished domestic policy pie. But the most direct threat to poverty knowledge came when the administration took aim against the institutional hub of the research industry, shrinking the analytic offices, like ASPE, that poverty experts had come to rely on for access and support. Deeply distrustful of the analytic networks that, thanks in no small part to the Nixon administration, had continued to flourish after the hopes of the Great Society had faded away, Reagan officials turned instead to a privately funded network of conservative think tanks that specialized in producing clear, uncomplicated, overtly ideological policy advice. "My friends," Reagan told the nation, crystallizing what they had to say, "some years ago, the federal government declared war on poverty, and poverty won."[3] Suddenly put on the defensive, poverty experts found themselves in the unavoidably ideological position of having to justify the very existence of the programs they had spent so much of the 1970s trying to replace or reform.

Unprepared though it was to meet the ideological challenge, the more fundamental problem for the poverty research industry was its own inability to respond to the transformations in political economy that could not be explained within the confines of an individualized analytic frame. The "Reagan recession" of 1981–82 was the deepest in post–World War II history, driving poverty to its highest measured rate, over 15 percent, since before the War on Poverty began. Contrary to what economic theory predicted, poverty conditions did not improve much in the ensuing economic "boom," which actually accelerated the decline in working-class wages, opportunities, and social protections, and left millions of workers earning well below a living wage.[4] The impact was most immediately visible in the swelling ranks of both the homeless and the "working poor," but it could also be seen in the harsh, sharply polarized political economy that the Reagan Revolution ushered in—which redefined 6–7 percent as a "natural" unemployment rate, and left the proverbial bottom fifth (actually, the bottom two-fifths) with steadily declining fortunes while redistributing power, wealth, and income to those at the very top.[5] The population in poverty also grew younger, more female, and more concentrated in racially segregated urban neighborhoods, reflecting the impact of economic and family restructuring as well as the long-standing gender and racial inequities in the postwar economy and welfare state. And yet, analysts continued to write about poverty only in the most individualized, apolitical terms, once again looking for clues to the "paradox" of poverty in the behavioral choices, human capital deficiencies, and ultimately in the social pathologies of the poor.

The discrepancy was more than simply a reflection of the narrow, individualized science that poverty knowledge had become. It was also a part of a broader ideological realignment that transformed the poverty debate, driving analysts to the "neutral" center in a spectrum that had shifted dramatically to the right. This ideological realignment was reflected in the renewed emphasis in poverty knowledge on "dependency," "illegitimacy," and intergenerational "transmission" as growth areas for research and reform. It also played a part in the scientific revival of a frankly pathologized vision of poverty in the debate over the urban "underclass." But the most far-reaching consequence of ideological realignment was the emergence of a "new consensus" on welfare, that sought to expand individual rather than social responsibility and that eventuated in President Clinton's market-affirming, neoliberal plan for bringing "welfare as we know it" to an end. In each of these instances, liberal poverty analysts not only acquiesced, but actively participated in what they hitherto had been trying to avoid: they repauperized the poverty problem and heightened the distinction between "undeserving" and "deserving" poor.

"APOCALYPSE NOW"?

"Apocalypse Now" was the heading on the internal memo from Institute for Research on Poverty director Eugene Smolensky when he broke the news to his staff in August 1981: ending a fifteen-year tradition of steady federal government support, the Reagan administration was effectively severing ties to the Institute by eliminating its annual $1.5 million grant. In the future, as the *Wall Street Journal* reported approvingly, ASPE would dole out its funding by ignoring liberal establishment networks and following a new competitive "regime." Now, poverty research grants would be smaller, more restricted to specific topics, and open to bids from institutions unencumbered by "the Great Society view that government alleviates poverty." ASPE officials denied that the move was ideologically motivated, but Smolensky had good reason to doubt. Just a few months before the announcement, the IRP had actually won the national competition, originally sponsored by the Carter administration's ASPE, that awarded it official recognition as a national poverty research center and $1.5 million for research in 1981–82. Reagan officials subsequently declared the competition nonbinding, and refused to make the award. That was where things stood when Smolensky told the staff that, without its core federal funding, the Institute would soon be closing its doors.[6]

The IRP's loss of federal revenue was devastating, but it was only a part of a more systematic attack on the Great Society knowledge industry that accompanied Reagan administration efforts to retrench the liberal welfare state. The Urban Institute topped what insiders called the "enemies list," losing three-quarters of its federal money—a drop of $8 million—between 1980 and 1982.[7] Agency budget cuts did even more damage, threatening the analytic enterprise at its source. Convinced that the career civil service would subvert the revolution before it began, Reagan authorized major reductions in nonmilitary government research offices and subordinated their activities to more ideologically dependable political appointees. ASPE alone shrunk to one hundred career policy analysts, one-third its former size, and was headed up, for the first time in its history, by an assistant secretary from outside the regular analytic ranks.[8] Budget cuts in turn threatened the loss of large, expensive data sets like the Panel Study of Income Dynamics, that constituted both the pride and the life-blood of poverty research.[9] Funding cuts also left evaluation "gravely eroded," the General Accounting Office reported, while confirming analysts' suspicion that Reagan officials had little interest in learning about the consequences of their "reforms." Perhaps most galling of all to the analytic sensibility was the administration's rejection of "value-neutral" policy planning in favor of an explicitly, indeed proudly, ideological approach.[10] From the standpoint of the poverty research industry, the change could not have been more stark. ASPE, once an ally, was now an adversarial force. The administration was barely interested in basic program evaluation, let alone the kinds of planned social experimentation that had given applied poverty research a truly scientific claim. And the prospects for new programs were singularly remote, as was anything approaching the analytic mobilization that in the 1970s had made guaranteed income the centerpiece of bureaucratic welfare reform.

Smolensky's news of the "apocalypse," however, was at best premature. Though cutting back drastically on research and administration, the poverty research industry survived through the crash of the early 1980s by becoming more entrepreneurial and political in the search for research funds. The IRP turned to Senator William Proxmire (D-Wisconsin), successfully lobbying for legislation forcing the administration to reinstate the $1.5 million contract the Institute had already officially won—the ritual would continue throughout the decade, leaving the Institute dependent on biannual legislation earmarking IRP funding as part of the ASPE appropriations bill. Congress also proved an ally in the struggle to preserve evaluation research, incorporating specific mandates for scientific evaluation into most major social welfare legislation.[11] Although hardly able to replace the government subsidy, liberal foundations did their part to salvage the poverty research industry as well. The Urban Institute fell back almost entirely on foundations, including an immediate infusion of nearly $7 million from the Ford and MacArthur Foundations when federal funding was at its lowest point. In a major feat of entrepreneurship, the MDRC used matching funds from the Ford Foundation to persuade several states to conduct, and pay for, controlled experimental evaluations of the "workfare" programs they were instituting in response to a clause in the 1981 OBRA legislation. In this and other ways analysts made a virtue of necessity, turning the Reagan Revolution into an opportunity for research. In 1981–82, the Urban Institute launched a major initiative called Changing Domestic Priorities, a comprehensive, Institute-wide project to assess Reagan's economic, social welfare, and new federalism policies. Codirected by economists John Palmer and Isabel Sawhill, the project lasted through the rest of the decade, published more than thirty volumes, and became the closest thing possible to a unified response from the liberal analytic community to the changes Reagan had wrought. In a sense, the project proved to be the Institute's salvation, not just as a continuing source of funding but as a safe, nonpartisan form of advocacy in the face of a wholesale attack on the liberal welfare state. That, to be sure, was what made it attractive to the mainstream foundations, for which analytic research became the first line in an exceedingly cautious, ideologically noncommital line of defense.

Of course, the question of whether the Urban Institute's style of analysis was in fact nonideological was open to debate. Reagan officials didn't think so, and routinely denounced Institute analysis as "political, biased, 'pseudo scientific,' "—anything but "objective" or "scientific" research.[12] Critics on the left were frustrated by its heavy reliance on a kind of econometric analysis that perpetuated a rationalistic, individualized view of social problems while treating the market as a natural, politically neutral force. The Institute, for its part, continued to emphasize its commitment to dispassion, nonpartisanship, and objectivity, for the most part avoiding the ideological underpinnings of its prevailing methods of research. And yet, in the polarized atmosphere of Reagan-era Washington, the inherently political nature of even the most hard-nosed statistical analysis was increasingly difficult to deny—and nowhere more so than when it came to measuring recent trends in wealth and poverty, and the role of Reagan administration policy therein. "Is it true," one congressman asked OMB director David Stockman, "that the rich are getting richer and that the poor are getting poorer and that the line between the two is becoming clearer?" Stockman replied that "it depends on what you want to believe. If you want to believe that the rich are getting richer and the poor are getting poorer, I can give you some statistics to prove it. If you want to believe something else, I can show you some pretty solid evidence that it is not the case at all." Stockman and other Reagan officials were more direct in their insistence that existing government measures vastly exaggerated the true extent of poverty by failing to include the value of "in-kind" benefits such as Medicaid, housing, school lunches, and Food Stamps in calculating household income. Including these benefits, conservatives had long been insisting, could cut official poverty rates—and hence the need for programs—nearly in half.[13]

Liberal poverty experts held the line against official maneuvers to define the problem out of existence, but they also moved to outflank their conservative counterparts in the administration by beefing up their own capacity to inject convincing numbers into the policy debate. In 1981, former Department of Agriculture analyst Robert Greenstein, who had run the Food Stamp program in the Carter administration, set up the Center on Budget and Policy Priorities as a kind of public interest think tank to deliver accessible, quick-turn-around analyses of administration policies and legislative proposals. Funded principally by liberal foundations, Greenstein's Center quickly established itself as a much less well heeled counterpart to the Heritage Foundation—if Heritage briefings could be read on the limousine ride between Capitol Hill and Washington's National Airport, went one description, the Center's would take up the just slightly longer subway ride—and as the analytic arm of a network of Washington-based advocacy organizations aligned in defense of a welfare state.[14] Similarly, under Democratic chairman Dan Rostenkowski, the House Ways and Means Committee began issuing an extensive annual report known as the Green Book with data on the entire array of social welfare programs within its jurisdiction. Compiled by staff analyst and IRP affiliate Wendell Primus, the Green Book was a dense compendium of government statistics, often referred to as "the Bible" within the analytic community after its 1981 debut. But the Green Book also served an important political purpose in the ongoing battle over numbers, drawing attention to problems the administration thought best to ignore—the polarization of incomes, the precipitous rise of child poverty rates, and the steadily declining status of the working poor, to name but a few.[15] Greenstein and Primus were widely respected for their ability to combine accuracy with advocacy and to get a hearing in legislative debates. Still, the prevailing culture among mainstream analytic experts was to let the facts speak for themselves, maintaining the veneer of apolitical neutrality, and in this way straddling the hazards of assessing Reagan administration policy while continuing to rely on federal government contracts for support. By the mid-1980s, the Urban Institute's federal funding was back up to more than 50 percent of its budget, thanks in part to its renowned technical proficiency at simulating variations on welfare reform.[16]

Ideological neutrality had its hazards, however, as became especially apparent in 1984 when, with much fanfare and well-orchestrated press attention, conservative social scientist Charles Murray published a missive on the Great Society entitled *Losing Ground.* Murray's argument was simple, accessible, couched very much in the logic of rational choice, and presented with the tone of measured detachment common to most analytic research. It also set out to overturn the prevailing analytic wisdom: the expansion of social welfare since the 1960s had not only failed to improve poverty conditions, claimed Murray, it had actually made things worse for the poor. Murray's solution was to eliminate social welfare programs (except for unemployment insurance) for nonelderly adults, in order to push the poor to learn how to fend for themselves.

If there was anything artful about Murray's argument, it was precisely in the way he used the conventions of liberal analysis (however inaccurately) to subvert liberal ends. For behind Murray's tables of aggregate statistics was a highly charged political tale of social policy gone wrong—an indictment of the "elite" (i.e., liberal) decision to "blame the system" for poverty and racial injustice, and to expand income transfer, affirmative action, legal services, and regulatory remedies in response. In 1964, Murray argued, liberals had changed "the rules of the game." The burden was no longer on the individual to make the best of every opportunity but on society to guarantee equal results. The new rules brought a massive change in behavior, reflected in the "rational (albeit wrong) decisions" that poor people made. Unemployment, illegitimacy, crime, and welfare dependency were more rational, in the short term, than marriage, respectability, individual responsibility, and low-wage work. In the long term, however, these rational choices bred the kind of bad behavior that fed on itself and became pathological, creating ever more poverty among the very people the Great Society presumed to help most. The looming black underclass served as Murray's case in point. Though pathological and self-perpetuating in behavior, the black underclass had its origins in guilt-ridden liberal policies that made it possible and acceptable to choose the path of unemployment, illegitimacy, and welfare dependency over marriage and low-wage work. It all came down to a simple "thought experiment," showing how a hypothetical couple named Harold and Phyllis would ineluctably make the "wrong" decisions by responding to the incentives of welfare as any rational couple would.[17]

The problem, Murray's critics hastened to point out, was that the numbers, even the thought experiment, did not say that at all. The poor had benefited from the vast growth in transfers—without it, the economic woes of the 1970s would have driven poverty rates higher than they were. Statistical analysis showed *no* link between social programs and an epidemic of out-of-wedlock births. In fact, Murray had used the wrong measure altogether, by pointing to the "illegitimacy ratio" (nonmarital births to all live births), which had risen, rather than the illegitimacy *rate* (nonmarital births to the number of women of childbearing age), which had declined. Murray had also included programs for the elderly in his calculations of social spending, and yet he failed to report on the welfare state's greatest achievement—the sharp decline in elderly poverty rates. Most telling, he conveniently failed to mention that the value of AFDC benefits had actually been *declining* since 1969—just at the time when progress against nonelderly poverty began to slow. Nor did he acknowledge that, contrary to their short-term interests, the vast majority of poor people did not "choose" welfare over work. The key point, then, in the case that analysts built up against Murray, was that the statistical basis for his argument was partial, deceptive, and for the most part just plain wrong. The real story behind the numbers, they argued, was the one poverty experts had been telling all along: that Great Society programs, however imperfectly, had helped poor people get through the 1970s, when the economy declined. No group, they took care to mention, had benefited more than the "deserving," elderly poor.[18]

The analytic response was strong, empirically grounded, and persuasive, but it missed an essential point. It mattered to analysts that Murray had calculated the illegitimacy *ratio* rather than the *rate*, but to the average reader it was a distinction without a difference; besides, to the extent that he even responded to his empirical critics, Murray simply charged that it was the same old liberal conventional wisdom at work. In the tenth anniversary edition, Murray said of *Losing Ground* that what in 1984 appeared controversial had actually become the new "conventional wisdom" by 1994; nothing needed revision, because nothing in the empirical analysis had been proven wrong.[19] More frustrating from the perspective of his critics was the way Murray had used the concepts and tools of analytic science to undermine even the most seemingly unassailable conclusions of poverty research. Thus, the statistical linchpin of Murray's argument—what he called "latent poverty"—was based on the measurements of "pre-transfer" poverty developed at the IRP. For IRP researchers, the measure was useful in demonstrating the degree (or lack) of "target efficiency" in antipoverty programs, but more importantly in reinforcing the growing importance of social welfare in keeping official poverty rates low. By some standards, that could be seen as a sign of progress against poverty, if not exactly success. For Murray, the very same measure was a sign of the failure of social programs because it illustrated the growing *dependence* of poor people on government benefits to get by.[20] Similarly, Murray used the NIT experiments as "unambiguous" proof that welfare undermined the work ethic and the family— pointing out that the hopes and expectations of liberal analysts had been irreversibly, scientifically dashed.[21] And in presenting the case of Harold and Phyllis, he was simply extending the rational choice logic that poverty researchers had themselves made the basis of a large-scale econometric modeling enterprise. Experts found fatal flaws in his argument, but it grew out of a logic that poverty experts had done a great deal to promote. Perhaps, after all, poverty knowledge was not quite as ideologically neutral as it made itself out to be.

More important, the significance of *Losing Ground* was much less in its facts than in what Gunnar Myrdal would have called its "valuations," and to these poverty knowledge could offer at best a partial response. *Losing Ground*, after all, was not just a critique of Great Society programs but an attack on the idea that "big government" liberalism could help the poor at all. Underlying this attack was a narrative that neoconservative intellectuals had been cultivating for years, featuring an insulated "new class" of liberal intellectuals who had taken the country disastrously to the left, subverting the American tradition of individual responsibility and opportunity with a mentality of entitlements and rights. The narrative in turn rested on the assumption that the market, not government, was more benevolent as the arbiter of the social good. Indeed, Murray argued that the economy was stronger in the 1970s than the liberals claimed; poor people would have done better had liberals simply let them live by the old "rules of the game." To this, analysts could offer empirical rebuttal, showing how government transfers offset the slow growth and high unemployment of the decade before. But poverty knowledge offered no positive ideological valuations, no alternative narrative explaining *why* the market economy in the 1970s had failed, and, at the time, no alternative to Murray's depiction of a pathological, morally bankrupt black urban "underclass." Nor could it lay claim to a coherent political agenda for achieving a more equitable welfare state.

To be sure, poverty experts were at a distinct institutional disadvantage in the ideological battle Murray had launched. Absorbed in the insistent objectivity that characterized liberal (though officially nonpartisan) think tanks, they operated from the assumption that their own work was nonideological, in an institutional culture that had come to value technical proficiency over clear, simple policy ideas. *Losing Ground*, in contrast, was very much a product of the new breed of conservative think tank that had recently taken Washington by storm, explicitly promoting a resurgent conservative ideology, and aiming with it to set federal policy on an entirely new course. With increasing momentum during the 1970s, organizations such as the Heritage Foundation, the Manhattan Institute, and the American Enterprise Institute had mobilized a network of conservative intellectuals within a movement to overturn Washington's liberal policy elite. "Ideas matter" became their mantra, implying that liberals had none, and the basis of a campaign to win renewed respectability for limited government, deregulation, and free market economics.[22] Unlike their liberal counterparts, they generally avoided federal contracts, relying instead on a well-heeled consortium of private foundations and individual donors who shared their passion for conservative ideas. By late 1980 the conservative think tanks had already scored several major coups, including, most prominently, the Heritage Foundation's 1,000-plus page compilation of policy recommendations known as the *Mandate for Leadership*, said to have provided a post-election blueprint for the Reagan revolution.[23] *Losing Ground* was considered an event of similar magnitude, this one carried off by a then-obscure think tank known as the Manhattan Institute with the help of an expensive, well-orchestrated media campaign. Murray's book was the "most important work on poverty and social policy since Michael Harrington's *The Other America*," pronounced the *New Republic*, calling it a book that would forever change the terms of the poverty debate.[24]

For all their proficiency in disputing the facts of Murray's case, then, poverty analysts did not offer a response to its ideological challenge—except to say that his calculations were ideologically skewed. Political constraints were part of the problem, as was the insular, nonideological institutional culture that surrounded poverty research. But the problem also stemmed from the confines of poverty knowledge, which had far more to say about the behavioral patterns of poor people than about the changing political, social, and economic conditions that sent "pre-transfer" or "latent" poverty on the rise. However flawed their analyses, neoconservative intellectuals like Murray had an alternative explanation—government policy—and they were willing to move aggressively to use it as the basis of social policy as well as a reformulated poverty debate.

"DEPENDENCY" REDISCOVERED

Well before *Losing Ground* was published, the poverty research industry was showing the impact of the ideological shift to the right, proving itself far more adept at accommodating than at anticipating and reshaping the terms of the policy debate. Reagan's ASPE set the tone with a research agenda that made welfare "dependency"—and its prevention—the administration's official, overriding concern. The research establishment responded quickly, shifting away from the emphasis on income and labor force participation that had prevailed in the 1970s to focus on welfare "dependency," family structure, teenage pregnancy, and the size, shape, and culture of the urban "underclass." By the late 1980s, ASPE's far-reaching influence could be seen in the industry at large.[25] Even economists were discovering that there was more to poverty than income, according to ASPE official Daniel Weinberg; the behaviors associated with the culture of poverty might be worth exploring after all.[26] One annotated bibliography summarized two hundred studies of dependency—most published after 1980, and most conducted within established venues of econometric, analytic research.[27] At the same time, ASPE was eager to "diversify" the poverty network, or at least to extend it beyond the reach of the IRP, by channeling big projects on dependency to Harvard's John F. Kennedy School of Government and the Heller School at Brandeis University, but also to institutions, like the neoconservative Hudson Institute, that would never have been in the official research orbit in the past.[28] ASPE also used its financial leverage to put an end to the IRP's comparatively free-wheeling ways, steering the Institute to a heavier focus on dependency than ever before.[29] Perhaps most dramatic, however, was the complete transformation in the meaning of welfare reform: the negative income tax was a distant memory, as was the notion of seriously petitioning to raise badly eroded benefit rates; the question on the table was "workfare"—not whether, but what kind, when, and how.

While adjusting to the conservative drift in the agenda, poverty knowledge did stand as important testimony to the severe erosion of the basic safety net, as well as to the vast inequities created by the administration's efforts to introduce fiscal austerity by slashing budgets for the poor.[30] Poverty expertise played a role, too, in defusing some of the more pernicious myths about poor people—or, at least, in temporarily preventing the myths from being written into law. Analysts put considerable effort, for example, behind gathering empirical evidence to disprove the age-old notion that welfare itself caused poverty, dependency, and out-of-wedlock births.[31]

More telling, however, was how the poverty research establishment accommodated the rightward turn in direction by making conservative voices part of the mainstream debate—ignoring, for the most part, scholarship from left of center that challenged assumptions within the analytic frame. Poverty think tanks put prominent conservatives onto their project advisory boards, as if to prove their research was not liberally biased, or at least to keep it in check. Liberal philanthropies were careful to prove their nonpartisanship, too, by "balancing" their portfolios with grants to institutions just (but not too far) to the right of center. Conference organizers regularly dipped into a pool of known conservatives, if only to provide the obligatory "alternative" point of view—not Murray (at the time, his proposals for ending welfare were considered beyond the pale) but more "reasonable" scholars such as political scientist Lawrence Mead, economist Glenn Loury, or Heritage Foundation staff members Stuart Butler and Anna Kondratas. What these scholars shared was not necessarily a common viewpoint, but the basic analytic credentials to take part in the mainstream poverty debate. Mead, for example, had worked at both ASPE and the Urban Institute, and was willing to acknowledge the need for a strong welfare state. He distinguished himself from hard-line neoconservatives by arguing that the problem was not government provision, but the permissiveness of Great Society programs in failing to enforce social obligations on the poor. In his 1986 book *Beyond Entitlement*, Mead advocated not less government, but a more authoritarian, paternalistic, possibly even expanded welfare state.[32] Butler and Kondratas, both economists, argued a more consistently neoconservative line, emphasizing the need for public aid to the "truly needy" and the virtues of free market individualism for everyone else.[33] And Loury, a professor at Harvard's John F. Kennedy School of Government, was among the small band of prominent African American neoconservatives who argued against government programs such as affirmative action and called for a greater spirit of self-reliance among blacks.[34] As regular (albeit "token") participants on the conference circuit, conservative scholars were accorded far more legitimacy in poverty circles than they had been in the past. Meanwhile, there was no comparable effort to recognize the legitimacy of scholarship or the need for "balance" from the left. Thus, while poverty knowledge continued to reflect the values of the liberal center, it was within a spectrum that had shifted lopsidedly to the right.

The true harbinger of ideological realignment, then, came more from changes within the poverty research establishment than from without. It came, for example, from an unpublished but extraordinarily influential 1983 paper on welfare dependency by economists Mary Jo Bane and David Ellwood from Harvard's John F. Kennedy School of Government, produced as part of a larger project on dependency conducted with ASPE support. In it, Bane and Ellwood developed a new approach to measuring dependency that seemed instantly to transform what had become the received wisdom in poverty knowledge. In the old view, based on over a decade of analysis, poverty and welfare were both "transitory" conditions, amenable to solution with a better system of income support. This view was considered one of the singular achievements of poverty research, not just because it was an artifact of better, longitudinal data, but also because it put the concept of a permanent culture of poverty to rest. "Dependency" was the "exception rather than the rule among welfare recipients," according to a team of University of Michigan researchers who tracked the year-to-year fortunes of low-income households using the Panel Study of Income Dynamics (PSID). On the whole, recipients were more like "us" than "them."[35] Now, with the same data and a different methodology, Bane and Ellwood were offering a considerably less sanguine view: "dependency," measured as a long "spell" of being on welfare, was a much bigger problem than it had first appeared. To be sure, only a minority of all recipients were on welfare for a long, unbroken "spell," but these "long-termers" represented the majority of welfare recipients at any given time. Together with the welfare "recidivists"—an incredibly stigmatizing way to talk about people who returned after a short time off the rolls—long-term recipients accounted for nearly two-thirds of the costs. Bane and Ellwood reported a key demographic difference between the "short-" and "long-termers" as well: the former were more likely to be white, divorced, and relatively well educated; the latter to be never-married single mothers, high school dropouts, and black.[36] At least *some* poor people were not so much "like us" after all.[37]

The report from Bane and Ellwood was just one in a whole series of studies and findings from the early 1980s, said with varying degrees of hyperbole to be transforming the way social scientists thought about the poor. Another was what Daniel P. Moynihan called an "earthquake" in family structure, but that poverty experts described in stripped-down demographic terms: more than half of the population in poverty lived in female-headed households, up from 30 percent two decades before.[38] By some reports as many or more poverty "spells" were initiated by a change in family structure (the "transition" to "female headship") than by loss of income from a job. Some analysts warned against making too much of these findings; antipoverty policy should avoid "hand wringing about the family" and focus on employment, wages, and labor force participation, wrote Mary Jo Bane, even though her own research with David Ellwood had directed researchers toward "household formation decisions" as a primary cause of poverty "spells."[39] Nevertheless, by identifying family breakup as itself an independent "cause" of poverty, they did help to confirm popular suspicions, and conservative allegations, that poverty was less an economic problem than a sign of disturbing new demographic and behavioral trends. Such suspicions were only heightened by the alarming sense of demographic destiny with which researchers overturned another element of liberal conventional wisdom, in a surge of studies showing that single motherhood did, after all, have negative consequences for children—and especially so if the mothers were poor and nonwhite. Single motherhood, the research concluded, put children at measurably "greater risk": of poverty, welfare dependency, teen pregnancy, school dropout, low achievement, and, depending on race and length of time with a single parent, of literally "growing up poor."

Since children were at greater risk of experiencing *single motherhood*, the ingredients for social disaster seemed at hand.[40] Moynihan, claimed students of family breakup, had been right all along.[41]

Much like the discovery that "dependency" was a problem, the analytic take on single motherhood was ostensibly ideology-free. Analysts were careful to avoid blaming the victim (after all, some had been single mothers themselves), without shying away from the dire consequences they associated with raising children in a female-headed home.[42] Most went to great lengths to establish that single motherhood was a legitimate, sometimes unavoidable, if not always "optimal" choice—except, that is, when the single mother was an adolescent, a "choice" analysts regarded with universal and growing alarm.[43] Nevertheless, especially amidst the conservative backlash of the 1980s, "single motherhood" and "dependency" were increasingly ideological terms.[44] Intentionally or not, they tapped into powerful and resurgent political opposition, to welfare, to poor people's reproductive freedom, and to the long-standing feminist objective of providing women with the means to gain independence from men. Alternatively, feminist scholarship explained the recent "feminization" of poverty, as a product not of demographic and behavioral "choices" but of long-standing gender inequities in the welfare state, the family, and the labor force. Structural problems such as unequal pay, job discrimination, and unequal responsibility for child care had *always* made women more vulnerable to poverty; within this context of gender inequality, post-1970s wage declines and changes in family structure had sent female poverty rates on the rise.[45] Mainstream poverty studies, in contrast, individualized and decontextualized the problem, and ended up reinforcing the stigma they sought to avoid.

As used by poverty experts, the very concept of "dependency" made receiving welfare a personal pathology, something that became harder to "escape" the longer it went on, while such descriptors as "long-termer" and "recidivism" virtually equated using welfare with a criminal offense. Nor was the concept of "dependency" particularly accurate, as subsequent research on women who receive welfare has confirmed. Rather, it rested on an entirely artificial polarity that pitted welfare, nonwork, and dependence against self-reliance and work. In reality, welfare recipients have always relied on other sources of income, often including work in the paid, sometimes in the underground, labor force to make ends meet—to learn this, however, poverty researchers had to look beyond the official statistics to speak with welfare recipients themselves. Nor is it at all realistic to expect employment to bring "independence" from government benefits, especially when the employment in question is low-wage, without benefits, and insecure.[46]

"Single motherhood" similarly marked off the unmarried mother as living in an unnatural state—whether as a breadwinner, or a woman trying to raise children on her own—and in turn provided the filter for defining the "absent father" as a man who failed to fulfill his masculine role as the psychological and economic family "head." As part of the discourse on welfare, all of these concepts carried unmistakable, if unacknowledged, connotations of race and social class. Though rarely called that, the black "matriarch" was clearly distinguishable in the literature as the mother who had *never* married, and was therefore more likely to be a "long-termer" on the welfare rolls than her white, divorced or widowed counterpart. Nevertheless, the analytic framework treated the growing concentration of poverty in nonwhite, female-headed families as a product of life course "events" and individual choices, as though the problem were unrelated to the structural inequalities of class, gender, and race. "Indeed, family structure now plays a far larger role than race in income differentials," noted a report from the American Enterprise Institute invoking findings from contemporary poverty expertise.[47] Nowhere in the highly descriptive, statistic-laden discourse was there even a nod to the idea that what turned up in the census as a rapid growth in female-headed families might represent a reasonable alternative to the "traditional" patriarchal structure, much less that its preponderance among blacks, as some anthropologists had been arguing since the 1940s, was a reflection of distinctive, and legitimate, African American lower-class norms.[48] The female-headed family had been identified as a direct "cause" of poverty and a whole host of other social pathologies, and that was enough to earn it the opprobrium of liberal and conservative analysts alike.

Even as a "merely" descriptive demographic category, then, family structure was hardly ideologically neutral, perhaps most importantly because it also served the ultimately ideological function of obscuring the deeply political and structural dimensions of poverty, while offering what analysts presented as a neutral conceptual framework for reform. Hence, the approach offered by David Ellwood in an analysis that identified family structure as the key fault line in understanding the poor. Ellwood's plan laid out one strategy for short-termer, two-parent, "working poor" families on the assumption that their problems were economic and thus relatively straightforward: they needed income, health care, and job assistance, which Ellwood packaged in the form of "non-welfare" (an increasingly common distinction that further stigmatized AFDC as a handout while masking the degree of government welfare for the nonpoor) supplements that would "make work pay." The long-term, female-headed, welfare-dependent families, on the other hand, were a much harder group to help, since "their" poverty was a product of single motherhood and all the disadvantages it brought. For these families Ellwood offered a proposal that was fast becoming the core of a new generation of liberal or, more accurately, neo-liberal (as in "new Democrat"), welfare reform: It would rely on expanded and more strictly enforced child support from the absent father, "transitional"— that is, time-limited—income support from the state, plus more aggressive work training to get mothers into the paid labor force. Once working, single welfare mothers would in turn benefit from the package of supplements Ellwood recommended for the working poor, such that they would be able to support their families while working part time. Taken as a whole, Ellwood claimed, this was a program that combined individual responsibility with family security, and reinforced the values of self-sufficiency and work. He called it the "divide and conquer" strategy—a strategy, as we shall see, that ultimately proved politically disastrous for AFDC recipients in the never-ending quest for welfare reform.[49]

WELFARE "CONSENSUS"

Ellwood's plan caught on as one of a new wave of mid-1980s proposals that were said to express a "new consensus" on welfare reform. The immediate context for these proposals was President Reagan's unexpected 1986 announcement that he was appointing a White House study group on welfare to recommend a complete overhaul—creating an opening, without warning, for renewed efforts at "comprehensive" welfare reform. The broader context for the "consensus," though, was the political transformation of poverty knowledge in the 1980s that had helped to make dependency and individual responsibility the key issues in the debate. The outcome was the Family Support Act of 1988 which, for politically pragmatic as well as more strictly "scientific" reasons, brought liberal poverty experts behind workfare as a strategy to get single mothers who were long-term welfare recipients "up and off" the rolls.

The much-trumpeted "new consensus" actually came from a spectrum ranging from the now-rightward-leaning, neoliberal center to the now moderate-appearing Right—conservatives, that is, for whom ending welfare à la Charles Murray was an unacceptable extreme. Its common themes were captured in the welter of commission reports and special studies sparked by Reagan's call for reform: "Up from Dependency" (the White House), "A New Social Contract" (New York Governor Mario Cuomo, Democrat), "Ladders Out of Poverty" (Arizona Governor Bruce Babbitt, Democrat), and "A Community of Self-Reliance" (the American Enterprise Institute), to name a few. Behind the consensus was a set of assumptions that were informed, or at least justified, by the "new" knowledge poverty experts had brought to light. One was the assumption that welfare did not work, not only, as liberals had been saying for years, because it was unfair to the working poor, but because it violated American values by fostering dependency, idleness, and antisocial behavior in an already-stigmatized segment of the poor.[50] A second assumption behind the "consensus" was about the need to "disaggregate" the poor, conceptually segregating two-parent, working, or what the AEI report called "involuntarily" poor families from the single-parent, long-term, or "behaviorally dependent" poor.[51] Liberal analysts, including Ellwood, offered a rash of proposals to "make work pay" for the working poor, but the true consensus on welfare held that reform should focus especially on the "dependent" welfare mothers—by all accounts the most difficult to reach. The focus on dependency in turn set the stage for a third set of shared assumptions, which constituted the operating principles for reform: absent fathers should take full financial responsibility for their children; all "able-bodied" welfare mothers should be expected, even required, to work; and welfare should be "transitional," not an open-ended guarantee. The first two principles made it into the 1988 Family Support Act. The third would reemerge eight years later, unencumbered by the imperative to "make work pay" above the poverty line, in far more extreme "reform" legislation than its neoliberal originators ever dreamed.

The "new consensus" brought reconstructed liberals much more in line with conservatives than the other way around, but it also papered over more differences than either side cared to admit. Liberals, for example, proposed to attach the reformed welfare system to an antipoverty program that included higher benefits, an expanded Earned Income Tax Credit for working poor families, and "last resort" job guarantees. Conservatives, for their part, were more concerned with "strengthening the family" by eliminating the "incentives" for single and teenage motherhood they believed unlimited access to benefits produced. Otherwise, the poor but "intact" family could be left to fend for itself. "Empirically, two-parent families are more likely to exit from and stay out of poverty," the AEI welfare commission explained. Presumably, since they presented "fewer problems for public policy," there was no reason to extend help.[52] But more striking than the differences was the extent to which liberal analysts had changed direction, while conservatives had hardly changed at all: the Reagan and Bush administrations did expand the Earned Income Tax Credit for low-income working families—but the EITC, after all, had originated in the mid-1970s as a conservative, and quite modest, alternative to the negative income tax.[53] Meanwhile, conservative parties to the welfare consensus got measures that liberal analysts had been resisting for years. For that matter, analysts had long resisted the movement to make "dependency" the center of welfare reform at all, promoting reforms to make the system more efficient, equitable, less categorical, and more expansive instead. Analytic welfare reform in the 1970s had embraced universalism as a goal, seeking to blur if not eliminate distinctions between the "deserving" and the "undeserving" poor. To do this, analysts had looked to the universal solvent—cash—and had basically accepted the "hazard" that at least some people would work less, or not at all, as a result. Finally, analytic reform in the 1970s had decidedly *not* been premised on the insistence that women—whether wives or working mothers—should be expected to work in the paid labor force; in an era of high unemployment, their concern was much more centered on sustaining labor force participation among men.[54] Now, although welfare participation rates were actually declining, and unemployment continued to hover near 6–7 percent, analysts had done an about-face on universal income proposals and were endorsing plans to put welfare mothers to work. Explaining their reasoning, analysts went beyond the revisionist view of poverty as a problem of dependency to invoke what some critics considered a perversely feminist tone: thanks to the women's movement, they reasoned, society was more willing to extend work opportunities—and expectations—to women rather than confining mothers to the home. Work requirements for welfare mothers, that is, were presumably extending expectations and responsibilities that all liberated women enjoyed. That, plus the reality that wives in two-parent working- and middle-class families had little choice but to supplement what would otherwise be declining household earnings, was fast becoming a leading liberal rationale for putting welfare mothers to work.[55]

This hardly meant that the new consensus incorporated anything of feminist thought; its "family values" were actually quite traditional. Thus, even liberal proposals for improved child support enforcement—a longtime feminist goal—reinforced the ideal of the male as the chief family breadwinner, premised as they were on the unlikely idea that support from the absent father would replace much if not all of the basic welfare grant. Similarly, one of the most prominent liberal explanations for single motherhood was the declining labor force participation—hence, "marriageability"—of black males, an explanation that, in the context of welfare, reinforced the notion that "dependency" was the poverty problem for women while joblessness was primarily a problem for men.[56] Nor did the welfare consensus do anything to acknowledge what feminists considered to be major barriers to according women independent means: unequal pay, opportunities, and workforce discrimination; and the failure to recognize child rearing as socially valued, remunerable work. Meanwhile, the idea that work requirements somehow recognized new, more liberated social expectations with regard to women and work completely ignored the reality that poor and working-class women had always been expected to work to contribute to family income—married or not.

Far more important than "feminist" values in the analytic turn to workfare was the imprimatur bestowed by analytic research. In 1986 the MDRC began an auspiciously timed campaign to release the findings from the multisite evaluation of state-level work and welfare programs it had initiated in the aftermath of the first round of Reagan's budget cuts. The findings themselves were hardly earth-shattering, but in the much-altered political atmosphere of the late 1980s, they were hailed as evidence of significant success: it was "feasible" to tie welfare to work and training obligations, and for at least some of the "hard to reach" welfare mothers, the programs produced "relatively modest" employment and income gains.[57] Summing up the policy influence of these findings, several observers, including the legislative assistant to Senator Daniel P. Moynihan, agreed that what had made them most convincing was the MDRC's reputation for rigor and neutrality, its ability to package them in accessible policy briefs, and, most important, "experimental design, experimental design, experimental design." Subsequently hailed as a major success story in the annals of policy research, MDRC's work was cited, along with Bane and Ellwood's research on dependency, as the most important factors in galvanizing a legislative welfare consensus behind the Family Support Act of 1988.[58]

But what appeared as a major victory for poverty knowledge had actually come at a substantial political price. For in responding to an agenda set by the Reagan administration, liberal analysts had played an active part in making family structure and "dependency" the issues in poverty policy while failing to address the problems of employment, wages, and growing inequality that consistently emerged in their own research. Still wedded to—and convinced of—their own ideological neutrality, they continued to reinforce rather than to shape the politically determined contours of federal policy and remained caught in the stranglehold of welfare reform. Acknowledging as much, IRP economist Sheldon Danziger issued a plea at the end of the decade for a policy agenda that genuinely embraced fighting poverty—rather than reforming welfare—as its goal.[59] But to do that would require an entirely different kind of poverty knowledge, focused on the issues of structural change, political economy, and institutionalized social inequality, that could not be measured within the existing confines of analytic poverty research.

POVERTY KNOWLEDGE AND THE REDISCOVERY
OF INEQUALITY

The welfare "consensus" that emerged in the 1980s thus grew out of an inseparable combination of welfare politics, ideological realignment, and new poverty knowledge that moved liberal experts considerably to the right. But just as significant in the new welfare consensus was the knowledge it ignored, knowledge that formulated the poverty problem not in terms of dependency and family breakup but in terms of economic stagnation, high unemployment, growing inequality, and the steady decline in work opportunities due to structural economic change. At least some elements of such an alternative formulation could be found in mainstream poverty research. Thus, concluded the experts (most of them economists) who gathered at a jointly sponsored IRP-ASPE conference in Williamsburg, Virginia, in late 1984, the Council of Economic Advisers had it right in 1964: Slow growth and high unemployment were still the driving forces behind poverty—surpassing welfare and changing family structure as poverty's leading "cause." Indeed, the poor suffered more than anyone from the combination of recession and slow growth that plagued the 1970s and early 1980s. Conversely, they stood to gain the most from the restoration of growth and employment that economists were projecting for the decade's latter half; the "rising tide," that is to say, would "lift all boats." The problem, in sharp contrast to the 1960s, was that nobody seemed to know how to stimulate the growth rates—and the employment—that would in fact lift the boats of the poor.[60]

Meanwhile, some poverty researchers were also pushing the economic diagnosis beyond the familiar themes of growth and unemployment to argue that the recent rise in income inequality was just as important in keeping poverty rates high. Accompanied as it was by the decline of working-class wages, the rise of inequality was diminishing the likelihood that economic recovery would easily translate into lower poverty rates.[61] Here again, convincing though they may have been in documenting economic decline and inequality, liberal poverty experts were hard put to explain these trends in the economy—or what policy should do in response. Nor could they explain why, contrary to what the econometric models predicted, poverty persisted and inequality *continued rising* in the 1980s after the return of economic growth. Thus, undeniable though the trend toward inequality was becoming, economist Isabel Sawhill characterized it as a "residual" explanation—what she offered as a "measure of our ignorance"—in a 1988 article reviewing the economic literature on poverty. Very much as they had in the 1960s, liberal economists continued to look to the combination of unemployment and human capital as economic explanations for poverty, and to growth rather than large-scale redistribution as the preferred policy response.[62]

Beneath Sawhill's "measure of ignorance" was a more extended debate about the economic roots of poverty and inequality that paralleled—in some ways it continued—the debate over structural unemployment that had emerged among liberal and left-liberal economists nearly three decades before. At issue, once again, was not whether slow growth and unemployment were causing poverty, but whether they were part of long-term structural changes in the economy that would make conventional growth and human capital measures inadequate as the leading edge of an antipoverty response. Few could any longer argue, as the Kennedy CEA had, that rising unemployment was principally due to the combination of inadequate growth and the normal flows of the business cycle rather than to structural changes in the economy. In the seemingly unending struggle to contain inflation since the mid-1970s, the officially accepted, or "natural rate" of unemployment (a phrase coined by economist Milton Friedman to pinpoint how low unemployment could go before triggering inflation) had crept steadily upward, from the 4 percent norm established by Keynesians in the 1960s to what would have been considered recessionary levels, 6–7 percent, as the mid-1980s recovery got under way. In explaining the upward creep in unemployment, economists may have minimized the role of politics and ideology, but they did lend new credence to structural hypotheses, such as technological displacement, job relocation, and changes in the size and composition of the wage-earning labor force, that the CEA had minimized in the 1960s.[63] Growing alarm over what one study referred to as "catastrophic" black youth unemployment rates also sent economists in more structural directions, and in particular to an idea, which had been subject to intense debate since economist John Kain proposed it in 1968, known as the "spatial mismatch" hypothesis: that industrial relocation from central city to the suburban fringe had undermined the employment prospects for low-skilled African Americans who remained stuck in segregated urban neighborhoods.[64]

But the development that was to draw the most sustained attention to the question of long-term structural change was one that defied all conventional expectations about the relationship between employment levels, wages, and overall economic growth.[65] It also shattered what economists had come to view as a remarkably stable feature of the postwar economy:[66] After three decades of stability, wages and income were becoming vastly more unequal, spurred on the one hand by a steady deterioration of wages at the bottom and on the other by sharp post-1980 gains at the top. Although initially subject to dispute among mainstream economists, the growing disparity of incomes had already garnered considerable attention in the popular press, particularly in the form of speculation about the decline, even the disappearance, of the great American middle class. Now, it was becoming clear to economists, the economic "recovery" and growth of the 1980s had not even begun to stem the trend toward inequality; if anything, the "rising tide" was making things worse.[67]

Once again, technology figured more prominently in the range of liberal explanations than it had in the past, this time in the idea that non–college-educated industrial workers were losing out because of a "mismatch" between their skills and the kinds of jobs that were paying a high "premium" for college education as the economy continued to shift away from traditional manufacturing to services and high-tech industries. Economists also pointed to the huge growth in the labor force during the 1970s, thanks to the rapid influx of coming-of-age baby boomers and women, in accounting for average wage declines. Still, liberal economists turned to structural explanations "reluctantly," as economist and former Kennedy CEA member James Tobin acknowledged, and when they did they remained very much within the framework of human capital and market-driven supply and demand.[68] Similarly, liberal economists were cautious about prescribing major restructuring or centralized planning as a policy solution. Better to concentrate on restoring overall growth and productivity while helping workers to respond to market "signals" with programs to upgrade their skills. Perhaps most important, liberal economists continued to invest faith in growth and employment—even if they weren't sure how to achieve them—convinced as they were that the U.S. economy had an enormous capacity to absorb and adjust to structural changes and, eventually, to generate job opportunities that would sustain a middle class way of life. To economist Frank Levy, who in 1987 published an influential and accessible account of recent economic decline, the stagnation, falling wages, and inequality that started in the 1970s were not signs of permanent economic restructuring, much less of fundamental structural flaws, but of a series of "shocks," like the 1973 oil crisis, that added up to a temporary, albeit extended, spate of economic "bad times."[69]

Meanwhile, an alternative kind of structural analysis was beginning to crystallize among economists associated with labor and the political left, cultivated in a handful of academic institutes and labor-affiliated think tanks that were either unrecognized, or considered to be "ideological," in the analytic mainstream.[70] Although well-versed in the methods of quantitative neoclassical economics, these economists embraced the historical, institutionalist tradition of political economy, with its emphasis on case studies and qualitative analysis, and its insistence that the market was a socially constructed, rather than a natural, force. While acknowledging the role of technology and demographics, their analysis put more emphasis on deindustrialization, globalization, and the shift from manufacturing to services as the structural roots of inequality and wage declines. But what truly distinguished theirs from liberal analyses was a narrative of recent political economy that focused on policies and institutions, rather than neutral markets, as the driving forces behind structural change.[71]

Thus, in the accounts of left-leaning economists Barry Bluestone, Bennett Harrison, Robert Kuttner, David Gordon, and others, a key to understanding the inequality and wage declines of the 1970s and 1980s was the collapse of the post–World War II "bargain" between management and labor, a bargain that had assured workers rising wages, workplace-based social benefits, and job security in exchange for cooperative relations, high corporate profits, a limited say in the workplace, and a residual welfare state. This bargain, based on the so-called "Fordist" (ironically, after the union-busting auto manufacturer Henry Ford) model of high wages and steady promotion from within, was sustained by postwar growth, U.S. dominance in the international economy, relatively high (by U.S. standards) rates of union membership, and a minimal but stable (again, by U.S. standards) New Deal government safety net. It began to give way, though, in the 1970s and 1980s as corporations under pressure from global competitors began aggressively to seek profits at labor's expense. At this point labor was already at a distinct disadvantage, as a result of deindustrialization, declining union membership, and, especially, government policies that set up barriers to unionization while actively promoting economic deregulation, corporate downsizing, wage-cutting, and outright relocation to countries where wages were unregulated and low. The result was a collapse in working- and middle-class wages and an accompanying polarization of income and wealth—not, as liberal "mismatch" theorists suggested, simply a product of the changing skill demands of the market, but of the willful dismantling of the political and institutional arrangements that had once sustained a prosperous labor force. Worse still, the now-heavily-deindustrialized U.S. economy was creating fewer and fewer *jobs* of the kind that could assure access to a middle-class standard of life. Instead, the labor market was itself increasingly segmented into "primary" and "secondary" sectors—one high-paying, unionized or professional, and upwardly mobile, the other low-paying, high turnover, nonunionized, and heavily minority and female—with no ladder connecting the two.

That these changes were made possible by technology, demographics, increasing global competition, and the economic shift from manufacturing to services did not, in this analysis, make them an inevitable by-product of natural market forces. To the contrary, by promoting globalization and industrial restructuring, government policy and corporate practice had helped to create the conditions for what Bluestone and Harrison called the "u-turn" in average American standards of living and to undermine the power of organized workers to exercise political clout. Economic growth and human capital investments might be part of a left-liberal strategy, but they were hardly enough. That strategy, as outlined in 1988 by Bluestone and Harrison in terms reminiscent of Progressive-era industrial reform, included industrial planning, workplace democracy, a reinvigorated trade union movement, and a renewed quest for universal public provision for basic social welfare needs.[72]

By the early 1990s, liberal and left economists had come to something of a consensus on the facts, if not the interpretation, of rising inequality and the collapse of wages for non–college-educated workers.[73] By all measures, income for the bottom fifth had declined drastically and steadily since the late 1960s, while the top fifth, and especially the top *1 percent*, had enjoyed a huge increase in both wealth and income since 1983. On at least some issues, despite significant and continuing disagreement, analysts also seemed to be approaching a meeting of the minds. Deindustrialization, technology, declining union membership, and federal policy *all* played some part in wage decline and inequality—the latter most measurably by shifting the direction of redistribution away from the bottom and toward the top.[74] But what turned out to be most immediately relevant for poverty knowledge were two other features in the inequality literature that cut across differences of interpretation and went beyond the well-documented stylized facts.

One was the race and gender blindness of its structural analysis: most economists, that is, treated deindustrialization, technology, skill mismatch, and industrial relocation as socially neutered variables that could in turn be used to account for disparities that were presumably due to economic, or "class" factors and *not* due to the disadvantages of race or gender. The genesis of the "spatial mismatch" hypothesis is instructive in this regard. As proposed by John Kain in 1968, the concept was by no means race neutral; Kain argued that institutionalized racism, in the form of residential segregation, would disadvantage blacks in the suburbanizing labor market—leading him to advocate residential integration, or what he unfortunately dubbed "ghetto dispersal," as a policy response. As operationalized in the subsequent literature, however, spatial mismatch was most often measured in terms of physical distance, commuting times, and access to transportation, rather than as a set of interlocking, racialized institutional barriers to employment opportunities for blacks. By such measures, "space" could be conceptualized as a race-neutral variable and juxtaposed against "race"—defined as employer discrimination—as an explanation for disparities in wages and employment. Thus, concluded David Ellwood in one frequently cited argument, "race, not space" was the more important labor market problem facing inner-city African American youth.[75] The larger point of the formulation was important—simply eliminating the geographic barrier was no guarantee that more blacks would get jobs. But it also underscored the degree to which the suburbanization of manufacturing employment was defined as itself a racially neutral development, a straightforward response to naturalized market forces rather than to industry practices and government policies that were themselves influenced by race. The problem of race, in the meantime, was being defined very much as both Gunnar Myrdal and mainstream economic theory suggested it should be: not as a structural dimension of the urban labor market, but as an individual, essentially irrational, act of discrimination rooted in personal prejudice. Thus, as came through most clearly in the emerging debate about the urban "underclass," measures of structural economic change such as deindustrialization, skills, and spatial mismatches became part of an explanation for growing concentrations of ghetto poverty that consistently minimized the "significance" of race.

The case of gender, on the other hand, was more literally a case of blindness: the virtual failure to deal with issues of gender beyond occasionally disaggregating the labor market statistics for women and men. Nevertheless, the literature on inequality and restructuring was itself highly gendered: its labor market analysis rested almost exclusively on the experience of *men*; when women did enter the picture, it was most often in the traditional role of secondary earners (wives) in two-parent households, or as competition in the deindustrialized labor market for low-skilled—especially African American—men.[76] To be sure, by conventional measures the story of wage decline and inequality was not as dramatic for women. Indeed, male/female earnings disparities actually narrowed in the 1980s and early 1990s—thanks in part to the gains made by college-educated women, but more significantly to the fact that male wages dropped more precipitously while women began to extend their hours in the paid labor force.[77] Conventional economic measures, however, failed to consider the impact of inequality, wage declines, and changing work patterns on the amount and organization of household labor—where women's *unpaid* "labor force participation" far exceeded that of men.[78] Nor did they systematically consider how the gender division of household and, especially, child care responsibilities affected wage earning opportunities for men and women. As a consequence, the literature offered little insight into how the stagnation, inequality, deunionization, and deindustrialization of the 1970s and 1980s—and the attendant decline of the single-earner "family wage"—was connected to the growing proportion of female heads of household (and their children) among the poor.[79] That, more often, was treated as a social or cultural development, and a separate "cause" of poverty in its own right.

In part for these reasons, a second feature of the literature about economic inequality and restructuring was its failure to have any visible impact on the mainstream poverty debate. Convinced though they might have been that declining wages, and not welfare, was the crux of the poverty problem, liberal economists failed to incorporate the poverty among female-headed households into their structural framework, and continued to draw artificial distinctions between the "working" and the "welfare" poor.[80] Meanwhile, combating "dependency" remained the driving obsession in poverty policy, even after the round of welfare reforms passed in 1988.[81] There can be little doubt that this was a reflection of the diminished political power of liberal knowledge brokers: thanks to the cutbacks, devolution, and anti-analytic ethos of the Reagan revolution, poverty analysts had long since lost the capacity to set the terms of the poverty debate. But the problem was also embedded in liberal knowledge, with its compartmentalization of poverty into structural and behavioral causes that only reinforced age-old political distinctions between the deserving (wage-earning, two-parent) and the undeserving (welfare "dependent," female-headed) poor. The distinction, as we have seen, carried over into policy solutions as well, not just in the "divide and conquer" strategy but in the wall that had emerged between economic and social policy beginning in the late 1970s, when the liberal Keynesian consensus, and with it the commitment to using macroeconomic policies for broadly redistributive ends, collapsed. The problem would only become more starkly evident in the next round of welfare reform, with the contradictory pulls of a policy that pushed people into a labor market that for over a decade had been "rewarding" low-end workers with diminishing wages, high turnover, few benefits, and less security than at any other time in the postwar period.

GHETTO PATHOLOGY REVISITED:
THE "UNDERCLASS" DEBATE

When structural analysis did enter the poverty debate in the late 1980s it was, once again, under cover of a concept that applied to a very limited, highly stigmatized segment of the poor, described in sociologist William Julius Wilson's 1987 *The Truly Disadvantaged* as the "urban underclass." Like Michael Harrington, Oscar Lewis, and, to a more limited degree, Daniel P. Moynihan, Wilson looked to structural conditions to explain the emergence of a population most people continued to think of in strictly behavioral and cultural terms. He was also geographically specific: the underclass was the inner-city, or "ghetto poor." Wilson's underclass was caught up in a discernible "tangle of pathology," but one that could be understood as the result of interlocking structural changes that had transformed the big-city ghetto after 1970.

The first, and most important, of the changes Wilson pointed to was urban deindustrialization and the massive loss of secure manufacturing jobs for the low-skilled, inner-city working class. The result could be described as a combination of skill *and* spatial mismatch for ghetto residents—men in particular—who were unsuited for work in the growing financial and services sectors and unable to get to suburban manufacturing jobs. Job loss had in turn robbed neighborhood residents of economic wherewithal and, equally important, of attachment to society's main source of meaning, discipline, and organization in daily life. It had also undermined the two-parent family, leaving women with a shrunken "pool" of "marriageable males" and leading directly to the rise of the impoverished female-headed home. The second major change Wilson wrote about was the rapid disappearance of middle-class residents once suburban housing markets began opening up to better-off blacks. Their departure, made possible by the decline of housing discrimination and as such a significant victory for civil rights, had also drained neighborhoods of the organizations, enterprises, and services that had once constituted the "institutional ghetto," and, especially, the role models that gave the poor a sense of what hard work could bring. The ghetto, that is, was no longer the lively, densely populated, class integrated "black metropolis" Drake and Cayton had written about. In its place was a new, more spatially concentrated form of poverty, in which the structurally rooted problems of joblessness, social isolation, and institutional breakdown had given rise to an all-encompassing "cycle" of welfare dependence, teen pregnancy, and crime that had become the ghetto way of life. The third factor in Wilson's explanation for ghetto poverty was more conspicuous for its absence than anything else: racial subordination, which had once confined all blacks to the ghetto, was now less important than the presumably race-neutral processes of economic restructuring—and the social pathologies it helped to bring about.[82]

Wilson was by no means the first to use the term "underclass" to describe an isolated, sub–working-class group of poor people. Indeed, Wilson's analysis resonated with two very different renditions of the term. On the one hand, there was the decidedly structural meaning that, thanks to Gunnar Myrdal and other left-liberal analysts, had gained some currency in the 1960s. For Myrdal, writing in the early 1960s, "underclass" referred to what he warned would be a growing number of unskilled, marginalized "unemployables" as the economy became increasingly automated and service-based—a prospect that pointed to the need for expanded social welfare and a greater degree of economic planning than most economists were willing to pursue. In 1969, the editors of the journal *Trans-action* devoted a special issue to the "American underclass," applying the term broadly to sub–working-class people "at the very bottom," and focusing heavily on racially segregated blacks, Latinos, and Native Americans. "Thinking people" should "stop deluding themselves," wrote editor Lee Rainwater, "that the underclass is other than a product of an economic system so designed that it generates a destructive amount of income inequality." On the other hand, and far more pervasive in terms of popular circulation, there was the meaning that had become familiar since the late 1970s, when journalists stripped it of its structural meaning and began using "underclass" as a new label for the old undeserving, dangerous, pauperized poor.[83] This was the meaning that Wilson did not so much reject as attempt to reformulate, by treating behavioral pathology as a response to the long-term joblessness that urban deindustrialization had wrought.

In contrast to the social scientists who would subsequently engage in excruciating debates about how to define, measure, label, and whether even to use underclass terminology, the journalists who popularized the term had a very specific set of descriptive associations in mind. To be underclass in popular usage was to be jobless, welfare dependent, uneducated, drug addicted, criminal, sexually promiscuous, inner-city and, overwhelmingly, black.[84] Poverty was neither a necessary nor a sufficient condition; deviant behavior was. " 'Underclass' describes a state of mind and a way of life," reported *Fortune* magazine in an article that displayed a photograph of a 16-year-old black expectant mother, her bare pregnant belly graced with the hand of her sleeping 13-month-old son. "It is at least as much a cultural as an economic condition."[85] Not surprisingly, by the mid-1980s, alarm over this "cultural condition" had been conflated with resurgent concern over teen pregnancy and the demise of the "traditional" black family—this time voiced by journalists and prominent African American civic leaders while social scientists presumably stood aside.[86]

To be sure, journalists and public officials did not suffer from a want of experts to call upon when they were so inclined. *Fortune* cited Charles Murray for his "pioneering" work on how welfare had contributed to the rise of the underclass. Daniel P. Moynihan was (once again) hailed as a prophet for having anticipated the fate of the black family twenty years before, and in 1985 he took the occasion of Harvard's prestigious Godkin lectures to expound upon the theme.[87] Journalist Nicholas Lemann interviewed Wilson for a controversial series in the *Atlantic* in which he portrayed the underclass as an inherited culture of poverty imported from the sharecropper South. And in his 1981 book *The Underclass*, *New Yorker* writer Ken Auletta categorized the population based on his encounters with the groups targeted for Supported Work, the experimental intervention that launched the Manpower Demonstration Research Corporation (MDRC). Still, few reporters were inclined to give the poverty experts the last—if any—word. Lemann, after all, had not only failed to acknowledge Wilson in his widely read *Atlantic* articles, he had gotten Wilson's argument wrong. The feeling, among social scientists as well as journalists, was that liberal academics, having abandoned the topic in the wake of Oscar Lewis and the Moynihan Report, had little to say about the alienated, socially deviant underclass. No one was more adamant about this than Wilson, who insisted that a reluctance to admit that the black poor exhibited behavioral deficiencies had led liberal experts to cede the dark ghetto to the "now dominant" conservative view.[88] In *The Truly Disadvantaged*, he vowed to reclaim the territory for serious empirical research—and to lay the basis for what he characterized as a social democratic policy response.

In reality, the scholarly retreat that Wilson and many others since him have lamented was more complicated than that. For while the reaction to the Moynihan Report certainly made the subject of race and poverty seem more politically hazardous, what liberal social science had subsequently abandoned was less the ghetto or the black family than the idiom of disorganization and pathology that Moynihan had invoked. Actually, for social historians in particular, one could argue that the late 1960s through the mid-1980s marked the heyday of "ghetto" research, featuring a number of detailed empirical studies that together offered a complex, ground-up perspective on changing patterns of black urban community formation, as well as analyses of the formal and informal processes through which segregation was maintained.[89] Nor could the abandonment of the pathological idiom simply be written off as a case of liberal ideological "correctness," or, as Wilson charged, a reluctance to confront "behavior construed as unflattering or stigmatizing to particular racial groups."[90] That was to diminish the importance of the research that did offer alternatives to the sociology of the Moynihan Report. It was also to diminish the deepseated flaws within the pathological idiom itself—among them, the proposition that poverty was being reproduced by single, female household heads.

One alternative to Moynihan was inspired by the broader movement to "decolonize" the ghetto—in reality as well as in social research—by rejecting the conventions of "white sociology" and emphasizing how capitalist political economy operated to perpetuate the subordination of blacks.[91] The lower-class black family was not pathological or broken in this literature. It was a viable, culturally adaptive alternative to the middle-class nuclear family, shaped not just by centuries of poverty and oppression but by cultural survivals from the African past. By ignoring its strengths, sociologists were reinforcing white oppression, while robbing blacks of the power to define themselves. In this way, liberal sociology merely replicated the colonial relationship that was embedded in white capitalist political economy, which exploited blacks for cheap labor and consumer markets while keeping ghetto residents in a state of dependency that prevented them from developing on their own. Rejecting the liberal focus on individual opportunity, the colonial analysis insisted that the key issue was power and that the solution was local, community-based development and political organizing to wrest control over economic and political institutions from the grasp of the white establishment.[92] By the late 1960s and for much of the 1970s, the colonialist analysis had gained popular as well as academic currency—indeed, it sounded the themes of exploitation earlier raised in Kenneth Clark's HARYOU Report, the proposal for Community Action funding that became the basis of *Dark Ghetto*.[93] Nevertheless, Wilson gave it barely a mention in *The Truly Disadvantaged*, where he characterized this so-called "black perspective" as an ideologically motivated celebration of black achievement that had diverted attention from ghetto pathology and the "dreadful economic situation of poor blacks."[94] Nowhere, however, did he actually engage the issues of power, racial subordination, autonomy, or even of political economy raised in the colonial analysis.[95] The economic decline of the ghetto, in Wilson's rendition, was the product of impersonal, apolitical, nonracial structural change.

Wilson similarly overlooked the feminist interpretation of the black family that had emerged in the work of Joyce Ladner, Carol Stack, and others in the 1970s.[96] Stack, an anthropologist who had studied with Oscar Lewis, had challenged the pathological idiom in her widely read 1974 study of families in a low-income black neighborhood, *All Our Kin*. Consciously seeking to break down the "neocolonial" relationship between researcher and subject, Stack wrote about family structure from the perspective of her (mostly female) informants and their day-to-day strategies to get by. Their families consisted of heavily feminized kin networks that extended well beyond the confines of any single household and were bound by an ethos of reciprocal cooperation even when, as often happened, they were riven by internal conflict, petty jealousies, or the frequent hardships of poverty and income loss. Far from perpetuating pathology, these networks offered a much greater degree of resource-sharing, child support, and economic security than the nuclear family household could provide. The pathology, Stack and others emphasized, lay not within the family but in the racism and chronic unemployment—and a welfare system—that made stable, monogamous relationships difficult to sustain. Nor did "The Flats" suffer from an "absence" of fathers—fathers were integrated within the kin networks, albeit hidden from conventional research when not playing the "traditional" role of breadwinner or household head. By writing about gender relations from a female perspective, Stack also complicated a story—of wandering unemployed men and lone welfare-dependent women—that had usually been told by and about men, revealing, for example, that even when looking to set up house with a male provider, women felt a competing pull from extended kin.[97] Wilson, however, incorporated none of Stack's insights into his analysis, making no mention of extended kin networks in characterizing the family structure of the underclass. Instead, relying on census statistics and expert consensus, he pointed to the dramatic rise of female-headed households as evidence of social disorganization, repeated Moynihan's contention that this problem had led to increases in poverty and the number of children in "fatherless" families, and explained it almost exclusively in terms of joblessness among black men.[98] Indeed, notwithstanding the national effort to turn welfare mothers into low-wage workers, the vast preponderance of underclass literature was premised on the notion that unemployment was a male (more precisely, a black male) problem—with a female counterpart in "dependency," out-of-wedlock pregnancy, and the female-headed home.

Certainly Wilson was not alone in neglecting, or rejecting, these alternative interpretations; the colonial analysis, after all, had always remained on the very fringes of academic respectability, and by the 1980s had all but faded from view.[99] Meanwhile Stack's work, while much more lasting and widespread in its impact, came near the end of a spate of anthropological ghetto studies that were eclipsed by the overwhelmingly quantitative, econometric turn in poverty research. The experts, as we have seen, had identified female-headed households as a "cause" rather than a response to poverty and had shown little interest or capacity for exploring the ties that linked those households to community and kin.

Still, Wilson's stance was an important indicator of just how far and how quickly poverty research had shifted away from the concerns about race and local empowerment that had motivated community activists in the 1960s—concerns that nevertheless continued to inform local community development efforts throughout the 1980s, in however deradicalized a form. It was here, mostly among neighborhood residents and activists, that awareness of the ghetto's institutionalized subordination and extended kin networks had been absorbed into practice, in movements to employ neighborhood residents as "paraprofessionals" rather than relying on trained social service providers, to design interventions around community "assets" rather than the traditional "deficit"-based models, and to fight against institutionally sanctioned redlining and other practices that restricted access to credit and other much-needed development resources.[100] Certainly these efforts did not shy away from the problems of poverty, family instability, crime, drugs, and neighborhood deterioration. Nevertheless, they had consistently resisted the pathological idiom as simplistic and damaging, not only because it failed to capture the diverse reality of the neighborhoods they worked in, but for the very practical reason that it undercut their efforts to rebuild from within. Wilson's underclass concept, though, effectively dismissed the legitimacy of alternative, nonpathological interpretations, and in the process revealed not just the ideological distance liberals had traveled, but the gulf between community-level antipoverty action and academic poverty research.

Liberal policy analysts, for very different reasons, had also rejected the notion of ghetto pathology, which in any case was not easily reconciled with the kind of quantitative, applied social research that did deal with the so-called underclass population, but focused on discrete policy areas and problem groups. Much of this research was tied directly to policy interventions. MDRC's Supported Work, for example, had targeted welfare mothers, just-released criminals, drug addicts, and young high school dropouts, conceptualizing them as distinct and divergent target groups. The evaluations, too (Ken

Auletta to the contrary), had emphasized the differences among Supported Work clients rather than their common membership in an underclass.[101] The problem of youth unemployment had also spawned quite an extensive, specialized research and evaluation literature since the 1960s, thanks in large part to the demand for experimentally designed interventions following a large influx of federal dollars during the Carter administration.[102] The same could be said about any number of discretely defined social problems areas, including early childhood education, substance abuse, housing, adolescent pregnancy—each of which had its own network of experts and specialized knowledge based on government and foundation-funded policy research. Attached, as it was, to a balkanized policy and funding infrastructure, this world of applied policy research had a kind of institutional resistance to conceptualizing populations in terms of interrelated problems or neighborhood dynamics that proved difficult to measure in standard data sets. So much of policy research, after all, was about designing a single point of intervention and isolating its effects. But neither had it yielded concrete statistical evidence of a shared culture or cluster of behavioral problems that engulfed a clearly definable subgroup of poor people—and if there were, analysts emphasized, it was a very small proportion of the poor.[103] There also remained the question of whether the pathological idiom was at all useful for liberal policy purposes: Charles Murray, after all, was only the most recent in a long line of conservative social scientists who had used the idea of a pathological subculture to lump poor people and social deviants together in support of either a do-nothing or an authoritarian policy stance.

In writing about the ghetto as a "tangle of pathology," then, Wilson was reviving a framework that many social scientists and activists had rejected, not only for fear of "blaming the victim" but because it raised conceptual, practical, and political objections that, at the very least, were themselves worthy of debate. Dismissing most objections as either blind or ideologically motivated, Wilson insisted that it was more important for liberals to reclaim the authority that had been appropriated by conservatives—the authority, that is, to write openly about social pathology—and to put it toward progressive policy aims. At the same time, Wilson was expressing a real and widely felt frustration with the kind of decontextualized statistical analysis that had become the norm in poverty research. On at least two fronts, then, *The Truly Disadvantaged* was reasserting a historic claim to the ghetto—not just for liberal social science, but for the tradition within liberal sociology that hearkened back to Chicago-school social ecology, and that would rekindle a whole series of disciplinary tensions that had been subdued by the recent demise of ethnographic, neighborhood-based research. Indeed, in Wilson's story of the "disorganization," "social isolation," and "concentration effects" caused by middle-class out-migration could be found elements of the old Chicago-school organization-disorganization-reorganization cycle—set now in the gloomy context of postindustrial disinvestment, and told from the perspective of the people left behind.[104] There was also something of a Chicago-school revival in the Urban Poverty and Family Structure Study, an ambitious program of surveys and ethnography that Wilson, with a large team of faculty and graduate students, launched in the neighborhoods surrounding the University of Chicago starting in 1985.

In practice, however, and in a by-then familiar pattern, the notion of a kind of poverty rooted in, or indelibly linked to, behavioral deviancy continually threatened to undermine Wilson's plan to draw attention to the structural origins of ghetto poverty and to put policy deliberations on a more social democratic course—if within social democracy can be included interventions that aim to reform markets rather than simply socializing poor people to existing market norms. Certainly this was the case in early efforts to "operationalize" Wilson's theory within the poverty research industry, which absorbed "underclass" into the social policy vocabulary in unmistakably behavioral terms. Soon after *The Truly Disadvantaged* was published, ASPE issued a notice listing teen pregnancy, school dropout, welfare dependency, drug use, and crime as examples of "underclass behaviors," and called for theoretical models linking them not to structural changes in the economy but to so-called "neighborhood effects" (such as what the "epidemic" theory referred to as a process of "social contagion" in poor neighborhoods).[105] Using these indicators of "bad behavior," researchers at the Urban Institute had come up with a way of distinguishing between neighborhoods that were merely "poor" and those that were "underclass"—which in turn became one of the standard measures for estimating the size (small but growing according to most estimates) of the underclass.[106] The IRP featured a lead article in its newsletter *Focus* reporting on a growing body of empirical literature based on the "behavioralist" approach to studying the underclass.[107] Defined as such, the underclass concept pointed more readily to policy proposals based on behavior modification, individual remediation, and workfare than to Wilson's agenda of guaranteed jobs, full employment, and economic reform.

Wilson went to some lengths to distance himself from the narrow, behavioralist direction of underclass research, continually emphasizing the structural dimensions of his argument, encouraging greater attention to the post-1970s transformation of urban economies, and criticizing the paternalist conservatives who proposed mandatory workfare, benefit cuts, and behavior modification as a solution to the underclass.[108] His own research project, in Chicago, aimed to provide empirical evidence of diminishing work opportunities for ghetto residents, including an extraordinarily telling survey of employer attitudes and hiring practices carried out by graduate students in face-to-face interviews.[109] Then, in what appeared to many a stunning reversal, he announced during his 1990 presidential address to the American Sociological Association that he was giving up the *term*, although not the concept, "underclass." In a speech that drew headlines in national newspapers, Wilson approvingly quoted sociologist Herbert Gans on the "dangers" of "underclass" as a label, admitting that it had become "hopelessly polluted in meaning" and a "pejorative" way of talking about inner-city blacks.[110] Now, he was giving up the term he had done so much to legitimize, in favor of one that was presumably less politically charged: "ghetto poor."[111] The shift in terminology, however, did not address a central tension within the concept itself: determine though he might to link the plight of the underclass to changes reverberating throughout the U.S. economy, Wilson's concept rested on the notion that there was a group of poor people whose lives were qualitatively different and cut off, not just from the majority of Americans, but from the majority of people who experienced poverty. And it was documenting and proving what—if anything—constituted the difference that would preoccupy the vast preponderance of underclass research, including the Chicago study itself. The centerpiece of the study was the Urban Poverty and Family Life survey, a questionnaire administered to households living in what the U.S. Census Bureau categorizes as "high poverty" neighborhoods, where 20 percent or more of the households have incomes below the official poverty line. Households outside these neighborhoods were not included in the survey—which, critics later noted, made it impossible to determine just how much of "ghetto-related" behavior was really "ghetto-specific" at all. Urban restructuring was presented as the context rather than as itself the central focus of empirical research, discernible in carefully assembled census statistics but for the most part treated as an inevitable and apolitical process divorced from policy choices and hence, by implication, not subject to reform. While drawing much-needed and overdue attention to what he later referred to as the disappearance of work, Wilson's Chicago project did not systematically examine working conditions among the substantial numbers of ghetto residents who were employed. The effect, however unintentional, was to sharpen the line between the underclass and the "working poor."[112]

Underclass research adhered more closely to Wilson's original concept in adopting his highly controversial argument, developed from and captured neatly in the title of his 1978 book *The Declining Significance of Race*. In that book, Wilson argued that class had become more important than racial status in determining "life chances" for blacks, pointing in particular to the emergence of an upwardly mobile black middle class as evidence that race-based subordination—at least in the economy—was getting to be a thing of the past. The underclass, though, was unable to take advantage of the demise of institutionalized racism because of the increased economic subordination of all low-skilled, uneducated workers in the wake of deindustrialization and other aspects of structural economic change.[113] Here, as later, Wilson was writing as a social democrat, arguing that liberal civil rights strategy had concentrated too narrowly on battling racial discrimination, while ignoring the problem of class subordination and the need for fundamental economic reform. He was also echoing themes earlier sounded by prominent black intellectuals, such as civil rights leader Bayard Rustin, and the Marxist sociologist Oliver Cromwell Cox: using terminology reminiscent of Cox's criticism of Gunnar Myrdal's racial "orthodoxy," Wilson excoriated the black intelligentsia at a 1979 University of Pennsylvania symposium, accusing scholars of protecting their own self-interest by propounding the "mythology" that race, rather than economics, was the single most important, and unifying, issue for blacks.[114] In the context of the late 1970s, however, and especially in the wake of the increasingly visible backlash against affirmative action, Wilson's arguments were construed less as a social democrat's attempt to draw attention to the economic disfranchisement of the black poor than as fodder for a neoconservative attack on liberal antidiscrimination policy. Equally important for the future course of poverty knowledge, they were absorbed into the much older, recently rekindled, "race vs. class" debate—a debate that, by treating race and class as alternative rather than mutually reinforcing variables, fed into an artificial polarization in politics as well as in social science.

Wilson sharpened his critique of what he characterized as a narrow, race-based civil rights agenda in *The Truly Disadvantaged*, arguing that antidiscrimination and affirmative action programs had helped the lower class or "truly needy" very little, while opening up significant opportunities for those in a position to take advantage of them—the more privileged, better educated middle class. For Wilson, this was a rationale not for government retreat but for a refocused policy agenda, making the economy rather than race relations the chief target for reform. Policies to end racial discrimination were not enough for the ghetto—in fact, since the discrimination that helped create the underclass was "historic" and not "contemporary," it was questionable whether they were relevant at all. Instead, Wilson called for a more expansive package of "race-neutral" programs—full employment, job training, child care, family allowances—that would make racial progress its "hidden agenda" since minorities would benefit disproportionately, and automatically, from these "universalistic" economic and social welfare reforms. In this, he was joined by a growing chorus of liberal centrists and new Democrats who, convinced that an overly aggressive racial agenda had torn the New Deal coalition apart, were urging the party to reconstitute itself as one that would face up to the racially fraught issues of crime and welfare while speaking for the interests of the white working and middle classes.[115]

Wilson's analysis reflected at least three assumptions that, despite heated contention from other scholars, were quickly becoming absorbed into mainstream poverty thought. One was the story of black class polarization into a secure, upwardly mobile "middle" and the jobless, usually single-parent, poor. This view, critics said, exaggerated the degree of security, occupational access, wealth, and status blacks had actually achieved—amenities reserved, in a still-racist society, for the *white* middle class. It also overlooked the existence of a substantial black working class, relegated by discriminatory practice to the lowest rungs of the occupational ladder, overrepresented among the working poor, and more closely connected—through family and neighborhood ties—to the jobless "underclass" than Wilson's theory implied.[116] Second was the assumption that the civil rights was indeed a narrow, noneconomic agenda, when in reality mainstream civil rights organizations had advocated such measures as full employment, national health insurance, skills training, and minimum income guarantees since the New Deal. Bayard Rustin, after all, had issued his call for a more expansive vision of political and economic justice from within the civil rights movement, and had played a central role in mobilizing support for the A. Philip Randolph Institute's 1966 Freedom Budget, which called for class-based coalition building without relinquishing the ongoing pursuit of antidiscrimination goals.[117] To be sure, there were real and deepening class divisions among African Americans, which were increasingly reflected in divergent political interests and views.[118] Nor had any of the major civil rights organizations been able to sustain a program that spoke convincingly to the economic needs of a mass, predominantly working-class, base. But to turn from there to a "nonracial" or "race-neutral" economic agenda was to diminish the extent to which racial distinctions were built into and perpetuated by the supposedly color-blind functioning of the economy, social policy, politics, and other structural dimensions of American life.

The third assumption in Wilson's analysis was that a truly "race-neutral" social policy was even a possibility in light of the historically racialized nature of U.S. social policy. Minorities, after all, were still unequal beneficiaries of such popular "universal" strategies as Social Security, full employment, and economic growth. From their perspective, those nontargeted programs were not "race neutral" but "white"—in the absence, that is, of specific and explicit policies to distribute their benefits across racial lines.[119] Nor was it likely that any underclass agenda, no matter how "hidden," would actually withstand the race-neutral test. The term itself, talk of a "white" or a "rural" underclass to the contrary, was already thoroughly racialized. It was widely recognized in political, popular, even in social scientific discourse as a code word for the black undeserving poor. Nevertheless, official measures of the underclass continued to treat it as a racially neutral term. Race, of course, figured prominently in demographic descriptions; according to all measures, underclass neighborhoods were never majority white. But as an explanatory "variable," race was virtually off the table, except when it was acknowledged as a "residual" only after the more readily measurable effects of low skills and "bad behavior" could be taken into account.[120] Underclass researchers even managed to strip the term "ghetto" of its historic meaning by defining it as an area of concentrated poverty, but not one restricted by race.[121] Thus could the overwhelmingly nonwhite composition of underclass neighborhoods be explained as a function of poverty and social pathology considered apart from institutionalized racial discrimination.

Touching on themes of economic restructuring, ghetto pathology, and the declining significance of race, the controversy that swirled around Wilson's underclass concept was in many ways a continuation of much older poverty debates. Several things distinguished this from earlier controversies, however, and help to explain why, in contrast to the quick rise and fall of Oscar Lewis's culture of poverty or the Moynihan Report, the controversy stirred by the underclass concept marked the beginning, rather than the end, of its career as an intellectually respectable idea. One was that Wilson's theory was considerably more than a recycled culture of poverty or a repackaged telling of black family deterioration. Wilson wrote about both as constituent elements of the underclass, but he also drew on, and stimulated, research on the structural transformation of the urban economy that had gotten little attention in poverty research—and that had been absent entirely from both mainstream political discourse and from conservative renderings of the underclass. Critics took issue with some or all of the argument, but its sheer scope made it impossible to dismiss on any single ground. And in presenting much of his analysis in the form of social scientific hypotheses, he created a road map for empirical research and for a discourse that could be framed in nonideological terminology. Wilson also had enormous credibility—as an established, widely respected sociologist, as an African American writing about racially charged issues, and as an avowed liberal sympathizer prepared to break the liberal silence about ghetto pathologies.

Perhaps more than any other single factor, the dramatically altered state of social politics helps to explain the staying power of the underclass concept. Writing, in contrast to Lewis and Moynihan, at a time when conservative politicians and analysts had succeeded in utterly redefining the terms of social policy debate, Wilson offered an alternative to the story of government-instigated welfare coddling and rampant individual immorality that Charles Murray and others had used to explain ghetto poverty. From the standpoint of large, historically liberal foundations in particular, Wilson's underclass theory presented an opportunity to take the social scientific high ground in a debate so far dominated by the Right. At the same time, it offered a venue for framing a discourse on poverty that, quite apart from Wilson's own politics, could be used to avert political danger in two ways. First, by providing a way to talk about ghetto poverty while diminishing, if not avoiding altogether, the importance of race as a structural divide. And second, by raising the larger problem of structural economic dislocation while also containing it within the confines of socially and economically isolated neighborhoods. As *the* latest, and hottest topic in poverty research by the late 1980s, the underclass (however unintentionally, from Wilson's perspective) easily overshadowed the rise of the deunionized, destabilized low-wage working class as the symbol of the "new American poverty" Michael Harrington had written about a few years before.[122]

A final important factor in the comparative staying power of the underclass has to do with the vast changes in the organization of social knowledge that had occurred since the mid-1960s. There had been, after all, no recognized poverty research industry to speak of when Oscar Lewis's culture of poverty and the Moynihan Report came to light—no Urban Institute, no Institute for Research on Poverty, not much by way of data for studying the poor. By the 1980s, in contrast, there was a large and established network of institutions that foundations could mobilize for what became a veritable cottage industry of underclass research and debate, an effort that drew on academics, graduate students, think tanks, and contract research organizations. A great deal of the ensuing research was devoted to sorting out and testing the various hypotheses in Wilson's multifaceted theory, often using the standard conventions of poverty research. Others took the occasion to challenge those conventions, by using the underclass concept as a springboard for introducing more structural and interdisciplinary ways of thinking about poverty. This was among the aims of what was by far the most ambitious of the underclass projects, the Social Science Research Council (SSRC) Program for Research on the Urban Underclass, a five-year, $6 million fellowship and research program launched with funding from the Rockefeller Foundation in 1987–88.

The SSRC project was one leg of an even more ambitious Rockefeller program to "build understanding" ("BU" in the internal shorthand), start Community Planning and Action Programs ("CPAPs") in six major cities, and influence national-level policy on behalf of the inner-city poor—an effort, that is, to restore something resembling the "iron triangle" of liberal philanthropy, expertise, and government policy in the hope that someday a more receptive administration would return.[123] As the principal academic research component of this initiative, the SSRC project underwrote interdisciplinary working groups, conferences, volumes, and more than one hundred undergraduate, pre- and postdoctoral fellows, all under the direction of a committee of well-known poverty researchers and a professional staff.[124] The result was a fairly wide-ranging mix of research and, through the fellowship program, opportunities for young and minority scholars working in otherwise marginalized areas of research. But the SSRC project also offers a case study in the politics of poverty knowledge in the late 1980s and early 1990s, which ultimately limited the capacity of social science to function, as the Rockefeller Foundation imagined, as a force for enlightened policy and social change.

The central issues for negotiation involved questions of what underclass research should encompass, who should conduct it, and how—complicated, in this instance, by ongoing contention over the quantitative methods and neoclassical economic models that had become the paradigm for "hard" poverty research. The SSRC had proposed to avoid falling into this paradigm by encouraging a more interdisciplinary, "multilevel" approach to research and by bringing new players into the field. Nevertheless, tensions quickly arose over perceptions of what one participant called a "pecking order" in Committee appointments, leadership, and funding decisions that favored "quantitative, analytic, ideally economistic rational choice models" over qualitative, contextual, or structural research.[125] This tension came to the surface in the wake of the Committee's first major public event, a 1989 conference at Northwestern University featuring papers from several well-known social scientists on various dimensions of Wilson's theory. Watching from an "outer circle" were several younger and less mainstream scholars who had been invited, but instructed not to speak—confirming, rather dramatically to those seated on the periphery, the general impression that the underclass discussion would be dominated by "the same old people" who had been writing about poverty without talking about the ghetto for years.[126] To be sure, ethnographers, even historians, had a presence on the project—historian Michael B. Katz was appointed project archivist, and edited a volume of historical essays with Committee support. But initially, at least, they came in as outsiders to a conversation already dominated by the methods, models, and the data sets that had become the lingua franca of mainstream poverty research.[127] Where, critics asked, was the research on urban politics and policy? Why the continued emphasis on "social isolation," "disorganization," and family "dysfunction" when ethnographic research had shown far more diversity and agency in "underclass" neighborhoods than that? Why not focus research on changes in neighborhood and labor market institutions rather than so exclusively on the individual outcomes they produced? Why neglect education, housing, and homelessness, even though all had been hot points in recent policy debates?

Meanwhile, much to the dismay of the Rockefeller Foundation, there was an underlying, ongoing tension within the Committee over whether "the underclass" existed at all. That dispute generated something more than academic controversy with the release of the much-publicized volume from the Northwestern conference, a Brookings Institution publication entitled *The Urban Underclass* coedited by Committee members Christopher Jencks and Paul Peterson (who was also the Committee chair). "This is a bunch of quantitative social scientists here," said Jencks at a press conference to release the volume. "When we can't count something, we're not sure it exists." Days later, Jencks summarized his own contribution to the volume in a *Wall Street Journal* article headlined "There Is No Underclass," where he argued that the concept confused a number of different problems that could not be empirically linked. Peterson was similarly skeptical, citing statistical evidence from national census data that the underclass was very small and shrinking—and in any case not a very useful way of understanding the "poverty paradox."[128] Both essays raised provocative issues, and did so within the norms of scholarly exchange. The controversy concerned their prominence in the press conference Brookings convened to announce the publication—and as the lead essays in an edited volume that subsequently proceeded to treat the concept as a valid basis for empirical research. From the headlines one would guess that the nation's premiere liberal think tank was debunking Wilson's underclass theory as a myth, at least implicitly calling into question the need for a concerted policy response.[129] Nevertheless, other volume contributors pointed to the opposite conclusion, including the closing essay by Wilson himself: poverty in ghetto neighborhoods had grown measurably worse. Charles Murray, commenting as a panelist at the Brookings session, pointed up just how complicated the political implications of these disagreements could be. Pronouncing Wilson right—things *were* getting worse in the ghetto—he used the occasion to argue that the data pointed to illegitimacy as the central problem and that in this case government should be more willing to intervene: not, to be sure, for purposes of "social engineering," but to remove children from single-mother homes. At least one point was not lost on the Rockefeller Foundation: with millions for research to "build understanding," the SSRC was still debating the validity of the underclass concept, while Charles Murray used the data for the simple, straightforward message that "bad mothers" were to blame.

Much of what was expressed in the Committee's academic exchanges was compounded by a less visible set of tensions about gender and race, centered to some degree on Committee representation and governance but more significantly on the failure to make gender and race central issues for substantive research. Only later, indeed, spurred partly by their absence on the underclass agenda, did gender and racial segmentation begin to get more explicit recognition.[130] The more immediate effect was to reinforce assumptions that were already deeply embedded in the research—employment and crime were the "black male" problems; single parenthood and welfare their female counterparts—and even more to reinforce the tendency in poverty research more generally to "explain" gender and race differences with such supposedly "neutral" measures of disadvantage as skill, education, family background, and space—as if these disadvantages were somehow independent of the structural restrictions experienced by women and nonwhites. Nor did the underclass project confront the enormous complexity in the category "race," particularly important in light of the demographic and cultural transformations that two decades of "new immigration" had generated in innercity neighborhoods. Indeed, the intergroup conflicts stirred by these transformations had something of a counterpart in academic debates about whether the "underclass" label should be imposed on Latinos, Asians, and other non–African American minority groups.[131] And yet, some considered the SSRC Committee to have helped make it less "dangerous" to study issues of race and poverty—especially in comparison to the ideologically divisive debates over the Moynihan Report.[132] As more precisely stated in an external evaluation, what the Underclass Committee had lessened was "the risk of studying the black family and the deviance of blacks," while otherwise minimizing the importance of race as a structural barrier.[133] And that, especially in the post–Civil Rights era of the 1980s, was in itself a statement of considerable ideological and political significance.

Ironically, the one area in which the SSRC Committee did address race explicitly was arguably its biggest success: the project had an express commitment to providing fellowship opportunities to young minority scholars, and it worked hard to carry that commitment out. This required concerted efforts to publicize the opportunity outside the standard SSRC venues. It also meant acknowledging that, even with the most meritocratic of intentions, social science opportunities are opened up through networks, peer and mentoring relationships, and a form of cultural recognition that all remain segmented by race and gender as well as by academic discipline. The project's summer dissertation workshop for minority graduate students was especially instructive in this regard. There, students got intensive analytic, methodological, and proposal-writing training. By far the most important part of the workshop, though, was the opportunity to interact and establish professional relationships with students and professors who similarly experienced isolation as minorities in a predominantly white profession. Here again, the work of the project mirrored its research in an interesting, albeit distant way, for in providing advice, role models, and networks for minority scholars, the workshop was institutionalizing precisely the kind of "social capital" the underclass was said to lack.

As the case of the fellowship program indicates, the SSRC underclass project did open up some possibilities for broadening the social scientific discourse on urban poverty, not just by diversifying the composition of networks but by introducing a wider range of disciplines, theoretical perspectives, and subject matter to the underclass debate. In its working groups, too, the project began to move toward interdisciplinary collaboration and to suggest new ways of framing questions for research. Developmental psychologists, economists, anthropologists, and sociologists collaborated in a Working Group on Communities and Neighborhoods, Family Processes, and Individual Development to "reinvent," as one commentator put it, the social ecology of "neighborhood effects."[134] The project also provided support for the Multi-City Study of Urban Inequality, an interdisciplinary study of labor markets, residential segregation, and racial attitudes that moved research beyond the boundaries of poor neighborhoods to the metropolitan area while making the intersection between economic, geographic, and racial barriers an explicit focus of empirical research.[135] And the project's volume of historical essays shifted the focus away from a preoccupation with measuring individual outcomes, drawing attention not just to long-term structural change, institutions, politics, and policy, but to the historical agency of poor people in mobilizing for change. What the SSRC did in these instances was to provide a venue for extended, often difficult, disciplinary negotiations, and occasionally to bring people to the table who had not been there before.

A third set of tensions set boundaries on the possibilities for innovation, however, and that was the struggle over what *kind* of knowledge mattered most in understanding, and changing, the plight of the urban poor. Underlying this struggle was an artificial, unspoken, yet deeply institutionalized hierarchy of knowledge that made the SSRC keeper of what was "basic" or "scientific" as distinct from MDRC and Urban Institute–style "applied" or "policy-relevant" research on the one hand, and on the other from what could be learned from living and/or working in urban neighborhoods—which academic social science had no way of recognizing as knowledge at all. The Rockefeller Foundation proposed to transcend this division by encouraging interaction among the three components of its program, and specifically by instructing the SSRC to address itself to policy and program concerns. Ideally, a reinvigorated "invisible college" of social science experts would provide the theory and empirical findings for policy makers in Washington as well as for the "ground level" practitioners who were part of the foundation's Community Planning and Action Program. Midway through the project, it was clear that, without major changes, such a smooth-running research-policy-practice link was not to be. For one thing, the SSRC committee was dominated by academics, who in their own as well as an outside evaluator's estimation had "only the foggiest conception of how to design social research that has policy relevance," and who had few direct links to the applied policy realm.[136] Nor did it make an effort to include, or even to acknowledge, policy research in its networks—suggesting the extent to which the SSRC project, with its primarily academic constituency, was unconnected to, even a bit disdainful of, applied research. Policy analysts, in turn, viewed the project with some skepticism, and considerable frustration at what appeared to be its refusal, or inability, to formulate a research agenda that would respond to policy concerns.

An even more basic rift divided SSRC research from Rockefeller's grantees in the Community Planning and Action Program (CPAP), in a clash of culture and political priority ("oil and water," as one Committee member recalled) that was in some ways reminiscent of the division between research and community action at the OEO.[137] For the most part, the SSRC committee did not take the CPAPs seriously—their language, of community mobilization and local participation, simply did not connect with the prevailing categories or the mood of research. Nor, coincidentally, were the CPAPs nearly as well funded—the six local organizations each received Rockefeller grants averaging $350,000 annually—less than half the amount allocated to the SSRC. For the SSRC actually to work with the CPAPs would have required substantial changes in the conventions of academic research: an agenda driven as much by local need as by theory-driven hypotheses, for starters; a language accessible to a nonacademic audience; and a willingness to collaborate with local activists to use research as a resource for change. It would also require revised terminology and measurement categories. All of the CPAPs rejected "underclass" as a label. They also discarded the census-based designations of neighborhood that quantitative social scientists used. And when criticized in an evaluation for concentrating on "issues involving children and women" to the exclusion of "prime-age male employment," they rejected the dichotomy as artificial and insensitive to their own need to find a point where they, as local actors with very limited resources, could intervene.[138] This is not to suggest that the CPAPs were without problems, and there is no question that the resistance to collaboration came from both sides. But neither were they innocent of the importance and power of research to mobilize—or demobilize—action, and for this reason they were unwilling to cede control over community study to "outside" social science expertise. The CPAPs did conduct surveys of local conditions, in partnership with nearby universities and quite independent of the SSRC. Near the end of the project, at an SSRC research conference, Angela Glover Blackwell of the Oakland-based Urban Strategies Council described one of these surveys and wondered whether, when the time came to interpret the data, the SSRC committee would be willing to help. By then, June 1992, few in the room could ignore the gap between academic research and local need. It had already come through quite starkly, in the absence of a coherent, mobilized social scientific response to the uprising in South Central Los Angeles neighborhoods following the not guilty verdict in the Rodney King police brutality trial just six weeks before.[139]

The Rockefeller Foundation soon grew impatient with the SSRC's apparent lack of "relevance," and expressed its dissatisfaction by informing the underclass Committee that funding would be terminated sooner than expected— after a five-year, rather than what had earlier been held out as a possible ten-year, span of annual grants. As always, the message was couched in indirect, programmatic logic: having "achieved a level of maturity," the SSRC had brought the field to its "saturation" point. The accompanying directives were more pointed: now, the foundation wanted a summary of the Ommittee's contribution to research, and what it all meant for policy and for practitioners in the field.[140]

In the course of responding to these directives, the underclass project finally made a brief, parting gesture toward a more collaborative approach to knowledge by sponsoring a policy conference that invited contributions from academics, policy analysts, and from some people who actually ran antipoverty programs in urban neighborhoods. The conference itself was the product of intensive planning and negotiation among these constituencies—allies in theory, but in truth fragmented, unaware or skeptical of one another, and decidedly unequal partners when it came to gaining a hearing from Washington's policy elite. Much of the work of planning involved finding ways to make the conversation hospitable for nonacademics—ruling out the time-honored presentation of "policy implications" at the end of lengthy social scientific exposition in favor of brief memos summarizing what could be learned from research, policy, and practical experience.[141] On this score, the conference was something of an accomplishment—at the very least, it was an official acknowledgment of the kind of collaboration and exchange that should have happened from the start. But there was also the question of what to *do* with this knowledge, at a time when policy possibilities actually, finally, appeared to be opening up: the conference was held in early November 1993, less than a year into the Clinton administration. Days before, William J. Wilson had met with the president at the White House. Policy agencies were once again staffed by allies, even some close colleagues, from the liberal social research industry. And the administration was asking the right kinds of questions, such as how to restore growth and jobs to neglected urban areas, how to make health insurance available to everyone, and how to "make work pay."[142] On this score, the SSRC conference accomplished little: the neglected work of negotiating and hammering out a policy agenda could hardly be accomplished in a day.

But the disconnect between underclass research and policy was as much due to broader trends in national politics and political culture as it was to problems within the SSRC project itself. The underclass research agenda was carried out in the near-complete policy vacuum created by the politics of governmental devolution, defunding, growing budget deficits, and neglect of the 1980s and early 1990s. For all his talk of a "kinder, gentler nation," President Bush floundered when it came to his own promised overhaul of antipoverty programs, or even to approving "enterprise zones" for South Central Los Angeles in 1992. Following consultations with poverty experts that generated ideas but no cash, one administration official offered this rendition of the White House policy stance: "Keep playing with the same toys. But let's paint them a little shinier."[143] At the same time, even after the 1992 presidential election, liberal groups remained internally divided along several lines, ranging from an old debate over whether policy should "disperse" or rebuild underclass neighborhoods to whether the Clinton administration, given the growing fixation on the middle-class suburban vote, should emphasize much of an identifiably "urban" agenda at all.[144] Most important, though, was that for all its connotations of pathology, a strong current of underclass research pointed to the need for a far more proactive agenda, of economic investment, labor market intervention, social welfare expansion, and, for some, antidiscrimination enforcement, than either administration was willing seriously to contemplate. Instead, what proved far more "relevant" from a policy perspective, was the poverty knowledge that fed into the undying political obsession with welfare reform.

CHAPTER 11

The End of Welfare and the Case for a
New Poverty Knowledge

IF EVER there were a case to be made for reconstituting poverty knowledge, it is the Personal Responsibility and Work Opportunity Reconciliation Act of 1996. That act, which brought an end to "welfare as we know it," was signed into law by President Clinton over the heated objections of the very experts he had invited to design the welfare "reform." Clinton's approval marked an especially cruel defeat for poverty knowledge, not because the legislation ignored, but because it was based on, premises that liberal experts had been promoting in their own research: that long-term "dependency" was the crux of the welfare problem and that it could be resolved by changing welfare to promote work and individual "self-sufficiency." In this formulation, poverty knowledge had departed considerably from its Progressive, New Deal, and Great Society roots: The experts who designed Clinton's welfare proposal remained committed to active government and to using rational knowledge on behalf of the poor, but they had come to accept and accommodate the conservative rhetoric of small government, individual responsibility, market benevolence, and of targeting welfare and welfare recipients rather than the economy and the opportunity structure for reform.

THE EXPERTS AND THE REFORM

It is difficult to exaggerate the hopes and expectations that President Clinton's 1992 election stirred in liberal poverty research circles. These were the hopes and expectations of social scientists come in from the cold. The exile of the long Reagan-Bush years was finally over: here was a president who could quote from their research, and wanted to put their expertise to work. As governor of Arkansas, Clinton had presided over one of the country's toughest "tough love" workfare programs, but he had also showcased it as one of MDRC's experimental evaluation sites, and himself as a proponent of knowledge-based reform. As a leading "new Democrat," he had fully embraced the mid-1980s "consensus" on welfare that poverty knowledge had helped to forge, emphasizing the importance of individual responsibility, parental support, public-private partnership, and labor market "self-sufficiency" in his own calls for reform.[1] The Clinton-Gore ticket had also adopted the central themes of poverty expertise in literature for the 1992 campaign, which talked about "empowering" poor Americans by improving wages and job opportunities while also expecting them to work.[2] Most important, he was actively recruiting from familiar research and advocacy networks for the brain trust that would put Democratic policy making back on the political map. Soon after the election he appointed the still-rising stars of the poverty research establishment, economists David Ellwood and Mary Jo Bane, as the HHS assistant secretary for planning and evaluation (head of ASPE) and assistant secretary for children and families, respectively. Ellwood was still teaching at Harvard's John F. Kennedy School of Government; Bane had become the New York State Commissioner of Social Services under Democratic Governor Mario Cuomo; both, since the early 1980s, had continued to write steadily about poverty and dependency and, at least indirectly, to advocate welfare reform. Also joining the agency were Wendell Primus, who as chief Democratic analyst on the House Ways and Means Committee had proved the single most effective staff person when it came to salvaging programs for the poor, and, later, Peter Edelman, a noted lawyer, human services administrator, and former aide to Robert F. Kennedy, who along with his wife, Marion Wright Edelman of the Children's Defense Fund, had been engaged in the liberal fight against poverty for more than thirty years. For the first time since the late 1970s, ASPE was firmly in the hands of liberal analysts, with a mandate to construct an antipoverty plan. The signs were encouraging. "If you work, you shouldn't be poor" had been a prominent campaign theme, and the first Clinton budget included a massive expansion of the experts' favorite "nonwelfare" program, the Earned Income Tax Credit (EITC). Upon appointing Bane and Ellwood, Clinton also asked them to join White House aide Bruce Reed as co-chairs of a high-level working group on welfare reform. All of this was good news for poverty analysts. If they wanted to get through to the administration, they could pick up the phone to ASPE and get a hearing among their own.

It was not long before the high expectations were dampened, as poverty experts watched welfare play second fiddle to reforming health care, getting tough on crime, and deficit reduction as administration goals. Few would have predicted, though, that just before the end of his first term in office three of Clinton's top poverty experts (Bane, Primus, and Edelman; Ellwood had already left the administration to return to Harvard) would resign in protest over his approval of a bill Daniel P. Moynihan characterized as welfare "repeal."[3] That bill, the Personal Responsibility and Work Opportunity Reconciliation Act of 1996, did away with the New Deal federal guarantee of assistance for families with children by imposing strict work mandates and time limits on eligibility, and by radically devolving responsibility for poor relief to the states. Poverty experts felt stunned and betrayed when Clinton actually signed the legislation—he had vetoed similar bills twice before—and were left scrambling for explanations of what went wrong. This was, as Peter Edelman put it, "the worst thing Bill Clinton has done."[4]

In David Ellwood's version of the story, the key turning point was the disastrous midterm election of 1994, which put control of the Congress in the hands of radically right-wing Republicans led by Georgia Representative Newt Gingrich. Demonizing welfare as the root of all evil, House Republicans proposed unprecedented spending cuts and behavioral restrictions, including the strict time limits and federal devolution that eventually made it into law.[5] Up until then, Ellwood claimed, the White House had the opening to push through its more progressive welfare legislation—only to squander it in misguided delays. "We got hit by a freight train," he wrote in reference to the post-1994 Republican onslaught, because "our own train moved too sluggishly."[6] Other versions of the story put the blame squarely on Clinton's shoulders: for trying to out-tough the Republicans; for signing legislation he knew would put millions of people, including children, in even greater hardship than before; for putting his own reelection before principle; and, especially, for promising a welfare overhaul in the first place, thus setting the stage for a dramatic takeover by the Right.[7] All of the experts agreed that the legislation was a triumph of politics over scientific knowledge and as such a devastating blow to the poor. What their explanations failed to come to terms with, however, was the complicity of poverty knowledge in the welfare repeal of 1996: first in making dependency the key reform issue and in severing ("disaggregating") it from the structural problem of labor market decline; second, in legitimating the reform obsession when earlier legislation had already put major changes in place; most important, in making time limits and other punitive measures part of the framework for neoliberal welfare reform.

That framework, of course, was captured in Bill Clinton's now-notorious campaign promise to "end welfare as we know it," the mantra reportedly coined and embraced as a "guiding star" by the White House welfare point man, Bruce Reed, yet referred to by other administration reformers by its initials—EWAKI—with more than a hint of disdain.[8] Along with two other campaign slogans, "two years and you're off," and "make work pay," Clinton's promise to "end" welfare was a neatly packaged, politically ambiguous adaptation of the antipoverty measures Ellwood, with broad support among poverty experts, had been proposing since 1988. Key to Ellwood's approach were the "make work pay" components—an expanded EITC, a higher minimum wage, and broader health insurance coverage—to guarantee that work would be a better-paying alternative to welfare while rewarding poor people who, as Ellwood liked to put it, "played by the rules." These proposals were touted as the heart of a "nonwelfare" agenda for helping the poor to attain "self-sufficiency," in combination with more rigorously enforced child support from absent parents ("deadbeat dads," in campaign talk) that would become a guaranteed government payment in the event that the parent couldn't pay.[9] The EITC in particular enjoyed broad bipartisan support; after all, it reinforced the work ethic and avoided visible expansion of the welfare state, all the while making up a little something for escalating disparities in income and wealth. Since the mid-1980s poverty experts had been at the front of the EITC bandwagon: this was in effect a repackaged negative income tax, now targeted to the working, or deserving, poor. In 1993, the administration won by far the biggest in a decade-long series of bipartisan EITC expansions—undoubtedly the single most important thing Clinton did to raise family incomes for the low-paid working class.[10]

But there were other aspects of the EITC expansion, and, more generally, the "make work pay" package, that portended far less well for the political fortunes of poor and low-wage workers. The EITC did nothing to reverse the long-term drop in wages, let alone the political disfranchisement of workers, while working safely outside the market to alleviate symptoms that stemmed from untrammeled market restructuring and the consequent earnings decline. If anything, it had been used to offset the administration's lukewarm, on-again/ off-again support for higher minimum wages, as well as the impact of budget cuts and tax hikes in other areas that did harm the working poor. It also fit a pattern of diminishing support for Keynesian social spending in favor of the more indirect and, for the poor, difficult-to-access tax expenditure route. And it sidestepped what concerned millions of Americans: the declining quality and security of *jobs*. In these ways, pushing the EITC helped Clinton to keep a distance from the "old," labor and left-liberal Democrats who sought more aggressive measures to protect workers from the globalizing, free market economy the administration was trying to promote.[11] Similarly, by restricting benefits to household heads in the paid labor force, the EITC completely ignored feminist proposals for valuing the household labor of welfare mothers and drove a political wedge between the "working" and the "welfare" poor—precisely the wedge poverty experts had tried avoiding throughout the 1960s and 1970s with more universalistic proposals such as the negative income tax.[12] Thus, in one of the great perversities of recent social policy, a significant benefit for low-wage workers with children could, and did, isolate "hard core," or "long-term" welfare dependents as a separate class of poor people and an independent target for punitive behavioral reforms—a consequence, had it not been so devoid of political analysis, poverty knowledge might have seen coming in the "divide and conquer" strategy as well as in Ronald Reagan's successful efforts to push the working poor off the welfare rolls. With the EITC expansion, but none of the other "make work pay" proposals in place, the administration had paved the way for yet another round of welfare reform that was more concerned about ending the "dependency" of poor women and their children than with reducing their poverty rates.

To be sure, Ellwood's initial vision of "ending welfare as we know it" was far different from the legislation Clinton eventually signed. For starters, in his version the "make work pay" proposals would precede the work of reform, and would be supplemented by health care coverage and the government guarantee of child support payments when absent parents could not pay. Only then should the government replace AFDC with a system of time-limited "transitional" assistance that combined temporary income support with a wide array of education, training, job placement, and work experience assistance to improve recipients' chances of making it in the paid labor force. AFDC's replacement would be generous with work-related supports such as child care, medical coverage, and transportation assistance, while sending a clear message that long-term cash assistance was not an option and that the government expected responsible behavior in return. At the end of two years or so of transitional assistance, recipients would either be off the dole and self-supporting, or they would be required to accept a government job at minimum wage—a feature of Ellwood's plan that later became known as "soft" time limits because it did not envision cutting people off from all forms of public assistance, as current law prescribes. For its part in upholding the "contract," the government would transform the organizational culture of welfare offices to make them job and training centers rather than check-writing and application processing sites. It would also spend substantially more money on work and training (as much as $16 billion, in addition to the EITC expansion) as an investment that would later yield taxpayer returns.[13] This was the vision that Ellwood, Bane, and other social scientists at ASPE brought to the table when they sat down with their counterparts on the administration's thirty-two-member interagency working group to hammer out a legislative proposal for welfare reform. It survived, albeit in a much watered-down version, to become the basis of the legislative proposal the administration finally unveiled in June 1994—which lacked, among other things, any mention of government child support assurance or guaranteed jobs, and had been scaled back to $10 billion in additional spending to be financed with other social program cuts. Ellwood professed himself "proud" of the Clinton proposal, even though he admittedly had lost many internal battles along the way.[14] By then, months before the Republican takeover, he and other poverty experts had already come up against the political pressures that would undermine their reform vision, and move the entire conversation further and further to the right.

One set of pressures came from widespread, deep-seated, and bipartisan opposition to spending more money, particularly on the undeserving poor—opposition that had thwarted many a past reform effort but that had become institutionalized in the post-Keynesian orthodoxy of the Reagan-Bush years. The Budget Law of 1990 forbade Congress from approving new spending without identifying an offsetting source of revenue—which meant higher taxes, or cuts in other parts of a social welfare budget that had already cut low-income programs to the bone. Clinton, though, was unwilling either to raise taxes for welfare or to touch such widely popular benefits as Social Security or home mortgage deduction rates. This left administration reformers in the truly absurd position of raiding Food Stamps, as well as immigrant, emergency shelter, and disability benefits for the sake of moving welfare mothers off the rolls—measures eventually avoided or minimized in the Clinton proposal, but restored and vastly expanded in the cost-cutting Republican legislation that eventually did pass.[15] Underlying the money struggle was a deeper political problem for the poverty experts, partly captured in Ellwood's personal realization that "only a tiny handful of people in the White House" really cared.[16] It was not just that the poverty experts lacked power in the administration, or that they represented a constituency that had no political standing at all. They were operating at cross-purposes with the overriding direction of an economic policy that made deficit reduction, low inflation, and deregulated global markets its primary goals, and that consistently avoided active measures to reach full employment and real, evenly distributed wage growth.[17] The contrast to the Kennedy and Johnson administrations could not have been more stark. Then, it was the Council of Economic Advisers calling for a war against poverty, with an economic policy of faster growth and full employment as its centerpiece. Now, administration poverty warriors were mostly confined to the second tier of the secretariat, and their most visible policy vehicle was not macroeconomic policy but welfare reform.

A second, enormously complicating set of pressures came from the fact that the "transformation" from welfare to work was already happening in the states. That was because of provisions in the Family Support Act of 1988, which, in addition to creating the Job Opportunities and Basic Skills Training (JOBS) program, allowed states to apply for federal waivers so that they might experiment with new approaches to getting people off the rolls and into jobs. At the time this carried something of a triumph for poverty experts: playing off the success of earlier MDRC research, the legislation required experimental design and random assignment in state-to-state JOBS evaluations, and imposed similar standards on waiver requests. In application, though, the waiver provision created a gigantic Pandora's box for federal reformers, and undermined the authority of expertise. First, it put local officials and legislatures in the limelight as policy innovators—given the pressures on state budgets, hardly a recipe for scientific reform. Although most waiver requests actually eased eligibility restrictions on poor families, they simultaneously sought permission for stricter mandates on participants, including immediate work-for-welfare, time limits on eligibility, and benefit reductions or absolute cutoffs for those who failed to "play by the rules." As welfare rolls began to swell in the early 1990s, state waiver requests increasingly turned to benefit cuts and to the "work first" model of reform, despite widely available evidence that low-cost, immediate placement programs did little to raise earnings and job security for the poor. Second, the waiver program opened the door to a flood of well-publicized "new paternalist" proposals from socially conservative governors, who in turn pushed to include them in federal-level reform. Wisconsin's "Learnfare" punished teenagers (and their families) for not attending school, while "Bridefare" rewarded young parents for getting married and penalized them for having babies while on the dole. In several states the so-called "family cap" reduced or refused benefits for additional children born to any mother on AFDC—defying reams of empirical studies showing little connection between welfare and higher single-parent birthrates.[18] That Clinton welfare officials had approved these "new paternalist" waivers only increased growing pressure from congressional conservatives, who themselves had declared war on illegitimacy and irresponsibility by including both family caps and strict time limits in their proposals for reform. Over expert objections, family caps made it into the Clinton administration's proposal, as an option for the states. So did "hard," or absolute time limits on mandatory work programs, but only for the most recalcitrant recipients, who continually refused to follow the rules.[19]

A third pressure bedeviling the poverty experts was the unrelenting push to move what was already a conservative, new-Democrat kind of proposal further to the ideological right—to prove, that is, that the administration was just as "tough" if not "tougher" on work, illegitimacy, and dependency than Republicans who were outdoing themselves with proposals to push people off the rolls. There is no question that this pressure intensified profoundly with the Republican electoral triumphs of 1994. Nor that the move toward devolution, cost-cutting, federal withdrawal, and mandatory absolute time limits gained momentum on the Republican watch. But all along, at least the seeds of this rightward pressure had been built into the logic of mainstream social scientific reform. That logic, after all, had defined long-term dependency and individual behavior as the problem, effectively dismissed any notion of legitimate entitlement in favor of individual responsibility, and, with the unquestioned assumption that it was always, inherently better for the able-bodied to work in the low-wage labor market than to rely on welfare for support, had subordinated the goal of fighting poverty to the more politically palatable welfare reform. That logic, too, drew social scientists into a major effort to "end welfare [dependency] as we know it" when the 1988 Family Support Act—greeted at the time as "landmark" legislation—had arguably provided at least the infrastructure to "transform" AFDC into a work and training program without ending its guarantee of federal protection for families in need. Why, indeed, with an economy barely out of recession and worsening labor market conditions for the majority of the working class, would poverty experts continue to fixate on welfare as the target of reform?

In reality, many poverty experts did not. For economists especially, wage stagnation and income inequality continued to be the big story of the early 1990s, leading some to call for at least modest "demand side," or labor market reforms.[20] The underclass debate, for all its problems, had reintroduced subjects like industrial restructuring, urban decline, and, especially after the Los

Angeles riots, racial discrimination into poverty discourse. Nevertheless, throughout its years of semi-exile, the poverty research establishment had put far more attention and energy into studying, evaluating, and experimenting with welfare than with strategies to reverse the growth in inequality, restore full employment at higher wages to the economy, stop low-end labor market decline—or even strategies to create jobs for all the welfare recipients they expected to move into the labor force. Nor had poverty analysts organized themselves to envision an alternative to the polarized, zero-sum political economy that, as their own research suggested, sustained low wages and high poverty rates. That was at least in part because, following the logic of analytic neutrality, the poverty research industry had developed a dependency problem of its own: a capacity, that is, to conform and respond to the shifting political agenda of the agencies it relied on for funding, but not to establish and gain support for an independent policy agenda for dealing with poverty at its roots.

Did social science end welfare as we know it? To say so would be a gross exaggeration of the political power of scientific knowledge. It would also ignore the powerfully orchestrated mobilization of political, ideological, and rhetorical forces against welfare mothers—the rhetoric had sunk so low by the 1990s as to introduce new variations on old subhuman analogies to congressional debate.[21] Indeed, by 1995 poverty knowledge had become an essential part of the polemic *against* Republican proposals, and up until the bitter end the analysts in ASPE were convinced that President Clinton would be swayed by their powerful evidence to veto the welfare repeal. But poverty knowledge had already played a central part, throughout the 1980s and 1990s, in the official redefinition of poverty as an individual pathology at a time when social and economic conditions were growing measurably worse. That this happened partly at the behest of a deeply conservative political regime did not make the experts less complicit; that it was couched in the language of scientific objectivity did not make it less of a political act. Coming as they did, then, near the end of a venture that should not have been started in the first place, the protests from poverty researchers came as too little, too late. Far from a triumph for poverty knowledge, the end of welfare was a humiliating defeat, less because politicians ignored than because they could find legitimation in liberal poverty expertise.

TOWARD A NEW POVERTY KNOWLEDGE

Much like the end of the War on Poverty, the end of welfare as we know it did not bring the production of poverty knowledge to a halt. To the contrary, poverty research remains heavily concentrated on welfare, mostly in the form of assessing what welfare repeal has meant for the poor. Nor has the end of welfare led major research organizations to rethink the basic outlines or the organization of poverty research; despite growing attention to the labor market prospects for welfare recipients, poverty research continues to concentrate overwhelmingly on the behavior and characteristics of the poor. Meanwhile, despite widely celebrated prosperity and a dramatic drop in the welfare rolls, officially measured poverty remains higher than it was for much of the economically stagnant 1970s, and even more for children. In this context, poverty knowledge offers an important reminder that the current political leadership has put far greater importance on ending "dependency" than on fighting poverty. The question remains, though, whether research that will no doubt be important to documenting the fate of the post-welfare poor is an adequate knowledge base for a more genuinely anti*poverty* policy—a knowledge base, that is, that ventures outside the constricted boundaries of what is now deemed to be politically feasible. For that, we must imagine a much different kind of poverty knowledge, altered in scope, in organization, in language, and above all in the way it defines the "poverty problem."

The single most important challenge for poverty knowledge in the post-welfare era is to put poverty on the national agenda as a legitimate *public* policy concern: not in the narrow sense of income deprivation, but as part of the larger problem of the steady and rapid growth of economic, political, and social inequality. Even more than some new policy "blueprint," meeting this challenge will require a basic reformulation of "the poverty problem" along several lines.

First, much like Progressive social investigation around the turn of the last century, current-day research faces the task of de-pauperizing poverty as a social problem at the outset, by making poverty knowledge a broad-guaged study of political economy rather than a narrow study of the poor. In shifting its focus from "dependency" to political economy, a new poverty knowledge would significantly expand the scope of inquiry, to examine the institutions, social and economic practices, work conditions, and especially the policy decisions that shape the economy and distribute economic opportunities. In so doing, it would open up a level of inquiry that has long been absent in poverty research: into markets as social and political as well as economic institutions, shaped by the relationships of class, gender, and race as much as by supply and demand; and into the historical, political and institutional origins of late-twentieth-century postindustrial capitalism that have generated such vast, and growing, inequalities of income and wealth. A new poverty knowledge would necessarily recognize class, gender, and race as legitimate "units of analysis"—not simply as demographic variables that can be isolated and controlled for, but as dimensions of social and economic stratification in their own right. Nor is it an inquiry that can rely so extensively on either the individualized household and administrative data or the model-building/hypothesis-testing approach that have become the common currency of poverty research. In a new poverty knowledge, factors now treated, if at all, as mere background—history, politics, public and private institutions, ideology—become much more the stuff of direct, and critical, scrutiny. Most of all, this is clearly not an inquiry that can be initiated with welfare "dependency" (or the mythical goal of post-welfare "self-sufficiency") as the central problematic. Far more fruitful, as a starting point, would be the problematic of work in the "new," post-welfare political economy, as a diminishing source of living wages and access to the requirements of social citizenship.

A second step toward reformulating "the poverty problem" in public consciousness is similarly to alter the lens of cultural analysis, this time to acknowledge the distorting effect of the "culture of poverty" and its variations, and to make poverty knowledge instead a study of the broader cultural dynamics that sustain, indeed encourage, social and economic inequality. The central concern in a new poverty knowledge would not be about whether poor people have a cultural affinity for poverty but about the cultural mechanisms for according status and privilege, deserving- and undeserving-ness, social value and denigration, based on class, gender, and race. At the same time, a reconstructed poverty knowledge would show greater appreciation of the role of social scientists as cultural brokers by declaring a moratorium on the stigmatizing language that riddles contemporary research with such loaded terms as "hard core," welfare "users," "recidivism," and "intergenerational transmission." On a deeper level this would also require thinking through the implications of such more benign-sounding terminology as "working poor," which not only plays into a sharp (and increasingly irrelevant) distinction between workers and welfare recipients, but, as a replacement for the term "working class," depoliticizes poor people by divorcing their interests in better wages and income from those of more organized labor groups. Equally important, a more culturally aware poverty knowledge would demand a more accurate but also a more humanistic and less distancing language that respects how poor people think of themselves—as citizens, workers, parents, and neighbors rather than as benighted, deviant, or somehow deficient "other" Americans.

A third task is to generate poverty knowledge within a far more diversified set of institutional arrangements, recognizing the limitations of the "research industry" model that continues to thrive on its ability to service government agencies and the existing policy debate. This is not simply a matter, as some would have it, of learning lessons from the far more effective policy think tanks of the Right. It is a matter of finding the institutional structure that can generate a genuinely independent and critical body of knowledge that aims to set rather than follow the agenda for policy debate. Crucial to this process is a willingness to break down the hierarchical relationship between social scientific ways of knowing and other forms of expertise—to recognize, that is, the legitimacy and importance of knowledge that is grounded in practice, in activism, and in the experience not only of material deprivation but of the everyday workings of the economy. This in turn requires a serious commitment from all sides to the difficult, even tedious, work of building long-term, collaborative relationships for setting as well as carrying out poverty research—a model that takes the production of knowledge out of or at least beyond traditional expert or academic venues and into a variety of communities.

Finally, a reconstructed poverty knowledge would acknowledge and embrace rather than deny its inherently political nature, not necessarily by adhering to a single, agreed-upon ideological alignment, but by opening up its usually buried interests and ideological assumptions to scrutiny and debate. For contemporary poverty knowledge in particular, that will require opening itself up to that part of the liberal tradition that has not been the prevailing voice: the part, that is, that has used poverty research to challenge and open up the ideological boundaries of liberalism rather than adhering to—thereby reaffirming—the preset boundaries of existing policy debates. It will also require poverty experts to come to terms with the role, and the potential, of knowledge as a political force—to move away from the existing model that relies so exclusively on building links to elite policy makers, and toward one that is willing to build links to social movements and ultimately to a much broader vision of political and economic reform.

Certainly this brief outline implies a significant departure from the current practice of poverty research—not just in substance, language, and organization, but in the way the "professors" relate to the "practitioners" and the "poor." It asks that researchers act as public intellectuals in a way that is neither customary nor rewarded in traditional social scientific venues. It asks, too, that recognized poverty experts relinquish the power and recognition that comes with an exclusive claim to objectivity, by opening knowledge to other forms of learning and experience. And it asks that they be explicit about their own ideological assumptions and interests as a way of improving poverty knowledge. It is worth recalling, then, that a reconstructed poverty knowledge has much in past and contemporary research to build on. Progressive Era poverty knowledge, for all its rudimentary methods and prejudices, offered at least the elements of a broad framework for investigating class, race, and gender inequities as problems of political economy. Additionally, a now significant body of economic research has documented the growing inequality of income and wealth. Community-based and ethnographic research, while eclipsed by the nationally representative survey, continues to offer a model not only for challenging the atomized vision of analytic poverty knowledge but also for making research a more genuinely collaborative enterprise. And a great deal of anthropological and historical research has looked beyond the wall of cultural "pathology" to investigate the wide variety of cultural, political, and community-building strategies in poor and working-class communities. These are the building blocks for a genuinely different kind of poverty knowledge, one that is less devoted to changing poor people than to a genuinely progressive struggle against inequality.

Improbable though it may seem, the late twentieth century may yet prove to be a propitious historical moment for making "the poverty problem" a matter of public and political consciousness without isolating and stigmatizing the poor—thanks, however perversely, to the end of welfare and the growth of inequality. For if welfare repeal makes it more difficult to blame poverty on "dependency," it also lays bare the reality that work is no guarantee out of poverty. So, too, amidst the vast inequities of late twentieth-century prosperity, is there an opening to draw attention to the maldistribution of wealth, power, and opportunity, and to the price of tolerating such yawning social disparities. Recognizing these as core issues in poverty is the first step toward the larger project of imagining, organizing, and mobilizing a new poverty knowledge.

Notes

Introduction

1. Daniel T. Rodgers, *Atlantic Crossings: Social Politics in a Progressive Age* (Cambridge, Mass.: Harvard University Press, 1998).

2. As noted in chapter 9, the "causes, consequences, and cures" formulation is very much a product of the War on Poverty, conveying as it does the notion that poverty could be routed out with the help of applied research.

3. Peter Edelman, "The Worst Thing Bill Clinton Has Done," *The Atlantic Monthly, March* 1997, 43–58.

4. Laurence Lynn, "Ending Welfare Reform As We Know It," *The American Prospect*, Fall 1993, 83–92.

5. Charles Murray, *Losing Ground: American Social Policy, 1950–1980* (New York: Basic Books, 1984).

6. For a discussion of the connection between the "new liberalism" and social investigation, see Michael J. Lacey and Mary O. Furner, "Social Investigation, Social Knowledge, and the State: An Introduction," in Michael J. Lacey and Mary O. Furner, eds., *The State and Social Investigation in Britain and the United States* (New York: Cambridge University Press, 1993), 3–62.

7. David Callahan, "State Think Tanks on the Move," *The Nation*, October 12, 1998, 15–19.

8. The notion that poverty exists as a "paradox" in the land of plenty was not itself new or unique to the 1960s. In earlier, and especially in Progressive Era renditions, however, the "paradox" was a way of drawing attention to the maldistribution of wealth or some other systemic flaw attributable to unregulated capitalism, rather than a way of drawing attention to the anomalous, pitiable status of the poor. See, for a particularly influential statement of the poverty paradox, Henry George, *Progress and Poverty*, Fiftieth Anniversary Edition (New York: Robert Schalkenbach Foundation, 1948).

Chapter 1
Origins

1. Daniel T. Rodgers, *Atlantic Crossings: Social Politics in a Progressive Age* (Cambridge, Mass.: Harvard University Press, 1998).

2. On the challenge to laissez-faire in the early years of professional social science, see Dorothy Ross, *The Origins of American Social Science* (New York: Cambridge, 1991), 53–140; Mary O. Furner, *Advocacy and Objectivity: A Crisis in the Professionalization of American Social Science, 1865–1905* (Lexington: University Press of Kentucky, 1975); Thomas L. Haskell, *The Emergence of Professional Social Science: The American Social Science Association and the Nineteenth-Century Crisis of Authority* (Urbana: University of Illinois Press, 1977); and William Leach, *True Love and Perfect Union: The Feminist Reform of Sex and Society* (New York: Basic Books, 1980), 297–300.

3. William Graham Sumner, *What Social Classes Owe to Each Other* (New York: Harper and Brothers, 1883).

4. On the "new economics," see Furner, *Advocacy and Objectivity*; Rodgers, *Atlantic Crossings*, chap. 3; and Ross, *Origins of Social Science*, 98–122.

5. Michael J. Lacey, "The World of the Bureaus: Government and the Positivist Project in the Late Nineteenth Century," and Mary O. Furner, "The Republican Tradition and the New Liberalism: Social Investigation, State Building, and Social Learning in the Gilded Age," in Michael J. Lacey and Mary O. Furner, eds. *The State and Social Investigation in Britain and the United States* (New York: Cambridge University Press, 1993), 127–70, 197–235.

6. Robert H. Bremner, *From the Depths: The Discovery of Poverty in the United States* (New York: New York University Press, 1956), 123–39.

7. Martin Bulmer, Kevin Bales, and Kathryn Kish Sklar, eds., *The Social Survey in Historical Perspective, 1880–1940* (Cambridge and New York: Cambridge University Press, 1991), 19.

8. For an extended discussion of Booth and *Life and Labour*, see Gertrude Himmelfarb, *Poverty and Compassion: The Moral Imagination of the Late Victorians* (New York: Alfred A. Knopf, 1991), chaps. 6–12. On Booth's old-age pension and labor colony proposals, see Rodgers, *Atlantic Crossings*, 213–14, 229–31.

9. Charles Booth, *Life and Labour of the People of London, First Series: Poverty* (London and New York: Macmillan and Co., 1892–97; reprint ed., New York: AMS Press, 1970), 33.

10. Himmelfarb, *Poverty and Compassion*, 107–20; Judith R. Walkowitz, *City of Dreadful Delight: Narratives of Sexual Danger in Late-Victorian London* (Chicago: University of Chicago Press, 1992), 30–38.

11. Residents of Hull House, *Hull House Maps and Papers* (New York and Boston: Thomas Y. Crowell & Co., 1895; reprint ed., New York: Arno Press, 1970), 11–12.

12. For an extended comparison of Booth and *Hull House Maps and Papers*, see Kathryn Kish Sklar, "Hull-House Maps and Papers: Social Science as Women's Work in the 1890s," in Bulmer, Bales, and Sklar, *The Social Survey in Historical Perspective, 1880–1940*, 122–24.

13. *Hull House Maps and Papers*, 15–19.

14. Ibid., 13.

15. Booth, *Life and Labour*, 4; Bulmer, Bales, and Sklar, *The Social Survey in Historical Perspective*, 23–25. On the institutional climate for generating policy knowledge, see Mary O. Furner, "Knowing Capitalism: Public Investigation and the Labor Question in the Long Progressive Era," in Mary O. Furner and Barry Supple, eds., *The State and Economic Knowledge: The American and British Experiences* (New York: Cambridge University Press, 1990), 241–86.

16. On the BLS and labor statistics, see Furner, "Knowing Capitalism," 246–47. On Kelley's career, see Sklar, "Hull-House Maps and Papers" and, for a more extended discussion, see Sklar, *Florence Kelley and the Nation's Work: The Rise of Women's Political Culture, 1830–1900* (New Haven: Yale University Press, 1995).

17. Addams quoted in *Hull House*, 184. Robyn Muncy, *Creating a Female Dominion in American Reform, 1890–1935* (New York: Oxford University Press, 1991), 3–37; Ellen Fitzpatrick, *Endless Crusade: Women Social Scientists and Progressive Reform* (New York: Oxford University Press, 1990), 71–91. On the settlement house

movement more generally, see Mina Carson, *Settlement Folk: Social Thought and the American Settlement Movement, 1885–1930* (Chicago: University of Chicago Press, 1990) and Allen F. Davis, *Spearheads for Reform: The Social Settlements and the Progressive Movement, 1890–1914* (New York: Oxford University Press, 1967).

18. On the Working People's Social Science Club, see the chapter Jane Addams devotes to "A Decade of Economic Discussion," in her memoir *Twenty Years at Hull House* (New York: The New American Library, 1961), 133–47. On Jane Addams and social science, see Dorothy Ross, "Gendered Social Knowledge: Domestic Discourse, Jane Addams, and the Possibilities of Social Science," in Helene Silberberg, ed., *Gender and American Social Science: The Formative Years* (Princeton: Princeton University Press, 1998), 235–64.

19. A good example of this is Isabel Eaton, who contributed her comparative study of cloakmakers to the Hull House volume as a young fellow of the College Settlement Association and a novice researcher—the essay was published after considerable revision in response to Ely's review—moving from there to become assistant to DuBois for his *The Philadelphia Negro* (Philadelphia: University of Pennsylvania Press, 1899; reprint ed., 1996), for which she conducted and published a pioneering study of black domestic service, the basis of her Master's degree at Columbia University. Similarly, Hull House residence proved excellent preparation for Edith Abbott, Sophonisba Breckinridge, and other women social scientists trained at the University of Chicago who embarked on ambitious surveys of Chicago housing and working conditions in careers that combined research and reform. Fitzpatrick, *Endless Crusade*, 166–200. For discussions of later settlement house research activity, see Mary Kingsbury Simkovitch, *Neighborhood: My Story of Greenwich House* (New York: W.W. Norton, 1938), 150–51; and Daniel J. Walkowitz, *Working with Class: Social Workers and the Politics of Middle Class Identity* (Chapel Hill: University of North Carolina Press, 1999), 38–39.

20. *Hull House Maps and Papers*, 12–13, 21; Sklar, "Hull-House Maps and Papers," 126; Ross, "Gendered Social Knowledge," 243–49.

21. *Hull House Maps and Papers*, vii–viii.

22. Ibid., 14.

23. Quoted in Fitzpatrick, *Endless Crusade*, 191.

24. Addams, *Hull House Maps and Papers*, 183–204.

25. Addams, *Twenty Years at Hull House*, chaps. 8–9; *Hull House Maps and Papers*, 183–204.

26. *Hull House Maps and Papers*, 22.

27. B. Seebohm Rowntree, *Poverty: A Study of Town Life* (London and New York: Macmillan and Company, 1901; reprint ed., New York: Howard Fertig, 1971), 117–51, 152–54, 176–80.

28. Robert Hunter, *Poverty* (New York: The Macmillan Company, 1904; reprint ed., New York: Harper Torchbooks, 1964), 11–17. For a discussion of Hunter, see James T. Patterson, *America's Struggle Against Poverty, 1900–1994* (Cambridge, Mass.: Harvard University Press, 1994), 6–15.

29. Hunter, *Poverty*, chap. 2.

30. DuBois, *The Philadelphia Negro*, 1–2.

31. David Levering Lewis, *W.E.B. DuBois: Biography of a Race, 1868–1919* (New York: Henry Holt and Company, 1993), 190; Martin Bulmer, "W.E.B. DuBois as a

Social Investigator: *The Philadelphia Negro*, 1899," in Bulmer, Bales, and Sklar, *Social Survey in Historical Perspective*, 170–88.

32. DuBois, *Philadelphia Negro*, 178.

33. For migration figures, see DuBois, *Philadelphia Negro*, 47–55. On the neighborhood and its transformation, see Michael B. Katz and Thomas J. Sugrue, "The Context of *The Philadelphia Negro*," in Michael B. Katz and Thomas J. Sugrue, eds., *W.E.B. DuBois, Race, and the City: The Philadelphia Negro and Its Legacy* (Philadelphia: University of Pennsylvania Press, 1998), 4–17.

34. For background on the study and DuBois's attitudes towards his sponsors, see Katz and Sugrue, "The Context of *The Philadelphia Negro*"; Lewis, *W.E.B. DuBois*, 179–90; Bulmer, "W.E.B. DuBois as a Social Investigator," 173–76; DuBois, *Dusk of Dawn: An Essay Toward an Autobiography of a Race Concept* (New York: Harcourt Brace, 1940), 57–63.

35. DuBois, *Philadelphia Negro*, 2–3.

36. Ibid., 2.

37. St. Clair Drake and Horace R. Cayton, *Black Metropolis: A Study of Negro Life in a Northern City* (Chicago: University of Chicago Press, 1945).

38. DuBois, *Philadelphia Negro*, 108–9, 147–63.

39. Ibid., 110–11.

40. Ibid., 140–46.

41. Ibid., 394.

42. Ibid., 170–72.

43. Ibid., 273–75.

44. Ibid., 284.

45. Ibid., 146.

46. Katz and Sugrue, "The Context of *The Philadelphia Negro*," 16–17. On race and the settlement movement more generally, see Elizabeth Lasch-Quinn, *Black Neighbors: Race and the Limits of Reform in the American Settlement House Movement* (Chapel Hill: University of North Carolina Press, 1993).

47. For an excellent discussion of the reviews, including those that did recognize his contributions to political economy, see Katz and Sugrue, "The Context of *The Philadelphia Negro*," 26–30. On the segregated patterns of reform networks, see Lasch-Quinn, *Black Neighbors*, and Linda Gordon, "Black and White Visions of Welfare: Women's Welfare Activism, 1890–1945," *Journal of American History* 78 (September 1991): 559–90.

48. On the more general neglect of *The Philadelphia Negro*, see Lewis, *W.E.B. DuBois*, 205–8; and Bulmer, "W.E.B. DuBois as a Social Investigator," 183–86.

49. Katz, *Shadow of the Poorhouse*, 165.

50. Linda Gordon, *Pitied But Not Entitled: Single Mothers and the History of Welfare* (New York: The Free Press, 1994), 88–92; Muncy, *Female Dominion*, Introduction, 38–65.

51. On the rise of corporate philanthropy, and its role in research and public policy, see Ellen Condliffe Lagemann, ed., *Philanthropic Foundations: New Scholarship, New Possibilities* (Bloomington and Indianapolis: Indiana University Press, 1999); Judith Sealander, *Private Wealth and Public Life: Foundation Philanthropy and the Shaping of American Social Policy from the Progressive Era to the New Deal* (Baltimore: Johns Hopkins University Press, 1997); David C. Hammack and Stanton Wheeler, *Social*

Science in the Making: Essays on the Russell Sage Foundation, 1907–1972 (New York: Russell Sage Foundation, 1994); Ellen Condliffe Lagemann, *The Politics of Knowledge: The Carnegie Corporation, Philanthropy, and Public Policy* (Middletown, Conn.: Wesleyan University Press, 1989); and John F. McClymer, *War and Welfare: Social Engineering in America, 1890–1925* (Westport, Conn.: Greenwood Press, 1980).

52. John M. Glenn, Lillian Brandt, and F. Emerson Andrews, *The Russell Sage Foundation, 1907–1946*, 2 vols. (New York: Russell Sage Foundation, 1947), vol. 1: 30, 24.

53. Glenn, Brandt, and Andrews, *Russell Sage Foundation*, vol. 1: 14–17; McClymer, *War and Welfare*, 50–52.

54. The Pittsburgh Survey was published in four monographs and two edited volumes, including Elizabeth Beardsley Butler, *Women and the Trades, Pittsburgh 1907–1908* (1909); Margaret Byington *Homestead: The Households of a Mill Town* (1910); Crystal Eastman, *Work-accidents and the Law* (1910); John Fitch, *The Steelworkers* (1910); and Paul U. Kellogg, ed., *The Pittsburgh District: Civic Frontage* (1914) and *Wage-Earning Pittsburgh* (1914). Several of the volumes have since been reprinted. The Survey is discussed at length in Maurine W. Greenwald and Margo Anderson, eds., *Pittsburgh Surveyed: Social Science and Social Reform in the Early Twentieth Century* (Pittsburgh: University of Pittsburgh Press, 1996). See also Steven R. Cohen, "The Pittsburgh Survey and the Social Survey Movement: A Sociological Road Not Taken," in Bulmer, Bales, and Sklar, *The Social Survey in Historical Perspective*, 245–68.

55. Sealander, *Private Wealth and Public Life*, 29.

56. Ibid., 109–11; Walkowitz, *Working with Class*, 58–9; Glenn, Brandt, and Andrews, *Russell Sage Foundation*, vol. 1: 125–35.

57. On van Kleeck's fascinating career, see Guy Alchon, "Mary van Kleeck and Social-Economic Planning," *Journal of Policy History* 3, no. 1 (1991): 1–23 and "The 'Self-Applauding Sincerity' of Overreaching Theory, Biography as Ethical Practice, and the Case of Mary van Kleeck," in Siverberg, ed., *Gender and American Social Science*, 293–325. For a description of the Women's Work-Industrial Studies Department, see Glenn, Brandt, and Andrews, *Russell Sage Foundation*, vol. 1:152–70.

58. Elizabeth Beardsley Butler, *Women and the Trades* (New York: Russell Sage Foundation, 1909), 24–27, 337–50.

59. Margaret Byington, *Homestead: The Households of a Mill Town* (New York: Russell Sage Foundation, 1910), 74–79, 107, 171–84.

60. Sealander, *Private Wealth and Public Life*,146.

61. Van Kleeck quoted in Glenn, Brandt, and Andrews, *Russell Sage Foundation*, vol. 1: 169.

62. Ewa Morawska, "The Immigrants Pictured and Unpictured in the Pittsburgh Survey," in Greenwald and Anderson, *Pittsburgh Surveyed*, 221–41; Paul Krause, *The Battle for Homestead, 1880–1892: Politics, Culture, and Steel* (Pittsburgh: University of Pittsburgh Press, 1992), 218–19. For a more sympathetic interpretation of the surveyors' views of immigrants, see Steven R. Cohen, "The Failure of Fair Wages and the Death of Labor Republicanism: The Ideological Legacy of the Pittsburgh Survey," in Greenwald and Anderson, eds., *Pittsburgh Surveyed*, 62–65.

63. DuBois, *Philadelphia Negro*, 310–15. On DuBois and cultural uplift, see Kevin Gaines, *Uplifting the Race: Black Leadership, Politics, and Culture in the Twentieth Century* (Chapel Hill: University of North Carolina Press, 1995).

64. Greenwald and Anderson, *Pittsburgh Surveyed*, 8–9, 12–13.

65. Stephen Turner, "The Pittsburgh Survey and the Survey Movement: An Episode in the History of Expertise," in Greenwald and Anderson, *Pittsburgh Surveyed*, 35–49; Ellen Condliffe Lagemann, *Politics of Knowledge*, 51–70; Martin Bulmer, "The Decline of the Survey Movement and the Rise of American Empirical Sociology," in Bulmer, Bales, and Sklar, *The Social Survey in Historical Perspective*, 291–315.

66. Martin Bulmer, *The Chicago School of Sociology: Institutionalization, Diversity, and the Rise of Sociological Research* (Chicago: University of Chicago Press, 1984), 1–11; Noel A. Cazenave, "Chicago Influences on the War on Poverty," *Journal of Policy History* 5, no. 1 (1993): 52–68.

67. William I. Thomas and Florian Znaniecki, *The Polish Peasant in Europe and America*, abridged, with an introduction by Eli Zaretsky (Urbana: University of Illinois Press, 1984).

68. On Thomas, see Dorothy Ross, *Origins of American Social Science*, 347–57.

69. Thomas and Znaniecki, *Polish Peasant*, 9.

70. Ibid., 226–33.

71. Ibid., 289; Ross, *Origins of American Social Science*, 354–56. On Polish and other immigrant groups in Chicago, including the various sources of resistance to Americanization, see Lizabeth Cohen, *Making a New Deal: Industrial Workers in Chicago, 1919–1939* (New York: Cambridge University Press, 1990).

72. Thomas and Znaniecki, *Polish Peasant*, 249–50.

73. On Thomas's relationship with Addams, see Mary Jo Deegan, *Jane Addams and the Men of the Chicago School, 1892–1918* (New Brunswick, N.J.: Transaction Books, 1988), 129–32.

74. Bulmer, *The Chicago School of Sociology*, 39; Muncy, *Female Dominion*, 66–92.

75. For Park's early career, see Fred Matthews, *The Quest for an American Sociology: Robert E. Park and the Chicago School* (Montreal: McGill-Queen's University Press, 1977), 1–84.

76. Robert E. Park, "The City: Suggestions for the Investigation of Human Behavior in the Urban Environment," in Robert E. Park, Ernest W. Burgess, and Roderick D. McKenzie, *The City* (University of Chicago Press, 1925), 38. For more on Park and his attitude toward reform, see Matthews, *Robert E. Park*, 97–104; Ross, *Origins of American Social Science*, 357–58; Stow Persons, *Ethnic Studies at Chicago, 1905–45* (Urbana: University of Illinois Press, 1987), 29–30; Deegan, *Jane Addams and the Men of the Chicago School*, 152–59.

77. Bulmer, *Chicago School of Sociology*, 68–74; Deegan, *Jane Addams and the Men of the Chicago School*, 144–52.

78. On the Laura Spelman Rockefeller Memorial and its impact on social science, see Martin Bulmer, "Support for Sociology in the 1920s: The Laura Spelman Rockefeller Memorial and the Beginnings of Modern, Large-Scale Sociological Research in the University," *American Sociologist* 17 (November 1982): 185–92; Barry D. Karl and Stanley N. Katz, "The American Private Philanthropic Foundation and the Public Sphere," *Minerva* 19 (Summer 1981): 236–71; Mark C. Smith, *Social Science in the Crucible: The American Debate Over Objectivity and Purpose, 1918–1941* (Durham: Duke University Press, 1994), 25–27. For a list of RSF grants, see Glenn, Brandt, and Anderson, *Russell Sage Foundation*, vol. 2: 685–97.

79. Ross, *Origins of American Social Science*, 359; Matthews, *Robert E. Park*, 130.

80. The principles of human ecology are laid out in Roderick D. McKenzie, "The Ecological Approach to the Study of the Human Community," in Park, Burgess, and McKenzie, *The City*, 63–79. See also Ross, *Origins of American Social Science*, 359–60; Persons, *Ethnic Studies at Chicago*, 60–64. On the concept of succession, see also Robert E. Park, "Succession, An Ecological Concept," *American Sociological Review* 1 (April 1936): 171–79.

81. Park, Burgess, and McKenzie, *The City*, 47, 4.

82. Ibid., 143.

83. Ibid., 50–56.

84. Ibid., 54.

85. Ibid., 45.

86. Ibid., 54.

87. Ibid., 31.

88. Hence, the title of Burgess's essay, "Can Neighborhood Work Have a Scientific Basis?"—he thought it could—in *The City*, 142–55.

89. For a more complete listing of significant Chicago school publications, see Bulmer, *Chicago School of Sociology*, 3–4.

90. Park, Burgess, and McKenzie, *The City*, 106, 110–11.

91. Bulmer, *Chicago School of Sociology*, 123–25.

92. Clifford R. Shaw and Henry D. McKay, *Juvenile Delinquency and Urban Areas* (Chicago: University of Chicago Press, 1942), 8–14.

93. Clifford R. Shaw et al., *Delinquency Areas* (Chicago: University of Chicago Press, 1929), 19–21, 205–6.

94. On the Chicago Area Project, see Shaw and McKay, *Juvenile Delinquency and Urban Areas*, 441–46; Steven Schlossman and Michael Sedlak, "The Chicago Area Project Revisited," Report prepared for the National Institute of Education (Santa Monica, Calif.: Rand Corporation, 1983); Robert Halpern, *Rebuilding the Inner City: A History of Neighborhood Initiatives to Address Poverty in the United States* (New York: Columbia University Press, 1995), 50–53; and Noel A. Cazenave, "Chicago Influences on the War on Poverty," 53–56.

95. On the Back of the Yards Neighborhood Council and Alinsky's critique of CAP, see Robert A. Slayton, *Back of the Yards: The Making of a Local Democracy* (Chicago: University of Chicago Press, 1986), 189–205; Saul D. Alinsky, "Community Analysis and Organization," *American Journal of Sociology* 46 (May 1941): 797–808.

96. For discussions of these links, see Alice O'Connor, "Community Action, Urban Reform, and the Fight Against Poverty: The Ford Foundation's Gray Areas Program," *Journal of Urban History*, 22 (July 1996): 586–625; Daniel Knapp and Kenneth Polk, *Scouting the War on Poverty: Social Reform Politics in the Kennedy Administration* (Lexington, Mass.: DC Heath, 1971), 25–42; Cazenave, "Chicago Influences on the War on Poverty."

Chapter 2
Poverty Knowledge as Cultural Critique

1. On the role of various Progressive intellectual networks in designing New Deal programs, see Daniel T. Rodgers, *Atlantic Crossings: Social Politics in a Progressive Age* (Cambridge, Mass.: Harvard University Press, 1998), chap. 10; Linda Gordon, *Pitied But Not Entitled: Single Mothers and the History of Welfare* (New York: Free

Press, 1994), 145–57, 167–72; Edward D. Berkowitz, *America's Welfare State: From Roosevelt to Reagan* (Baltimore: Johns Hopkins University Press, 1991), chap. 2; and Jess Gilbert, "Organic Intellectuals in the State: A Collective Biography of Midwestern Social Scientists in the New Deal Department of Agriculture," unpublished paper delivered at the Social Science History Association Meeting, October 1997.

2. E. Wight Bakke, *The Unemployed Worker* (New Haven: Yale University Press, 1940) and *Citizens Without Work* (New Haven: Yale University Press, 1940).

3. For discussions of the central issues that absorbed New Deal economic policy intellectuals, see Alan Brinkley, *The End of Reform: New Deal Liberalism in Recession and War* (New York: Knopf, 1995); and William J. Barber, "Government as a Laboratory for Economic Learning in the Years of the Democratic Roosevelt," in Mary O. Furner and Barry Supple, eds., *The State and Economic Knowledge: The American and British Experiences* (New York: Cambridge University Press, 1990), 103–37.

4. James T. Patterson, *America's Struggle Against Poverty: 1900–1994* (Cambridge, Mass.: Harvard University Press, 1994), 40–41.

5. On the legacy of the "two-tiered" nature of the U.S. welfare state, see Gordon, *Pitied But Not Entitled*, 287–306; Patterson, *America's Struggle Against Poverty*, 75–77; and Michael B. Katz, *In the Shadow of the Poorhouse: A Social History of Welfare in America* (New York: Basic Books, 1996), 242–55.

6. Robert S. Lynd and Helen Merrell Lynd, *Middletown: A Study in American Culture* (New York: Harcourt Brace Jovanovich, 1929). On Veblen, and his influence on the Lynds, see Dorothy Ross, *The Origins of American Social Science* (New York: Cambridge University Press, 1991), 204–16; and Mark C. Smith, *Social Science in the Crucible: The American Debate Over Objectivity and Purpose, 1918–1941* (Durham: Duke University Press, 1994), 133–34.

7. Richard Wightman Fox, "Epitaph for Middletown: Robert S. Lynd and the Analysis of Consumer Culture," in Richard Wightman Fox and T. J. Jackson Lears, eds., *The Culture of Consumption: Critical Essays in American History, 1880–1980* (New York: 1983), 106–18; Smith, *Social Science in the Crucible*, 128–32.

8. Lynd and Lynd, *Middletown*, 23–24.

9. Ibid., 76–89, 458, 486–87.

10. Ibid., 458–70, 497.

11. Robert S. Lynd and Helen Merell Lynd, *Middletown in Transition* (New York: Harcourt Brace, 1937), 72–73, 46.

12. Lynd and Lynd, *Middletown: A Study in American Culture* (1929), 499–500.

13. Lynd and Lynd, *Middletown in Transition* (1937), 102–43; Fox, "Epitaph for Middletown," 129–36.

14. On Lynd's consumer activism and its impact on his thinking about the social role of research, see Smith, *Social Science in the Crucible*, 145–52.

15. James West (pseud. for Carl Withers), *Plainville, USA* (New York: Columbia University Press, 1945), 259.

16. Lynd and Lynd, *Middletown*, vi.

17. Ellen Condliffe Lagemann, *The Politics of Knowledge: The Carnegie Corporation, Philanthropy, and Public Policy* (Chicago: University of Chicago Press, 1989), 154–58.

18. On Warner's early career, see Richard Gillespie, *Manufacturing Knowledge: A History of the Hawthorne Experiments* (New York: Cambridge University Press, 1991),

154–57. On the sources of funding for his fieldwork and his understanding of social class, see W. Lloyd Warner and Paul S. Lunt, *The Social Life of a Modern Community* (New Haven: Yale University Press, 1941), 1–7, 79–82. For an example of his later efforts to demonstrate the utility of his research for advertising, see W. Lloyd Warner, Marchia Meeker, and Kenneth Eells, *Social Class in America: The Evaluation of Status* (New York: Harper Torchbooks, 1960). For a statement about Warner's influence, see Herbert J. Gans, "Relativism, Equality, and Popular Culture," in Bennett M. Berger, ed., *Authors of Their Own Lives: Intellectual Autobiographies by Twenty American Sociologists* (Berkeley: University of California Press, 1990), 439–41.

19. For a description of Warner's measurement techniques, see Warner, Meeker, and Eells, *Social Class in America*, 34–43.

20. W. Lloyd Warner and Paul S. Lunt, *The Status System of a Modern Community* (New Haven: Yale University Press, 1942), 49; Warner and Lunt, *Social Life in a Modern Community*, 82.

21. W. Lloyd Warner, *The Social System of the Modern Factory* (New Haven: Yale University Press, 1947).

22. Warner et al., *Democracy in Jonesville: A Study of Quality and Inequality* (New York: Harper and Brothers, 1949), 294; Warner, *Modern Factory*, 188–89.

23. Warner, Meeker, and Eells, *Social Class in America*, 5.

24. Robert J. Havighurst et al., *Growing Up in River City* (New York: John Wiley and Sons, 1962), viii.

25. Allison Davis, "The Motivation of the Underprivileged Worker," in William F. Whyte, ed., *Industry and Society* (New York: McGraw Hill, 1946), 94.

26. Davis, *Social-Class Influences Upon Learning* (Cambridge, Mass.: Harvard University Press, 1948), 30.

27. Davis, "Underprivileged Worker," 86, 94, 104.

28. William F. Whyte, *Street Corner Society: The Social Structure of an Italian Slum*, rev. ed. (Chicago: University of Chicago Press, 1955), 272–75.

29. Allison Davis and John Dollard, *Children of Bondage: The Personality Development of Negro Youth in the Urban South* (Washington, D.C.: American Council on Education, 1940).

30. Allison Davis and Robert J. Havighurst, "Social Class and Color Differences in Child Rearing," *American Sociological Review* 11 (December 1946), 707; Allison Davis, "American Status Systems and the Socialization of the Child," *American Sociological Review* 6 (June 1941), 353.

31. Davis and Dollard, *Children of Bondage*.

32. Davis, *Social-Class Influences*, 32; "American Status Systems and the Socialization of the Child," 352.

33. Whyte, *Street Corner Society*, 274.

34. Ibid., 275.

35. Bakke, *Citizens Without Work*, 85–106, 109–225.

36. National Emergency Council, *Report on Economic Conditions of the South* (Washington, D.C.: 1938). On the significance of the report for federal intervention in the South, see Bruce J. Schulman, *From Cotton Belt to Sunbelt: Federal Policy, Economic Development, and the Transformation of the South* (New York: Oxford University Press, 1991), 50–62. For criticisms, see George B. Tindall, "The 'Colonial Economy' and the Growth Psychology: The South in the 1930s," *Southern Atlantic*

Quarterly 64 (1965): 465–77; Clarence Danhoff, "Four Decades of Thought on the South's Economic Problems," in Melvin C. Greenhut and W. Tate Whitman, eds., *Essays in Southern Economic Development* (Chapel Hill: University of North Carolina Press, 1964), 35–44; James C. Cobb, *The Selling of the South: The Southern Crusade for Industrial Development, 1936–1980* (Baton Rouge: Louisiana State University Press, 1982), 34. The Report has recently been reprinted in a compilation of related documents, entitled *Confronting Poverty in the Great Depression*, ed. with an introduction by David L. Carlton and Peter A. Coclanis (Boston: Bedford Books, 1996).

37. Daniel J. Singal, *The War Within: From Victorian to Modernist Thought in the South, 1919–1945* (Chapel Hill: University of North Carolina Press, 1981), 115–52, 302–38; Morton Sosna, *In Search of the Silent South: Southern Liberals and the Race Issue* (New York: Columbia University Press, 1977), 20–41, 60–87; Rupert Vance, Oral History, 1971, Columbia University Library, New York; Guy Johnson, *Research in Service to Society: The First Fifty Years of the Institute for Research in Social Science* (Chapel Hill: University of North Carolina Press, 1980). For a brief statement of regionalist goals, see Howard W. Odum, "The Way of the South," *Social Forces* 23 (March 1945): 258–68.

38. Rupert Vance, "Cotton Culture and Social Life and Institutions of the South," in John Shelton Reed and Daniel J. Singal, eds., *Regionalism and the South: Selected Papers of Rupert Vance* (Chapel Hill: University of North Carolina Press, 1982), v–xvi, 19–27.

39. Vance, "Cotton Culture and Social Life"; Arthur Raper, *Preface to Peasantry*, with a foreword by Will Alexander (Chapel Hill: University of North Carolina Press, 1936), 171–72.

40. Richard S. Kirkendall, *Social Scientists and Farm Politics in the Age of Roosevelt* (Columbia: University of Missouri Press, 1966); Sidney Baldwin, *Poverty and Politics: The Rise and Decline of the Farm Security Administration* (Chapel Hill: University of North Carolina Press, 1968).

41. Rupert Vance, *Human Geography of the South: A Study of Regional Resources and Human Adequacy* (Chapel Hill: University of North Carolina Press, 1932), 498–500; NEC, *Report*, 8.

42. Vance, *Human Geography*, 508–10.

43. NEC, *Report*, 61.

44. Margaret Jarman Hagood, *Mothers of the South: Portraiture of the White Tenant Farm Woman*, reissued with an introduction by Anne Firor Scott (Charlottesville: University of Virginia Press, 1996), 1–2, 242–44.

45. Ibid. 2, 4.

46. Vance, "Cotton Culture and Social Life," 20; Arthur Raper and Ira de Augustine Reid, *Sharecroppers All* (Chapel Hill: University of North Carolina Press, 1941), 79.

47. Tindall, "Growth Psychology"; Danhoff, "Four Decades of Thought on the South's Economic Problems," 51; Southern Regional Council, *The South: America's Economic Opportunity Number One* (Atlanta, 1945); Guy Johnson, Oral History, 1973, Columbia University Library, New York, 137–38; James C. Cobb, *The Selling of the South*, 34.

48. Rupert Vance, "The Regional Concept as a Tool for Social Research," in *Regionalism and the South*, 155–75; Michael B. Katz, *The Undeserving Poor: From the War*

on *Poverty to the War on Welfare* (New York: Pantheon, 1989), 52–65; Tindall, "Growth Psychology," 476; Alice O'Connor, "Modernization and the Rural Poor," in Cynthia Duncan, ed., *Rural Poverty in America* (New York: Auburn House, 1992), 215–33.

Chapter 3
From the Deep South to the Dark Ghetto

1. Gunnar Myrdal, *An American Dilemma: The Negro Problem and Modern Democracy* (New York: Harper and Row, 1944, rev. ed. 1962), 205. For a discussion of Du-Bois's efforts to lay the empirical groundwork for a comprehensive sociological understanding of the American Negro, see his *Dusk of Dawn* (New York: Harcourt Brace, 1940), 59–68.

2. Of course, the most renowned of the philanthropic studies of race during this period was Gunnar Myrdal's *American Dilemma* funded by the Carnegie Corporation, but several other foundations had earlier turned to race relations research as well. The idea for the Myrdal study originated in trustee discussions of how the foundation could expand on its educational work to deal with Negro problems, and specifically the potential for interracial conflict, in the North. Walter Jackson, *Gunnar Myrdal and America's Conscience: Social Engineering and Racial Liberalism, 1938–1987* (Chapel Hill: University of North Carolina Press, 1990), 16–26; Ellen Condliffe Lagemann, *The Politics of Knowledge: The Carnegie Corporation, Philanthropy, and Public Policy* (Chicago: University of Chicago Press, 1989), 123–46.

3. James R. Grossman, *Land of Hope: Chicago, Black Southerners, and the Great Migration* (Chicago: University of Chicago Press, 1989); William M. Tuttle, Jr., *Race Riot: Chicago in the Red Summer of 1919* (New York: Atheneum Press, 1977); Allan H. Spear, *Black Chicago: the Making of a Negro Ghetto, 1890–1920* (Chicago: University of Chicago Press, 1967).

4. This classic example of riot-inspired race relations research, directed by Chicago-trained sociologist Charles S. Johnson, was produced as a result of the Chicago race riot of 1919. Chicago Commission on Race Relations, *The Negro in Chicago: A Study of Race Relations and a Race Riot* (Chicago: University of Chicago Press, 1922). More than a decade later, following the Harlem riot of 1935, E. Franklin Frazier was appointed research director of an investigative commission appointed by New York Mayor Fiorello Laguardia, to produce *The Negro in Harlem: A Report on Social and Economic Conditions Responsible for the Outbreak of March 19, 1935* (New York: Arno Press, 1968). More recently, the Kerner Commission, appointed by President Lyndon B. Johnson to explain several consecutive summers of racial violence in the 1960s, drew on social scientific theory to portray blacks as the enraged, psychologically damaged victims of institutionalized white racism. For a discussion of the social science in the Kerner Commission report, see Ellen Herman, *The Romance of American Psychology: Political Culture in the Age of Experts* (Berkeley: University of California Press, 1995), 208–37.

5. On the influence of World War II and other factors on the sociology of race relations, see David W. Southern, *Gunnar Myrdal and Black-White Relations: The Use and Abuse of An American Dilemma, 1944–1969* (Baton Rouge: Louisiana State University Press, 1987), 52–54; St. Clair Drake and Horace R. Cayton, *Black Metropolis: A Study of Negro Life in a Northern City* (Chicago: University of Chicago Press, 1945; rev. ed.

1993), 762–67; E. Franklin Frazier, "Race Contacts and the Social Structure," *American Sociological Review* 14 (February 1949): 1–11.

6. Daryl Michael Scott, *Contempt and Pity: Social Policy and the Image of the Damaged Black Psyche, 1880–1996* (Chapel Hill: University of North Carolina Press, 1997), 62–66; Walter Jackson, *Gunnar Myrdal and the American Conscience*, 261–71; Lee D. Baker, *From Savage to Negro: Anthropology and the Construction of Race* (Berkeley: University of California Press, 1998), 127–87.

7. George M. Frederickson, *The Black Image in the White Mind: The Debate on Afro-American Character and Destiny, 1817–1914* (Middletown, Conn.: Wesleyan University Press, 1987), 330–31; Lee Baker, *From Savage to Negro*, 99–126; Allison Davis and John Dollard, *Children of Bondage: The Personality Development of Negro Youth in the Urban South* (Washington, D.C.: American Council on Education, 1940), 3–4.

8. Hortense Powdermaker, *After Freedom: A Cultural Study in the Deep South* (New York: Viking Press, 1939), xv–xvii. Powdermaker later wrote a fascinating description of her experience in Indianola in her autobiographical book, *Stranger and Friend: The Way of an Anthropologist* (New York: W.W. Norton, 1966), 129–205.

9. On the "liberal orthodoxy" and Myrdal's role in shaping it, see Jackson, *Gunnar Myrdal and America's Conscience*, 272–311; Stephen Steinberg, *Turning Back: The Retreat from Racial Justice in American Thought and Social Policy* (Boston: Beacon Press, 1995), 21–49.

10. Oliver Cromwell Cox, *Caste, Class and Race: A Study in Social Dynamics* (New York: Doubleday, 1948), 462–538.

11. For the most comprehensive statement of African/African American cultural continuity of the time, see Melville J. Herskovits, *The Myth of the Negro Past* (Boston: Beacon Press, 1941). For a brief overview of the scholarship on race relations on the eve of Myrdal's project, see Jackson, *Gunnar Myrdal and America's Conscience*, 94–106.

12. E. Franklin Frazier, *The Negro Family in the United States* (Chicago: University of Chicago Press, 1939; rev. and abridged ed. New York: The Dryden Press, 1948), 366; Charles S. Johnson, "The Present Status of Race Relations in the South," *Social Forces* 23 (October 1944): 27–32.

13. Robert E. Park, "Racial Assimilation in Secondary Groups," in *Race and Culture* (Glencoe, Ill.: Free Press, 1950), 204–20.

14. For Park's views on race, and how they changed over time, see Park, *Race and Culture*; E. Franklin Frazier, "Sociological Theory and Race Relations," *American Sociological Review* 12 (June 1947): 265–71; and Stow Persons, *Ethnic Studies at Chicago, 1905–45* (Urbana: University of Illinois Press, 1987), 60–64.

15. For comprehensive discussions of the 1919 riot, see Chicago Commission, *The Negro in Chicago*; and Tuttle, *Race Riot*. On the riot and the Commission response, see Drake and Cayton, *Black Metropolis*, 65–76; Persons, *Ethnic Studies at Chicago*, 64–67; Spear, *Black Chicago*, 201–22.

16. David Levering Lewis, *When Harlem Was in Vogue* (New York: Alfred A. Knopf, 1981), 45–49, 89–98, 125–29.

17. Richard Robbins, "Charles S. Johnson," in John E. Blackwell and Morris Janowitz, eds., *Black Sociologists: Historical and Contemporary Perspectives* (Chicago: University of Chicago Press, 1974), 60.

18. Chicago Commission on Race Relations, quoted in *Black Metropolis*, 71.

19. Charles S. Johnson, *Growing Up in the Black Belt: Negro Youth in the Rural South* (Washington, D.C.: American Council on Education, 1941), 47–52.

20. For background on Johnson's career, see Robbins, "Charles S. Johnson," 56–84; Walter Jackson, *Gunnar Myrdal and America's Conscience*, 102–3; Lewis, *When Harlem Was in Vogue*, 45–49.

21. E. Franklin Frazier, *The Negro Family in the United States*, 364.

22. Walter A. Jackson, "Between Socialism and Nationalism: The Young E. Franklin Frazier," *Reconstruction*, 1 (1991), 124–34; Jackson, *Gunnar Myrdal and the American Conscience*, 103–4, 225–27; G. Franklin Edwards, "E. Franklin Frazier," in Blackwell and Janowitz, *Black Sociologists*, 85–117; Scott, *Contempt and Pity*, 42–51, 74–76; Stowe Persons, *Ethnic Studies at Chicago*, 131–43.

23. E. Franklin Frazier, "The Changing Status of the Negro Family," *Social Forces* 9 (March 1931): 386–93.

24. E. Franklin Frazier, *The Negro Family in Chicago* (Chicago: University of Chicago Press, 1932).

25. For a more extended discussion of Frazier's view of the matriarchy as adaptive, see Scott, *Contempt and Pity*, 46–51.

26. Frazier, *The Negro Family in the United States*, 255.

27. Johnson, *Growing Up in the Black Belt*, 58–59.

28. E. Franklin Frazier, *Negro Youth at the Crossways* (Washington, D.C.: American Council on Education, 1940), 52; Johnson, *Black Belt*, 224–25.

29. Frazier, *The Negro Family in the United States*, 367.

30. For a discussion of how Frazier and other intellectuals at Howard University rejected cultural relativism, see Baker, *From Savage to Negro*, 168–87.

31. Jackson, *Gunnar Myrdal and America's Conscience*, 102–3.

32. W. Lloyd Warner, "American Caste and Class," *American Journal of Sociology*, 42 (September 1936): 234–37.

33. John Dollard, *Caste and Class in a Southern Town* (New Haven: Yale University Press, 1937), 171, chap. 7; Allison Davis, Burleigh B. Gardner, and Mary B. Gardner, *Deep South: A Social Anthropological Study of Caste and Class* (Chicago: University of Chicago Press, 1941), 38, 44; Powdermaker, *After Freedom*, 145–46.

34. Dollard, *Caste and Class*, 84–85, 391–92.

35. Ibid., 186–87.

36. Allison Davis and John Dollard, *Children of Bondage*. Other volumes in the series, all published by the American Council on Education, included Frazier, *Negro Youth at the Crossways*; W. Lloyd Warner, Buford Junker, and Walter A. Adams, *Color and Human Nature: Negro Personality Development in a Northern City* (1941); Johnson, *Growing Up in the Black Belt*; and Robert L. Sutherland, *Color, Class and Personality* (1942). For background on the studies and their purpose, see Scott, *Contempt and Pity*, 66–69.

37. Davis and Gardner, *Deep South*, 13, 234; Dollard, *Caste and Class*, 67; Powdermaker, *After Freedom*, 61–64, 148.

38. Frazier, "Race Contacts and the Social Structure," 3. For other contemporary critical reviews of the caste and class framework, see Cox, *Caste, Class and Race: A Study in Social Dynamics*, 462–538; and Maxwell R. Brooks, "American Class and Caste: An Appraisal," *Social Forces* 25 (December 1946): 207–11.

39. Elaine Ogden McNeil and Horace R. Cayton, "Research on the Urban Negro," *American Journal of Sociology* 47 (September 1941): 176–83. John H. Bracey, Jr., August Meier, and Elliott Rudwick, *The Black Sociologists: The First Half Century* (Belmont, Calif.: Wadsworth Publishing Company, 1971); Everett C. Hughes, "Introduction to the 1962 Edition," in Drake and Cayton, *Black Metropolis*, xxxvii.

40. Horace R. Cayton, *Long Old Road* (New York: Trident Press, 1965), 236–40.

41. Ibid, 238.

42. Drake and Cayton, *Black Metropolis*, xiii-xv, 89–97, 755, 760–64.

43. Richard Wright, "Introduction," in Drake and Cayton, *Black Metropolis*, xvii–xxxiv; Scott, *Contempt and Pity*, 98–99.

44. Drake and Cayton, "Author's Preface to the 1962 Edition," in *Black Metropolis*, xli.

45. Drake and Cayton, *Black Metropolis*, 17–18.

46. Ibid., 97.

47. Ibid., 206, 211.

48. Ibid., 390, 581–84, 593, 600–57, 718.

49. Ibid., 742–44, 753.

50. Significantly, W. Lloyd Warner came to a more pessimistic conclusion in an appendix to *Black Metropolis*, his only real visible presence in the book. Drawing attention to the discouraging parallels between South and North, Warner argued that despite evidence of black advancement in northern cities, "the *type* of status relations controlling Negroes and whites remains the same and continues to keep the Negro in an inferior and restricted position . . . there is still a status system of the caste type." The caste system was "deeply implanted in the lives of all of us," he went on to say, leaving off only with the typically rhetorical, but totally unspecified, observation that it would be up to the "next generation" to take on the "hard and painful" task of "destroying color-caste in the United States." Warner, appendix to Drake and Cayton, *Black Metropolis*, 781–82.

51. Jackson, *Gunnar Myrdal and America's Conscience*, 272–311; Steinberg, *Turning Back*, 42–43; Myrdal, *An American Dilemma*, 1023–24, 1035–64.

52. Myrdal, *An American Dilemma: The Negro Problem and Modern Democracy*, 667–705, 930–35.

53. Ibid., 928–29.

54. Ibid., 700–701.

55. Myrdal introduced the vicious circle as his "main hypothesis" in his chapter on economic inequality, then used it throughout. The accompanying "principle of cumulation" was explained more fully in an appendix. Myrdal, *An American Dilemma*, 207–9, 1065–70.

56. Ibid., 75–78, 208.

57. Ibid., 60–67, 589–92.

58. Jackson, *Gunnar Myrdal and America's Conscience*, 285. Reflecting more general trends in social science, this turn to psychology was encouraged, as Jackson notes, by the influence of postwar European emigrés, by federal agency and foundation funding priorities, and by a political climate that discouraged large-scale institutional reform. On the growing emphasis on psychological damage and its policy implications, see Scott, *Contempt and Pity*, esp. chaps. 5–7.

Chapter 4
Giving Birth to a "Culture of Poverty"

1. President's National Advisory Commission on Rural Poverty, *The People Left Behind* (Washington, D.C.: U.S. Government Printing Office, 1967).

2. James T. Patterson, *Grand Expectations: The United States, 1945–1974* (New York: Oxford University Press, 1996), 61–70; Robert H. Zieger, *American Workers, American Unions* (Baltimore: Johns Hopkins University Press, 1994), 138.

3. David M. Potter, *People of Plenty: Economic Abundance and the American Character* (Chicago: University of Chicago Press, 1954).

4. For a discussion of the retreat from a more expansive government role in economic management, see Alan Brinkley, *The End of Reform: New Deal Liberalism in Recession and War* (New York: Knopf, 1995). On the turn toward growth rather than redistribution, see Robert M. Collins, "The Emergence of Economic Growthmanship in the United States: Federal Policy and Economic Knowledge in the Truman Years," in Mary O. Furner and Barry Supple, eds., *The State and Economic Knowledge: The American and British Experiences* (New York: Cambridge University Press, 1990), 138–70. On labor's bargain, see Nelson Lichtenstein, "From Corporatism to Collective Bargaining: Organized Labor and the Eclipse of Social Democracy in the Postwar Era," in Steve Fraser and Gary Gerstle, eds., *The Rise and Fall of the New Deal Order, 1930–1980* (Princeton: Princeton University Press, 1989), 140–44.

5. Richard H. Pells, *The Liberal Mind in a Conservative Age: American Intellectuals in the 1940s and 1950s* (New York: Harper and Row, 1985), 130–47; Godfrey Hodgson, *America in Our Time* (Garden City, N.Y.: Doubleday, 1976), 67–98.

6. Simon Kuznets, *Shares of Upper Income Groups in Income and Savings* (New York: National Bureau of Economic Research, 1950).

7. John K. Galbraith, *The Affluent Society* (Boston: Houghton Mifflin, 1958), 96–97; Pells, *The Liberal Mind*, 186.

8. Lee Rainwater, Richard P. Coleman, and Gerald Handel, *Workingman's Wife: Her Personality, World and Life Style* (New York: MacFadden Books, 1962); "A Sociologist Looks at an American Community," *Life*, September 12, 1949, 108–19; W. Lloyd Warner, *Social Class in America: The Evaluation of Status* (New York: Harper Torchbooks, 1960).

9. On the functionalist view, see Kingsley Davis and Wilbert E. Moore, "Some Principles of Stratification," *American Sociological Review* 10 (1945): 242–49; R. J. Havighurst et al., *Growing Up in River City* (New York: John Wiley and Sons, 1962).

10. Patterson, *Grand Expectations*, 62–64.

11. Robert Lampman, "Recent Changes in Income Inequality Reconsidered," *American Economic Review* 44 (June 1954): 251–68; Jeffrey G. Williamson and Peter H. Lindert, *American Inequality: A Macroeconomic History* (New York: Academic Press, 1980), 82–94; Sheldon Danziger and Peter Gottschalk, eds., *Uneven Tides: Rising Inequality in America* (New York: Russell Sage Foundation, 1993), 6–8. Until the sharp fall-off of the 1980s, the income share of the bottom fifth (20%) of earners was just over 5%.

12. Mark J. Stern, "Poverty and Family Composition Since 1940," in Michael B. Katz, ed., *The "Underclass" Debate: Views from History* (Princeton: Princeton University Press, 1993), 237.

13. Jacqueline Jones, "Southern Diaspora: Origins of the Northern 'Underclass,' " and Thomas J. Sugrue, "The Structures of Urban Poverty: The Reorganization of Space and Work in Three Periods of American History," in Katz, *The "Underclass" Debate*, 27–54, 85–117.

14. Lichtenstein, "The Eclipse of Social Democracy," 144–45; Zieger, *American Workers, American Unions*, 137–47.

15. Claudia Goldin, *Understanding the Gender Gap: An Economic History of American Women* (New York: Oxford University Press, 1990), 62–63; Daphne Spain and Suzanne M. Bianchi, *Balancing Act: Motherhood, Marriage, and Employment among American Women* (New York: Russell Sage Foundation, 1996), 82, 108–12.

16. St. Clair Drake and Horace Cayton, *Black Metropolis* (Chicago: University of Chicago Press, 1993), 793–825.

17. For an extensive discussion of the influence of psychology in postwar social science and social policy, see Ellen Herman, *The Romance of Psychology: Political Culture in the Age of Experts* (Berkeley: University of California Press, 1995). See also Daryl Michael Scott, *Contempt and Pity: Social Policy and the Damaged Black Psyche, 1880–1996* (Chapel Hill: University of North Carolina Press, 1997), 71–74.

18. Ellen Condliffe Lagemann, *The Politics of Knowledge: The Carnegie Corporation, Philanthropy, and Public Policy* (Chicago: University of Chicago Press, 1989), 153–79.

19. Herman, *Romance of Psychology*, 126–30; Peter J. Seybold, "The Ford Foundation and the Triumph of Behavioralism in American Political Science," in Robert F. Arnove, ed., *Philanthropy and Cultural Imperialism* (Boston: G. K. Hall and Co.), 305–30; Gene M. Lyons, *The Uneasy Partnership: Social Science and the Federal Government in the Twentieth Century* (New York: Russell Sage Foundation, 1969), 277–82.

20. C. Wright Mills, *The Sociological Imagination* (New York: Oxford University Press, 1959).

21. The battle over whether the social sciences should have their own separate branch in the National Science Foundation is one of several episodes in which the legitimacy of the social sciences was called into question, while McCarthy-era congressional investigations into foundation giving used social scientists' support for "subversive" activity, including sociological inquiry, to call for stricter regulation. Lyons, *The Uneasy Partnership*, 124–36.

22. This was the language used by the Ford Foundation in its description of what it had designated as Area V, The Behavioral Sciences, in its original mandate. Statement on Area V, December 1951, Ford Foundation Archives, New York.

23. David C. Hammack and Stanton Wheeler, *Social Science in the Making: Essays on the Russell Sage Foundation, 1907–1972* (New York: Russell Sage Foundation, 1994), 24–25, 81–94; Guy Alchon, "Mary Van Kleeck and Social-Economic Planning," *Journal of Policy History* 3, no. 1 (1991): 1–23.

24. Herman, *Romance of Psychology*, 138.

25. See, for example, Margaret Mead and Martha Wolfenstein, eds., *Childhood in Contemporary Cultures* (Chicago: University of Chicago Press, 1955).

26. *The American Soldier: Adjustment During Army Life* was actually the first of four volumes published under the general series title of Studies in Social Psychology in World War II. Other titles in the series include *The American Soldier: Combat and*

Its Aftermath (vol. II), *Experiments in Mass Communication* (vol. III), and *Measurement and Prediction* (vol. IV) (New York: John Wiley and Sons, 1949).

27. Lagemann, *Politics of Knowledge*, 176–77; Frederick Osborn, foreword to *The American Soldier*, ix.

28. Alchon, "Mary Van Kleeck and Social-Economic Planning," 14.

29. Herman, *Romance of Psychology*, 48–53.

30. Theodor Adorno, *The Authoritarian Personality* (New York: Harper, 1950); Herman, *Romance of Psychology*, 58–60.

31. Margaret Mead, *And Keep Your Powder Dry: An Anthropologist Looks at America* (New York: William Morrow, 1942), 24.

32. Herman, *Romance of Psychology*, 124–25.

33. Seymour Martin Lipset, *Political Man* (New York: Doubleday, 1960), chap. 4. For early criticism of the idea, see S. M. Miller and Frank Riessman, "Working-Class Authoritarianism: A Critique of Lipset," and Lipset, "Working-Class Authoritarianism: A Reply to Miller and Riessman," *British Journal of Sociology* 12 (September 1961): 263–81. Within a few years the concept had come under extensive criticism on theoretical as well as methodological grounds, and Lipset himself seemed to back away from it. See, for example, the brief, dismissive discussion of authoritarianism in Lipset and Reinhard Bendix, *Social Mobility in Industrial Society* (Berkeley: University of California Press, 1966), 71. *The Authoritarian Personality*, too, came under strong attack for its method and for its attempt to root politics in personality structure. Richard Christie and Marie Jahoda, *Studies in the Scope and Method of "The Authoritarian Personality"* (New York: Free Press, 1954).

34. Mead, *And Keep Your Powder Dry*, 37–41; Florence Kluckhohn, "Dominant and Substitutive Profiles of Cultural Orientations: Their Significance for the Analysis of Social Stratification," *Social Forces* 28 (May 1950), 382–83.

35. On the links between child rearing and racial prejudice, see Ruth Feldstein, "Antiracism and Maternal Failure in the 1940s and 1950s," in Molly Ladd-Taylor and Lauri Umansky, eds., *"Bad" Mothers: The Politics of Blame in Twentieth-Century America* (New York: New York University Press, 1998), 150–51.

36. The findings from the Harvard child rearing research are reported in Robert R. Sears et al., *Patterns of Childrearing* (Evanston, Ill.: Row, Peterson and Co., 1957), and discussed in Allison Davis and Robert J. Havighurst, "A Comparison of the Chicago and Harvard Studies of Social Class Differences in Childrearing," *American Sociological Review* 20 (August 1955): 438–42; and Urie Bronfenbrenner, "Socialization and Social Class Through Time and Space," in Eleanor Maccoby et al., *Readings in Social Psychology* (New York: Henry Holt, 1958), 400–425. For earlier findings from Havighurst and Davis, see their "Social Class and Color Differences in Child Rearing," *American Sociological Review* 11 (December 1946): 698–710.

37. John R. Seeley et al., *Crestwood Heights* (New York: Basic Books, 1956), 167.

38. Talcott Parsons and Robert F. Bales, *Family, Socialization and Interaction Process* (Glencoe, Ill: Free Press, 1955).

39. On the "domestic consensus" and its relationship to Cold War politics and culture, see Elaine Tyler May, *Homeward Bound: American Families in the Cold War Era* (New York: Basic Books, 1988).

40. W.E.B. DuBois, *The Philadelphia Negro: A Social Study* (Philadelphia: University of Pennsylvania Press, 1996), 110–11.

41. Martha May, "The 'Good Managers': Married Working Class Women and Family Budget Studies, 1895–1915," *Labor History* 25 (Summer 1984): 351–71; Margaret Byington, *Homestead: The Households of a Mill Town* (New York: Russell Sage Foundation, 1910; reprint, University of Pittsburgh, 1974); Elizabeth Beardsley Butler, *Women and the Trades* (New York: Russell Sage Foundation, 1909; reprint, Arno Press, 1969), 375.

42. Margaret Hagood, *Mothers of the South* (Chapel Hill: University of North Carolina Press, 1939; reprint, University of Virginia, 1996).

43. E. Wight Bakke, *Citizens Without Work* (New Haven: Yale University Press, 1940), 109–225.

44. Frazier, *The Negro Family in the United States* (rev. and abridged ed., New York: The Dryden Press, 1948), 334–55.

45. For some of the more extreme charges brought against improper mothering, see Jennifer Terry, "Momism and the Making of Treasonous Homosexuals," in Ladd-Taylor and Umansky, *"Bad" Mothers*, 169–90.

46. Scott, *Contempt and Pity*, 74–75. For Frazier's earlier analysis of delinquency, see *The Negro Family in the United States*, 268–80.

47. Lawrence L. LeShan, "Time Orientation and Social Class," *Journal of Abnormal and Social Psychology* 47 (July 1952): 589–92.

48. For an explanation of n Achievement and how it was developed, see David C. McClelland et al., *The Achievement Motive* (New York: Appleton-Century-Crofts, 1953) and *The Achieving Society* (New York: Van Nostrand, 1961). For examples of its application in studying social class, see J. W. Atkinson, *Motives in Fantasy, Action and Society* (New York: Van Nostrand, 1958). For an overview of McClelland's career, see Nicholas Lemann, "Is There a Science of Success?" *The Atlantic Monthly*, February 1994, 83–98.

49. For a review, see Elizabeth Herzog and Cecilia E. Sudia, "Fatherless Homes— A Review of Research," *Children* 15 (September/October 1968): 177–82; Margaret Thomes, "Children with Absent Fathers," *Journal of Marriage and the Family* 30 (February 1968): 89–96.

50. For various methods of measuring achievement motivation, see J. W. Atkinson, ed., *Motives in Fantasy, Action and Society*; Bernard Rosen, "The Achievement Syndrome," *American Sociological Review* 21 (April 1956): 203–11; and "Race, Ethnicity and the Achievement Syndrome," *American Sociological Review* 24 (February 1959): 47–60.

51. Walter Mischel, "Father-Absence and Delay of Gratification: Cross-Cultural Comparisons," *Journal of Abnormal and Social Psychology* 63 (July 1961): 116–24; Thomas F. Pettigrew, *A Profile of the Negro American* (New York: Van Nostrand, 1964), 17.

52. John H. Rohrer and Munro S. Edmonson, *The Eighth Generation Grows Up: Cultures and Personalities of New Orleans Negroes* (New York: Harper and Row, 1960). This study, designed as a follow-up to Allison Davis and John Dollard's *Children of Bondage*, used the psychoanalytic interviews Davis and Dollard conducted in the 1930s to predict, and then check up on, how the children would turn out as adults.

53. For critical perspectives on the psychological literature, see Vernon L. Allen, ed., *Psychological Factors in Poverty* (Chicago: Markham Publishing Co., 1970); S. M. Miller et al., "Poverty and Self-Indulgence: A Critique of the Non-

Deferred Gratification Pattern," in Louis Ferman et al., *Poverty in America* (Ann Arbor: University of Michigan Press, 1965), 416–32; Frank Riessman and S. M. Miller, "Social Class and Projective Tests," in Frank Riessman, ed., *Mental Health of the Poor: New Treatment Approaches for Low-Income People* (New York: Free Press, 1964), 248–58.

54. For an extended discussion of the psychological "turn" in the literature on the black family, see Scott, *Contempt and Pity*, chap. 5.

55. Abram Kardiner and Lionel Ovesey, *The Mark of Oppression* (New York: W.W. Norton, 1951; reprint Meridian Books, 1962), 381–87.

56. Kardiner and Ovesey, *Mark of Oppression*, 387; Scott, *Contempt and Pity*, 107–8.

57. Rickie Solinger, *Wake Up Little Susie: Single Pregnancy Before Roe v. Wade* (New York: Routledge, 1992), 59–76.

58. Dwight D. Eisenhower, Message to Congress, June 23, 1954.

59. Oscar Lewis to Ruth Benedict, April 26, 1944, reprinted in Susan Rigdon, *The Culture Facade* (Urbana: University of Illinois Press, 1988), 200–201.

60. Oscar Lewis, *Five Families: Mexican Case Studies in the Culture of Poverty* (New York: Basic Books, 1959), 2.

61. Robert Redfield, *Tepoztlàn, A Mexican Village* (Chicago: University of Chicago Press, 1930).

62. Oscar Lewis, *Life in a Mexican Village: Tepoztlàn Restudied* (Urbana: University of Illinois Press, 1951).

63. Edward Banfield, *The Moral Basis of a Backward Society* (Chicago: Free Press, 1958), 9.

64. Examples of these studies include Kenneth Morland, *Millways of Kent* (Chapel Hill: University of North Carolina Press, 1958); Herman Lantz, *People of Coaltown* (Carbondale: Southern Illinois University Press, 1958); Jack Weller, *Yesterday's People* (Lexington: University Press of Kentucky, 1965). For further discussion of the literature, see Alice O'Connor, "Modernization and the Rural Poor: Some Lessons from History," in Cynthia Duncan, ed., *Rural Poverty in America* (New York: Auburn House, 1992), 220–23.

65. Richard Hofstadter, *The Age of Reform* (New York: Vintage Books, 1955).

66. Herman, *Romance of Psychology*, 137–38, 142–43.

67. Mead, *Childhood in Contemporary Cultures*, 5.

68. McClelland, *The Achieving Society*, 202.

69. Ibid., 393–94.

70. Ibid., x.

71. The specifics of the achievement motivation seminars, as well as the withdrawal of funding by AID and Ford, are discussed in David McClelland and David G. Winter, *Motivating Economic Achievement* (New York: Free Press, 1969).

72. Oscar Lewis, *Five Families*, 2.

73. Oscar Lewis, *The Children of Sanchez: Autobiography of a Mexican Family* (New York: Random House, 1961), xxiv–xxv; *Anthropological Essays* (New York: Random House, 1970), 78.

74. It is not easy to keep track of Lewis's trait list, or to understand why he thought that continually adding to it would add to his argument that a distinctive culture of poverty unified certain subgroups of poor people across local boundaries. For a comprehensive compilation, see Susan Rigdon, *The Culture Facade*, 114–15.

75. Oscar Lewis, "The Culture of Poverty," in Daniel P. Moynihan, ed., *On Understanding Poverty* (New York: Basic Books, 1969), 188.

76. The following is drawn from Rigdon, *The Culture Facade*, chaps. 1–2.

77. For a full list, see Lewis, *Life in a Mexican Village*, xix–xx.

78. Lewis, *La Vida: A Puerto Rican Family in the Culture of Poverty, San Juan and New York* (New York: Random House, 1966), xxviii.

79. Rigdon, *Culture Facade*, 117–18. For a description of the household inventory, see Lewis, *La Vida*, xxii–xxiii.

80. Ibid., xlv, xlix.

81. Ibid., xlviii.

82. Ibid., xxvi.

83. Michael Lapp, "The Rise and Fall of Puerto Rico as a Social Laboratory, 1945–1965," *Social Science History* 19 (Summer 1995), 190–94.

84. Lewis, *La Vida*, xi.

85. Ibid., xxxvii–xlii. For Lewis's private correspondence on this issue, see Rigdon, *Culture Facade*, 256–63.

86. See, for example, the experiences reported by Cruz during a temporary stay in Florida. Lewis, *La Vida*, 619. For an earlier, more systematic treatment of the migrants' encounter with race, see C. Wright Mills et al., *Puerto Rican Journey: New York's Newest Migrants* (New York: Harper and Brothers, 1950), 125–38.

87. Rupert Vance, "The Region's Future, A National Challenge," in Thomas R. Ford, ed., *The Southern Appalachian Region: A Survey* (Lexington: University of Kentucky Press, 1962), 289–99.

88. Michael Harrington, *The Other America* (New York: Macmillan, 1962), 146, 167.

89. Lewis, *La Vida*, xi.

90. Harrington, *The Other America*, 183–84.

Chapter 5
Community Action

1. On the roots of the Community Action Program, see Daniel P. Moynihan, *Maximum Feasible Misunderstanding: Community Action in the War on Poverty* (New York: The Free Press, 1969); Peter Marris and Martin Rein, *The Dilemmas of Social Reform: Community Action and Poverty in the United States* (New York: Atherton Press, 1967); Daniel Knapp and Kenneth Polk, *Scouting the War on Poverty: Social Reform Politics in the Kennedy Administration* (Lexington, Mass.: D.C. Heath, 1974); Michael B. Katz, *The Undeserving Poor: From the War on Poverty to the War on Welfare* (New York: Pantheon Books, 1989), 95–101; Alice O'Connor, "Community Action, Urban Reform, and the Fight Against Poverty: The Ford Foundation's Gray Areas Program," *Journal of Urban History* 22 (July 1996): 586–625.

2. Readers may note the absence of the word "implementation"—one of the many problems for which community action, like many other types of intervention, would be taken to task.

3. Noel A. Cazenave, "Chicago Influences on the War on Poverty," *Journal of Policy History* 5, no. 1 (1993), 53–56; Knapp and Polk, *Scouting the War on Poverty*, 26–32;

Leonard S. Cottrell, "The Competent Community," paper delivered at the University of North Carolina, November 30, 1972, included in "Summary Planning and Materials," Poverty Urban Conference (1973), Brandeis University, John F. Kennedy Library, Boston; Nelson N. Foote and Leonard S. Cottrell, Jr., *Identity and Interpersonal Competence: A New Direction in Family Research* (Chicago: University of Chicago Press, 1955).

4. David C. Hammack and Stanton Wheeler, *Social Science in the Making: Essays on the Russell Sage Foundation, 1907–1972* (New York: Russell Sage Foundation, 1994), 131–32.

5. Gerald Grob, *From Asylum to Community: Mental Health Policy in Modern America* (Princeton: Princeton University Press, 1991), 48–54, 61–69; Marris and Rein, *Dilemmas of Social Reform*, 131–32.

6. Knapp and Polk, *Scouting the War on Poverty*, 28–31; Cottrell, "Community Competence," 8–10.

7. Lloyd E. Ohlin, "The Development of Indigenous Social Movements Among Residents of Deprived Urban Areas," Ford Foundation Archives, New York.

8. As Merton puts it, Cloward had managed "the improbable feat of 'crossing 120th street'" to get Merton on his dissertation committee. Robert K. Merton, "Opportunity Structure: The Emergence, Diffusion, and Differentiation of a Sociological Concept, 1930s-1950s," reprint from Freda Adler and William S. Laufer, eds., *The Legacy of Anomie Theory*, vol. 6 of *Advances in Criminological Theory* (New Brunswick, N.J.: Transaction Books 1995), 47–48.

9. Robert K. Merton, "Social Structure and Anomie," *American Sociological Review* 3 (October 1938): 672–82. Cloward's dissertation was entitled "Social Control and Anomie: A Study of the Prison Community."

10. Richard A. Cloward and Lloyd E. Ohlin, *Delinquency and Opportunity: A Theory of Delinquent Gangs* (Glencoe, Ill.: Free Press, 1960), 211.

11. For example, in 1955, with the help of Merton, Cloward's work as a graduate student came to the attention of Helen Witmer, Chief of the Division of Research for the Department of Health, Education and Welfare (HEW) Children's Bureau, which had just set up a Division of Juvenile Delinquency Service to fund research and demonstration projects. On this and the role of networks in delinquency research and policy, see Helen L. Witmer and Ruth Kotinsky, eds., *New Perspectives for Research on Juvenile Delinquency* (Washington, D.C.: Children's Bureau, 1955); Merton, "Opportunity Structure," 49–51; Knapp and Polk, *Scouting the War on Poverty*, 32–35.

12. On the emergence of juvenile delinquency as a national issue, see James Gilbert, *Cycle of Outrage: America's Reaction to the Juvenile Delinquent in the 1950s* (New York: Oxford University Press, 1986).

13. Knapp and Polk, *Scouting the War on Poverty*, 32–36; Marris and Rein, *The Dilemmas of Social Reform*, 20; Frances Fox Piven, "Dilemmas in Social Planning: A Case Inquiry," *Social Service Review* 42 (June 1968): 197–206.

14. The charges against the MFY staff were originally levied by the New York *Daily News*, then taken up by Daniel P. Moynihan in *Maximum Feasible Misunderstanding*. Along with allegations of financial mismanagement, the supposed links to the Communist Party were the basis of an outside investigation, which found both to be highly exaggerated. The controversy nevertheless took a toll on MFY, and led to staff changes and board restructuring. For a discussion of these matters, and of MFY's efforts to

develop a feasible action strategy in light of powerful economic forces, see George A. Braeger and Francis P. Purcell, eds., *Community Action Against Poverty: Readings from the Mobilization Experience* (New Haven: Yale University Press, 1967).

15. The interrelated processes of industrial restructuring, technological change, and migration patterns that, along with government policies, contributed to the decline of central cities and the growth of suburbs in the post–World War II years have been well documented in the historical literature, including Mark Gelfand, *A Nation of Cities: The Federal Government and Urban America, 1935–1965* (New York: Oxford University Press, 1975), chap. 5; Arnold R. Hirsch, *Making the Second Ghetto: Race and Housing in Chicago, 1940–1960* (New York: Cambridge University Press, 1983); Kenneth T. Jackson, *Crabgrass Frontier: The Suburbanization of the United States* (New York: Oxford University Press, 1985); Thomas J. Sugrue, "The Structures of Urban Poverty: The Reorganization of Space and Work in Three Periods of American History," in Michael B. Katz, ed., *The "Underclass" Debate: Views from History* (Princeton: Princeton University Press, 1993), 85–117; and *The Origins of the Urban Crisis: Race and Inequality in Postwar Detroit* (Princeton: Princeton University Press, 1996); Leonard Wallock, "The Myth of the Master Builder: Robert Moses, New York, and the Dynamics of Metropolitan Development Since World War II," *Journal of Urban History* 17 (August 1991): 339–62. For a sampling of some of the best journalistic coverage from *Fortune* magazine, see William H. Whyte et al., eds., *The Exploding Metropolis* (Garden City, N.Y.: Doubleday, 1958). On the "new migrants," see Jacqueline Jones, *The Dispossessed: America's Underclasses from the Civil War to the Present* (New York: Basic Books, 1992), 205–65.

16. For a summary of the "gray areas" idea, see Raymond Vernon, "The Changing Economic Function of the Central City," in James Q. Wilson, ed., *Urban Renewal: The Record and the Controversy* (Cambridge, Mass.: MIT Press, 1966), 3–23. Vernon's article was a distillation of an earlier New York Regional Plan Association project funded by the Ford Foundation, the findings of which were presented in Edgar M. Hoover and Raymond Vernon, *Anatomy of a Metropolis* (Cambridge, Mass.: Harvard University Press, 1959).

17. Leonard J. Duhl, Preface to the Proceedings of Conferences on Environmental Determinants of Mental Health (Washington, D.C.: NIMH), May 28–29, 1956. I am grateful to Dr. Duhl for giving me access to his copy of the transcripts from these and other NIMH meetings. Among the most renowned of the many important urban studies funded by the NIMH during this period was a study of the impact on urban renewal on Boston's West End neighborhoods, reported in Marc Fried, "Grieving for a Lost Home," in Wilson, ed., *Urban Renewal*, 359–79; and Herbert J. Gans, *The Urban Villagers* (New York: The Free Press, 1961; rev. ed., 1982). For the results of another important NIMH-funded housing study, this as part of an evaluation of social services programs attached to the infamous St. Louis Pruitt-Igoe housing project, see Lee Rainwater, *Behind Ghetto Walls: Black Families in a Federal Slum* (Chicago: Aldine Publishing Co., 1970).

18. Leonard J. Duhl, ed., *The Urban Condition: People and Policy in the Metropolis* (New York: Basic Books, 1963), vii–xiii.

19. The five cities funded under the Gray Areas program were Boston, New Haven, Oakland, Philadelphia, and Washington, D.C. Each eventually received grants totaling

$1.5 to $2.5 million over approximately four years. In 1963, the foundation awarded $7 million to the state of North Carolina to set up gray areas programs in rural and urban areas around the state.

20. For a more detailed discussion of the Gray Areas program, see O'Connor, "Community Action, Urban Reform, and the Fight Against Poverty." For a classic contemporary discussion of "executive-centered" mayoralty, set in the Gray Areas–grantee city of New Haven, see Robert A. Dahl, *Who Governs? Democracy and Power in an American City* (New Haven: Yale University Press, 1961). See also Clarence N. Stone and Heywood T. Sanders, "Reexamining a Classic Case of Development Politics: New Haven, Connecticut," in Clarence N. Stone and Heywood T. Sanders, eds., *The Politics of Urban Development* (Lawrence: The University Press of Kansas, 1987), 159–82.

21. The early community action evaluations consisted mostly of a relatively informal but consistent process of observation, site visits, and conferences. Although hardly "scientific" according to the norms applied to evaluation today, the results of these observations, conveyed in letters and memos in the Ford Foundation archives, were invaluable to the learning process that accompanied community action. See, for example, the correspondence between Paul Ylvisaker and foundation consultant Clifford Campbell, Grant File PA62–29, Ford foundation Archives. For a more detailed discussion of early "lessons" from the evaluations, see Alice O'Connor, "The Ford Foundation and Philanthropic Activism in the 1960s," in Ellen Condliffe Lagemann, ed., *Philanthropic Foundations: New Scholarship, New Possibilities* (Bloomington: Indiana University Press, 1999), 179–83; See also Marris and Rein, *Dilemmas of Social Reform.*

22. Knapp and Polk, *Scouting the War on Poverty,* 85–87.

23. Joseph Helfgot, *Professional Reforming: Mobilization for Youth and the Failure of Social Science* (Lexington, Mass.: D.C. Heath, 1981), 74–77.

24. Saul D. Alinsky, "Community Analysis and Organization," *American Journal of Sociology,* 46 (May 1941), 801. For a contemporary perspective on the divergent approaches to resident participation, see Frances Fox Piven, "Participation of Residents in Neighborhood Community Action Programs," *Social Work* 11 (January 1966): 73–80.

25. For one example of how race entered into the politics of neighborhood participation in New Haven's Gray Areas project, see Edgar S. Cahn and Jean C. Cahn, "The War on Poverty: A Civilian Perspective," *Yale Law Journal* 73 (July 1964): 1317–52; and Marris and Rein, *Dilemmas of Social Reform,* 171–77.

26. Charles E. Silberman, *Crisis in Black and White* (New York: Random House, 1964), 10, 37, 351–54.

27. For further discussion of the problems raised in evaluating community action, see Alice O'Connor, "Evaluating Comprehensive Community Initiatives: A View from History," in James P. Connell et al., *New Approaches to Evaluating Community Initiatives* (Queenstown, Md.: Aspen Institute), 23–63.

28. Michael P. Brooks, "The Community Action Program as a Setting for Applied Research," *Journal of Social Issues* 21 (January 1965), 37; Marris and Rein, *Dilemmas of Social Reform,* 199–202.

Chapter 6
In the Midst of Plenty

1. Hylan Lewis, "The Family: New Agenda, Different Rhetoric," in *Children of Poverty, Children of Affluence* (New York, 1967), 1.

2. Theodore W. Schultz, "Investing in Poor People: An Economist's View," in *The Economics of Poverty* (Washington, D.C.: American Economic Association, 1964), 510–20.

3. James T. Patterson, *America's Struggle Against Poverty, 1900–1994* (Cambridge, Mass.: Harvard University Press, 1994), 94–95, 127–29; Henry J. Aaron, *Politics and the Professors* (Washington, D.C.: The Brookings Institution, 1978), 111–45; Sar A. Levitan and Robert Taggart, *The Great Society's Poor Law: A New Approach to Poverty* (Baltimore: Johns Hopkins University Press, 1969), 3–48.

4. Carl M. Brauer, "Kennedy, Johnson and the War on Poverty," *Journal of American History* 69 (June 1982): 98–119.

5. On the journalistic appropriation of the "new economics" to describe older trends in the field, see James Tobin, *The New Economics One Decade Older* (Princeton: Princeton University Press, 1972), 6–7; Seymour Harris, ed., *The New Economics* (New York: Knopf, 1947).

6. On the "neoclassical synthesis" that became dominant in postwar U.S. economics, see Ira Katznelson, "Was the Great Society a Lost Opportunity?" in Steve Fraser and Gary Gerstle, eds., *The Rise and Fall of the New Deal Order, 1930–1980* (Princeton: Princeton University Press, 1989), 191–92; James Tobin and Robert M. Solow, "Introduction," in Tobin and Murray Weidenbaum, eds., *Two Revolutions in Economic Policy* (Cambridge, Mass.: MIT Press, 1988), 5–7. For discussions of "social" as compared to "commercial" Keynesianism, see Robert Lekachman, *The Age of Keynes* (New York: Random House, 1966), 286–87; Fraser and Gerstle, *Rise and Fall of the New Deal Order*, xiv–xvi; Theda Skocpol and Edwin Amenta, "The Limits of the New Deal System and the Roots of Contemporary Welfare Dilemmas," in Margaret Weir, Ann Shola Orloff, and Theda Skocpol, *The Politics of Social Policy in the United States* (Princeton: Princeton University Press, 1988). On the emergence of American Keynesianism in relation to shifting reform ideology, see Margaret Weir, *Politics and Jobs: The Boundaries of Employment Policy in the United States* (Princeton: Princeton University Press, 1992), 27–61; Alan Brinkley, *The End of Reform: New Deal Liberalism in Recession and War* (New York: Knopf, 1995) 3–8, 128–31, 227–64; Robert M. Collins, "The Emergence of Economic Growthmanship in the United States: Federal Policy and Economic Knowledge in the Truman Years," in Mary O. Furner and Barry Supple, eds., *The State and Economic Knowledge: The American and British Experiences* (New York: Cambridge University Press, 1990), 146–52.

7. Weir, *Politics and Jobs*, 42; Tobin, *The New Economics*, 18–27; Arthur M. Okun, Oral History, Lyndon Baines Johnson Presidential Library (hereafter LBJ Library), Austin, Texas, 1969, 10–15. Walter Heller, Oral History, LBJ Library, 1970, 28–35.

8. On the institutionalist influence in labor economics, see Paul J. McNulty, *The Origins and Development of Labor Economics: A Chapter in the History of Social Thought* (Cambridge, Mass.: MIT Press, 1980), 153–76; Bruce E. Kaufman, ed., *How Labor Markets Work: Reflections on Theory and Practice by John Dunlop, Clark Kerr,*

Richard Lester and Lloyd Reynolds, (Lexington, Mass.: D.C. Heath, 1988); Gunnar Myrdal, *Against the Stream: Critical Essays on Economics* (New York: Random House, 1972), 6–7.

9. Bruce E. Kaufman, "The Postwar View of Labor Markets and Wage Determination" in Bruce E. Kaufman, ed., *How Labor Markets Work*, 145–204; Glen G. Cain, "The Challenge of Segmented Labor Market Theories to Orthodox Theory: A Survey," *Journal of Economic Literature* 14 (December 1976), 1227–28. As Kaufman and others have noted, the "bridge" generation steadfastly eschewed the institutionalist or neoinstitutionalist label, preferring to think of themselves as "realists" operating within the neoclassical framework.

10. On human capital theory, see McNulty, *Labor Economics*, 192–97; Kaufman, "The Postwar View of Labor Markets," 184–85; Mark Blaug, "The Empirical Status of Human Capital Theory: A Slightly Jaundiced Survey," *Journal of Economic Literature* 14 (September 1976): 827–55. While Blaug and others credit Theodore Schultz with first "announcing" its arrival in 1960, the classic text in the field is Gary Becker, *Human Capital* (New York: Columbia University Press, 1964). The importance of human capital theory to CEA thinking is discussed in Tobin and Weidenbaum, *Two Revolutions in Economic Policy*, 11–12.

11. Lloyd G. Reynolds, "Labor Economics Then and Now," in Kaufman, *How Labor Markets Work*, 129–32.

12. Arthur M. Okun, *The Political Economy of Prosperity* (Washington, D.C.: Brookings Institution, 1970), 21–23. On modeling, see Kenneth L. Kraemer et al., *Datawars: The Politics of Modeling in Federal Policymaking* (New York: Columbia University Press, 1987), 65–70. An excellent statement of the promise of economics as a nonideological science is in Daniel P. Moynihan, "The Professionalization of Reform," *The Public Interest*, no. 1 (Fall 1965): 6–16.

13. For discussions of the Employment Act and the creation of the CEA, see Weir, *Politics and Jobs*, 53–56; Lekachman, *Age of Keynes*, 165–75. Between them, Kennedy's CEA appointees had an impressive record of public service and a good deal of political engagement. Heller had been a Treasury Department analyst and a Marshall Plan administrator in Germany; Gordon was on the staff of the Temporary National Economic Committee and the Office of Price Administration during the New Deal and early war years. Even Tobin, who thought of himself and his career as more strictly "ivory tower," had some engagement in Democratic party politics. Like Heller and Gordon, he had been called in as an occasional advisor to candidates Adlai Stevenson, Hubert Humphrey, and to Kennedy himself during the 1960 campaign. For more on the backgrounds of Kennedy CEA members, see Council of Economic Advisors Oral History, John F. Kennedy Library, Boston.

14. Keynesian economists had been unable to establish a stable institutional foothold for themselves in the government bureaucracy before the 1960s. The CEA was strictly an advisory body, and during the 1950s its role in economic policy had been circumscribed by the laissez-faire stance of the Eisenhower administration. Lekachman, *Age of Keynes*, 174–75; Weir, *Politics and Jobs*, 54–56. The policy role of any given CEA was largely determined by the administration, but also by the chairman's predilections. Truman's first chairman, Edwin G. Nourse, favored scientific detachment and nonpartisanship for the Council, an approach that was reversed by his successor, Leon Keyserling, who himself played a strong advocacy role both within and outside administration

circles, and regarded academic ideas with skepticism if not disdain. The Eisenhower Council under Arthur F. Burns and Raymond J. Saulnier was considerably more restrained in its stance, emphasizing stability and inflation control as policy goals and regarding congressional testimony and other public statements as improper. On Truman's CEA, see Collins, "Emergence of Economic Growthmanship," 146–50, 160–62. On Edwin Nourse and his approach to the CEA, see Robert H. Nelson, "The Economics Profession and the Making of Public Policy," *Journal of Economic Literature* 25 (March 1987), 65–66. On the contrast between Kennedy and Eisenhower CEA approaches, see CEA Oral History, 258–70.

15. CEA Oral History, 135.

16. Schultz, "Investing in Poor People."

17. The CEA program is reflected in the presidential message proposing "A Program to Restore Momentum to the American Economy," February 2, 1961, OEO Agency Records, LBJ Library, box 7.

18. Heller, Oral History, Interview II, 1971, LBJ Library, 35.

19. On Kennedy's appointments and instinctive conservatism, see CEA Oral History, 170–79, 186.

20. Kennedy's CEA was concerned and alarmed by the pervasiveness and "instinctive appeal" of structural unemployment arguments and the automation scare, enough so to develop a detailed statistical refutation of the concept in 1961, updated versions of which were included in subsequent economic reports through the mid-1960s. Okun, *Political Economy of Prosperity*, 35–36; Tobin, *The New Economics*, 15–17; CEA Oral History, 282–88, 316–22.

21. Heller, Oral History, Interview II, 34–35; Okun, *Political Economy of Prosperity*, 52–53.

22. CEA Oral History, 316–22; Okun, "Potential GNP: Its Measurement and Significance," reprinted in *Political Economy of Prosperity*, 132–45. Historian Michael Bernstein discusses the significance of Okun's article as part of a more comprehensive exploration of the thinking and the impact of Kennedy's CEA in his forthcoming *Economics and Public Purpose in Twentieth-Century America* (Princeton: Princeton University Press), chap. 6.

23. Nelson, "The Economics Profession," 66; Okun, *Political Economy of Prosperity*, 45.

24. The CEA oral history provides a useful chronology of events leading up to Kennedy's acceptance of the tax cut, 379–406. "Question: Is a Tax Cut What the Country Needs?" *Newsweek*, July 16, 1962, 57–60.

25. John Kenneth Galbraith, *The Affluent Society* (Boston: Houghton, Mifflin, 1958), 189.

26. Ibid., 96–97.

27. For a discussion of various approaches to measuring poverty at the time, see Gordon Fisher, "From Hunter to Orshansky: An Overview of (Unofficial) Poverty Lines in the United States from 1904–1965," unpublished paper presented at the Association for Public Policy Analysis and Management Meetings, October 28, 1993, 48–51. Fisher, who has done the most comprehensive research on poverty lines, reports that the $2,000 poverty line used by the Subcommittee on Low Income Families of the Congressional Joint Committee on the Economic Report in 1949 was generally accepted as standard, with some notable exceptions like Walter Reuther, who argued for a $3,000 line in

1953. However, Galbraith may have taken the $1,000 figure from the CEA Annual Report of 1955 which, despite having used the $2,000 figure the year before, used $1,000 as its gauge for estimating poverty. It is also possible that Galbraith used $1,000 because he was focused primarily on the rural/farm poor, for whom it was standard practice to use lower poverty lines.

28. Galbraith, *Affluent Society*, 325–27.

29. Ibid., 332.

30. In contrast to Galbraith's imagery of a sparse residuum, Lampman's statistical analysis revealed a still substantial poverty rate of 19%, a low-income population that, though disproportionately composed of disadvantaged subgroups, broadly reflected the population at large. Lampman found a close and continuing link between the postwar advance in overall economic growth and the reduction of poverty. Steady economic expansion accounted for the near 10% decline in poverty since 1947. In fact, recent slowdowns in poverty reduction were directly attributable to sluggish annual growth rates after 1953. Growth, he concluded, was not only essential to reducing poverty; inadequate growth was responsible for its persistence. By maintaining its high postwar growth levels, he predicted, the U.S. could achieve a poverty rate of 10–12% by 1977. Robert Lampman, "The Low Income Population and Economic Growth in the United States" (Washington, D.C.: Joint Economic Committee of Congress, 1959).

31. Gunnar Myrdal, *Challenge to Affluence*, rev. ed. (New York: Vintage Books, 1965), 11–12, 36–38, 64–66.

32. James L. Sundquist, *Politics and Policy: The Eisenhower, Kennedy and Johnson Years* (Washington, D.C.: Brookings Institution, 1968); Sar A. Levitan, *Federal Aid to Depressed Areas* (Baltimore: Johns Hopkins University Press, 1964); Alice O'Connor, "Modernization and the Rural Poor: Some Lessons from History," in Cynthia M. Duncan, ed., *Rural Poverty in America* (New York: Auburn House, 1992), 215–33.

33. Thomas F. Jackson, "The State, the Movement, and the Urban Poor: The War on Poverty and Political Mobilization in the 1960s," in Michael B. Katz, ed., *The "Underclass" Debate: Views from History* (Princeton: Princeton University Press, 1993), 430–31. On the centrality of jobs, equal employment opportunities, and income guarantees to the evolving civil rights agenda, see Charles V. Hamilton and Dona C. Hamilton, "Social Policies, Civil Rights and Poverty," in Sheldon H. Danziger and Daniel H. Weinberg, eds., *Fighting Poverty: What Works and What Doesn't* (Cambridge, Mass.: Harvard University Press, 1986), 287–311, and Dona Cooper Hamilton and Charles V. Hamilton, *The Dual Agenda: Race and Social Welfare Policies of Civil Rights Organizations* (New York: Columbia University Press, 1997).

34. Allen J. Matusow, *The Unraveling of America: A History of Liberalism in the 1960s* (New York: Harper and Row, 1984), 119–20; Brauer, "Kennedy, Johnson and the War on Poverty," 105.

35. National Policy Committee On Pockets of Poverty, Press Release, March 5, 1964, Wilbur J. Cohen Papers, Wisconsin State Historical Society (hereafter WSHS), box 125, folder 1; John Kenneth Galbraith, "Wealth and Poverty," Address to the National Committee on Pockets of Poverty, December 13, 1963, Cohen Papers, WSHS, box 125, folder 3, 2–3.

36. The results of Ornati's study were eventually published in *Poverty Amid Affluence* (New York: Twentieth Century Fund, 1966), 43, 50, 125, 132. But his analyses were circulating in Washington earlier. Draft chapters were reviewed by staff members

for HEW undersecretary Wilbur Cohen and by CEA economist Robert Lampman. Eugenia Sullivan to Wilbur J. Cohen, June 6, 1963; Robert J. Lampman, "Comments on *Poverty in an Affluent Society*," n.d., Cohen Papers, WSHS, box 124, folder 11.

37. Michael Harrington, *The Other America: Poverty in the United States* (New York: MacMillan, 1962), 2.

38. Harrington, *The Other America*, 10, 18–19, 167–71, 199.

39. Ibid., 168, 172–76.

40. Dwight Macdonald, "Our Invisible Poor," *New Yorker*, January 19, 1963, 82–132; Brauer, "Kennedy, Johnson and the War on Poverty," 103.

41. Macdonald, "Invisible Poor," 86.

42. Significantly, these early discussions of poverty were less concerned about accuracy in numbers than they were about how to characterize the problem. In later years, issues of measurement would loom much larger, as the implications of poverty lines for welfare spending became more immediately relevant, and as quantitative precision was more highly valued in defining social problems more generally.

In fact, though, where and how the poverty line was drawn had enormous implications for how the problem was characterized, especially in its effect on what the composition of the poor population would look like. The lower and more "fixed" the line, the more "hard core" and "other" the poor would appear. Conversely, the higher and more relative the line, the more "normal" or "representative" of the wider population the distribution would be. This point was brought up by economist Herman Miller in a critique of the fixed poverty line ($3,000) used by the CEA. He studied the concentration of demographic characteristics at three different levels of deprivation—less than $500, less than $2,000, and less than $4,500, finding that the "cumulative risk factor" rose considerably with lower income levels. The $3,000 figure eventually used by the CEA was a somewhat arbitrary compromise position, later supplanted by a more "scientific" method of calculation. Mollie Orshansky, "Children of the Poor," *Social Security Bulletin*, July 1963; "Counting the Poor: Another Look at the Poverty Profile," *Social Security Bulletin*, January 1965, 3–29; "Recounting the Poor—A Five-Year Review," *Social Security Bulletin*, April 1966, 2–19; and "How Poverty is Measured," *Monthly Labor Review*, February 1969, 37–41.

43. Robert Lampman, Oral History, Interview I, 1983, LBJ Library, 3; Brauer, "Kennedy, Johnson, and the War on Poverty," 103–4.

44. *Economic Report of the President* (Washington, D.C.: U.S. Government Printing Office, 1962), 10.

45. Robert Lampman, "Comments on the Twentieth Century Fund Project," May 17, 1963, Cohen Papers, WSHS, box 124, folder 11. Liberal economist and former Truman CEA chair Leon Keyserling also warned against distinguishing between unemployment and poverty in a pamphlet circulated in 1962, which estimated that slow growth and unemployment had put 40% of American households at "poverty" (below $4,000) or "deprivation" (below $6,000) levels during the Eisenhower years. Patterson, *America's Struggle Against Poverty*, 112.

46. Having completed his undergraduate degree at the University of Wisconsin in 1942, Lampman returned for graduate study just after the war. During these years he worked with Edmund Witte, Selig Perlman, and Elizabeth Brandeis in a department still strongly committed to institutionalist economics, antagonistic toward neoclassical theory, and skeptical about Keynesianism. Lampman's dissertation, entitled "Collective

Bargaining of West Coast Sailors, 1885–1947," was straight out of the Wisconsin tradition. It was not until after his formal training, while teaching at the University of Wisconsin, that he became more fully exposed to Keynes and to neoclassical labor market theory. Interview with author, June 1995.

47. Lampman seemed to have a penchant for moving into uncharted territory, as well as for taking issue with the claims of eminent economists. In 1957, he spent a year as a Carnegie Fellow at the National Bureau of Economic Research examining changes in the concentration of wealth in the U.S. since the 1920s. His analysis challenged news of the "income revolution" heralded by economist Simon Kuznets by showing that wealth holdings remained highly concentrated at the top. Lampman, "Recent Changes in Income Inequality Reconsidered," *American Economic Review* 44 (June 1954): 251–68; *The Share of Top Wealth-holders in National Wealth, 1922–1956* (Princeton: National Bureau of Economic Research, 1962); Lampman Oral History, Interview II, 1984, University of Wisconsin Archives, 155–57. On Heller's balance between Keynesianism and the Wisconsin school, see Brauer, "Kennedy, Johnson, and the War on Poverty," 103–4. An interesting, if selective, self-assessment of the Wisconsin economics department was compiled for its centenary. Lampman, ed., *Economists at Wisconsin: 1892–1992* (Madison: University of Wisconsin Press, 1993).

48. Lampman, "The Low Income Population and Economic Growth."

49. Brauer, "Kennedy, Johnson, and the War on Poverty," 104.

50. Lampman to Heller, June 10, 1963, Legislative Background: Economic Opportunity Act (hereafter EOA) of 1964, LBJ LIbrary, box 1.

51. Lampman to Heller, June 3, 1963, Legislative Background: EOA of 1964, LBJ Library, box 1.

52. Ibid.

53. Lampman, Oral History, Interview I, 1983, LBJ Library, 6–8.

54. Lampman to Heller, June 10, 1963; Heller to Agency Secretaries, "1964 Programs for 'Widening Participation in Prosperity,'—An Attack on Poverty," November 5, 1963, Legislative Background: EOA of 1964, LBJ Library, box 1. On the August 1963 March on Washington as an effort to highlight the issues of employment and poverty, see Hamilton and Hamilton, *The Dual Agenda*, 123–28.

55. The Department of Labor was pushing for intensified training, targeted economic development, a substantial job creation initiative, and a more comprehensive approach to labor market policy. HEW, having achieved passage of 1962 reforms that significantly elevated the role of rehabilitative services in the welfare program, was proposing a legislative agenda focused on increasing social security benefits, health insurance for the elderly, added vocational training for welfare families, and federal aid to education. On Labor's efforts to define a more comprehensive labor market policy, see John C. Donovan, *The Politics of Poverty* (New York: Pegasus, 1967), 25–26. HEW's initial approach to the poverty program is reflected in a memo from Secretary Wilbur Cohen to Heller, November 19, 1963, Cohen Papers, WSHS, box 149, folder 5. According to historian Edward D. Berkowitz, the War on Poverty "was little more than an incidental concern for Wilbur Cohen and others who were trying to pass Kennedy's education and health legislation in 1963." Berkowitz, *Mr. Social Security: The Life of Wilbur J. Cohen* (Lawrence: University Press of Kansas, 1995), 145–53, 188–202.

56. Heller to Agency Secretaries, November 5, 1963.

57. Capron to Heller, December 12, 1963, Legislative Background: EOA of 1964, LBJ Library, box 1.

58. Heller to Theodore Sorenson, "Poverty Program," December 20, 1963; "Points for Meeting on Poverty Program," Legislative Background: EOA of 1964, LBJ Library, box 1.

59. "Some Notes on a Program of 'Human Conservation,' " November 2, 1963, Legislative Background: EOA of 1964, LBJ Library, box 1.

60. *Economic Report of the President* (Washington, D.C.: U.S. Government Printing Office, 1964), 55; Lampman Oral History, LBJ Library, 15.

61. *Economic Report* (1964), 29.

62. Ibid. (1964), 85–111, and Appendix, 166–90.

63. *Economic Report* (1964), 55.

64. Ibid. (1964), 72.

65. Ibid. (1964), 77.

66. For a discussion of the tendency to define the poor as a group cut off from mainstream society, see June Axinn and Mark J. Stern, *Dependency and Poverty: Old Problems in a New World* (Lexington, Mass.: Lexington Books, 1988), 95–100.

67. Capron to Heller, December 2, 1963, LBJ Library, Legislative Background: EOA of 1964, LBJ Library, box 1.

68. Patterson, *America's Struggle Against Poverty*, chap. 9.

69. James L. Sundquist, "The Origins of the War on Poverty," in James L. Sundquist, ed., *On Fighting Poverty* (New York: Basic Books, 1969), 22.

70. Daniel Knapp and Kenneth Polk, *Scouting the War on Poverty: Social Reform Politics in the Kennedy Administration* (Lexington, Mass.: DC Heath, 1974), 109.

71. Paul Ylvisaker, "Social Bargaining and Community Welfare," *Economic and Business Bulletin*, September 1963, 8. Ylvisaker also noted that the poverty label "can be restrictive. Many of the problems of the urban newcomers go beyond poverty; discrimination is one example." Nevertheless, "breaking the cycle of poverty" became the official catchphrase of the Ford Foundation's Gray Areas programs in 1964. Peter Marris and Martin Rein, *Dilemmas of Social Reform: Poverty and Community Action in the United States* (New York: Atherton Press, 1967), chap. 2.

72. David Hackett to Robert F. Kennedy, "Participation in the Heller Study of Poverty," November 6, 1963, document included with Summary Planning and Materials for Poverty and Urban Conference (1973), Brandeis University, JFK Library.

73. Brandeis University conference transcript, JFK Library, 225–26; Knapp and Polk, *Scouting the War on Poverty*, 111–12.

74. David Hackett to Robert F. Kennedy, November 6, 1963.

75. William Cannon, Oral History, 1982, LBJ Library, 2–5.

76. David Hackett to Robert F. Kennedy, November 6, 1963.

77. David Hackett to Walter Heller, "Attack on Poverty," December 1, 1963, Legislative Background: EOA of 1964, LBJ Library, box 1.

78. CEA/BOB memo to Theodore Sorenson, December 23, 1963, Legislative Background: EOA of 1964, LBJ Library, box 1.

79. William Cannon, Oral History, LBJ Library, 11–13.

80. Robert Lampman, Oral History, LBJ Library, 15–17.

81. "Gray Areas Review," Report #002845, Ford Foundation Archives, New York, 17.

82. Marris and Rein, *Dilemmas of Social Reform*, 211.

83. Campbell to Ylvisaker, December 2, 1964; Planning documents, Puerto Rico conference, both in Ford Foundation Archives, PA # 62–29.

84. John Wofford, "The Politics of Local Responsibility: Administration of the Community Action Program, 1964–1966," in Sundquist, *On Fighting Poverty*, 70–102.

Chapter 7
Fighting Poverty with Knowledge

1. Robert Haveman, *Poverty Policy and Poverty Research: The Great Society and the Social Sciences* (Madison, Wis.: University of Wisconsin Press, 1987), 31–35.

2. James Tobin, "It Can Be Done!: Conquering Poverty in the U.S. by 1976," *The New Republic*, June 3, 1967, 14.

3. Capron to Walter Heller, "Poverty Program Issues," January 4, 1964, White House Central Files (WHCF), Lyndon B. Johnson Library, Austin, Texas, microfilm reel 1; White House to Department Secretaries, "Specifications for a Bill to Combat Poverty," January 21, 1964, Wilbur B. Cohen Papers, Wisconsin State Historical Society (WSHS), box 125, folder 6.

4. Adam Yarmolinsky, Oral History, July 13, 1970, LBJ Library, 10–12.

5. John G. Wofford, "The Politics of Local Responsibility," in James L. Sundquist, ed., *On Fighting Poverty* (New York: Basic Books, 1969), 88.

6. William F. Haddad, "The Savage Politics of Poverty," *Harpers,* December 1965, 45. Christopher Weeks had slightly different versions of Shriver's motto: "Nice guys don't win ball games," and "There's no place on this team for good losers." Christopher Weeks, *Job Corps: Dollars and Dropouts* (Boston: Little, Brown, 1967), 163.

7. Haddad, "Savage Politics," 45.

8. Weeks, *Job Corps*, 184–86.

9. Adam Yarmolinsky, "The Beginnings of OEO," in Sundquist, *On Fighting Poverty*, 34–51.

10. Allen J. Matusow, *The Unraveling of America: A History of Liberalism in the 1960s* (New York: Harper Torchbooks, 1984), 247.

11. Wofford, "The Politics of Local Responsibility," 77.

12. Sanford Kravitz, "The Community Action Program," in Sundquist, *On Fighting Poverty*, 60.

13. Kravitz, "The Community Action Program," 61, 65; Wofford, "Politics of Local Responsibility," 88–92.

14. "119 Projects Launch Poverty War in All Sections of the Nation," OEO Press release, WHCF, LBJ Library, box 124; *OEO Administrative History*, LBJ Library, 59–62; 475n. 30.

15. Wofford, "Politics of Local Responsibility," 79.

16. Haddad, "Savage Politics," 44; Matusow, *Unraveling*, 246.

17. Matusow, *Unraveling*, 246.

18. William C. Selover, "The View from Capitol Hill: Harassment and Survival," in Sundquist, *On Fighting Poverty*, 166.

19. "Antipoverty Program Stirs Wide Controversy," *New York Times*, May 2, 1965.

20. Eric Tolmach, Oral History, Interview III, 1969, LBJ Library, 1.

21. Sanford Kravitz, interview by author, May, 1995.

22. Kravitz, interview by author; "Project Head Start," *OEO Administrative History*, 229–65.

23. Tolmach, Oral History, Interview III, 1–3; *OEO Administrative History*, 325–49.

24. Tolmach, Oral History, Interview II, 1969, 29.

25. *OEO Administrative History*, 87; Tolmach, Oral History, Interview II, 29 and Interview III, 3–6; Matusow, *Unraveling*, 248.

26. For background and correspondence relating to the controversy surrounding the grant to The Woodlawn Organization, see Bertrand Harding Papers, LBJ Library, box 49.

27. Matusow, *Unraveling*, 248.

28. Charles Schulze to LBJ, September 18, 1965, War on Poverty 1964–1968, microfilm, WHCF, LBJ Library, reel 1; Matusow, *Unraveling*, 250.

29. Robert Levine, *The Poor Ye Need Not Have With You: Lessons from the War on Poverty* (Cambridge: Mass.: MIT Press, 1970), 63.

30. James A. Smith, *The Idea Brokers: Think Tanks and the Rise of the New Policy Elite* (New York: Free Press, 1991), 8–19, 98–121.

31. Smith, *Idea Brokers*, 117–21.

32. Alain Enthoven, "The Planning, Programming, and Budgeting System in the Department of Defense: Some Lessons from Experience," in *The Analysis and Evaluation of Public Expenditures: The PPB System*, vol. 1 of papers submitted to the Joint Economic Committee of Congress (Washington, D.C.: U.S. Government Printing Office, 1969), 901–3. Enthoven's paper is part of an extremely useful collection that provides an excellent overview of the PPB system and attitudes towards it. My thanks to Robert Haveman for bringing this compendium to my attention. For a more extended, and critical, perspective on the analytic approach to policy, see Laurence H. Tribe, "Policy Science: Analysis or Ideology?" *Philosophy and Public Affairs* 2 (Fall 1972), 66–110.

33. Smith, *Idea Brokers*, 134–36.

34. Alan Schick, "A Death in the Bureaucracy: The Demise of Federal PPB," *Public Administration Review* 33 (March/April 1973), 146.

35. On PPBS, see Walter Williams, *Social Policy Research and Analysis: The Experience in the Federal Social Agencies* (New York: American Elsevier Co., 1971), 18–35; Haveman, *Poverty Policy and Poverty Research*, 31–35; Schick, "A Death in the Bureaucracy."

36. *New York Times*, August 25, 1965, quoted in Williams, *Social Policy*, 5.

37. Bureau of the Budget, Bulletin #66–3, "Planning-Programming-Budgeting," October 12, 1965, OEO Microfilm Collection, LBJ Library, reel 1.

38. The following discussion draws principally on Schick, "A Death in the Bureaucracy"; Williams, *Social Policy*, 18–35; and Aaron Wildavsky, "Rescuing Policy Analysis from PPBS," in Joint Economic Committee, *The PPB System*, 835–52.

39. Enthoven, "The Planning, Programming, and Budgeting System," 907.

40. Williams, *Social Policy*, 29.

41. Alice M. Rivlin, "The Planning, Programming, and Budgeting System in the Department of Health, Education, and Welfare: Some Lessons from Experience," in Joint Economic Committee, *The PPB System*, 913.

42. Alice M. Rivlin, *Systematic Thinking for Social Action* (Washington, D.C.: Brookings Institution, 1971), 5.

43. Shriver's handwritten comment is on a memo of August 25, 1965, announcing the coming of PPBS. OEO Microfilm Collection, LBJ Library, reel 2.

44. Yarmolinsky, Oral History, 5.

45. Ibid., 17–18; Weeks, *Job Corps*, 132–41.

46. Robert Levine, Oral History, 1969, LBJ Library. OEO was not the only domestic agency to recruit analysts from the Department of Defense. Among the other prominent "crossover" appointments were Joseph Califano, who went from Defense to become a Johnson White House domestic advisor and later became head of HEW under President Jimmy Carter, and William Gorham, a defense analyst who was appointed as the first Assistant Secretary for Planning and Evaluation (ASPE) at HEW, and later became the first director of the Urban Institute, a position he would hold for more than thirty years.

47. Levine, Oral History; Otis Singletary (director of the Job Corps) Oral History, 1970, LBJ Library, 9–26; Weeks, *Job Corps*, 205.

48. Robert Levine, *The Poor Ye Need Not Have With You*, 59.

49. Robert Levine, interview by author, May 1995.

50. Walter Williams, interview by author, June 1995.

51. Myron Lefkowitz, interview by author, April 1995; Alvin Schorr, interview by author, May 1995. For more on Schorr's expertise and reform proposals, see Alvin Schorr, *Explorations in Social Policy* (New York: Basic Books, 1968).

52. "The OEO Programming System," WHCF, FG 11–15: OEO 8/15–11/17/65, LBJ Library, box 124.

53. *OEO Administrative History*, 618–19.

54. Levine, *The Poor Ye Need Not Have*, 60–62.

55. "National Anti-Poverty Plan," June 1966, Sargent Shriver Papers, LBJ Library, Introduction.

56. "The First Step," OEO Congressional Report, April 1965, Agency Records: OEO, LBJ Library, box 1, 78–79.

57. Levine, *The Poor Ye Need Not Have*, 61.

58. Ibid., 62.

59. *OEO Administrative History*, 609.

60. Wofford, "The Politics of Local Responsibility," 70.

61. Levine, *The Poor Ye Need Not Have*, 71.

62. "National Anti-Poverty Plan," introduction, Section IV, 1–3.

63. *OEO Administrative History*, 610–12.

64. Walter Heller to LBJ, "What Price Great Society?" December 21, 1965, WHCF, Confidential Files, LBJ Library, box 98, WE9.

65. Levine, *The Poor Ye Need Not Have*, 81–82; Levine, interview by author.

66. Levine, "Policy Analysis and Economic Opportunity Programs," Joint Economic Committee, *The PPB System*, 1194.

67. Levine, Oral History, 8.

68. OEO, "The First Step," 78–79.

69. An account of the sequence of research developments leading Orshansky to develop the poverty line is reported in detail in Gordon M. Fisher, "The Development of the Orshansky Poverty Thresholds and Their Subsequent History as the Official U.S. Poverty Measure," unpublished paper, May 1992, 20–27. For a definitive overview of poverty measurements since the early twentieth century, see Fisher, "From Hunter to Orshansky: An Overview of (Unofficial) Poverty Lines in the United States from 1904

to 1965." I am very grateful to Fisher for making these and other papers on the evolution of the poverty line available to me.

70. Eugene Smolensky, Proceedings of the 23rd Interstate Conference on Labor Statistics, June 15–18, 1965, quoted in Fisher, "Orshansky Poverty Thresholds," 22n. 62.

71. Naomi Aronson, "Nutrition as a Social Problem: A Case Study of Entrepreneurial Strategy in Science," *Social Problems* 29 (June 1982): 474–87; Linda Gordon, *Pitied But Not Entitled: Single Mothers and the History of Welfare, 1890–1935* (New York: The Free Press, 1994), 167–81.

72. Mollie Orshansky, "How Poverty is Measured," *Monthly Labor Review*, February 1969, 37; Fisher, "Orshansky Poverty Thresholds," 31; U.S. Chamber of Commerce, *The Concept of Poverty* (Washington, D.C.: 1965).

73. Mollie Orshansky, "Counting the Poor: Another Look at the Poverty Profile," *Social Security Bulletin*, January 1965. The "multiplier" of three was based on survey evidence indicating that most families spent approximately one-third of their budgets on food.

74. Memo to the CEA from James T. Bonnen, "OEO's New Definition of Poverty," May 17, 1965. I am grateful to Professor Bonnen for providing me with a copy of this memo.

75. Orshansky, "Counting the Poor," 10.

76. For summary discussions of the major critiques of the poverty line, see Patricia Ruggles, *Drawing the Line: Alternative Poverty Measures and Their Implications for Public Policy* (Washington, D.C.: The Urban Institute, 1990); Haveman, *Poverty Policy and Poverty Research*, 74–79; Constance F. Citro and Robert T. Michael, *Measuring Poverty: A New Approach*, (Washington, D.C.: National Academy Press, 1995).

77. Citro and Michael, *Measuring Poverty: A New Approach*.

78. Robert J. Lampman, "What Does It Do for the Poor? A New Test for National Policy," *Public Interest*, 34 (Winter 1974): 81; James Tobin, quoted in Haveman, *Poverty Policy and Poverty Research*, 56.

79. Edward A. Suchman, *Evaluative Research: Principles and Practice in Public Service and Social Action Programs* (New York: Russell Sage Foundation, 1967), 23. The correspondence regarding these early attempts to come up with an evaluation plan for CAP are in the OEO Microfilm Collection, LBJ Library, reel 1.

80. Joseph Kershaw to Theodore Berry, November 9, 1965, OEO Microfilm Collection, LBJ Library, reel 6; Robert Levine to RPP&E Staff, January 10, 1968, Institute for Research on Poverty (hereafter IRP) Archives; Williams, *Social Policy*, 108–9.

81. For an overview of Head Start's early history, including the "fade-out" controversy, see *OEO Administrative History*, 229–65. See also Head Start director Jule M. Sugarman, Oral History, 1969, LBJ Library. An extremely helpful discussion of the evaluation conflict is Walter Williams and John Evans, "The Politics of Evaluation: The Case of Head Start," *The Annals of the American Academy* 385 (September 1969): 118–32.

82. Levine to Shriver, "Compendium on Evaluation," January 13, 1967, IRP Archives, 3.

83. Williams and Evans, "Politics of Evaluation," 124; Williams, *Social Policy*, 111–13.

84. Williams and Evans, "Politics of Evaluation," 125–26; Nixon quoted in Williams, *Social Policy*, 114.

85. M. A. Farber, "Head Start Report Held 'Full of Holes,' " *New York Times*, April 18, 1969, A1.

86. Robert B. Semple, Jr., "White House and Advisors Stand By Report Critical of Head Start," *New York Times*, April 27, 1969, A 44.

87. Ibid.

88. Council for Urban Affairs, "Report of the Subcommittee: Future of the Poverty Program and the Office of Economic Opportunity," February 1, 1969, Arthur Burns Papers, Urban Affairs Council (13), Gerald Ford Library, Ann Arbor, Michigan.

89. Resource Management Corporation, *Evaluations of the War on Poverty: Status and Prospects at the Office of Economic Opportunity* (Santa Monica, Calif.: 1969), v, 23, 30.

90. Robert Perrin to Cabinet members, "OEO Reorganization," August 11, 1969, Arthur Burns Papers, Office of Economic Opportunity, Ford Library.

91. William R. Shadish, Jr., Thomas D. Cook, and Laura C. Leviton, *Foundations of Program Evaluation* (London: Sage Publications, 1991), 25–27.

92. Ibid., 28–29.

93. "National Anti-Poverty Plan," Section III-I, 1–8.

94. Rivlin, *Systematic Thinking for Social Action*, 86–119.

95. National Advisory Council on Economic Opportunity, *Focus on Community Action* (Washington, D.C.: 1968), 15–20; *OEO Administrative History*, Addendum, 6.

96. Council for Urban Affairs, "Report of the Subcommittee: Future of the Poverty Program and the Office of Economic Opportunity," February 1, 1969, Arthur Burns Papers, Urban Affairs Council, box 13, Ford Library; Thomas Glennan, interview by author, June 1995; Edward Gramlich, interview by author, June 1995; and Robert Levine interview by author.

97. Council for Urban Affairs, "Report of the Subcommittee."

98. Daniel P. Moynihan, "The Professionalization of Reform," *Public Interest*, 1 (1965): 6–16.

99. Daniel P. Moynihan, "The Professors and the Poor," in Daniel P. Moynihan, ed., *On Understanding Poverty* (New York: Basic Books, 1969), 3–35.

100. Council for Urban Affairs, "Future of the Poverty Program."

101. Robert Perrin to Cabinet Members, "OEO Reorganization," August 11, 1969, Arthur Burns Papers, Office of Economic Opportunity, Ford Library.

102. The phrase is Hugh Heclo's in "OMB and the Presidency—The Problem of 'Neutral Competence,' " *Public Interest*, 38 (Winter 1975): 80–98.

103. Arnold J. Meltsner, *Policy Analysts in the Bureaucracy* (Berkeley: University of California Press, 1976), 190–92; Glennan and Gramlich interviews by author.

104. Walter Williams, *Mismanaging America: The Rise of the Anti-Analytic Presidency* (Lawrence: University Press of Kansas, 1990), 48; Glennan interview by author.

105. Glennan, interview by author; Glennan to PR&E staff, "Five Year Plan," October 13, 1971, IRP Archives.

106. John Wilson to Donald Rumsfeld, "Proposed Plan for Research in PR&E, October 1, 1969, IRP archives; Williams, *Mismanaging*, 48; Glennan and Gramlich interviews by author.

107. William Plissner to OEO Employees, "Narrative Description of the Impact on OEO of the 1974 budget," n.d., IRP Archives.

Chapter 8
Poverty's Culture Wars

1. Daniel P. Moynihan, ed., *On Understanding Poverty* (New York: Basic Books, 1969); James Sundquist, ed., *On Fighting Poverty* (New York: Basic Books, 1969).

2. Daniel P. Moynihan, "The Professors and the Poor," and Harold Watts, "An Economic Definition of Poverty," both in Moynihan, ed., *On Understanding Poverty*, 5, 19, 316–17.

3. The Hemingway/Fitzgerald exchange is rendered in, among other places, Moynihan, "Professors and the Poor," and in Lee Rainwater, *Behind Ghetto Walls: Black Families in a Federal Slum* (Chicago: Aldine Publishing Company, 1970), 364. On the question of race, poverty, and the limitations of income-based definitions of poverty, see especially Otis Dudley Duncan, "Inheritance of Poverty or Inheritance of Race?" and Marc A. Fried, "Deprivation and Migration," both in Moynihan, *On Understanding Poverty*, 85–110, 111–59.

4. On the demise of the culture of poverty as a liberal idea, see Michael B. Katz, *The Undeserving Poor: From the War on Poverty to the War on Welfare* (New York: Pantheon, 1989), 17–35.

5. Zahava Blum and Peter H. Rossi, "Social Class Research and Images of the Poor: A Bibliographic Review," in Moynihan, *On Understanding Poverty*, 22, 38–39.

6. Oscar Lewis, *The Children of Sanchez* (New York: Random House, 1961), 30. Eleanor Leacock, ed., *The Culture of Poverty: A Critique* (New York: Simon and Schuster, 1971), 19.

7. Walter B. Miller, "Implications of Urban Lower-Class Culture for Social Work," *Social Service Review* 33 (1959): 231, and "Lower-Class Culture as a Generating Milieu of Gang Delinquency," *Journal of Social Issues* 14, no. 3 (1958): 5–19.

8. Oscar Lewis, "The Culture of Poverty," in Moynihan, *On Understanding Poverty*, 187–220.

9. Herbert J. Gans, *The Urban Villagers: Group and Class in the Life of Italian-Americans* (New York: Free Press, 1962), 267–68. As noted below, Gans later retracted his analysis of this lower-class subculture, stating that he was dissatisfied with his generalizations about the relationship between family structure and class, and arguing that class differences were based in economics. See the revised (1982) edition, 281.

10. For the situationalist perspective, see Herbert J. Gans, "Culture and Class in the Study of Poverty: An Approach to Anti-Poverty Research," and Lee Rainwater, "The Problem of Lower-Class Culture and Poverty War Strategy," both in Moynihan, *On Understanding Poverty*, 201–59. On the "value stretch," see Hyman Rodman, "The Lower-Class Value Stretch," *Social Forces* 42 (December 1963): 205–15, and *Lower-Class Families: The Culture of Poverty in Negro Trinidad* (New York: Oxford University Press, 1971), 4–7.

11. Hylan Lewis, *Blackways of Kent* (Chapel Hill: University of North Carolina Press, 1955), 153–54, 311–12, 327.

12. For a fuller discussion of "damage" psychology, see Scott, *Contempt and Pity*, chap. 6.

13. Abram Kardiner and Lionel Ovesey, *The Mark of Oppression* (New York: W.W. Norton, 1951), 381–85; Scott, *Contempt and Pity*, 76–79.

14. Thomas F. Pettigrew, *A Profile of the American Negro* (New York: Van Nostrand and Company, 1964); Scott, *Contempt and Pity*, 80.

15. Dreger and Miller, Psychological Bulletin 1960, cited by Laura Carper, "The Negro Family and the Moynihan Report," in Lee Rainwater and William L. Yancey, eds., *The Moynihan Report and the Politics of Controversy* (Cambridge, Mass.: MIT Press, 1967), 466–74.

16. The findings from these studies, some of which were conducted in Trinidad for comparative reasons, are reported in Walter Mischel, "Preference for Delayed Reinforcement and Social Responsibility," *Journal of Abnormal and Social Psychology* 62 (January 1961): 1–7; "Delay of Gratification, Need for Achievement and Acquiescence in Another Culture," *Journal of Abnormal and Social Psychology* 62 (May 1961): 543–52; "Father-Absence and Delay of Gratification: Cross-Cultural Comparisons," *Journal of Abnormal and Social Psychology* 63 (July 1962): 116–24.

17. Pettigrew, *A Profile of the American Negro*, 16–19.

18. For a more extended discussion of the liberal use of damage imagery, see Scott, *Contempt and Pity*, chap. 8.

19. Kenneth B. Clark, *Dark Ghetto: Dilemmas of Social Power* (New York: Harper and Row, 1965), xxxvi; Gerald Markowitz and David Rosner, *Children, Race, and Power: Kenneth and Mamie Clark's Northside Center* (Charlottesville: University Press of Virginia, 1996), 197–99.

20. Rainwater, *Behind Ghetto Walls*, vii.

21. Lee Rainwater, "Crucible of Identity: The Negro Lower-Class Family," *Daedalus* 95 (Winter 1966): 176–216.

22. Clark, *Dark Ghetto*, chaps. 4–5.

23. Rainwater, "Crucible," 207–9.

24. See, for example, Pettigrew, *Profile*, 16–17.

25. *The Negro Family: The Case for National Action* (Washington, D.C.: Office of Policy Planning and Research, March 1965), reprinted in Rainwater and Yancey, *The Moynihan Report and the Politics of Controversy*, preamble, 3, 5–6.

26. Scott, *Contempt and Pity*, 150–56.

27. The phrase was Kenneth Clark's, used initially in HARYOU reports and then in *Dark Ghetto*, published in 1965. Daniel P. Moynihan, *Miles to Go: A Personal History of Social Policy* (Cambridge, Mass.: Harvard University Press, 1996), 178.

28. *The Negro Family*, 16, 39–40.

29. Ibid., 48.

30. Ibid., 34–43.

31. Moynihan, *Miles to Go*, 180.

32. *The Negro Family*, 5.

33. James T. Patterson, *America's Struggle Against Poverty, 1900–1994* (Cambridge, Mass.: Harvard University Press, 1994), 78–84; Gilbert Steiner, *Social Insecurity: The Politics of Welfare* (Chicago: Rand McNally, 1966), 31–32; Carper, "The Negro Family and the Moynihan Report," 468; Elizabeth Herzog, "Unmarried Mothers: Some Questions To Be Answered and Some Answers To Be Questioned," *Child Welfare* 41 (October 1962): 339–50.

34. See, for example, the graph comparing white vs. nonwhite male/female employment ratios, *The Negro Family*, 33, as compared to the figures on job distribution in

St. Clair Drake and Horace Cayton *Black Metropolis* (Chicago: University of Chicago Press, 1993), 225–32.

35. Carper, "The Negro Family and the Moynihan Report," 467–68; William J. Wilson and Kathryn M. Neckerman, "Poverty and Family Structure: The Widening Gap Between Evidence and Public Policy Issues," in Sheldon H. Danziger and Daniel H. Weinberg, eds., *Fighting Poverty: What Works and What Doesn't*, (Cambridge, Mass.: Harvard University Press, 1984), 258–59.

36. President's Task Force on Manpower Conservation, *One-Third of a Nation: A Report on Young Men Unqualified for Military Service* (Washington, D.C.: U.S. Government Printing Office, 1964).

37. "To Fulfill These Rights," June 4, 1965, reprinted in Rainwater and Yancey, *The Moynihan Report*, 125–32.

38. Elizabeth Wickenden, "Confidential Notes on the Planning Session for White House Conference 'To Fulfill These Rights,' " November 23, 1965, Wilbur Cohen Papers, Wisconsin State Historical Society, box 113, folder 8.

39. Moynihan, *Miles to Go*, 178; Rowland Evans and Robert Novack, "Inside Report," August 18, 1965, in Rainwater and Yancey, *The Moynihan Report*, 375–76; Ellen Herman, *The Romance of American Psychology: Political Culture in the Age of Experts* (Berkeley: University of California Press, 1995), 206–7.

40. Wickenden, "Confidential Notes," 1.

41. See, for example, columns by CORE director James Farmer in Rainwater and Yancey, *The Moynihan Report*, 409–13.

42. For a detailed discussion of the efforts of civil rights organizations to push an economic and social welfare agenda, see Dona Cooper Hamilton and Charles V. Hamilton, *The Dual Agenda: Race and Social Welfare Policies of Civil Rights Organizations* (New York: Columbia University Press, 1997).

43. Ibid., 139.

44. Christopher Jencks, "The Moynihan Report," in Rainwater and Yancey, *The Moynihan Report*, 443.

45. Hylan Lewis, "The Family: Resources for Change," and Mary Dublin Keyserling, "The Negro Woman at Work: Gains and Problems," November 11, 1965, White House Conference "To Fulfill These Rights" Collection, LBJ Library, boxes 4 and 72.

46. Herbert J. Gans, "The Negro Family: Reflections on the Moynihan Report," in Rainwater and Yancey, *The Moynihan Report*, 445–57.

47. Among the earlier, and most influential, scholarly projects providing systematic evidence to refute the Moynihan Report are Herbert G. Gutman, *The Black Family in Slavery and Freedom, 1750–1925* (New York: Vintage Books, 1976) and Carol Stack, *All Our Kin: Strategies for Survival in a Black Community* (New York: Harper and Row, 1974). While Gutman and Stack embarked on their research in the mid-to-late 1960s, when scholarly controversy over the Report was at its height, more recent scholarship continues to invoke Moynihan in disputing and providing alternatives to the larger tradition of black lower-class pathology. See, for example, Jacqueline Jones, *Labor of Love, Labor of Sorrow: Black Women, Work, and the Family, From Slavery to the Present* (New York: Basic Books, 1985) and Robin D. G. Kelley, *Yo' Mama's Disfunktional!: Fighting the Culture Wars in Urban America* (Boston: Beacon Press, 1997).

48. Alice O'Connor, "The False Dawn of Poor Law Reform: Nixon, Carter, and the Quest for a Guaranteed Income," *Journal of Policy History* 10, no. 1 (1998): 104–5.

49. Daniel Patrick Moynihan, "The Crisis in Welfare," *The Public Interest*, no. 10 (1968): 3–29.

50. Hylan Lewis, "Child Rearing Practices among Low-Income Families in the District of Columbia," and "Culture, Class and the Behavior of Low-Income Families," both reprinted in *Culture, Class and Poverty* (Washington, D.C.: Crosstell, 1967), 1–12, 13–42. Both essays are based on an NIMH project Lewis directed in low-income Washington, D.C., communities, which also provided the basis for Eliot Liebow's *Tally's Corner: A Study of Negro Streetcorner Men* (Boston: Little, Brown, 1967).

51. Herbert J. Gans "Poverty and Culture: Some Basic Questions About Methods of Studying Life-Styles of the Poor," in Peter Townsend, ed., *The Concept of Poverty: Working Papers on Methods of Investigation and Life-Styles of the Poor in Different Countries* (London: Heineman Press, 1970), 149; and *Urban Villagers*, rev. ed. (1982), 281.

52. Oscar Lewis, responding to Charles Valentine in *Current Anthropology* 10 (April–June 1969), 191–92. For a more extended discussion, see Susan Rigdon, *The Culture Facade: Art, Science and Politics in the Work of Oscar Lewis* (Urbana: University of Illinois Press, 1988), 87–108.

53. Charles A. Valentine, *Culture and Poverty: Critique and Counter-Proposals* (Chicago: University of Chicago Press, 1968); Leacock, *The Culture of Poverty*; Katz, *Undeserving Poor*, 37–43, 251n. 17.

54. William Ryan, *Blaming the Victim* (New York: Random House, 1971); Lee Rainwater, "Neutralizing the Disinherited" in Vernon Allen, ed., *Psychological Factors in Poverty* (Chicago: Markham Publishing Co., 1970), 9–28; Thomas Gladwin, Review of Charles A. Valentine's *Culture and Poverty*, *Current Anthropology* 10 (April–June 1969), 185.

55. Edward Banfield, *The Unheavenly City* (Boston: Little, Brown, 1970) and *The Unheavenly City Revisited* (Boston: Little, Brown, 1974).

56. William Julius Wilson, *The Truly Disadvantaged: The Inner City, The Underclass, and Public Policy* (Chicago: University of Chicago Press, 1987).

Chapter 9
The Poverty Research Industry

1. Robert H. Haveman, *Poverty Policy and Poverty Research* (Madison: University of Wisconsin Press, 1987), 38–39; Edward F. Lawlor, "Income Security," in Laurence E. Lynn, Jr., ed., *Studies in the Management of Social R&D: Selected Policy Areas* (Washington, D.C.: National Academy of Sciences, 1978), 11–59. For an overview of federal spending patterns for social research more broadly, see volume I of the report by the National Research Council Study Project on Social Research and Development, *The Federal Investment in Knowledge of Social Problems* (Washington, D.C.: National Academy of Sciences, 1978), 17–29.

2. For an extensive review of poverty research and its contribution to social scientific methodology, see Haveman, *Poverty Policy*.

3. Gary Burtless, "Public Spending for the Poor: Trends, Prospects, and Economic Limits," in Sheldon H. Danziger and Daniel H. Weinberg, eds., *Fighting Poverty: What Works and What Doesn't* (Cambridge, Mass., 1986), 18–49.

4. "New Study Field: Policy Sciences," *New York Times*, August 9, 1970.

5. "Policy Analysis Explosion," *Trans-action*, September/October 1979; Peter de-Leon, "Policy Sciences: The Discipline and Profession," *Policy Sciences* 13 (February 1981): 1–7; Aaron Wildavsky, "The Once and Future School of Public Policy," *The Public Interest* 79 (Spring 1985): 25–41; Robert H. Haveman, "Policy Analysis and the Congress: An Economist's View," *Policy Analysis* 2 (Spring 1976): 235–50; Sidney M. Milkis, "Remaking Government Institutions in the 1970s: Participatory Democracy and the Triumph of Administrative Politics," *Journal of Policy History* 10, no. 1 (1998): 51–74.

6. The text is Aaron Wildavsky, *Speaking Truth to Power: The Art and Craft of Policy Analysis* (Boston: Little, Brown, 1979). Among the most penetrating of criticisms are Charles E. Lindblom and David K. Cohen, *Usable Knowledge: Social Science and Social Problem Solving* (New Haven: Yale University Press, 1979); Harold Orlans, *Contracting for Knowledge* (San Francisco: Jossey-Bass, 1973); Laurence H. Tribe, "Policy Science: Analysis or Ideology?" *Philosophy and Public Affairs* 2 (Fall 1972): 66–110; and Henry J. Aaron, *Politics and the Professors: The Great Society in Perspective* (Washington, D.C.: The Brookings Institution, 1978).

7. Wildavsky, "Once and Future School," 29–32.

8. Richard Elmore, "A Political Scientist's View of the Income Maintenance Experiments," in Alicia Munnell, ed., *Lessons from Income Maintenance Experiments*, 206–13. For an excellent discussion of changes in policy making more generally, see Hugh Heclo, "Issue Networks and the Executive Establishment," in Anthony King, ed., *The New American Political System* (Washington, D.C.: American Enterprise Institute, 1978), 87–124.

9. For more on Nixon's FAP and the politics of race, see Jill Quadagno, *The Color of Welfare: How Race Undermined the War on Poverty* (New York: Oxford University Press, 1994), 121–34.

10. The relationship between politics and analytic research has been a central issue in the growing literature on "knowledge utilization," most of it debunking the notion of "neutral competence" that informed the analytic ideal. See, for just a small sampling, Carol H. Weiss, "Ideology, Interests, and Information: The Basis of Policy Positions," in Daniel Callahan, ed., *Ethics, Social Science and Policy Analysis* (New York: Plenum Press, 1983); Hugh Heclo, "OMB and the Presidency—The Problem of 'Neutral Competence,'" *The Public Interest*, 38 (Winter 1975): 80–98; Bruce Bimber, *The Politics of Expertise in Congress: The Rise and Fall of the Office of Technology Assessment* (Albany: State University of New York Press, 1996), chaps. 1–2.

11. "A Think Tank that Thinks for the Poor," *Business Week*, June 22, 1968, 106.

12. Robert A. Levine to Sargent Shriver, August 15, 1966, Harding Papers, LBJ Library, box 41.

13. For discussions of how the Wisconsin Idea had played out in policy, see Jess Gilbert, "Democratic Planning in the New Deal: The Federal-County Agricultural Planning Program, 1938–1942," Paper delivered at the Newberry Library, Chicago, February 1994, 13, and Edward D. Berkowitz, *America's Welfare State From Roosevelt to Reagan* (Baltimore: Johns Hopkins University Press, 1991), 33–36.

14. This move, which mirrored the trend toward quantification universitywide, was heralded by the department's recruitment of noted MIT econometrician Guy Orcutt, who arrived in Madison in 1959 and helped to establish the Social Systems Research Institute as a multidisciplinary center devoted to quantitative research and statistical model-building. This and other efforts to make the social sciences more "scientific" were heavily subsidized by the Ford Foundation and the National Academy of Sciences, although Orcutt himself was continually frustrated by what he saw as the insufficiency of financial support.

15. "Think Tank for the Poor," 107; Robert A. Levine, Memo of conversation at University of Wisconsin, March 9, 1965, Institute for Research on Poverty (hereafter IRP) Archives.

16. Robert Lampman, "The Institute for Research on Poverty," in Charles E. Higbie, ed., *Conference on Poverty Research, Communications and the Public* (Madison: University of Wisconsin Press, 1966), 121.

17. Robben Fleming to Faculty, September 27, 1965, IRP Archives; "Request for Grant for Poverty Studies," n.d., IRP Archives.

18. Institute for Research on Poverty, "Research Progress," July 1966, IRP Archives.

19. "Report of Inspection Made October 23–25, 1967, The Institute for Research on Poverty," February 9, 1968, IRP Archives, 1.

20. "Report of Inspection," 1–2, 7.

21. Ibid., 12–17, 26.

22. Kershaw to Levine, March 5, 1968, IRP Archives.

23. "Report of Inspection," 33.

24. Advisory Committee for Assessment of University-based Institutes for Research on Poverty, National Academy of Sciences, "Interim Report," June 1970, IRP Archives, 35–36.

25. "Interim Report," 28–29.

26. Subsequent experiments were conducted in rural North Carolina and Iowa; Gary, Indiana; and jointly in Seattle and Denver (SIME/DIME).

27. For more on the negative income tax and its genesis, see Christopher Green, *Negative Taxes and the Poverty Problem* (Washington, D.C.: The Brookings Institution, 1967). On OEO sponsorship, see Alice O'Connor, "The False Dawn of Poor Law Reform: Nixon, Carter, and the Quest for a Guaranteed Income," *Journal of Policy History* 10, no.1 (1998): 110–12; Office of Economic Opportunity, "National Anti-Poverty Plan, FY 1968–1972," June 1966, Sargent Shriver Papers, LBJ Library.

28. These conclusions are reflected in the reports of two successive interagency task forces on income maintenance, in 1965 and 1966, both in the LBJ Library. For brief summaries, see memo and attachments from CEA Chairman Gardner Ackley to Joseph Califano, Califano Office Files, LBJ Library, box 19.

29. Robert Lampman, "The Decision to Undertake the New Jersey Experiment," in David Kershaw and Jerilyn Fair, eds., *The New Jersey Income Maintenance Experiment*, vol. I (New York: Academic Press, 1976), xvi.

30. Robert Levine to Sargent Shriver, May 6, 1967, IRP Archives.

31. Robinson Hollister, interview by author, May 1995.

32. Harold Watts Oral History, University of Wisconsin (hereafter UW) Archives, 22; "Think Tank for the Poor," 106; Harold Watts, Statement before the Fiscal Policy

Subcommittee of the Joint Economic Committee of Congress, June 13, 1968, IRP Archives; IRP National Advisory Committee meeting minutes, May 1968, IRP Archives.

33. Kershaw and Fair, *New Jersey Experiment*, 8–11.

34. Ibid., 14–15; David Kershaw to John Wilson, July 1, 1970, New Jersey NIT Experiment, (hereafter NJ Experiement) UW Archives, box 9, Site Selection folder.

35. The riots did affect the experiment in other ways: Newark was ruled out as a site, for fear of potential racial turmoil, and the initial payment schedule was changed from spring to early September 1968 for fear that another long hot summer would create administrative problems. Kershaw and Fair, *New Jersey Experiment*, 24; Letter from William Baumol to Harold Watts, November 14, 1967, NJ Experiment, UW Archives, box 9, Correspondence folder.

36. Richard M. Nixon, "Address to the Nation on Domestic Programs" ("New Federalism" Speech), August 8, 1969, *Public Papers of the Presidents, 1969* (Washington, D.C.: U.S. Government Printing Office, 1971), 637–45.

37. On Nixon's attempts to "tame" the bureaucracy, see Richard Nathan, *The Plot That Failed: Nixon and the Administrative Presidency* (New York: John Wiley and Sons, 1975).

38. Memo from Richard Redinius to John Wilson, March 20, 1970, IRP Archives; Harold Watts to Wilson, April 27, 1970, IRP Archives. For more on the CAP evaluation and its political uses, see Alice O'Connor, "Evaluating Comprehensive Community Initiatives: A View from History," in James P. Connell et al., *New Approaches to Evaluating Community Initiatives* (Queenstown, Md.: Aspen Institute, 1995), 45–46.

39. Thomas Glennan, interview by author, July 1995.

40. Kershaw and Fair, *New Jersey Experiment*, 183–86; Memo by David Kershaw, "Administrative Relations with Existing Public Assistance Agencies in New Jersey," December 1970, NJ Experiment, UW Archives, box 7, folder 1.

41. For an overview of the "explosion" and changing demographics of the welfare rolls, see James T. Patterson, *America's Struggle Against Poverty, 1900–1994* (Cambridge, Mass.: Harvard University Press, 1994), 171–84.

42. Daniel P. Moynihan, the Family Assistance Plan's chief sponsor at the White House, laid out the "dependency" argument in "The Crises in Welfare," *The Public Interest*, 10 (Winter 1968): 3–29.

43. For an account of the exchange with Moynihan, see Fred J. Cook, "When You Just Give Money to the Poor," *New York Times Magazine*, May 3, 1970, 110.

44. "Preliminary Results of the New Jersey Graduated Work Incentive Experiment," February 18, 1970, Needham Papers, Gerald R. Ford Library, Ann Arbor, Michigan, box 5.

45. "Chronology—General Accounting Office and Senator Williams," NJ Experiment, UW Archives, box 3; Kershaw and Fair, *New Jersey Experiment*, 187–89 and Appendix A.

46. On FAP's demise, see Daniel P. Moynihan, *The Politics of a Guaranteed Income: The Nixon Administration and the Family Assistance Plan* (New York: Random House, 1973); Quadagno, *Color of Welfare*, 131–34; Gareth Davies, *From Opportunity to Entitlement: The Transformation and Decline of Great Society Liberalism* (Lawrence: University Press of Kansas, 1996), 226–33.

47. David N. Kershaw, "A Negative-Income-Tax Experiment," *Scientific American* 227 (October 1972): 19–24.

48. For descriptions of the experiments as they were about to go into the field, see the forum on "Current Status of Income Maintenance Experiments," *American Economics Review* (May 1971): 15–42. On the motivations for conducting additional experiments, see David Greenberg and Marvin Mandell, "The Income Maintenance Experiments," Paper presented at the Association of Public Policy and Management Annual Meeting, October 1995, 13–15.

49. The issue of experimental design has in fact been the subject of ongoing debate in policy analysis, and particularly in evaluation circles. See, for example, James J. Heckman, V. Joseph Hotz, and Marcelo Dabos, "Do We Need Experimental Data to Evaluate the Impact of Manpower Training on Earnings?" *Evaluation Review* 11 (August 1987): 395–427, and Charles F. Manski and Irwin Garfinkel, eds., *Evaluating Welfare and Training Programs* (Cambridge, Mass.: Harvard University Press, 1992).

50. William Plissner (OEO Controller) to OEO Employees, undated memo, IRP Archives.

51. Walter Williams, *Mismanaging America: The Rise of the Anti-Analytic Presidency* (Lawrence: University Press of Kansas, 1990), 44–46; Beryl A. Radin, "Policy Analysis in the Office of the Assistant Secretary for Planning and Evaluation in HEW/ HHS: Institutionalization and the Second Generation," unpublished paper, Department of Health and Human Services Record Center, Washington, D.C.

52. National Advisory Committee Meeting Minutes, April 19, 1974, IRP Archives; Department of Health Education and Welfare, "Policy Research Studies," *Federal Register* 39 (September 27, 1974).

53. HEW, "The Income Supplement Program: 1974 Welfare Replacement Proposal," 1974, HHS Record Center.

54. National Research Council, *Evaluating Federal Support for Poverty Research* (Washington, D.C.: National Academy of Science, 1979), 16.

55. Haveman, "Policy Analysis and the Congress: An Economist's View"; Bimber, *The Politics of Expertise*, 78–92.

56. On the significance of and increasing reliance on contract arrangements as a mechanism for procuring research, see James A. Smith, *The Idea Brokers: Think Tanks and the Rise of the New Policy Elite* (New York: Free Press, 1991), 113–14; National Academy of Sciences Study Group on Social Research and Development, *The Federal Investment in Knowledge of Social Problems* (Washington, D.C.: National Academy of Sciences, 1978), 50–51.

57. The concerns over "diversification" and generating large research projects are reflected in several internal IRP documents, including Irv Garfinkel to Research Committee, January 8, 1976, IRP Archives.

58. For general background on the Urban Institute, see Smith, *The Idea Brokers*, 151–54, 291–92. The Urban Institute Archives in Washington, D.C. also contain helpful documents, including an in-house history (untitled), written by Grace Bassett.

59. Transcript of News Conference with Joseph A. Califano, Washington, December 6, 1967, Urban Institute Archives.

60. Frederick O'R Hayes and Anthony F. Japha, "The Urban Institute: An Evaluation," 1977, Ford Foundation Report #003743, Ford Foundation Archives, 11.

61. Califano interview, quoted in Bassett, History, Part II, 7. The idea for a government-financed institute on urban development had been circulating in foundations for

years. It was formally proposed by LBJ's 1964 Task Force on Cities, which was chaired by MIT political scientist and later HUD undersecretary Robert C. Wood, and included several prominent urbanologists. The idea came up again in a 1967 Task Force chaired by the Ford Foundation's Paul Ylvisaker. For a discussion of the various task force recommendations, see Bassett, History, Part I, 2–4.

62. The other incorporators included Cummins Engine CEO Irwin Miller, Ford Motor Company President Arjay Miller, Brookings Institution President Kermit Gordon, and New York attorney Cyrus Vance. Bassett, History, Part II, 35–39.

63. Bassett, History, Part II, 43–44; Memorandum for The Board of Trustees, The Urban Institute, April 8, 1968, Urban Institute Archives.

64. Bassett, History, Part II, 78–84.

65. Despite the continued funding, the whole issue of project-specific vs. basic or "mission" research was a continuing source of tension between the Institute and the Ford Foundation as well, a tension outlined in a memorandum from foundation staff member Fred Bohen to McGeorge Bundy, October 24, 1969, Bundy Papers, Ford Foundation Archives, series II, box 21.

66. Hayes and Japha, "The Urban Institute: An Evaluation," 3–8; Randall Bovbjerg, "A Brief History of the Urban Institute," September 1983, Urban Institute Archives, 3–8.

67. For accounts of the initial development and use of microsimulation models for policy purposes, see Kenneth L. Kraemer et al., *Datawars: The Politics of Modeling in Federal Policymaking* (New York: Columbia University Press, 1987), 33–42; and Haveman, *Poverty Policy and Poverty Research*, 217–21.

68. Moynihan, *Guaranteed Income*, 190.

69. Haveman, *Poverty Policy and Poverty Research*, 220; Kraemer et al., *Datawars*, 42–46.

70. Hayes and Japha, "Urban Institute: An Evaluation," 34–35; Haveman, *Poverty Research*, 222.

71. Kraemer et al., *Datawars*, 49–62.

72. "The 'Modern Miracle' of Microsimulation," *Focus* 4 (Summer 1980): 10–13. On the role of competing models in Carter's PBJI, see Kraemer et al., *Datawars*, 140–43.

73. On the costs of modeling, see Haveman, *Poverty Research*, 228, and David Betson, David Greenberg, and Richard Kasten, "A Simulation of the Program for Better Jobs and Income," ASPE Technical Analysis Paper #17, HHS Record Center, p. 1.

74. Hayes and Japha, "Urban Institute: An Evaluation," 22–25; George E. Peterson, "Intergovernmental Financial Relations," in George Galster, ed., *Reality and Research: Social Science and U.S. Urban Policy Since 1960* (Washington, D.C.: The Urban Institute Press, 1995), 217.

75. Mitchell Sviridoff, Oral History, Ford Foundation Archives; Sviridoff to McGeorge Bundy, March 7, 1978, Bundy Papers, Ford Foundation Archives, series II, box 18, folder 228.

76. Mitchell Sviridoff, "A Perspective on the Seventies," *Ford Foundation Annual Report* (New York: Ford Foundation, 1969): 17–22.

77. On the Ford Foundation's efforts to build a working-class program, see "The Working Class Program," National Affairs Committee, June 1975, Report #010981, Ford Foundation Archives.

78. "National Affairs Programs: Some Comments on Background and Rationale," Report #006510, November 1975, Ford Foundation Archives. For a good statement of the intermediary philosophy, see William J. Grinker, "The Use of Nonprofit Intermediaries in the Development of Social Policy" (Manpower Demonstration Research Corporation Library).

79. On the genesis of Supported Work, see Edward M. Brecher, *The Manpower Demonstration Research Corporation: Origins and Early Operations* (New York: Ford Foundation, 1978), 1–6; Joseph Ball, "Implementation of the Supported Work Program Model," in Robinson G. Hollister, Jr., Peter Kemper, and Rebecca A. Maynard, *The National Supported Work Demonstration* (Madison: University of Wisconsin Press, 1984), 51–52; Richard P. Nathan, *Social Science in Government: Uses and Misuses* (New York: Basic Books, 1988), 97–98.

80. Margaret Weir, *Politics and Jobs: The Boundaries of Employment Policy in the United States* (Princeton: Princeton University Press, 1992), 67–69.

81. The Department of Labor was the "lead" and by far the largest funder, contributing just under $10 million at the start. Other agencies were the Department of Justice (Law Enforcement Assistance Administration), the National Institute on Drug Abuse, HEW, HUD, and the Department of Commerce (Economic Development Administration).

82. MDRC, 1977 *Annual Report*, 8; Sviridoff to Bundy, March 7, 1978.

83. MDRC, 1977 *Annual Report*, 8.

84. Robinson G. Hollister, Jr., "The Design and Implementation of the Supported Work Evaluation," in Hollister, Kemper, and Maynard, *The National Supported Work Demonstration*, 20–21; Heckman, Hotz, and Dabos, "Do We Need Experimental Data?"

85. See, for example, Lloyd Ulman, "The Uses and Limits of Manpower Policy," *The Public Interest*, 34 (Winter 1974): 83–105.

86. The advisory group was chaired by Columbia University manpower economist Eli Ginsburg, who was initially the lone skeptic about emphasizing research as opposed to program goals. Other board members were IRP's poverty expert Robert Lampman, MIT economist Robert Solow, Gilbert Steiner from the Brookings Institution, economist Phyllis Wallace from MIT's Sloane School of Management (the only African American and the only woman on the original board), and former Nixon advisor Richard Nathan, a political scientist then at Brookings.

87. For a comparison of the two, see "Assessment of Two Intermediary Organizations: The Corporation for Public Private Ventures and the Manpower Demonstration Research Corporation," Report #006675, Ford Foundation Archives.

88. MDRC, *Summary and Findings of the National Supported Work Demonstration* (Cambridge, Mass.: Ballinger, 1980), 1–15; Ken Auletta, *The Underclass* (New York: Random House, 1982).

89. O'Connor, "False Dawn of Poor Law Reform," 118–19.

90. Aaron, *Politics and the Professors*, 159.

91. Weir, *Politics and Jobs*, 123–24.

92. For discussions of the disputes between ASPE and the Department of Labor, see Kraemer et al., *Datawars*, 126–43 and Laurence Lynn and David Whitman, *The President as Policymaker: Jimmy Carter and Welfare Reform* (Philadelphia: Temple University Press, 1981), 49–51.

93. Linda E. Demkovich, "The Numbers Are the Issue in the Debate over Welfare Reform," *National Journal*, April 22, 1978, 633.

94. Moynihan quoted in *The New York Times*, November 16, 1978, A23. The marital breakup findings were formally reported in late 1977 and picked up by the press a year later. A substantial debate emerged a decade later, following an IRP reanalysis that disputed the findings but had little impact on public perceptions or political support for the idea. Michael T. Hannan et al., "Income and Marital Effects: Evidence from an Income Maintenance Experiment," *American Journal of Sociology* 82 (May 1977): NIT 1186–1211; *Washington Post* May 2, 1978, A6; Glen Cain and Doug Wissoker, "A Reanalysis of Marital Stability in the Seattle-Denver Income Maintenance Experiment," *American Journal of Sociology* 95 (March 1990): 1235–69.

95. See, for example, Charles Murray, *Losing Ground: American Social Policy, 1950–1980* (New York: Basic Books, 1984), 148–53.

96. Robert J. Lampman, "What Does It Do for the Poor?: A New Test for National Policy," *The Public Interest* 34 (Winter 1974): 66–82.

97. For a useful summary of these trends, see Laurence E. Lynn, Jr., "A Decade of Policy Developments in the Income-Maintenance System," in Robert H. Haveman, ed., *A Decade of Federal Antipoverty Programs: Achievements, Failures, and Lessons* (New York: Academic Press, 1977), 55–117. See also Robert D. Plotnick and Felicity Skidmore, *Progress Against Poverty* (New York: Academic Press, 1975).

98. Donald Lambro, "Doing Well by Doing Good Through Consulting," *The Heritage Foundation Policy Review* (Winter 1979): 107.

99. The most influential of these models was the "status attainment model" developed by Otis and Beverly Duncan in the mid-1960s, and further elaborated in dozens of subsequent studies. A straightforward explanation of this model and its findings, along with references to the ensuing modifications, is in David L. Featherman and Robert M. Hauser, "Design for a Replicate Study of Social Mobility in the United States," in Kenneth C. Land, ed., *Social Indicator Models* (New York: Russell Sage Foundation, 1975), 219–51. For a use of these and even more elaborate models to make a case for an aggressively redistributive, egalitarian social policy, see Christopher Jencks et al., *Inequality: A Reassessment of the Effect of Family and Schooling in America* (New York: Basic Books, 1972).

100. For example, researchers in Nixon's OEO were actively discouraged from developing a major program of research and experimentation on the question of residential segregation and the so-called "spatial mismatch" between ghetto residents and suburban jobs. Arnold J. Meltsner, *Policy Analysts in the Bureaucracy* (Berkeley: University of California Press, 1976), 106–10; "Research on Race and Ethnicity: Reports on Federal Agencies," Report #004592, Ford Foundation Archives. The OEO research in question was conducted by Harvard economist John F. Kain, and was one of the earliest analyses of a problem that has only recently gained much wider attention, largely due to the underclass debate. John F. Kain, "Housing Segregation, Negro Employment, and Metropolitan Decentralization," *The Quarterly Journal of Economics* 82 (May 1968): 175–97. At Wisconsin, the main focus of research on poverty and race was residential segregation, conducted by IRP affiliates Karl E. Taeuber and Franklin Wilson, which was part of a much more extensive, heavily demographic literature on racial residential segregation more generally. The starting point for much of this literature, at least in terms of method and basic concepts, is in Karl E. Taeuber and Alma F. Taeuber, *Negroes*

in Cities: Residential Segregation and Neighborhood Change (Chicago: Aldine Publishing, 1965). For an overview of the major themes and debates in the area, see W.A.V. Clark, "Residential Segregation in American Cities: A Review and Interpretation," *Population Research and Policy Review* 5, no. 2 (1986): 95–127 and George Galster, "Residential Segregation in American Cities: A Contrary View," *Population Research and Policy Review* 7, no. 2 (1988): 93–112. On the absence of segregation from the poverty debate more generally, see Douglas S. Massey and Nancy A. Denton, *American Apartheid: Segregation and the Making of the Underclass* (Cambridge, Mass.: Harvard University Press, 1993), 1–16.

101. Then program officer, now Ford Foundation President Susan Berresford made the comment in a letter to Urban Institute staff researcher Heather Ross on October 9, 1973, instructing Ross that a recent $100,000 grant for the study of female-headed households should focus more on poor and minority women than on older women and the rising divorce rate. Grant File PA 73–44, Ford Foundation Archives. The Urban Institute project did produce one of the first comprehensive studies on female-headed households, Heather Ross and Isabel V. Sawhill, *Time of Transition: The Growth of Families Headed by Women* (Washington, D.C.: The Urban Institute, 1975). The main focus of poverty research, however, was on poor families, welfare dependency, and whether welfare was causing the numbers to go up. See, for example, Isabel V. Sawhill et al., "Income Transfers and Family Structure" (Washington, D.C.: The Urban Institute, 1975).

102. Concerns about the lack of racial diversity are reflected in internal memos from the late 1970s, at which point the IRP had only two full-time minority faculty associates, a small number in temporary or research associate positions, and no minority representation on its research committee. See Research Committee Meeting Notes, September 8, 1978; "Report on Minority Participation," n.d. memo; Minority Recruitment Committee Memo to Irv Garfinkel, IRP Director, January 17, 1980, IRP Archives. See also *Evaluating Federal Support for Poverty Research*, 64–66.

Chapter 10
Dependency, the "Underclass," and a New Welfare "Consensus"

1. For a breakdown of agency support for poverty research, see Appendix A of the National Research Council, *Evaluating Federal Support for Poverty Research* (Washington, D.C.: National Academy of Sciences, 1979).

2. Eugene Smolensky to Institute Staff, July 15, 1980, IRP Archives.

3. Ronald W. Reagan, State of the Union Address, January 25, 1988, *Public Papers of the Presidents of the United States: Ronald Reagan, 1988* (Washington, D.C.: U.S. Government Printing Office), 87.

4. Rebecca M. Blank, "Why Were Poverty Rates So High in the 1980s?" in Dimitri B. Papadimitriou and Edward N. Wolff, eds., *Poverty and Prosperity in the USA in the Late Twentieth Century* (London: Macmillan Press, 1993), 21–55; Blank, and *It Takes a Nation: A New Agenda for Fighting Poverty* (New York: Russell Sage Foundation, 1997), 53–64.

5. The upward redistribution has been well documented, but is captured most powerfully in Kevin Phillips, *The Politics of Rich and Poor: Wealth and the American Electorate in the Reagan Aftermath* (New York: Random House, 1990). See also Sheldon H.

Danziger and Daniel H. Weinberg, "The Historical Record: Trends in Family Income, Inequality, and Poverty," in Danziger, Gary Sandefur, and Weinberg, eds., *Confronting Poverty: Prescriptions for Change* (Cambridge, Mass.: Harvard University Press, 1994), 21–25.

6. "Federal Fund Cutoff Dooms UW Poverty Research Institute," *The Capital Times*, September 16, 1981; "Golden Fleeced," *Wall Street Journal*, January 20, 1983.

7. "The Urban Institute, 1978–1987," Report prepared for the Ford Foundation by Thomas J. Anton, 3, and William D. Carey, "Appendix: Perceptions of the Urban Institute," 5, both in the Ford Foundation Archives.

8. Assistant Secretary Robert Rubin was an M.D., and made no secret of his hostility to mainstream poverty research.

9. ASPE dropped the PSID in the early 1980s, after which funding was pieced together from the National Science Foundation and several foundations. Charles Brown, Greg J. Duncan, and Frank P. Stafford, "Data Watch: The Panel Study of Income Dynamics," *Journal of Economic Perspectives* 10 (Spring 1996), 156.

10. Beryl A. Radin, "Policy Analysis in the Office of the Assistant Secretary for Planning and Evaluation in HEW/HHS: Institutionalization and the Second Generation," unpublished paper, Department of Health and Human Services Record Center, Washington, D.C., 7–8; Walter Williams, *Mismanaging America: The Rise of the Anti-Analytic Presidency* (Lawrence: University Press of Kansas, 1990), 13–18.

11. Williams, *Mismanaging America*, 14–15.

12. Carey, "Perceptions of the Urban Institute," 9.

13. The exchange was between Stockman and Representative Frank J. Guarini (D-New Jersey) during special hearings on rising poverty rates called by the House Ways and Means Committee in 1983. For that and Stockman's testimony on poverty measures, see U.S. Congress, House of Representatives, Hearings before the Subcommittees on Oversight and on Public Assistance and Unemployment Compensation of the Committee on Ways and Means, November 3, 1983, 220–22, 234–37, 278–80. The controversy over including in-kind benefits in the poverty measure dates back to the 1970s, when those programs had expanded considerably, leading Hoover Institution analyst and former Nixon administration staffer Martin Anderson to charge the Census Bureau with a "deliberate 'cover-up' of the true extent of poverty"—which was virtually nonexistent, he claimed, when in-kind benefits were counted: indeed, the war on poverty had actually been "won." Martin Anderson, *Welfare: The Political Economy of Welfare Reform in the United States* (Palo Alto: Hoover Institution, 1978), 19–20. For a sharply critical review of the controversy, see Michael Harrington, *The New American Poverty* (New York: Holt, Rinehart, and Winston, 1984), 77–88.

14. For a discussion of antipoverty advocacy in the 1980s, see Douglas R. Imig, *Poverty and Power: The Political Representation of Poor Americans* (Lincoln: University of Nebraska Press, 1996). On "advocacy tanks," including the quip about Heritage and the limousine ride, see Kent Weaver, "The Changing World of Think Tanks," *PS: Political Science and Politics*, (September 1989): 563–79.

15. The Green Book is published each March by the U.S. House of Representatives under the title *Background Material and Data on Programs within the Jurisdiction of the Committee on Ways and Means*. Its 1989 edition included a special study on income distribution that flatly contradicted Stockman's earlier remarks, offering the conclusion

that "the rich are in fact getting richer and the poor getting poorer," according to the accompanying release.

16. Randall Bovbjerg, "A Brief History of the Urban Institute," September 1983, Urban Institute Archives, 4, 10.

17. Charles Murray, *Losing Ground: American Social Policy: 1950–1980* (New York: Basic Books, 1984).

18. For an overview of the many statistically based critiques of Murray, see "Are We Losing Ground?" in the IRP newsletter *Focus* 8 (Fall and Winter 1985), 1–12. Among the most comprehensive, and devastating, reviews were Robert Greenstein, "Losing Faith in Losing Ground," *The New Republic*, March 25, 1985, 12–17, and Christopher Jencks, "How Poor Are the Poor?" *New York Review of Books*, May 9, 1985.

19. Murray, *Losing Ground*, 10th anniversary ed. (1994), xvi.

20. On Murray's use of "latent" poverty, which was subject to a great deal of criticism, see Jencks, "How Poor Are the Poor?" and Sanford F. Schram, *Words of Welfare: The Poverty of Social Science and the Social Science of Poverty* (Minneapolis: University of Minnesota Press, 1995), 108–9.

21. Murray, *Losing Ground*, 147–53.

22. Gregg Easterbrook, "Ideas Move Nations," *The Atlantic Monthly*, January 1986, 66–80.

23. Donald T. Critchlow, "Think Tanks, Antistatism, and Democracy: The Nonpartisan Ideal and Policy Research in the United States, 1913–1987," in Michael J. Lacey and Mary O. Furner, eds., *The State and Social Investigation in Britain and the United States* (Washington, D.C.: Woodrow Wilson Center and Cambridge University Press, 1993), 313–22.

24. Chuck Lane, "The Manhattan Project," *The New Republic*, March 25, 1985, 14–15.

25. Office of the Assistant Secretary for Planning and Evaluation, Department of Health and Human Services, "Current Policy Research," October 1988.

26. Daniel H. Weinberg, "A Poverty Research Agenda for the Next Decade," in Sheldon H. Danziger and Weinberg, eds., *Fighting Poverty: What Works and What Doesn't* (Cambridge, Mass.: Harvard University Press, 1986), 351; David T. Ellwood, "Understanding Dependency: Choices, Confidence or Culture?" Report prepared under contract to ASPE, 1987.

27. *Annotated Bibliography on Welfare Dependency*, prepared for ASPE by the Center for Human Resources, Heller Graduate School, Brandeis University, 1987.

28. *Welfare Dependency: Behavior, Culture and Public Policy*, Report prepared for ASPE by the Hudson Institute, September 1987.

29. ASPE instructed the IRP to use part of its core grant for a small grants competition, as a way of assuring that the funds would not remain in-house. Sheldon Danziger, interview by author, June 1995.

30. Indeed, among the more forceful critics of Reagan fiscal priorities was American Enterprise Institute analyst Jack Meyer, who excoriated the administration for cutting means-tested programs while leaving the vastly larger middle-class entitlements untouched. See Meyer's testimony before the House Ways and Means Subcommittees on Oversight and on Public Assistance and Unemployment Compensation, October 18, 1983, 130–35.

31. David Ellwood and Mary Jo Bane, "The Impact of AFDC on Family Structure and Living Arrangements," in Ron G. Ehrenberg, ed., *Research in Labor Economics* (Greenwich, Conn.: JAI Press, 1985); Robert Moffitt, "Incentive Effects of the U.S. Welfare System: A Review," *Journal of Economic Literature* 30 (March 1992): 1–61.

32. Lawrence M. Mead, *Beyond Entitlement: The Social Obligations of Citizenship* (New York: The Free Press, 1986).

33. Stuart Butler and Anna Kondratas, *Out of the Poverty Trap: A Conservative Strategy for Welfare Reform* (New York: Free Press, 1987). Butler is currently a vice president at the Heritage Foundation. Kondratas, who subsequently ran the food stamp program in the Bush administration, has since joined the staff of the Urban Institute.

34. Loury has consistently identified himself with a conservative political agenda, emphasizing the values of free enterprise, self-help, moral responsibility, and small government in his work. Since the early 1990s, however, he has gone to some length to distance himself from conservative racial politics, resigning from the board of the American Enterprise Institute in protest over the publication of Dinesh D'Souza's *The End of Racism*, and publishing a harsh review of *America in Black and White* by Stephan and Abigail Thernstrom, both of which argue that racism is a thing of the past. For Loury's evolving views on these and other issues, see Glenn C. Loury, *One by One from the Inside Out* (New York: Free Press, 1995).

35. Greg Duncan et al., *Years of Poverty, Years of Plenty* (Ann Arbor, Mich.: Institute for Social Research, 1984), 71–93. See also Greg Duncan, "On the Slippery Slope," *American Demographics*, May 1987, 30–35. For a use of PSID data as proof against the culture of poverty, see Mary Corcoran et al., "Myth and Reality: The Causes and Persistence of Poverty," *Journal of Policy Analysis and Management* 4 (Summer 1985): 516–36.

36. Mary Jo Bane and David Ellwood, "The Dynamics of Dependency: Routes to Self Sufficiency," unpublished report prepared for the U.S. Department of Health and Human Services, JFK School of Government, 1983. The language of recidivism has become well-entrenched in the poverty literature. See, for example, Rebecca M. Blank and Patricia Ruggles, "Short-term Recidivism Among Public-Assistance Recipients," *The American Economic Review* 84 (May 1994): 49–53.

37. The findings on dependency did not go uncontested at the time. See, for example, Rebecca Blank, "How Important Is Welfare Dependence?" IRP Discussion Paper #821–86 (Madison: Institute for Research on Poverty, 1986). Nevertheless, they were enormously influential, both because Bane and Ellwood enjoyed wide respect in the research community and because they introduced a pioneering research methodology to overturn what had become conventional wisdom in the field.

38. Moynihan, in a statement about the rise in child poverty rates, was quoting from an address by demographer Samuel H. Preston, who had referred to the "earthquake that shuddered through the American family in the past 20 years." *Focus*, Spring 1988, 5.

39. Mary Jo Bane and David Ellwood, "Slipping Into and Out of Poverty: The Dynamics of Spells," *The Journal of Human Resources* 21 (Winter 1986): 1–23; Mary Jo Bane, "Household Composition and Poverty," in Danziger and Weinberg, *Fighting Poverty*, 231.

40. David Ellwood, *Divide and Conquer: Responsible Security for America's Poor* (New York: Ford Foundation, 1987); Irwin Garfinkel and Sara S. McLanahan, *Single*

Mothers and Their Children: A New American Dilemma (Washington, D.C.: The Urban Institute, 1986). For a more recent, more pointed follow-up to these studies, see Sara McLanahan and Gary Sandefur, *Growing Up with a Single Parent: What Hurts, What Helps* (Cambridge, Mass.: Harvard University Press, 1994).

41. McLanahan and Sandefur, *Growing Up*, 7–8; William J. Wilson and Kathryn M. Neckerman, "Poverty and Family Structure: The Widening Gap between Evidence and Public Policy Issues," in Danziger and Weinberg, *Fighting Poverty*, 232–33.

42. McLanahan, for example, identified herself as "a single mother for ten years" in *Single Mothers and Their Children*, xix.

43. On the emergence of adolescent pregnancy as an issue across the political spectrum, see Constance A. Nathanson, *Dangerous Passage: The Social Control of Sexuality in Women's Adolescence* (Philadelphia: Temple University Press, 1991); Kristin Luker, *Dubious Conceptions: The Politics of Teenage Pregnancy* (Cambridge, Mass.: Harvard University Press, 1996); and Arline T. Geronimus, "Teenage Childbearing and Personal Responsibility: An Alternative View," *Political Science Quarterly* 112 (Fall 1997): 405–30. Geronimus, in particular, came under fire in the 1980s and early 1990s for challenging the notion that teenage childbearing was an unmitigated disaster that had reached epidemic proportions, and a cause of poverty that should be targeted for immediate preventive action.

44. Nancy Fraser and Linda Gordon, "A Genealogy of Dependency: Tracing a Keyword of the U.S. Welfare State," *Signs* 19 (Winter 1994): 309–36.

45. For the article most often credited with coining the phrase "feminization of poverty," see Diana Pearce, "The Feminization of Poverty: Women, Work, and Welfare," *Urban and Social Change Review* 11 (February 1978): 28–36. For several essays that develop the strands of the argument in more depth, see Linda Gordan, ed., *Women, the State, and Welfare* (Madison: University of Wisconsin Press, 1990). For in-depth historical data on women in the labor force, see Claudia Goldin, *Understanding the Gender Gap: An Economic History of American Women* (New York: Oxford University Press, 1990).

46. Kathryn Edin and Laura Lein, *Making Ends Meet: How Single Mothers Survive Welfare and Low-Wage Work* (New York: Russell Sage Foundation, 1997); Michael B. Katz, *Improving Poor People: The Welfare State, the "Underclass," and Urban Schools as History* (Princeton: Princeton University Press, 1995), 144–72.

47. Michael Novak et al., *A Community of Self-Reliance: The New Consensus of Family and Welfare* (Washington, D.C.: American Enterprise Institute, 1987), 46.

48. Melville J. Herskovits, *The Myth of the Negro Past* (Boston: Beacon Press, 1990), 167–86; Andrew T. Miller, "Social Science, Social Policy, and the Heritage of African-American Families," in Michael B. Katz, ed., *The "Underclass" Debate: Views from History* (Princeton: Princeton University Press, 1993), 254–89.

49. David T. Ellwood, *Divide and Conquer* and *Poor Support: Poverty in the American Family* (New York: Basic Books, 1988).

50. Liberal poverty experts, especially, showed a sudden fascination with values as a justification for welfare reform—albeit less as a reflection of their own value commitments than as an objective statement of what "Americans," based on opinion polls or focus groups, believed. Most often, they presented these values in the form of an age-old "dilemma," or "conundrum" between the conflicting values of compassion

for the needy and the aversion to dependency. See, for example, Ellwood, *Poor Support*, 14–44.

51. Novack, *A Community of Self Reliance*, 3–13.

52. Ibid., 45.

53. If anything, it was liberals who were the latecomers to the EITC bandwagon, promoting it as one of their "nonwelfare" devices for subsidizing low incomes only after the repeated defeat of more comprehensive negative income tax proposals. For a discussion of the legislative career of the EITC, see Dennis J. Ventry, Jr., "The Strange Political Career of the Earned Income Tax Credit: Tax Policy, Social Policy, and Welfare Politics, 1969–1998," unpublished paper, January 1999.

54. Recall, for example, that the first NIT experiment was conducted with only two-parent families, on the assumption that it was not as important to focus on the behavioral response of welfare mothers since they probably *would* maintain a relatively low labor force participation with the NIT. It is also of interest that Supported Work, the experiment that got MDRC started, was not originally designed to include welfare recipients in the sample; project designers were initially quite reluctant to include poor single mothers at all.

55. Barbara Ehrenreich, "A Step Back to the Workhouse?" *Ms*, November 1987, 40–42.

56. Wilson and Neckerman, "Poverty and Family Structure."

57. Judith M. Gueron, *Reforming Welfare with Work* (New York: Ford Foundation, 1987).

58. The MDRC experiments in particular were the focus of a mostly celebratory symposium on the role of research in making the Family Support Act of 1988 possible, reprinted in the *Journal of Policy Analysis and Management* 10 (Fall 1991). The remark about experimental design is reported by symposium participant Peter Szanton, 598.

59. Sheldon Danziger, "Introduction," *Focus* 11 (Spring 1988): 1–2.

60. See David Ellwood and Lawrence H. Summers, "Poverty in America: Is Welfare the Answer or the Problem?," Rebecca M. Blank and Alan S. Blinder, "Macroeconomics, Income Distribution, and Poverty," and Edward M. Gramlich, "The Main Themes," all in Danziger and Weinberg, *Fighting Poverty*, 78–105, 180–208, 341–47.

61. Peter Gottschalk and Sheldon Danziger, "Macroeconomic Conditions, Income Transfers, and the Trend in Poverty," in D. Lee Bawden, ed., *The Social Contract Revisited* (Washington, D.C.: Urban Institute Press, 1984), 185–215.

62. Isabel V. Sawhill, "Poverty in the United States: Why Is It So Persistent?" *Journal of Economic Literature* 26 (September 1988): 1073–1119.

63. On the natural rate of unemployment, see the symposium in the *Journal of Economic Perspectives* 11 (Winter 1997): 3–108.

64. A useful entry point to the extensive literature on black youth unemployment is Richard B. Freeman and Harry J. Holzer, eds., *The Black Youth Employment Crisis* (Chicago: University of Chicago Press, 1986). For an entree into the similarly voluminous literature on spatial mismatch, see John F. Kain, "Housing Segregation, Negro Employment, and Metropolitan Decentralization," *Quarterly Journal of Economics* 82 (May 1968): 175–97 and "The Spatial Mismatch Hypothesis: Three Decades Later," *Housing Policy Debate* 3, no. 2 (1992): 371–460; Harry J. Holzer, "The Spatial Mismatch Hypothesis: What Has the Evidence Shown?" *Urban Studies* 28 (February 1991): 105–22.

65. An important postwar statement of the notion that growth would lead to greater equality was made by Simon Kuznets in his presidential address to the American Economic Association in 1954. Kuznets, "Economic Growth and Income Inequality," *American Economic Review* 45 (March 1955): 1–28.

66. On the postwar stability of income distribution, see Jeffrey Williamson and Peter Lindert, *American Inequality: A Macroeconomic History* (New York: Academic Press, 1980).

67. On the turnaround in the conventional wisdom about inequality, see Frank Levy and Richard J. Murnane, "U.S. Earnings Levels and Earnings Inequality: A Review of Recent Trends and Proposed Explanations," *Journal of Economic Literature* 30 (September 1992): 1333–81; Sheldon Danziger and Peter Gottschalk, eds., *Uneven Tides: Rising Inequality in America* (New York: Russell Sage Foundation, 1993), 3–17.

68. James Tobin, "Poverty in Relation to Macroeconomic Trends, Cycles, and Policies," in Danziger, Sandefur, and Weinberg, eds., *Confronting Poverty*, 147–67.

69. Frank Levy, *Dollars and Dreams: The Changing American Income Distribution* (New York: Russell Sage Foundation, 1987). Recently, Levy has published an updated and revised version, in which he pays much more attention to inequality as a long-term structural issue. *The New Dollars and Dreams: American Incomes and Economic Change* (New York: Russell Sage Foundation, 1998).

70. The Economic Policy Institute was established in 1986 with strong labor union backing and a mission to reflect the interests of low-income and working-class people in its research agenda. Although EPI has since gained broader acceptance, mainstream foundations were at first wary of its labor connections, and only reluctantly accepted it as a source of impartial research.

71. The following discussion draws on Barry Bluestone and Bennett Harrison, *The Deindustrialization of America: Plant Closings, Community Abandonment, and the Dismantling of Basic Industry* (New York: Basic Books, 1982); Bennett Harrison and Barry Bluestone, *The Great U-Turn: Corporate Restructuring and the Polarizing of America* (New York: Basic Books, 1988); Robert Kuttner, "The Declining Middle," *The Atlantic Monthly*, July 1983, 60–72; Michael A. Bernstein and David E. Adler, eds., *Understanding American Economic Decline* (New York: Cambridge University Press, 1994).

72. Harrison and Bluestone, *U-Turn*, 181–93.

73. Levy and Murnane, "U.S. Earnings Levels." By then the only real dispute about the factual basis of the trend toward inequality was coming from the Right. Paul R. Krugman, "The Rich, the Right and the Facts: Deconstructing the Income Distribution Debate," *The American Prospect*, Fall 1992, 19–31.

74. For a helpful overview of the various explanations, and points of agreement, about inequality, see Barry Bluestone, "The Inequality Express," *The American Prospect*, Winter 1995, 81–93. A central dispute, at least among liberal economists, is whether the wage collapse at the lower end of the labor market can be explained primarily by the low skills and education of workers, as opposed to political and institutional factors such as economic and labor policy, deunionization, and shifts in monopoly power. Levy emphasizes skills mismatch in *The New Dollars and Dreams*. For a critique of the skills "orthodoxy," see David R. Howell, "The Skills Myth," *The American Prospect*, Summer 1994, 81–90, and James K. Galbraith, *Created Unequal: The Crisis in American Pay* (New York: Free Press, 1998), 23–36. On the declining progressivity

of U.S. tax and transfer policy, see Edward M. Gramlich et al., "Growing Inequality in the 1980s: The Role of Federal Taxes and Cash Transfers," in Danziger and Gottschalk, *Uneven Tides*, 234–40.

75. For an example of how space was defined as a race-neutral variable by leading scholars of the spatial mismatch hypothesis, see Keith R. Ihlanfeldt and David L. Sjoquist, "The Impact of Job Decentralization on the Economic Welfare of Central City Blacks," *Journal of Urban Economics* 26 (July 1989): 110–30. Ellwood's quip, which was quickly absorbed in the literature, was based on research for his doctoral dissertation, later reported in "The Spatial Mismatch Hypothesis: Are There Teenage Jobs Missing in the Ghetto?" in Freeman and Holzer, *The Black Youth Employment Crisis*, 147–90.

76. Maria Cancian, Sheldon Danziger, and Peter Gottschalk, "Working Wives and Family Income Inequality Among Married Couples," in Danziger and Gottschalk, *Uneven Tides*, 195–221; George Borjas, "Demographic Determinants of the Demand for Black Labor," in Freeman and Holzer, *The Black Youth Employment Crisis*, 214–16.

77. Levy and Murnane, "U.S. Earnings Levels," 1333–34; Daphne Spain and Suzanne M. Bianchi, *Balancing Act: Motherhood, Marriage, and Employment Among American Women* (New York: Russell Sage Foundation, 1996), 107–40.

78. Spain and Bianchi, *Balancing Act*, 169–73.

79. For a discussion of the gender gap in conventional economic measures, see Martha MacDonald, "The Empirical Challenges of Feminist Economics: The Example of Economic Restructuring," in Edith Kuiper and Joland Sap, eds., *Out of the Margin: Feminist Perspectives on Economics* (London: Routledge, 1995), 175–97.

80. For an analysis that focuses on the problem of wage declines for both male- and female-headed families, see Rebecca M. Blank, "Why Were Poverty Rates so High in the 1980s?"

81. Sheldon Danziger, "Fighting Poverty and Reducing Welfare Dependency," in Phoebe H. Cottingham and David T. Ellwood, eds., *Welfare Policy for the 1990s* (Cambridge, Mass.: Harvard University Press, 1989), 41–44.

82. William Julius Wilson, *The Truly Disadvantaged: The Inner City, the Underclass, and Public Policy* (Chicago: University of Chicago Press, 1987).

83. Gunnar Myrdal, *Challenge to Affluence*, (rev. ed. New York: Vintage Books, 1965); Lee Rainwater, "Looking Back and Looking Up," *Trans-action*, February 1969, 9. For a more detailed discussion of the genesis of the term "underclass," see Herbert J. Gans, *The War Against the Poor* (New York: Basic, 1995), 27–35. See also Michael Katz, *The "Underclass" Debate*, 4–5.

84. Among the most important, widely discussed, and, at least among poverty experts, controversial journalistic reports on the underclass are Ken Auletta, *The Underclass* (New York: Random House, 1982), originally published as a series of articles in *The New Yorker* magazine; and Nicholas Leman, "The Origins of the Underclass," *The Atlantic Monthly*, June 1986, 31–55 and July 1986, 54–68, later published as part of *The Promised Land: The Great Black Migration and How It Changed America* (New York: Random House, 1991).

85. Myron Magnet, "America's Underclass: What to Do?" *Fortune*, May 11, 1987, 130–50.

86. Two especially attention-getting examples are Eleanor Holmes Norton, "Restoring the Traditional Black Family," *New York Times Magazine*, June 2, 1985, 43 and a

television documentary by reporter Bill Moyers, "Crisis in Black America," which aired in January 1986. See also a front-page series of articles on teen pregnancy by *Washington Post* reporter Leon Dash in January 1986, and Marion Wright Edelman (founder of the Children's Defense Fund), *Families in Peril: An Agenda for Social Change* (Cambridge, Mass.: Harvard University Press, 1987).

87. Daniel P. Moynihan, *Family and Nation* (New York: Harcourt, Brace, Jovanovich, 1996).

88. Wilson, *The Truly Disadvantaged*, 3–19.

89. Among the most prominent studies of ghettoization published during this period are Gilbert Osofsky, *Harlem: The Making of a Ghetto Negro, New York, 1890–1930* (rev. ed. New York: Harper and Row, 1971); Allan H. Spear, *Black Chicago: The Making of a Negro Ghetto, 1890–1920* (Chicago: University of Chicago Press, 1967); Kenneth L. Kusmer, *A Ghetto Takes Shape: Black Cleveland, 1870–1930* (Urbana: University of Illinois Press, 1976); and Arnold R. Hirsch, *Making the Second Ghetto: Race and Housing in Chicago, 1940–1960* (New York: Cambridge University Press, 1983). For an excellent critical overview of this literature that offers an alternative interpretive framework, see Joe William Trotter, Jr., "Afro-American Urban History: A Critique of the Literature," in Joe William Trotter, Jr., *Black Milwaukee: The Making of an Industrial Proletariat, 1915–45* (Urbana: University of Illinois Press, 1985), 264–82, and "Blacks in the Urban North: The 'Underclass Question' in Historical Perspective," in Katz, *The "Underclass" Debate*, 55–81. For more recent studies that have emphasized the need to look beyond the ghetto formation framework to examine the complexities and, above all, the historical agency of the African American urban working class, see James R. Grossman, *Land of Hope: Chicago, Black Southerners, and the Great Migration* (Chicago: University of Chicago Press, 1989); Earl Lewis, *In Their Own Interests: Blacks in Twentieth-Century Norfolk* (Berkeley: University of California Press, 1991); and Tera Hunter, *To Joy My Freedom: Southern Black Women's Lives and Labors after the Civil War* (Cambridge, Mass.: Harvard University Press, 1997).

90. Wilson, *The Truly Disadvantaged*, 4.

91. For an overview of the movement in sociology to "decolonize" the ghetto, see Joyce Ladner, ed., *The Death of White Sociology* (New York: Random House, 1973) and Robert Blauner, *Racial Oppression in America* (New York: Harper and Row, 1972).

92. On the black family, see Joyce Ladner, *Tomorrow's Tomorrow: The Black Woman* (New York: Doubleday, 1973); Robert B. Hill, *The Strength of Black Families* (New York: Emerson Hall, 1972); Andrew Billingsley, *Black Families in White America* (Englewood Cliffs, N.J.: Prentice-Hall, 1968). On the political economy of the ghetto, see William K. Tabb, *The Political Economy of the Black Ghetto* (New York: W.W. Norton, 1970). For a synthetic discussion of the colonialist literature, see Michael B. Katz, *The Undeserving Poor* (New York: Pantheon, 1989), 52–65.

93. Blauner, *Racial Oppression in America*, 82–89.

94. Wilson, *Truly Disadvantaged*, 9, 127.

95. Interestingly, these were the very issues that had absorbed Wilson in his first book, a comparative study of U.S. and South African race relations entitled *Power, Racism and Privilege: Race Relations in Theoretical and Sociohistorical Perspectives* (New York: Macmillan, 1973).

96. Joyce Ladner, *Tomorrow's Tomorrow*; Carol Stack, *All Our Kin: Strategies for Survival in a Black Community* (New York: Harper and Row, 1974).

97. Stack, *All Our Kin*, 108–23. For contemporary ethnographies written from the male perspective, see Charles Keil, *Urban Blues* (Chicago: University of Chicago Press, 1966); Eliot Liebow, *Tally's Corner: A Study of Negro Street Corner Men* (Boston: Little, Brown, 1967); and Ulf Hannerz, *Soulside: Inquiries into Ghetto Culture and Community* (New York: Columbia University Press, 1969). An important, later, exception is John Langston Gwaltney, *Drylongso: A Self-Portrait of Black America* (New York: Vintage, 1980).

98. Wilson, *Truly Disadvantaged*, chap. 3. For penetrating critiques of Wilson's underclass concept from anthropological perspectives, see Brett Williams, "Poverty among African Americans in the Urban United States," *Human Organization* 51, no. 2 (1992): 164–74, and Katherine S. Newman, "Culture and Structure in *The Truly Disadvantaged*," *City and Society* 6, no. 1 (1992): 3–25.

99. Katz, *Undeserving Poor*, 64–65.

100. Robert Halpern, *Rebuilding the Inner City* (New York: Columbia University Press, 1995), 175–81; John McKnight, *The Careless Society: Community and Its Counterfeits* (New York: Basic Books, 1995); Margaret Weir, "Power, Money, and Politics in Community Development," in Ronald F. Ferguson and William T. Dickens, eds., *Urban Problems and Community Development* (Washington, D.C.: Brookings Institution, 1999), 139–92. For a discussion of empowerment strategies in a rural setting, see John Gaventa, *Power and Powerlessness: Quiescence and Rebellion in an Appalachian Valley* (Urbana: University of Illinois Press, 1980).

101. Robinson G. Hollister, Jr., Peter Kemper, and Rebecca A. Maynard, *The National Supported Work Demonstration* (Madison: University of Wisconsin Press, 1984).

102. Public/Private Ventures, a research and evaluation firm established with money from the Labor Department and the Ford Foundation in 1978, was a direct outgrowth of the increased demand for youth-oriented applied research, and represented an effort to replicate the MDRC model in this more specialized area.

103. Corcoran et al., "Myth and Reality." For a more recent, statistically based caution against exaggerating the correlation among social problems, see Christopher Jencks, "Is the American Underclass Growing?" in Christopher Jencks and Paul E. Peterson, eds., *The Urban Underclass* (Washington, D.C.: Brookings Institution, 1991), 28–100.

104. The 1980s and 1990s have seen a major revival of Chicago-school social ecology, especially in the area of delinquency and crime. See, for example, Robert J. Sampson and W. Byron Groves, "Community Structure and Crime: Testing Social-Disorganization Theory," *American Journal of Sociology* 94 (January 1989): 774–802.

105. Department of Health and Human Services, "Problems of the Underclass: Applications for Grants," *Federal Register* 53 (September 15, 1988), 35905. On the "epidemic" theory, see Jonathan Crane, "The Epidemic Theory of Ghettos and Neighborhood Effects on Dropping Out and Teenage Childbearing," *American Journal of Sociology* 96 (March 1991): 1226–29.

106. Erol R. Ricketts and Isabel V. Sawhill, "Defining and Measuring the Underclass," *Journal of Policy Analysis and Management* 7 (Spring 1988): 316–25; Idem and Douglas A. Wolf, "The Underclass: Definition and Measurement," *Science*, April 27, 1990, 450–53. See also Gans, *The War Against the Poor*, 62–63.

107. William A. Prosser, "The Underclass: What Have We Learned?" *Focus* 13 (Summer 1991): 1–17.

108. See, for example, the collection of articles Wilson assembled for a special issue of *The Annals* in 1989, especially Loic J. D. Wacquant and William Julius Wilson, "The Cost of Racial and Class Exclusion in the Inner City"; John D. Kasarda, "Urban Industrial Transition and the Underclass"; Lawrence M. Mead, "The Logic of Workfare: The Underclass and Work Policy"; and William Julius Wilson, "The Underclass: Issues, Perspectives and Public Policy," all in *The Annals of the American Academy of Political and Social Science* 501 (January 1989): 8–25, 26–58, 156–69, 182–92.

109. Joleen Kirschenman and Kathryn M. Neckerman, "We'd Love to Hire Them But . . . ": The Meaning of Race for Employers," in Jencks and Peterson, *The Urban Underclass*, 203–32.

110. Wilson, "Social Theory and Public Agenda Research: The Challenge of Studying Inner-City Social Dislocations," Presidential Address, Annual Meeting of the American Sociological Association, August 12, 1990, 9–14.

111. William Julius Wilson, ASA Presidential Address, 20–21.

112. William Julius Wilson, *When Work Disappears: The World of the New Urban Poor* (New York: Alfred A. Knopf, 1996). For a discussion of findings from a subsequent research on work opportunities and conditions for ghetto residents, see Katherine S. Newman, *No Shame in My Game: The Working Poor in the Inner City* (New York: Alfred A. Knopf and Russell Sage Foundation, 1999).

113. William J. Wilson, *The Declining Significance of Race: Blacks and Changing American Institutions* (Chicago: University of Chicago Press, 1980). The book caused a tremendous controversy among black sociologists in particular, especially after it was awarded the American Sociological Association's Spivack Award for a work contributing to the understanding of race. For a compilation of critical essays, including a denunciatory statement from the Association of Black Sociologists, see Charles V. Willie, *The Caste and Class Controversy* (New York: General Hall, Inc., 1979). On the book's influence in sociology, see Aldon Morris, "What's Race Got To Do With It?" in Dan Clawson, ed., *Required Reading: Sociology's Most Influential Books* (Amherst: University of Massachusetts Press, 1998), 157–65.

114. Bayard Rustin, "From Protest to Politics: The Future of the Civil Rights Movement," *Commentary* 39 (February 1965): 25–31; Oliver Cromwell Cox, *Caste, Class, and Race: A Study in Social Dynamics* (New York: Doubleday, 1948). Wilson's statement at the University of Pennsylvania symposium was reported in Carl Gershman, "A Matter of Class," *New York Times Magazine*, October 5, 1980, 98–99.

115. Wilson, *Truly Disadvantaged*, 140–64, and "Race Neutral Policies and the Democratic Coalition," *The American Prospect*, Spring 1990, 74–81. For an influential analysis of how Great Society racial politics undermined the old liberal coalition by caving in to the demands of black and left-wing activists, see Thomas Byrne Edsall with Mary D. Edsall, *Chain Reaction: The Impact of Race, Rights, and Taxes on American Politics* (New York: W.W. Norton, 1991), 47–73. Although the Edsalls' account has been challenged by historians, it reflected the conventional wisdom in new Democratic circles that liberals had gone "too far," or taken a "wrong (left) turn" in the mid-1960s, alienating the party's traditional white, blue-collar base. For alternative accounts of the roots of white working-class disaffection, see Arnold R. Hirsch, "Massive Resistance in the Urban North: Trumbull Park, Chicago, 1953–1966," and Thomas J. Sugrue, "Crabgrass-Roots Politics: Race, Rights, and the Reaction against Liberalism in the Urban North, 1940–1965," *Journal of American History* 82 (September 1995): 522–

78. On the new Democrat race agenda and how it played out in Clinton administration policies, see Linda Faye Williams, "Race and the Politics of Social Policy," in Margaret Weir, ed., *The Social Divide: Political Parties and the Future of Activist Government* (Washington, D.C.: Brookings Institution, 1998), 417–63.

116. On the black vs. white middle class, see Cora Marrett, "The Precarious Position of the Black Middle Class," *Contemporary Sociology* 9 (January 1980): 16–19 and Melvin L. Oliver and Thomas M. Shapiro, *Black Wealth/White Wealth: A New Perspective on Racial Inequality* (New York: Routledge, 1995). For critiques of the notion of black "polarization," see Steven Schulman, "Race, Class and Occupational Stratification: A Critique of William J. Wilson's *The Declining Significance of Race*," *The Review of Radical Political Economics* 13 (Fall 1981): 21–31, and Reynolds Farley, *Blacks and Whites: Narrowing the Gap?* (Cambridge, Mass.: Harvard University Press, 1984), 190–91.

117. Dona Cooper Hamilton and Charles V. Hamilton, *The Dual Agenda: The African-American Struggle for Civil and Economic Equality* (New York: Columbia University Press, 1997). The need to pursue what the Hamiltons describe as a "dual agenda" was the central theme of the 1966–67 hearings on the "urban crisis" before the Senate Government Operations Committee's Subcommittee on Executive Reorganization. Chaired by Senator Abraham Ribicoff (D-Conn.), the hearings became a prominent platform for a broad-gauged critique of Johnson administration urban policy, prominently featuring Senators Robert F. Kennedy (D-N.Y.) and Jacob Javits (R-N.Y.). The hearings pointed to the need for full employment, a federally guaranteed income, economic development in ghetto neighborhoods, and cross-race coalition-building on behalf of civil and economic rights. U.S. Senate, Committee on Government Operations, Subcommittee on Executive Reorganization, *Hearings on the Federal Role in Urban Affairs*, 21 vols. (Washington, D.C.: U.S. Government Printing Office, 1967).

118. For a systematic discussion, see Michael C. Dawson, *Behind the Mule: Race and Class in African-American Politics* (Princeton: Princeton University Press, 1994).

119. For a discussion of "universalism" and African Americans, see Hamiltons, *Dual Agenda*, 244–54.

120. The major exception in the early underclass debate was sociologist Douglas Massey, who in the early 1990s published an article on racial residential segregation as a key structural underpinning of the underclass, an argument he and coauthor Nancy Denton later expanded in their book *American Apartheid: Segregation and the Making of the Underclass* (Cambridge, Mass.: Harvard University Press, 1993). Douglas S. Massey and Mitchell L. Eggers, "The Ecology of Inequality: Minorities and the Concentration of Poverty, 1970–1980," *American Journal of Sociology* 95 (March 1990): 1153–88.

121. Paul A. Jargowsky and Mary Jo Bane, "Ghetto Poverty in the United States, 1970–1980," in Jencks and Peterson, *The Urban Underclass*, 235–73.

122. Harrington, *The New American Poverty*.

123. Interestingly, the Rockefeller Foundation turned to people who had been tied to early community action and War on Poverty programs as evaluators for its initiative, including Peter Marris, Frederick O'R Hayes, Robinson Hollister, and Peter Rossi. For the most part, however, the foundation minimized the similarities between its own and earlier community action efforts, identifying instead with a new, more professional, and less overtly political generation of community-based programs.

124. This account draws on my experience as an SSRC/Urban Underclass project staff member, a position I assumed in early 1991 when the project was already under way, as well as an extensive collection of oral history interviews conducted by historian Michael Katz, who at the Council's invitation served as the project archivist. The interviews and other project documentation have been deposited at the University of Minnesota Social Welfare History Archives (hereafter SWHA), Minneapolis–St. Paul, Minnesota.

125. For the original mission statement of the SSRC project, see Martha A. Gephart and Robert W. Pearson, "Contemporary Research on the Urban Underclass," *Social Science Research Council Items*, June 1988, 1–10; Lawrence Aber, Oral History, SWHA, 2.

126. Melvin Oliver, Oral History, SWHA, 17.

127. An outside evaluator, himself a quantitative social scientist, put the prevailing sentiment succinctly when, in questioning the wisdom of the Committee-supported historical volume, he wrote "Surely history is important, but is it central?" Peter H. Rossi, "An Assessment of the SSRC Committee on the Underclass," April 4, 1990, 18. Actually, support for the volume absorbed a very small portion of Committee funds, totaling less than $25,000. Katz, *The "Underclass" Debate*. For Katz's discussion of his experience as project archivist, see *Improving Poor People*, 60–98.

128. Jencks quoted in Joe Klein, "Life without Father," *New York*, April 29, 1991, 16; Christopher Jencks, "There Is No Underclass," *Wall Street Journal*, April 17, 1991; Paul E. Peterson, "The Urban Underclass and the Poverty Paradox," in Jencks and Peterson, *The Urban Underclass*, 3–27.

129. "Study Counters Many Theories on Underclass," *Los Angeles Times*, April 16, 1991, A1; "Overrated Statistics on the Underclass?" *Washington Times*, April 15, 1991, D1.

130. For one example of research stimulated by the absence of race on the underclass agenda, see the preface to Massey and Denton, *American Apartheid*. Massey had written a paper on residential segregation and the underclass for the Northwestern conference that was not included in the subsequent volume. See also Irene Browne, ed., *Latinas and African American Women at Work: Race, Gender, and Economic Inequality* (New York: Russell Sage Foundation, 1999).

131. Edwin Melendez, *Understanding Latino Poverty* (London: Sage Publications, 1993); Joan Moore and Raquel Pinderhughes, eds., *In the Barrios: Latinos and the Underclass Debate* (New York: Russell Sage Foundation, 1993).

132. Paul E. Peterson, Oral History, SWHA, 1.

133. Rossi, "An Assessment," 17.

134. Jeanne Brooks-Gunn, Greg J. Duncan, and J. Lawrence Aber, eds., *Neighborhood Poverty* 2 vols. (New York: Russell Sage Foundation, 1997).

135. For a brief description of the project aims, see Alice O'Connor, "Studying Inequality in American Cities," *Social Science Research Council Items*, December 1992. The findings are reported in a series of volumes published by the Russell Sage Foundation, including Alice O'Connor, Chris Tilly, and Lawrence Bobo, eds., *Urban Inequality: Evidence from Four Cities* (New York: Russell Sage Foundation, 2000).

136. Rossi, "Assessment," 22.

137. James Johnson, Oral History, SWHA, 12.

138. Peter Rossi and Aida Rodriguez, "The Underclass and Persistent Poverty Program: Mid-Course Assessments, Syntheses and Implications," October 1, 1990, 29–31.

139. See, for a discussion, a Point of View essay by Peter Marris in *The Chronicle of Higher Education*, May 20, 1992, A40; Katz, *Improving Poor People*, 62.

140. The message, which came quite without warning and took the SSRC very much by surprise, was delivered in a series of meetings, summarized in a letter from Rockefeller program officer Erol Ricketts to SSRC staff member Martha Gephart, January 23, 1991.

141. Martha A. Gephart, Alice O'Connor, and Richard R. Peterson, "Persistent Urban Poverty: Integrating Research, Policy, and Practice." This, and the other summary memos are available through the National Center for Children in Poverty, 154 Haven Avenue, New York, NY 10032.

142. For an excellent overview of policies in these and other areas, see Weir, *The Social Divide*.

143. Robert Pear, "White House Spurns Expansion of Nation's Anti-Poverty Efforts," *New York Times*, July 6, 1990, A1, A12.

144. Jeffrey S. Lehman, "Updating Urban Policy," in Danziger et al., *Confronting Poverty*, 226–52; John H. Mollenkopf, "Urban Policy at the Crossroads," in Weir, *The Social Divide*, 464–505.

Chapter 11
The End of Welfare and the Case for a New Poverty Knowledge

1. Clinton was the co-chair of the National Governors Association working group of welfare reform that played an aggressive role in pressing for reform in the mid-1980s and in shaping the Family Support Act of 1988.

2. Bill Clinton and Al Gore, *Putting People First* (New York: Time Life, 1992), 164–68. By the time Clinton used it, the word "empower" had undergone quite a political odyssey, having been appropriated from the Left by Bush administration officials and free market Republicans in arguments for "cutting red tape," and privatizing welfare and housing in order to put the fate of the poor in their own hands. In the early 1990s, prominent conservatives Jack Kemp and William Bennett cofounded an organization called Empower America to advocate for these and other reforms. Clinton's use of the term had similarly market-oriented connotations: For new Democrats, the goal of "empowerment" was economic "self-sufficiency" rather than political agency and social change.

3. Moynihan made the remark on the Senate floor during debate of the bill, as reported in the *New York Times*, August 2, 1996. Primus quit shortly after Clinton signed the bill in August; Bane and Edelman waited until a month later, after the Democratic National Convention, reportedly to avoid political embarrassment to the president. Alison Mitchell, "2 U.S. Officials Quit to Protest New Welfare Law," *New York Times*, September 12, 1996, A1; E. J. Dionne, "Resigning On Principle," *Washington Post*, September 17, 1996, A15.

4. Peter Edelman, "The Worst Thing Bill Clinton Has Done," *The Atlantic Monthly*, March, 1997, 43–58.

5. For the blueprint for Republican reform, see *Contract with America* (New York: Times Books, 1994), 65–77. Although some bills proposing strict cutoffs appeared before the 1994 elections, the real momentum behind the "Personal Responsibility Act"

started in 1995. For a comprehensive discussion, see Kent Weaver, "Ending Welfare As We Know It," in Margaret Weir, ed., *The Social Divide: Political Parties and the Future of Activist Government* (Washington, D.C.: Brookings Institution, 1998), 361–416.

6. David T. Ellwood, "Welfare Reform As I Knew It," *The American Prospect*, May–June, 1996: 22–29.

7. Edelman, "The Worst Thing." Reports on the welfare bill prepared by the Urban Institute and by ASPE, made available to the president, and discussed in strategically timed op-eds, predicted that at least 1 million children would be plunged into poverty as a result, and that as many as 11 million households would lose income. Sheila Zedlewski et al., "Potential Effects of Congressional Welfare Reform Legislation on Family Incomes" (Washington: Urban Institute, 1996).

8. Jason DeParle, "The Clinton Welfare Bill: A Long, Stormy Journey," *New York Times*, July 15, 1996, A-1, A-18; Ellwood, "Welfare Reform As I Knew It," 26.

9. Having initially presented these proposals in his 1988 book *Poor Support*, Ellwood reiterated and honed them in subsequent publications, including a volume he and Mary Jo Bane published while they were in office. Mary Jo Bane and David T. Ellwood, *Welfare Realities: From Rhetoric to Reform* (Cambridge, Mass.: Harvard University Press, 1994), 143–62.

10. For recent data, see Robert Greenstein and Issac Shapiro, "New Research Findings on the Effects of the Earned Income Tax Credit" (Washington: Center on Budget and Policy Priorities, 1998).

11. On the appeal and "offsetting" nature of the EITC, see Weaver, "Ending Welfare," 180; Christopher Howard, "Happy Returns: How the Working Poor Got Tax Relief," *The American Prospect*, Spring 1994, 46–53. On Clinton's strategy of "keeping labor at arm's length" and withdrawal from minimum wage hikes, see Margaret Weir, "Wages and Jobs: What Is the Public Role?" in *The Social Divide*, 268–311.

12. On recognizing welfare mothers as workers, see Gwendolyn Mink, *Welfare's End* (Ithaca: Cornell University Press, 1998).

13. For more detail on all of these proposals, see Bane and Ellwood, *Welfare Realities*.

14. De Parle, "The Clinton Welfare Bill," A18.

15. Jason DeParle, "Democrats Face Hard Choices in Welfare Overhaul," *New York Times*, February 22, 1994, A16.

16. Ellwood, "Welfare Reform As I Knew It," 26.

17. For a critique of Clinton's economic policy from a veteran of the War on Poverty, see Robert A. Levine, "The Economic Consequences of Mr. Clinton," *The Atlantic Monthly*, July 1996, 60–65.

18. On waiver requests, and their increasingly cost-cutting and "paternalist" drift, see Mark Greenberg, "Racing to the Bottom? Recent State Welfare Initiatives Present Cause for Concern," and "Welfare Reform in an Uncertain Environment" (Washington: Center for Law and Social Policy, 1996); Nancy E. Rose, *Workfare or Fair Work: Women, Welfare, and Government Work Programs* (New Brunswick, N.J.: Rutgers University Press, 1995), 155–66; Thomas J. Corbett, "Welfare Reform in Wisconsin: The Rhetoric and the Reality," in Donald F. Norris and Lyke Thompson, eds., *The Politics of Welfare Reform* (Thousand Oaks, Calif.: Sage Publications, 1995), 19–54; and Lawrence Mead, ed., *The New Paternalism: Supervisory Approaches to Poverty* (Washington, D.C.: Brookings Institution, 1997). On the work/welfare initiatives, including the

JOBS program, see "The Jobs Evaluation: Early Lessons from Seven Sites," Report prepared for ASPE, 1994; Ladonna Pavetti and Amy-Ellen Duke, "Increasing Participation in Work and Work-Related Activities: Lessons from Five State Welfare Reform Demonstration Projects" (Washington: Urban Institute, 1995); Judith M. Gueron and Edward Pauly, *From Welfare to Work* (New York: Russell Sage Foundation, 1991); Daniel Friedlander and Gary Burtless, *Five Years After: The Long-Term Effects of Welfare-to-Work Programs* (New York: Russell Sage Foundation, 1995).

19. DeParle, "The Clinton Welfare Bill." Reducing out-of-wedlock pregnancy, particularly among poor teenagers, became truly a bipartisan preoccupation in the 1990s, as did the propensity to tie it to everything from welfare to crime control. Charles Murray, "The Coming White Underclass," *Wall Street Journal*, October 29, 1993; Kristin Luker, *Dubious Conceptions: The Politics of Teenage Pregnancy* (Cambridge, Mass.: Harvard University Press, 1996); Arline T. Geronimus, "Teenage Childbearing and Personal Responsibility: an Alternative View," *Political Science Quarterly* 112 (Fall 1997): 405–30.

20. See, for example, Robert H. Haveman, "The Clinton Alternative to 'Welfare As We Know It': Is It Feasible?" in Demetra Smith Nightingale and Robert H. Haveman, eds., *The Work Alternative: Welfare Reform and the Realities of the Job Market* (Washington, D.C.: Urban Institute Press, 1995), 185–202, and Robert M. Solow, *Work and Welfare* (Princeton: Princeton University Press, 1998), 39–43.

21. Michael Katz, *In the Shadow of the Poorhouse: A Social History of Welfare in America*, (New York: Basic Books, 1996), 326.

POLITICS AND SOCIETY IN TWENTIETH-CENTURY AMERICA

Civil Defense Begins at Home: Militarization Meets Everyday Life in the Fifties
by Laura McEnaney

Cold War Civil Rights: Equality as Cold War Policy, 1946–1968
by Mary Dudziak

Divided We Stand: American Workers and the Struggle for Black Equality
by Bruce Nelson

*Poverty Knowledge: Social Science, Social Policy, and the Poor in
Twentieth-Century U.S. History*
by Alice O'Connor